*touchpoints
three to six*

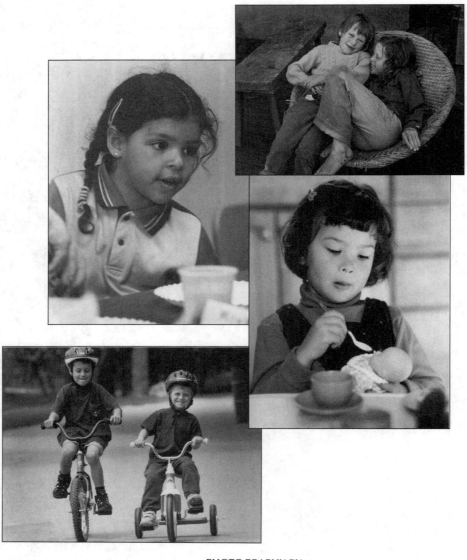

PHOTOGRAPHY BY
DOROTHY LITTELL GRECO
MARILYN NOLT
SAM OGDEN
JANICE FULLMAN

touchpoints three to six

For Ellen!

YOUR CHILD'S
EMOTIONAL
AND
BEHAVIORAL
DEVELOPMENT

T. Berry Brazelton, M.D.

Joshua D. Sparrow, M.D.

A MERLOYD LAWRENCE BOOK

PERSEUS PUBLISHING
A Member of the Perseus Books Group

Copyright © 2001 by T. Berry Brazelton, M.D. and Joshua D. Sparrow, M.D.

Cataloging-in-Publication Data is available from the Library of Congress

ISBN 0–7382-0678-4

Perseus Publishing is a member of the Perseus Books Group.

Find us on the World Wide Web at http://www.perseuspublishing.com

Perseus Publishing books are available at special discounts for bulk purchases in the U.S. by corporations, institutions, and other organizations. For more information, please contact the Special Markets Department at the Perseus Books Group, 11 Cambridge Center, Cambridge, MA 02142, or call (617)252-5298.

Text design by Jeff Williams

Set in 11-point Times by the Perseus Books Group

First paperback printing, September 2002

1 2 3 4 5 6 7 8 9 10—04 03 02

*This is book is dedicated to
Dr. Brazelton's grandchildren, and to
Dr. Sparrow's wife and children.*

acknowledgments

We would like to acknowledge the tremendous contribution of our mentor and editor, Merloyd Lawrence. She has prodded, edited, and supported us through this process.

Thanks also go to Brian Smith, Susan Ivey, and Kurt Werthmuller, who faithfully typed the manuscript.

contents

2   Four Years Old: New Power, New Fears   91

3   Five Years Old: Who I Am Matters 173

4   Six Years Old: Entering the Real World   239

Two FACING CHALLENGES AS A FAMILY

INTRODUCTION

Ever since *Touchpoints: Your Child's Emotional and Behavioral Development* presented a map of child development during the first two years, readers have asked me to continue the map into the following years. This book extends the touchpoints concept through the crucial first-grade year. In writing this sequel, I have had the opportunity to work with a colleague, Joshua Sparrow, M.D., a child psychiatrist at Children's Hospital in Boston, and have deepened my thinking and approach to children of these ages. It has been a rare opportunity to combine our approaches, and I hope that readers will see the benefits of our collaboration. Together we have had a great time exploring children's development and potential for the future.

The Touchpoints Concept

Readers of the first book found comfort in the knowledge that the regressions in behavior infants display just before a burst in development are healthy and constructive. It is reassuring to view periods of regression as an opportunity to reorganize in preparation for an area of rapid development. Each new spurt in motor, cognitive, or emotional development is likely to be heralded by disorganization and regression in the child's behavior; understanding these sequences of events and predicting them has proved helpful to those caring for young children.

We call these potentially vulnerable periods "touchpoints" because they present an optimal time for professionals to join with parents in understanding the child's progress. Parents feel support when professionals point out the purpose of these disturbing periods; in this way touchpoints become a positive opportunity for cementing not only parent-child but also parent-physician bonds. This book addresses the predictable touchpoints in the years three, four, five, and six.

In recent years, at more than thirty sites around the country, we have been training caregivers in preventive healthcare settings and childcare centers to see these touchpoints of development as opportunities to deepen their relationships with parents. When caregivers can share distressing but hopeful moments, parents can feel more confident and enjoy their child's development. The barriers of "gatekeeping," or competition between parent and supplementary caregiver, are more readily overcome when caregivers reach out to parents with an understanding of the challenges a child faces as he or she grows. Touchpoints present major opportunities for communicating about the child's temperament, the stage of development, and the special abilities or needs that help or hinder progress.

Touchpoints are based on a concept involving energy. If extra energy is needed to fuel a new, rapid development, where does it come from? For example, learning to walk is an expensive achievement; it demands all the forces the child can muster. At night, the child is up and down, crying out every three to four hours, hanging onto the crib rails. During the day, the child screams every time you don't help. These determined efforts are constant and use up the family's energy. The child is frustrated, angry, near the edge of temper tantrums night and day. But when he or she finally walks, everything changes. The child walks, walks, walks, arms wide and high, face lit up, with happiness, chortling with triumph, the goal achieved! Everyone can sleep again. Everyone relaxes and admires this great feat—after the house is baby-proofed anew.

Each new step in any line of development carries such a cost— and such a reward. If parents can anticipate their child's touchpoints, worry about the regression and accompanying misery can be turned into excitement and appreciation of the child's efforts to move forward. If parents can share these moments with caring professionals and relatives, they will derive greater enjoyment from the milestones. Their appreciation, in turn, transforms each step into a firm base for children's belief in themselves and in their future. Children and parents feel empowered.

Four Children

In this volume, we have imagined four children who reflect the range of temperamental differences. The concept of temperament, first proposed by Stella Chess and Alexander Thomas in 1951 and supported by subsequent decades of research, has flourished as a way of understanding each child's individual differences. Temperament affects the way each child receives, digests, and reacts to important stimuli. It is a reflection of the way the child's mind and body work to handle goals, dreams, and spurts in development—as well as the child's response to nurturing and stressful events. Our four unique, fictional children respond to each touchpoint differently. We hope they represent a range of potential responses, and that they capture your child's style, temperament, and way of reacting to the world. Your child might be a mixture of two or three of these, or you might find that none quite captures your child's temperament. If you don't find aspects of your child here, the omission is likely to reflect our shortcoming, not your child's. But we hope that the four children we present will give you some insight into how children with great differences in temperament adapt to their worlds and learn. We also hope that each story conveys a sense of the wonder and excitement of growing up, as well as the vicissitudes and work of adjusting to each new step.

Billy, with his dancing curls and bright brown eyes, seems to be a born winner. When he enters a room, he is masterful. He looks around, watches long enough to size up the situation, and enters the conversation with a sure conviction that he should be a part of it. He shows his sensitivity to others, both in gestures and in words. His manners and his direct way of soliciting with voice and body language when he looks at another child or adult are infused with self-assurance. This approach tends to make him a leader. Other children almost immediately like him and choose to be with him. Adults love him, for his bright eyes shield a deeper sensitivity that he demonstrates whenever events summon it.

In his second year, Billy witnessed an abusive father and a struggling, depressed mother. Mrs. Stone has since remarried; her new husband is a wonderfully caring man who stepfathers Billy as if he were his own. Both parents are white, middle-class Americans. When Billy is three, a new baby sister, Abby, is born. We will watch as he adjusts to her and learns to be both competitive and caring in his responses to her. Their relationship can be a bellwether as to Billy's emotional state, for his eyes grow sad when he is anything but loving toward Abby. At times, the hurt he still feels about the loss of his own father lingers just below the surface. Billy is athletic and coordinated. He is bright and enjoys school, where he assumes responsibility in helping the teachers hold the other children's attention and maintain order. He commands respect from his classmates.

Billy is in many ways a healthy, appealing, typical boy. His attempt to handle his aggression, his fears, and his sensitivity rooted in early experience gives him broader dimensions. Everyone wants a Billy!

Minnie is a lively, active child, on the borderline of hyperactive. As she charges toward her goals, she can appear somewhat insensitive to others around her. These are largely motor goals, and she is a competent, fearless athlete, which delights her father. Mr. Lee (an Asian man and an athlete himself) and Minnie have a devoted, devouring relationship. Minnie's mother (Caucasian) finds Minnie difficult. Mrs. Lee has felt from the first that Minnie never seems to need her. Minnie's older sister (five years Minnie's senior), May, has always been close to her mother. She was easy, "feminine," and she made Mrs. Lee feel irreplaceable. Mrs. Lee's own sisters excluded her as a child, and Minnie revives this feeling in her mother. Boys like Minnie, but she has to struggle to be accepted by other girls. Her intense attachment to her father seems to offer her enough support. Mrs. Lee worries about Minnie's adjustment to school and wonders whether her daughter's teachers will also find Minnie remote and driven. As Minnie exuberantly confronts first grade, we see her gravitate toward sports and gradually adapt to the rules and requirements of school.

Minnie's assertive, energetic nature will be a great asset as she learns to channel it into schoolwork and athletics.

Marcy is a tall, graceful and outgoing child. She is African American, with a close-knit, supportive family. Both parents work and are successful. Marcy's quiet, sensitive older brother, Amos, is very different in temperament and he has worried his outgoing mother. Marcy expects to be accepted, and she is popular with her peers. She engages other outgoing children (Billy is one of her friends) and she is quietly sensitive to Tim, a shy child. As an African-American child growing up in a community where she is in the minority, Marcy will have to face the responses of other children to differences in her hair and skin color.

To get her way, Marcy is actively demanding. But sometimes she is frightened when she succeeds. In learning to curb her demands, Marcy turns to her imaginary friends to help her. In first grade, Marcy becomes her teacher's favorite. It comes as a real surprise, however, when the teacher announces to Mr. and Mrs. Jackson that Marcy has a learning difficulty. No one could have predicted this, and both she and her parents are shaken by the news. After a period in which they are all raw and vulnerable, they muster their resources. Marcy is strong and not easily undermined. Her charm, resilience, and leadership help her face all obstacles.

Tim is a shy, quiet, highly intelligent child. He is easily overwhelmed, especially in a social setting. He tries to isolate himself in his mother's lap, and he is dependent on his thumb and blanket. Tim's older brother, Philip, teases him and is ashamed of him when among his own peers. Tim's father has had a difficult time understanding and accepting Tim, but they eventually become closer through computer games. Tim is so bright that his father is not always able to beat him.

Tim works valiantly to overcome the almost overwhelming pain that social situations cause him. His mother hovers and risks exacerbating his vulnerability as a frightened child who cannot fit in with his peers. But Billy's and Marcy's acceptance of Tim and his personality pave the way for his entry into the school group.

Tim senses that he is a disappointment to his father and brother. His mother responds instinctively to his needs, which helps him tolerate his interactions with the world. When Tim is three, Mrs. McCormick goes to work; Tim has to adjust to separation and to fitting in with other three-year-olds. With the help of a similarly shy child, he learns to adjust to a group of peers as he sits watching on the sidelines. Tim learns to participate visually, not motorically. He, too, has an imaginary friend, who becomes the repository of his feelings after such an effort.

Tim's father's pride in Tim's strong intellect helps Tim begin to feel he can manage with less help from his mother. Because he already knows how to read by the time he enters first grade, his classmates are impressed, especially Billy. The two form a wonderful friendship, bolstering one another and exchanging strengths. Tim's devoted parents and his evident academic skills form a firm base for future self-confidence.

Individuality from the Beginning

Our insights into the individuality of small children derive from work with newborn babies and from the Neonatal Behavioral Assessment Scale. In newborns we can observe states of consciousness that cover the adjustments we all make, even as adults, physiologically and psychologically. Our responses to our environment are dependent on which state we are in. Babies' temperaments are demonstrated by their abilities to maintain and circulate through these states. The capacity to take in and use stimuli from the world outside is correlated with certain alert states in infants and children. Each baby and child has a threshold below which he or she can receive, assimilate, and respond to stimuli and experiences. Above this, the child may be unavailable. Too far above the threshold, the child may be overwhelmed. This threshold varies—from the low threshold of a fragile child (such as Tim) to a high threshold with a driven child (such as Minnie). Recognizing and respecting this threshold becomes a crucial task for parents; otherwise, either life events can be too overwhelming or children may seem hard to reach. Thresholds may shift over time, but remain individual.

Individuality in temperament is not simply genetic; many environmental variables shape experience, and experience shapes temperament. Nature and nurture are rarely separable. Genetic endowment is already shaped by intrauterine experiences: nutrients, drugs, maternal health, infections, and other factors that affect the parent also affect the developing fetus. The newborn's behavior is thus not simply genetically determined, but has already been shaped by the early environment. Parents must adjust to an individual temperament that has been formed both by genes and experience.

The balance between nature and nurture shifts as the child grows older. In the first two years, biological forces strongly influence many of the child's accomplishments. Many of these accomplishments, though far from all, involve visible (sitting, standing, walking) or audible (talking) developments that are based, at least in part, on motor activity. Although the child masters obvious skills like these in the next few years (riding a bike, tying one's own shoes), others are subtler and take place in the child's thoughts and feelings. The greatest surge in brain cell interconnections occurs in the first two years and continues at least through age six, leveling off by age ten, according to our current understanding of brain development. Nonetheless, the touchpoints of ages three through six are perhaps somewhat more subject to influence by other forces, and as a result show greater variability. It is true that some children walk first, others talk first. For children ages three to six, though, the specific sequence of achievements is likely to be even more individual. External factors, such as the birth of a sibling, the influence of an older sibling, or the return of a parent to the workforce, are bound to affect the timing and course of the touchpoints during these years. A family's evolution depends on an intricate interweaving of each member's developmental steps, the reorganization they require, and the energy they bring.

Ghosts from the Nursery

As intense, passionate parents engage with their growing child, they will attempt to set up an environment that is sensitively nurturing to the temperament and individuality of their child. As they do so, their own past experiences begin to influence their responses. Whenever parents feel besieged or anxious about a small child's behavior, it is time to reflect upon the ghosts from their own nursery. The term *ghosts from the nursery* was used by Selma Fraiberg and others to capture important experiences from the past that can dominate parents' behavior. These ghosts influence the biases and approaches of the parents. These are experiences the parents had with their own parents, or with past challenges reminiscent of the one they now find themselves facing with their own child. Biases dominate our behavior much more completely if we aren't aware of them. Bringing them to consciousness gives us a choice: conform to the bias or resist it. Ghosts from each parents' nursery differ from each other. They had better be faced openly so each parent can support the other in such important areas as discipline, feeding, sleep patterns, and toilet training.

Intent of the Book

In this second *Touchpoints*, we first take up those specific issues of child rearing in the years three through six that are a part of normal development. Sibling rivalry, crying, tantrums, waking at night, fears, getting stuck emotionally, lying, or bedwetting may take hold when parents attempt to control situations that really belong to the child. Often, these kinds of behavior are part of the struggle for autonomy. We suggest techniques that parents can adopt to remove themselves from the struggle and thus defuse it.

Parents become locked in battle with their children not because they don't care, but because they care so much. As children explore the reactions of adults and struggle towards autonomy, they are bound to hit upon areas that are difficult for parents. When parents find themselves overreacting, the time has come to pull back and to reconsider the reason for the tension associated with the child's behavior: Is it appropriate for the child's developmental stage? What is the hidden message behind the behavior? Does the behavior represent the child's struggle with an emerging developmental competence? In other words, a parent's first job is to understand the child; then, parents can reevaluate their own reactions. Once they have done so, they are in a better position both to support the child and to set necessary limits. These issues are likely to occur in all families. If this book can help parents understand the underlying issues both for themselves and for the child, it will help families to avoid getting "stuck."

The characters in Part I of this book are all composites. They are intended to typify the many children we've cared for over the years—as a pediatrician (Berry Brazelton) and a child psychiatrist (Joshua Sparrow), but are not based on any single child. The observations are our own. The ideas of development beyond touchpoints are drawn from many scholars (Freud, Erikson, Benjamin, Winnicott, Piaget, Fraiberg, and many more recent ones). The parents, teachers, and caregivers in the book have, for the most part, been portrayed as responding optimally. We hope they serve as role models, but without setting unattainable expectations for parents.

In Part II, topics appear in alphabetical order; they are either perennial concerns or current issues raised in urgent tones by the parents we see in our offices and whenever we speak to groups. The topics are discussed in the context of the touchpoints theory of development. These sections are written for parents who see themselves or their child at risk of becoming mired in a particular difficulty. They are intended to help families find their own solutions and strengths and avoid becoming locked into destructive patterns or incapacitating anxiety. None of the individual sections—such as those on depression, developmental disabilities, or speech and hearing problems—are meant to be comprehensive. They are intended only to help parents distinguish between normal variations in behavior and problems that require expert help.

one

THE YEARS FROM
THREE TO SIX

1

THREE YEARS OLD

What I Do Matters

On the Playground

The playground was teeming: Children running about with their caregivers or nannies, and the at-home mothers clustered in groups on the benches. Children were mostly under four. Their siblings were in school—preschool and "real" school. Freed from the pressure of their older siblings' domination, the two- and three-year-olds raced from one activity to another. Watchful parents or caregivers needed to race back and forth with them to maintain conversation. Children were stimulated to keep up with each other's activities. The sandboxes were the quiet areas. The slides and merry-go-round were active spots. Four children, two boys and two girls—our four major actors in this book—were part of this melee. An active boy and a quiet boy, Billy and Tim, an intense, driving girl, Minnie, and a cheerful and outgoing girl, Marcy, played with the other children.

Billy, a joyful, active little boy, arrived on this scene with his mother. His round face had a cherubic look. His soft, full cheeks and wide eyes, his tumbling hair, busy-talk, and finger in the mouth—all seemed designed to make him endearing and pick-up-able. It was difficult not to want to hug Billy. When he was ready, it was okay. But when he wasn't, away he'd wriggle. He wanted to be free to roam, to inquire, to find out about his world. He still stood with feet apart, though more steadily now. Occasionally, he stumbled. He was in a hurry. He hadn't yet mastered motor planning, anticipating how his body would have to move in time for him to get where he was going. At three, getting there is more important than figuring out how. For the most part, though, his motor development allowed him to move about with greater certainty and aplomb. As a result, he wanted to *be* with everyone, but not always with people who represented hugs. He needed to explore the world; and, for him, the most important part of the world was people.

Billy was always smiling and outgoing. He charged up to a group of three-year-olds in the sand pile. "Hi. I'm Billy." No one looked up. Undaunted, he sat beside a boy who was making a sandcastle. As if in imitation, he began to make a castle just like the other child's. Never looking at each other, the boys became more and more aware of each other's moves. Billy took a cup, filled it with sand, and patted the sand down; when he turned the cup over, the sand formed a molded tower. The other child was clearly impressed. The two moved closer to each other and began to build together. Billy's mother was struck with Billy's ability to "move on in."

As soon as Billy had made a friend, the other children seemed to recognize their strength as a pair. "Billy, look here." "Tommy, can you help me build?" They moved closer. Another child, a girl, recognized a kindred soul in Billy. "You got curly hair. Did your mommy do it?" "Do what?" "Curl it up like she does. My hair is curly, too, but kids tease me." Billy returned to his sand building as if this were to be ignored. The girl moved next to him. "Wanna ride my big wheel?" Billy looked up, brightening. "Sure." She raced over to her tricycle. Billy followed as fast as he could. She held on to one handlebar while he climbed on. As soon as he was astride, he tried to pedal. At first, his foot slipped. The girl grinned. Billy looked around, embarrassed. Placing his feet more squarely on the pedals, he began to move, but backwards. She laughed, "Not that way." Billy realized his mistake, and began to pedal forward. Proud of his achievement, he began to yell, "Look out!" The other three-year-olds stopped to watch with admiration.

Learning to pedal a three-wheeler is quite an achievement. From walking to running to pushing a kiddie-car are a two-year-old's milestones. Then, a year later, to be able to push, to alternate feet, to cycle with one's own legs, and to be able to reverse the motion is a major victory for a three-year-old. No wonder Billy was proud. His ability to restrain his own behavior to match that of the other children, and to enter their play, is a measure of his adaptability. He is hungry to win these children over to play with him. His persistence and determination to succeed in social interaction is one window into his temperament.

Billy's mother sat on the bench with the other mothers. She was confident that Billy could take care of himself. Did he already know how to reassure her with his competence? As she watched Billy with the other three-year-olds, she realized how nurturing he was. At one point, a child threw a handful of sand at him. Billy looked down at the culprit. "No! No throwing." Mrs. Stone was fascinated that he'd taken in her admonition and was now ready to use it to protect himself. Instead of throwing sand back, he'd used words he'd heard before. The other child looked up in surprise, listened, and stopped.

Marcy was already on the jungle gym. Although she still toddled at times—falling back on her wide-based gait, on rather clumsy footing, she was handsome to watch. If she stumbled, she'd fall down and get up in one motion without stopping. Her eyes sparkled. Her smile was contagious. She climbed with deliberate concentration, but slipped if distracted. She whipped up and down the slide. She rode her tricycle with dexterity. At home, she could put pieces in her puzzles, although she had to fumble around, and could untie her own shoes. She could pile as many as ten blocks on top of each other in a tower, placing each corner precisely on top of the corner below it.

Like her mother, Marcy was tall—tall for her age. Her skin was a light chocolate color, her tight, soft curls were shiny black. She was winning in her ways. Her pretty face with her appealing, dark eyes looked at you with trust. As her face broke into a smile, your heart flip-flopped. She was eagerly responsive and everyone in turn seemed to respond to her.

As she came onto the playground, she bounced. Her limbs were soft and strong, with dimples still in her elbows and beside her knees as she started off to a run. Then, the slight widening to her gait seemed to disappear, or nearly. This almost imperceptible immaturity makes an adult feel more protective than she will feel about Marcy at four and five. But Marcy's movements are so purposeful and enthusiastic. Boisterousness is mixed with adventure, and all Marcy's activities seem aimed at playful fun.

Every new object needs to be examined, to be tried out. A large leaf must be dislodged and turned over for scrutiny. A rock becomes an object of curiosity—"Is it heavy? Is it rough? Is it muddy? What's under it?" That squirmy worm must be picked up and examined. Active wonder marks every experience. Each leaf is a first.

Marcy ran up to each child. "I'm here!" She waited for a response before she went to the next child. When she approached a little boy who was sitting in his mother's lap, she greeted him. As he withdrew and turned in to his mother, she followed her greeting by appealing to his mother. Sensitively, she dropped her voice to say, "I'm Marcy. I'm shy, too." She obviously wasn't.

Of course, the other toddlers and three-year-olds began to be aware of her. Several of them followed her around. She quickly became a leader of those her age. She took her role seriously. "Let's play on the jungle gym." The others followed. "Let's climb through the tunnel." They followed. "Let's ride on my big wheel." They followed. They all tried to climb on the tricycle at once. It turned over. No one got to ride.

All of Marcy's achievements were accompanied by her good nature. Although she often had to work hard to complete a task, she finished with a grin. It seemed as if she was not only pleased with herself but wanted to share her joy in success with others. This was not done with any braggadocio, but more with the feeling of "Isn't it fun to be alive?" No wonder she was popular with her peers and with adults who met her. "Is she always like this?" people would ask. "She always has been delightfully easy," her mother would reply. "As a baby she seemed to appreciate all we did for her. Her brother was just the opposite. He's easier now, but he wasn't in the beginning. Everyone loves Marcy. Her brother would like to make her life miserable, but she worships him, and she learns so much from him. He can't stay mad at Marcy too long."

Tim sat watching the other children from his mother's lap. He had been to the playground once before, but there had been only one other child present. He had clung to his mother, hiding his face in her shoulder. After a few minutes, he'd begun to peek out at the other child. His mother sensed how hungry he was to know and understand other children. She'd brought Tim again today, expecting him to be shy. He was. Even around his older brother, he clung to his mother or his father. Everyone in the house was aware of Tim's shyness. It daunted them all. As a newborn baby, he was too quiet, too easily overwhelmed by noise and people. His parents had protected him because it seemed too painful to push him. If they took Tim to a noisy party or into a crowd of people, he'd quiver. He'd shun those who came near, averting his face and eyes. At home, he was just as quiet and retiring. He was clear about his needs, however—hunger and sleep—and made few demands. In that respect, his parents felt he'd been easy. At first they'd taken him everywhere, as they had his older brother. But he was too quiet, too unresponsive when they were out with him. People wondered why he was so quiet. When the family returned home, Tim would cry a great deal, in long sobs, which wrenched his parents' hearts. It was easier just to stay at home with him.

Tim had walked at the expected time. He had talked on time. Each milestone in his development reassured his parents that he was doing fine. This quiet child was so gentle. When a new person came into the house, he hid his face or covered his ears. When he could walk, he would quietly disappear. Her own mother reassured Mrs. McCormick; she called her grandson "her quiet, sensitive Tim."

Tim's older brother, Philip, teased him. Tim would brighten at his attention. His brother's intentions weren't so benign, however. He'd look for Tim's weaknesses. When Philip saw Tim open up to him, he'd increase the teasing. "Nyah, nyah, nyah. Look at Tim, he's a baby." Tim would look worried. Then Philip would grab Tim's blanket. Tim couldn't stand it. He'd curl up in a little ball to protect the blanket. He'd whimper silently and suck his thumb loudly—his most overt plea for help. Mrs. McCormick would rush to Tim to pick him up. She'd sit down in a rocking chair, rocking him with a tender, crooning song. Tim would visibly relax. His face would brighten. He would look around and show interest in everything around him, but only as long as he was enclosed in the safe envelope of his mother's lap. Mrs. McCormick knew she was needed. Tim's older brother would then slink off, angry and unfulfilled. "Tim always gets his way."

When Mrs. McCormick held Tim in her lap at the playground, she sat alone on a bench across from the other mothers as if she were ashamed of Tim's clinging. She knew that if she sat by other mothers, they would all give her advice: "Just put him down and let him cry—he'll get over it." "My little girl was just like that but she finally got used to other kids." "Get him a play date. He can learn about other children that way."

They watched the other children play, and as Mrs. McCormick relaxed, Tim's vigilance began to diminish. He grabbed for his blanket. It was at home, so he grabbed his mother's dress, clutched it in one hand, and sucked on his thumb with the other. As he did so, he began to relax. He watched and watched. He even began to talk about the children he was watching. "He don't like that slide. He don't want to climb it." He wasn't speaking to her, but she could tell that this was Tim's attempt at participation with the other children.

Some of the other three-year-olds were curious about Tim and his mother. They watched them out of the corners of their eyes. After one little girl hurt herself on the jungle gym, she cringed in her mother's lap; she sucked her thumb and fingered her mother's dress, as if imitating Tim. As the other children watched, they glanced back and forth at Tim and the little girl. They had made the connection. Tim's utter dependency was a threat to all of them because they had only recently struck out on their own. One little boy rushed up to Mrs. McCormick: "Put him down! Make him play!" At this age, all children are still working on their independence. It is frightening to see someone acting out your own struggle.

Minnie raced into the playground. Her legs and arms were flying, her face eager. As she ran, she leaned forward, as if her legs couldn't keep up to get her where she wanted to go. "Hey, let's go!" she shouted, to no one in particular. Her mother walked silently behind her. She did not expect to keep up with her. For three years now, Minnie's mother had wondered where Minnie had come from. Minnie's sweet, patient, and engaging big sister, May, had not prepared her parents for Minnie. She was unlike anyone else Mrs. Lee had ever experienced. A steamroller, she never stopped moving. She climbed, she jumped, she tested every piece of furniture, every curbstone, every jungle gym or slide in a playground. As her mother watched her, she gasped at her audacity. "Minnie, don't climb up to the top until I get there!" fell on deaf ears. Minnie seemed to be caught by the physical excitement of movement. She had a kind of recklessness that made it nerve-wracking for her mother to watch. By the time Mrs. Lee got to the "big" slide, Minnie had gone up and come down at the other end. The harder Mrs. Lee tried to keep up with her, the more Minnie seemed to be on the run. As Minnie returned to climb up, her mother grabbed her arm in an attempt to make her slow down; Minnie wrenched it away and kept climbing. Her heedlessness, mixed with her ability to achieve these physical accomplishments, made her mother feel disconnected and somewhat useless.

Minnie's father loved Minnie's athletic prowess. He admired her intensity. He valued her ability to achieve athletic goals, and she knew it. That was an unspoken bond between them. From time to time he'd say, "Minnie, you're amazing! I can't believe how fast you climbed that slide!" She never appeared to respond to him, either, although he thought he detected a slight smile after his words of encouragement. Minnie paid little attention to her father when he tried to slow her down with words. Instead, he'd throw her up in the air. She squealed with delight. He'd get more and more audacious. She loved it. They invented all sorts of games together. When she wanted a ride, she'd ask for the "wheelbarrow." He'd hold her by the ankles, dip her down and she'd run across the floor on her hands. Then, exhausted, she'd plop down on the ground so hard that her father would wonder whether he'd hurt her. Not at all. She chortled, "More! More!"

In desperation, Mrs. Lee would enlist her husband when she needed to discipline Minnie, but his attempts at discipline were likely to go almost as unheeded as hers. Trying to stop this energetic little girl was like trying to dam a rushing stream.

The playground is often a child's first venture into the wide, wide world. Here, children learn from and about other children, about each other's individuality. Humans are social animals from the very beginning. From the start, infants are "wired" to seek out and engage in relationships. By three years, they have not only learned but can think about the importance of communication and of relationships. "You're my best friend." Nurturing relationships with their parents set the tone. A child knows how rewarding it can be to look, to talk, to listen, to touch, and to demand attention from an important adult. Siblings have been models for learning about ambivalent relationships—sometimes rivalrous, sometimes loving, but always *exciting*. A sibling provides the positive and negative sides of a passionate relationship as well as the enticing opportunity for involving a parent, who will try to break up the rivalry!

Peers offer children a window they can look into and see themselves. They are often at the same stage of development, struggling with the same issues, facing the demands of the next developmental steps. Yet they are also different. The differences offer a kaleidoscope of experiences, a way of testing what one's own feelings might be. A child can see himself in a mirror as he experiences the other child's reactions. The chance to play with and to model on the peer's reactions and styles of learning offers the opportunity for learning about oneself.

Three-year-olds are now less dominated by tortured negativism. No longer bound to the parallel play of the two-year-old (although even at this age, children are already more interactive than was once thought), they are now able to pay attention to the other child in a more complicated way—reading cues, matching rhythms of response, waiting and watching for another response—the rhythm of interaction. They can learn to read the other child's cries and respond to them appropriately. From the beginning, the infant learns from interactions with attentive caregivers; but learning how to capture and respond to peers with their own agendas is a major step.

With peers, a child can try out and experiment with his own impact on the world around him. He can begin to learn about himself as an active participant in the world, no longer just within his own family.

Temperament

At the playground, children make very clear their individual differences in their play, in the way they make relationships. The way children take on the developmental steps to come will vary with their individuality, pressing their parents to face each "touchpoint" differently, too. Temperament, a valuable concept for parents, describes the differences in how children receive, digest, and express their experiences. Understanding the variations of each child's temperament can give us insight into the way the child needs to handle new developmental experiences, into his responses to each challenge he encounters as he develops.

Certain developmental changes, certain touchpoints, are likely to be unsettling not only to the parents but to the whole family. But parents who have learned to understand the child's temperament can rely on each child's individual way of addressing a challenge, turning the turmoil into a more predictable event. Temperament is made up of many factors: activity level, distractibility, persistence, approach/withdrawal, intensity, adaptability, regularity, sensory threshold, mood. These traits are probably largely inborn. Stella

Chess and Alexander Thomas identified these elements of children's temperaments and pointed out how powerfully they affect the parent-child relationship. Chess and Thomas coined the term *goodness of fit* to describe how temperaments of child and parent can match in a close and supportive relationship. My first book, *Infants and Mothers,* demonstrates how the baby's style or temperament affects the parent's reactions from the very first days. In the process of adjusting to each other, the baby and the parent develop a predictability of expectations with each other. Parents' understanding of their child's temperament limits the unpredictability of the forms that developmental changes will take.

If parents can accept and value their child's way of greeting and mastering her life, they make a positive contribution to the child's sense of conquest and self-esteem. If parents can treasure their child's style of protecting herself from feelings or experiences that overwhelm her, they support her sense of security. A parent's first and most important job is to understand the child as an individual. This means watching, listening, observing each change in her development, and the individual ways in which she masters her environment. The new energy required for each new task is fueled when a child has found her own strategies for dealing with change. The stable aspects of a child's temperament supply the foundation from which the child can learn to deal with the instability and excitement that come with each new touchpoint.

Is temperament fixed? Is it predictive for the future? To some degree it is. But many things influence temperament; these include the ways parents understand their child and interact with her, and the experiences (positive and negative) that challenge their child's coping strategies.

By the age of three, temperament has become a reliable and recognizable part of the parent-child relationship. No longer can it be overlooked. No longer can a parent hope to change it. The child's powerful contribution affects every aspect of interaction: communication, caring, caretaking, and discipline. Unless its power is understood, a parent can easily feel manipulated and helpless.

Parents are helped in understanding a child's temperament when they view the child as an active participant in their relationship. The chances of being able to adjust to that child's rhythms and behavioral language—the "goodness of fit"—is then significantly enhanced. It also helps when parents are able to understand their particular styles and to see their own reactions as subjective.

Three clusters of characteristics vary with each child and affect how she deals with her world. These, along with the individual rhythms of sleep, hunger, and other bodily functions, define her temperament:

1. Task orientation—attention span and persistence, distractibility, and activity level.
2. Social flexibility—approach/withdrawal (how a child handles stimuli from the outside) and adaptability.
3. Reactivity—sensory threshold of responsiveness (high or low), quality of mood, and intensity of reactions.

Look at the differences in the ways the four children we have just met would approach entering a swimming pool. Marcy, for example, would approach the task with a determination to succeed. If she had to conquer her fears about going into a swimming pool, she'd watch the other children near her age. She'd approach them with, "Is it fun?" "Is it cold?" When they acknowledged her with a response, whatever it was, she would feel a bond that helped her master her anxiety. She would look to her brother, Amos, and to her parents to see whether they were behind her. She'd put a foot in the water to test it. Leaving it in until she was used to the water and to the temperature, she'd then slip into the shallow water. She'd look up at the others for approval. If no one responded, she'd sidle up to another child in the water. Soon, they would be splashing around together.

Tim's temperament would be clearly evident in his avoidant approach to the pool. He would be overwhelmed by the many reverberating sights and sounds: the smell of chlorine, the loud cries and echoing splashes, the frenzied joyousness. Struggling even tighter into his mother's arms, he might cover his face with her blouse. As he gradually relaxed in her lap, however, he might peep out from behind the curtain he'd drawn. With one eye, he'd watch the other children. When they squealed, he'd shudder. If anyone sat beside his mother, he'd retreat further into her lap. If his father or his brother tried to coax him away from his haven, his face would pucker. He'd curl into a fetal position and leave as little skin showing as possible. His mother, without meaning to, would reinforce this behavior by shielding him from the pressure his father or brother were putting on him. "He just isn't ready. He's too sensitive." Meanwhile, with one eye, Tim would take in all the other children's activity in the pool.

Billy, however, would rush to the pool. "Hi, kids!" Standing on the edge of the pool, he'd look around for a friend. He'd watch the activity with fascination, so interested that he might lean too far forward and fall into the pool. If this happened, his mother would rush to pull him out. Sputtering and choking, red in the face, Billy would let out a wail and a moment later he'd say, "Let me go. I'm ready." Soon he would become a leader as he splashed around in the shallowest part of the pool. Giggling, he might splash his mother. "Billy, stop it. Remember to keep your head up! Look at you now. You're going to choke." As if remembering fleetingly the near tragedy, Billy would look anxious for a moment, but then turn away to the other children. "Let's play!"

Minnie, of course, would race to the pool, heedless, her mother in alarmed pursuit. "Minnie, look out! This isn't just a wading pool. It's a real one. Don't run into it. Let me help you!" But Minnie would simply collide with the water. The water had to give. Splashing, spitting out water, she would stand up to propel herself forward. Ignoring the other children, she would splash water excitedly. The more she splashed, the more she would choke. Undeterred, she would flail around while ignoring her mother, yet fueled by her anxious pleas to "settle down." Minnie might make so much commotion in the water that the other children would even avoid her.

Each of these children, with their different temperaments, have almost as much of an effect on their parents as their parents have on them. They are shaping the kind of parenting that they are receiving, as well as their own futures. Parents' inevitable anxiety about the future can often be alleviated if they can learn to accept—and even appreciate—their child's temperament and way of responding to difficulties and new experiences.

A "Difficult Child"

Minnie's parents faced issues of temperament early. An intense child, her energy directed toward motor achievements, Minnie was always in trouble. By the age of three, she'd fallen seriously three times—once she had sustained a concussion, once she had broken an arm, and the third time, she had tumbled into a gravel pile and scratched her face and arms. She always recovered, though, undaunted and ready to go. It was her mother who bore the traces of Minnie's misadventures.

Minnie's drive often resulted in her being far away from adult help. She was hard to keep up with. But even nearby, she could find trouble. When she was 15 months old, her mother was cooking in the kitchen. Minnie was quiet. That should have been a sign that something was wrong, as Mrs. Lee reconstructed it, but Minnie had pushed her for so long that she was relieved to be left alone. Minnie was playing in the corner, so that seemed safe. When Mrs. Lee glanced at her daughter, she saw to her horror that Minnie was busily drinking from a bottle of detergent. Mrs. Lee was terrified and called 911. By the time the emergency squad arrived, Minnie was bubbling so much that she was barely able to breathe. She was rushed to the emergency room, and she spent the next week in intensive care, bubbling. She had to be placed on a ventilator so that oxygen could get past the bubbles and into her lungs. Minnie's survival always seemed tenuous.

Minnie's parents felt pressed against the wall. Did she learn from this crisis? No. Did her parents learn from it? Yes. They learned never to trust her. They learned they couldn't let her out of their sight even for a split second. They searched for traps and poisons and took precautions that had never been necessary for their first daughter, May. They locked closets. They cleaned out shelves and closets. They covered all electrical outlets. They followed the rules in the booklet about poisons and accidents sent out by a children's hospital. They got down on their hands and knees and looked at the world from a toddler's eye view. In spite of all this, Minnie still found ways to get herself into trouble.

Minnie's parents thought of their daughter as "accident-prone." Mrs. Lee found herself on edge when she was with Minnie. Every kind of discipline—from "time out" to confining Minnie to her bedroom, from scolding to withholding rewards—failed. Minnie was too driven for such brief disciplinary actions. During time out, she tried to wait patiently, but soon pushed ahead as if nothing had happened. Her parents began to realize that Minnie was paying little attention to their understandably worn-out tune: "Watch out! Be careful or you're going to get yourself into trouble again". They saw

that their job was to try to engender a sense of responsibility and awareness in her.

The danger in having to watch a child all the time until she is able to assume responsibility for herself is that all this attention from parents perpetuates the reckless activity. How can parents be on a constant lookout for the next catastrophe without inadvertently pushing the child into it? The child begins to experience reckless activity as a way of holding on to her parents' focus. This was especially a risk for Minnie, who could see that her older sister was so much more rewarding for her parents to attend to.

Minnie was not just reckless. She was very adept at physical accomplishments. They were her opportunity for recognition. Other children admired her. But she rarely responded to them. A boy her age might say: "Hi! Let's slide together." Ignored. "Hey, want to play with me?" Ignored. Minnie's parents wondered whether their daughter's hearing was impaired, she seemed so unavailable. But her parents saw that when she had only one child of her age to play with, she was quite aware of the other child. Still, she didn't seem interested in her playmate. Perhaps she didn't yet know how to show her interest in another child. When her father tried a new activity, such as throwing a ball, it was apparent that she was watching carefully. She learned his way of throwing from watching him. No wonder Mr. Lee was "hooked."

Minnie's limited social repertoire alienated others and left her isolated. Other children, for example, were already aware that they must line up for turns at the slide. Their parents reminded them and held them back. They needed their parents close by to dare the big slide. Not Minnie. She shoved other children out of the way as she rushed to the slide. Mrs. Lee felt unable to control her, and was embarrassed. She tried saying, "Minnie! Wait! It's not your turn! Come here and I'll wait with you." No response from Minnie. Mrs. Lee wilted inside. She felt that Minnie made her role at the playground that of an observer, not a participant. She watched the faces of the other three-year-olds, envying their recognition of their parents' directions. When a parent said, "No, just wait in line," the three-year-old would dutifully stop, reach for a parent's hand, sometimes putting a thumb in his mouth. The pair would be in a kind of understanding and closeness that Mrs. Lee longed for.

Minnie climbed up on the slide again. Mrs. Lee winced at a split-second of clumsiness. Minnie slipped on a step, but quickly righted her feet and her balance. Her mother had to admire her resilience. She had watched Minnie walk early at nine months. She had watched her climb stairs at twelve months and let herself back down adeptly. She had watched her climb out of her crib at eighteen months. Minnie had been so pleased with herself that Mrs. Lee could rejoice with her. But her remoteness bothered her mother. Did Minnie really need her? She was still so caught up in her drive toward activity.

Any of the other parents could have told Mrs. Lee to be firm and resolved. Why couldn't she? Minnie would have listened, in her own way, taking something in even if she wasn't yet ready to use it. But this was hard for Mrs. Lee to recognize, because Minnie was a child who still communicated what she was learning through her activity more than through words. Parents of three-year–olds are already beginning to rely on language to know when their children are learning. Minnie's learning was still expressed by motor behavior. This, coupled with Minnie's ignoring her, made Mrs. Lee feel useless. Feeling useless as a parent creates a kind of angry desperation, and desperation can make a parent even less effective. Mrs. Lee would hold back, or respond only tentatively because she was afraid to express her anger towards Minnie. They did not have an easy relationship.

Learning

Curiosity

Why do the stars stay up in the sky? Excitement at learning about his world is evident in a three-year-old's questions about everything. His curiosity never seems satisfied. "Why?" is a recurrent theme over and over, all day and even into the night.

A problem for parents at this age may be to give answers that are meaningful for a three-year-old. Trying to explain why a car goes can be a major job. Remember the causality of a two-year-old? "If you wind up a toy, it will go. If you don't it won't." If translated into the question, "Why does the car go?" The answer would be simple: "Because you turn the key." But Billy's stepfather now adds, "Do you hear the noise of the engine? It starts when I turn the key. The key starts the engine. The engine is what drives the car to make it go. Hear it? When I turn it off, it stops." Billy's face is awestruck. "Ohhh." His stepfather can watch Billy take it in. He recognizes the power of the key, of the hand that turned it, of the unseen engine, and of the adult who knows all this. Billy looks at his stepfather's face as if to ask the next question: "But why does it go if you turn the key?" How would Billy ever understand that? Instead, he blurts out, "I wanna do it." After a few tries at turning the key, he jumps off his stepfather's lap to run to his play car. He jumps into the seat and makes the car go with his feet. If that wasn't enough, and it wasn't, he got on his tricycle to push on the ground then to try to pedal it to "make it go." The connection between the original "why" and making the tricycle go may have been lost on the observing adult. Not for him. Instead of remaining overwhelmed by what he can't understand, Billy has put this simple communication into an action he can achieve himself.

Billy has to absorb the causal relation between the turning of the key and the car's moving. His eagerness to understand these steps, and his stepfather's ambitious explanations, drive him to the tricycle, over which he has control. He is trying hard to make the connection in his own way. Billy knows he can learn by doing. He doesn't push his stepfather further because he senses the limits of his explanatory powers. Mr. Stone is relieved to be let off the hook.

Another kind of learning is trying something out: "Let me do it all by myself!" With this comes the irresistible plea: "Help me! Show me!" Billy and his mother were at the parking garage of a huge shopping mall near their house. Billy was worn out, and Mrs. Stone was rushing to get him home before he disintegrated. As she dragged him aboard the elevator, he tripped and fell forward. She picked him up. "Come on, Billy. We are going home." He whimpered. Mrs. Stone pushed the button without thinking; The three-year-old beside her dissolved into a roaring tantrum. "*I* wanted to!" Billy yelled. His mother was tired, too. "Next time." Billy kept on screaming. She recognized his "missed opportunity." They rode up to the stop. She then let Billy press the button to go back down; he was back in control and gleefully he pushed and pushed and pushed.

Having become aware that the button "makes it go," Billy's next step is to see that if "I push the button, I can make it go." A sense of power! A three-year-old demands that power and has a hard time giving it up. Having wondered, "Why does the elevator go?" he finds his answer: "I did it!" "I made it go!"

A three-year–old's intense drive for mastery is a touchpoint in his development and presents new complexities for his parents. Along with his new drive to understand "why," and "what makes things go" is a new capacity to test these questions. With this comes frustration and falling apart as he faces what he can't understand, or what he will not be allowed to do to understand and to exercise his mastery.

Mrs. Stone's next dilemma was how long she should let Billy work the elevator. Another family got on. The little girl tried to push Billy away, and another tantrum was about to start. The little girl's mother tried to hold her back. Billy triumphed. But Billy's mother sensed the importance of limiting his actions. She pulled him in close. "Billy, you've had your turn. It's this little girl's turn now." "I wanna do it! I wanna do it!" The other family was intimidated by his passionate demands. Mrs. Stone held him tightly. "I'm sorry, Billy. It's her turn."

For the parent, there is a new balance to be weighed. When is it time to support exploration? How can a parent tell when exploration has gone too far and must be stopped? One parent may tip towards the peace of mind that comes with limiting exploration, but another—for fear of shutting down curiosity important to learning—may tolerate risk or havoc wild enough to scare the child. Both parents may fear losing a certain closeness.

Must the child be allowed to try everything out? Should every question be answered? A parent would like to encourage a quest for knowledge, but without overwhelming a child with complicated answers. The most important thing to remember is that the child will want to get a sense of mastering it himself. His world still makes sense only as it relates to *him*. In order to understand, he may have to act, to use his body, to see his body make things happen, and also hear his questions answered. Neither limiting exploration nor giving free rein is right all the time. Parents will have to find a balance that they can tolerate and that fits their child's style of learning.

One day, Marcy asked her father, "How do those people get inside the TV? Are they real people?" Mr. Jackson hardly knew how to answer her. "What a good question! Click the machine on and you've got a picture of those people. When you click it again they are gone. They are just play-acting for us, somewhere far away, and the TV show they're acting is the picture. They're real people, but they're not inside the TV." Marcy turned the television on and off. "Where do they go?" Father: "They are still there. You are seeing the picture of them. When you turn off the picture they go out of sight. But they're still there somewhere. They'll still be play-acting. But we won't see them." How could anyone understand this? Mr. Jackson's fumbling answer didn't seem adequate to him. Nor did it to Marcy. But he wanted to encourage her to ask such questions. What should he do? His goal was not to try to help her understand completely, but to encourage her inquisitive wondering. Many parts of our lives are complex and difficult to understand at any age. If Marcy's father joins her with his own wonder, she is unlikely to give up on her curiosity. Turning it on and off helped her master the question. Answers were only a tease.

(As a child I wondered, in the days before television, where the people in the family radio were. My younger brother and I took the whole thing apart to find out. When my mother came home and found the treasured radio in pieces on the floor, we sheepishly explained, "We were looking for the announcer." I remember how hard she tried to hide her smile.)

Tim was sitting on the porch with his father. A caterpillar fell off a tree onto the table where they sat. He and his father watched as the caterpillar humped himself across the table. "Look at him go," Tim whispered excitedly. Mr. McCormick admired Tim's intent observing and said coyly, "Tim, how do you know this caterpillar is a boy?" Tim answered quickly, "Oh, it's a boy." "How can you tell?" "His hair sticks up straight—just like mine."

*Gender
Differences*
Three-year-olds understand things in concrete terms that are based
on their perceptions; one visible characteristic is enough to put
something in one category. Genital differences are out of sight most
of the time, so they are not uppermost in the minds of three-year-
olds. If he were pressed to name the differences between a boy and
a girl, Tim would refer to the attributes he sees the most: "Long hair.
Girls have dresses, boys don't. Girls play with dolls, boys don't."
Simple characteristics distinguish important differences.

An important realization for a three-year–old is that everyone is a
boy or a girl, and they are different. "How do you tell if it's a girl?"
"Because she's not a boy." "But how do you know?" "I just look."
"Is Mommy a girl?" "No, she's a mommy!" "Well, who is a girl?"
"Susie." "Is Daddy a boy?" "No, silly. He's a daddy." "Who is a
boy?" "Me".

A three-year-old knows that boys and girls aren't alike, and never
will be, although he can coyly say, "When I grow up I want to be a
girl." He knows, and he knows we know.

Who presents the most obvious, living differences? Mommy and
Daddy. No wonder one of the first jobs in a three-year–old's quest
for himself and his gender is to learn about Mommy and Daddy, and
to recognize their different meanings to him.

The differences have been there from the beginning. Fathers and
mothers have different rhythms. As early as two months of age, babies learn their parents' differences in communication and play.
From early infancy, babies react with surprise and delight to a
change in their expectation of the rhythm they have learned to interact with. They can distinguish mother and father through the rhythm
patterns of their interactions.

When her baby is six to eight weeks old, a mother will act in a
certain way as she plays with him. If he is nestled in a baby chair,
she'll sit down quietly in front of the baby, lean over him to make a
quiet envelope of her voice, her face, even her hands, around the
baby. She'll say, "Hello! Can you say hello to me?" "Coo." "That's
right. Now another." "Coo." "One more." The baby looks at her with
gentle eyes. Arms, legs, face brighten and reach out, to withdraw in
easy quiet rhythms. These soothing rhythms become what the baby
expects from his mother.

Not with fathers. A father naturally excites. When fathers sit
down in front of an infant, they lean back as if they weren't entirely

comfortable. Then, as if to alert the too-quiet infant, they start poking at him. They poke from feet to the top of the head. The two-month old infant startles, then alerts to look eager and surprised. His face alerts, shoulders up, fingers and toes pointed out toward his father. The father starts the poking again—foot to head. Three times he pokes. The baby squeals with delight each time. His whole body shows the different expectations that have been set by this predictable difference in play routines. By eight weeks of age, a baby will get a look of heightened anticipation when he hears his father's voice or sees his face. From then on, his father greets him with vigorous playfulness.

Violations of rhythms, violations of expectancies that have been built upon rhythmic play since infancy become a sure source for humor. Even with babies, first we set up a rhythm when we play peek-a-boo. Rhythm molds the expectancy. Then, when we violate expectancy by breaking the rhythm, the baby chortles. Such games become even more likely by the end of the first year.

Violations become opportunities for the baby to learn about expectancies. Violations elicit behavior from the baby to restore what he expected. The humor comes from a shared knowledge: the baby knows that we know that he knows that what he expected to happen has changed. Fathers use this repeatedly because it always gets a reaction. Any infant knows this as one difference between fathers and mothers. Fathers tend to convey humor naturally. From the first, they offer the child a "violation" of what he expects. Mothers are for cooing, feeding, and other serious business. Fathers are for play—even when the baby is as young as two months!

Mr. Lee loved to play with Minnie. When she was an infant, he found that she'd respond to him when he surprised her. They went from peek-a-boo to singing games in which they would burst out with an exclamation to surprise the other, to rocking games at night before bedtime. He'd rock, rock, rock, until Minnie seemed to settle. Then he'd stop to tease her. She'd get so excited that she wouldn't sleep. Her mother had to put a stop to this game.

As soon as she could walk, Minnie would clamber up her father's knee whenever he sat down. "Ri! Ri!" He knew it was "Ride, ride to Boston; Ride, ride to Lynn; Ride, ride to Boston; Oops! Fall in!" On the "Oops," he'd throw Minnie in the air with his foot. He'd catch her as she collapsed. She loved all these games. So did he.

Expectancies are learned and they are important to learning at any age; they are made to be broken and to be experimented with. In this way, a child learns the importance of rules for living. Humor surely helps. A child gets used to daily routines. They are comforting, and when they are broken, they can even be fun. Fathers like Mr. Lee have a special role in this learning.

Mr. Lee found that the seesaw was made for such learning. He would set the expectancy with regular ups and downs. Then, he would break the rhythm by stopping the seesaw in the middle or by banging it on the ground. Minnie's gestures and paroxysms of laughter made Mr. Lee feel like a king.

It is easy to recognize how readily each child has already begun to absorb gender differences. By two years, a little boy strides like his father, arms swinging. A girl not only walks like her mother—watch a mother and daughter walk away from you—but she gently tilts her head when she wants to be appealing. Her gestures (especially under pressure) easily mimic the female members of her family, including older sisters. It has always amazed me how quickly a small child models behavior on an older one. Whereas a two- or three-year-old masters a task in steps when an adult presents it, the three-year-old absorbs the entire task when a four- or five-year-old performs it. What, then, influences a three-year-old girl like Marcy to learn a "feminine" way of performing when her older brother is such a powerful model for her? Her sense of herself as female rather than male must already be a powerful determinant. For example, when she imitates Mommy, Daddy may become more available and intrigued. If she stomps around like her brother, no one really approves of it. This is not expressed overtly in many families, but subtly. The subtle but definite differences in expectations from birth can also be a parent's response to subtle but real differences in the newborn baby's behavior.

At three years of age, subtle differences in behavior are already treated differently by parents. When Marcy postured like her mother, or imitated her mother's language, both parents would have a rewarding response. "Marcy, you sound just like your Mommy."

Her father's remark might come with a nurturing pat, an accepting tone of voice. Marcy would recognize a kind of communication with him that would be difficult for her to elicit any other way.

At the playground, Marcy joined contentedly with the other children her age, and they set up a playhouse. They used utensils from the sandbox and imagined a house and a make-believe stove. Each child had his own recipe. Marcy said, "Here's your tea, dear. Drink it." So much of this was in imitation of her mother. Mrs. Jackson had to laugh as she watched and listened from across the playground. Marcy's gestures were accurate. When Marcy patted her hair with one hand, Mrs. Jackson recognized herself.

When Mr. Jackson arrived on the scene, Marcy's behavior changed. Her movements, which had had a soft, fluid quality to them, became more vigorous, more muscular. She ran over to the big slide. "Watch, Daddy. This one's scary. I can do it." She teetered clumsily up the ladder to the top. Mr. Jackson rushed over to catch her in case she fell. She looked down at him with a forced smile. "I'm not scared. See me?" She leaned over the last step up, to lie on her stomach as she came down the slide. This was her first try at this new technique and she was unaware of the possibility of landing on her face at the bottom. Mr. Jackson rushed to grab her as she landed. As he caught her, she looked up at him gratefully. In an attempt to be triumphant, she said, "I wasn't scared." But her father was.

Marcy's brave move attracted another little girl. Minnie whirled over to the slide to imitate Marcy's triumph. Mrs. Lee jumped off her bench to protect her accident-prone child. Minnie stormed up the ladder, sat, and slid down. Now, it was up to Marcy to imitate her. Mr. Jackson wished he could lead her away. No luck! Up Marcy climbed, slipping once. Mr. Jackson's heart stopped. Mumbling to herself, she sat and edged down the slide. "Now Marcy, you've done it. Let's do something else." Marcy gave Minnie a parting look, but followed her dad across the playground. Her stride was a little like his. Her gestures even became more like his. She looked up at him adoringly. She'd used words to talk herself out of being afraid. Her father almost believed her, and so did she.

Language and Speech

Learning about language is an exciting new adventure for a three-year-old. A child of this age tries to elicit reactions with his speech. He is discovering that speech influences others. Language is also shaping his understanding of the world around him, and helping him shape his own thoughts. Words give a child new power over himself and the world, just as he is becoming aware of how powerful the world around him can be.

Further into her third year, a new development in Minnie caught Mrs. Lee by surprise. She hadn't imagined that at some point Minnie's driving pace would diminish as her interest in language developed. Now a few words from her mother would catch Minnie's attention. Minnie would often respond to such suggestions as "Can you slide down the big slide?" This resulted in Minnie's demonstrating it, to her mother's amazement. But if the line at the slide was too long, or if there was any other distraction at all, Minnie would veer away as if she'd never heard the question. If the request involved something less compelling, Minnie might barely notice that she'd been spoken to. When Mrs. Lee saw that Minnie was capable of taking in and responding to verbal directions, she was puzzled by the fact that sometimes she did and sometimes she didn't. She couldn't help but take the times Minnie didn't listen as a rejection. She did not yet understand that Minnie's capacity to follow directions depended on how much else was going on around her, and on her own inner drives.

When Minnie was preparing to dash off, Mrs. Lee tried various tactics: "Let's play with your ball." "Pick up your dolly and hold her." Or she'd say something surprising to catch Minnie's interest: "Watch that little boy run! I bet you can run faster than he can!" Minnie began to imitate her. "Boys running." "That's right, Minnie. The boy is running." Minnie slowed down enough to talk about the boy who was going so fast. Then she ran off after him. Minnie was still more action than talk.

But Minnie's mother was beginning to use Minnie's new openness to language to shape her behavior. If she had directly corrected Minnie's speech, Minnie would have pulled away and stopped listening. But repeating her sentence while incorporating a subtle correction says that Minnie has been heard, and that her words are important: it carries a message of respect. Minnie began to listen more for this reward of being listened to.

Speech, and using words authoritatively, is crucial to the three-year–old. Without thinking, parents help them feel even more masterful by expanding their children's vocabulary. After a three-year-old has blurted out a noun and a verb, he will be able to complete the sentence. The three-year-old is eager to take in the added new words that mean she's been understood. This is indeed how children learn to make sentences and to enlarge their vocabularies. Exposure to language is necessary for learning it. Equally important are the emotions that go with a communication. The inner satisfaction of being understood, and the external reinforcement of the power of words propel language learning along. A three-year–old is delighted with both. Both are supported by the astonishing capacity of children in these years to absorb new language, a capacity that far exceeds that of their parents!

Children of this age nearly always pick up the essential active words of an adult sentence. "Take your pants off" may change to "Pants off." "Put your shoes on" to "Shoes on." Or an order, "Seat belts on, Grandpa." Along with the many new words a child learns in the third year, he learns new ways of stringing them together into sentences. Her speech rhythms and inflections will also mimic those of the adults around him. "I don't WANT that" or "Don't

PUSH me." This big step from a two-year-old's monotonic productions and could easily be overlooked. It's another sign of the child's strong need to communicate. The feeling of controlling the world through language is exciting to a child. But when she can speak and can imitate the speech and the gestures of others around her, she becomes part of their world.

The rapid burst in language since the second year is another touchpoint for the three-year-old. Learning how to attract and charm people is such a motivation. The discovery that speech can make things happen is a momentous one. She knows by now how powerful words can be not only in expressing herself, but also in controlling what happens around her. However, the frustration with her still limited capacity to use the power of language can lead to stammering, stuttering, and even tantrums. She knows what she wants to say, which makes not being able to say it even harder to bear. When she falls apart, it is her awareness that she is unable to live up to this power that leaves her so devastated. This is when parents may find that they try to protect the child from her frustration by supplying words for her, or by carrying out her wishes before she has expressed them. It is a time for parents to pull back and rely on frustration to motivate the child to master this step herself.

Billy wanted so much to communicate and to woo adults around him that he often stuttered. He'd get going with "A-a-a-a-I can't." At times he'd be so frustrated that he'd fling himself down screaming, "I can't say it." He was determined, but his ideas raced ahead of his ability. His face would screw up, his hands would flutter. He would look anxious and miserable. Mrs. Stone tried to help him. "Slow down, Billy, you can do it." He'd plead with his eyes. She'd search for what he might want. He sensed her desperation as well as his own. But when at last he relaxed, his words spilled out.

Many three-year-olds go through a phase of stuttering or dysfluency (difficulty in starting to speak). Is their desire to speak ahead of their capacity? If no one becomes too involved in this, or puts more pressure on an already pressured area, the stuttering and dysfluency are likely to pass after a few months.

Billy's stuttering seemed to subside as he found more speech. It was as if his words had to catch up with the new ideas and questions spinning around in his head. He danced as he talked; he used his hands, his face, his whole body. When he emphasized a noun in his speech, his shoulders would go up, his hands almost portraying the word. Mrs. Stone was amazed by her son's sudden increased vocabulary and the new concepts he could portray. "Cow jumped over the moon"—Billy jumped and pointed to the sky. "Where did Billy learn it? Was he acquiring these theatrical concepts from daycare? Every parent of a three-year-old experiences wonder and awe at the child's spongelike absorption of everything new. When the three-year-old absorbs something they have offered, parents know they matter.

Billy learned how to charm everyone. "Hi. I'm Billy." When this didn't work by itself, he learned to hold out his hand to attract adults. He learned to use words in his play to attract his peers. Body language offered another set of meanings to extend the effect of his words. He'd ask for a toy from another child. "Can I?" No answer. "I want it." No answer. "It's mine. I take it." No answer. Billy tightened his fists, leaned forward, and glared insistently. When the other child dissolved in tears, Billy might even say, "Sorry," and pat the crying child to soothe him. But he'd walk away with the toy.

As an expressive mother, Mrs. Stone contributed at least three things: (1) She modeled exciting concepts with her own behavior; (2) she offered Billy scaffolds for remembering and expressing ideas by reading to him (cow and the moon); (3) she elicited speech through her questions and she added her own vital excitement to everything they read or talked about.

For Tim, language and speech were both exciting and scary. Tim was silent in social situations. He protected himself in a noisy environment and was quiet when he was in a group. But when he was at home, his speech was well developed. Tim could speak in sentences with verbs and nouns appropriately placed. He could use sophisticated words and concepts: "Mommy, I watched the moon. What makes it light up?"

When he had been speaking for several months, he began to stutter. "I-I-I-I have to g-g-g-go to the bathroom." His parents were taken aback. "Tim, slow up. You don't need to hurry so. Then you won't stutter like that." "I-I-I-I can't help it." "That's all right. But if you'll slow down, it will get easier." It was almost as if Tim needed to demonstrate his problem, and he chattered at every opportunity. He was even a bit more outgoing. But with each utterance came the stuttering.

Mrs. McCormick became impatient. "Tim, just try. Don't keep on stuttering." The more she worried and let Tim see her worry, the more he stuttered. He began to screw up his face, to perk up his shoulders, to tense before he spoke. These gestures of "maturity" added to Mrs. McCormick's concern. The stuttering was a constant reminder of Tim's disconcerting differences, which she found hard to face. She consulted Tim's doctor, who tried to reassure her. But it didn't work. She couldn't help herself. Tim's struggling continued. At last, Mr. McCormick attempted to relieve the situation. "Don't add to it. He's already worried. I think your anxiety is adding to his." "But what happens if he goes on stuttering? How do you know that I don't help him by trying to slow him down?" "Because he just seems to get worse and more contorted when you try." Mr. McCormick was right; pressure does not help a child's stuttering. It is wise to be patient and wait (before seeking a speech specialist's help) to see whether it resolves spontaneously. Stuttering often disappears when a child's oral motor ability catches up with his mental ability.

"What a chatterbox!" Marcy is a nonstop talker now. Her constant talk shows how driven she is to learn to communicate successfully. She is almost desperate to bring her new language capacities in line with the new things she can do, or almost do, or wishes she could do. Every sentence represents an enormous thrust in learning about her world and how to affect it. Sometimes saying something makes up for not being ready to do it yet.

"Don't tell me to go potty" says Marcy to stop her mother's pressure on her to go to the toilet. Her mother will have to think twice now before she asks Marcy about going to the potty. Marcy learns how powerful her speech can be in influencing others. But she may find that when she talks, she will have to live up to what she has said. She may blurt out, "I don't *need* go potty now" as a response to her mother's pressure. But, once she has said it, she's stuck. She can't go to the potty right now or she will let herself down. Speech becomes a powerful way to create expectations and obligations for herself.

Mrs. Jackson began to notice that Marcy used different inflections with different people. With a peer: "I want it." With her mother: "Get it for me, Mommy." With her father, it was never an order, but more a plea: "Can I have it, Daddy?" And to her mother's surprise, she asked her grandmother, "Grandma, can I play with that please?" Marcy was beginning to learn manners. Mrs. Jackson realized that Marcy was already differentiating people and adjusting what she said to them.

Marcy was learning that words could push her parents into action. She could use her ability to mimic speech effectively. Marcy called out to her father with the same rhythm, the same tones that her mother used. Mr. Jackson called back as if he were talking to his wife. Marcy said, "Come here, dear." He came. Both of them giggled.

A three-year-old can discover other ways in which words are powerful. Marcy's babysitter reported that Marcy was saying "damn" and "shit" when her parents were out one night. When she corrected Marcy, the child said, "Mommy and Daddy won't let me say them, either." She was trying out new words she had heard from her older brother, testing their power, testing her babysitter. Marcy had in her grasp a whole new way of reaching adults. Marcy's curiosity about these words whose power was evident, even though their meaning escaped her, was driving the testing and the learning.

A three-year-old also discovers the power of the written word, especially when she has been exposed to books. By the time a child is three, books have long stopped being for chewing, scrunching, or dragging around. A three-year-old who has been exposed to books knows that they have stories to tell, that the stories have a beginning, and, if she can listen and wait, an end. She may even have some sense that the black marks on the page are called letters and that "reading" is when parents look at the letters and know what to say. The three-year-old knows that she can't read, but may be so captivated by the power of the mysterious symbols to tell a story that she pretends she can read. With repetition, she may try to memorize simple stories, as if she could already make her wish to be able to read come true. A three-year-old like this will not need to be pushed; her own motivation—which can so easily turn to frustration—must be protected.

Time and Space

He can't read a clock, but the three-year-old can use words to organize *time*. He can try out his ideas about time with words and see whether they work or cause parents to interrupt with their objections. The routines of a child's day also contribute to his learning about time. Snack time, nap time, supper time, bath time, bedtime—these are the hours on a three-year-old's clock. He's ready to expect them. Their dependable, predictable nature help him give up the activity he is engrossed in and move on to the next. By making times invariable, yet pointing out that they inevitably end, parents can lessen the struggles that come with the unwanted regular times. "You always take your nap after lunch." "Why?" "Because it's nap time." "But I'm not tired." "You can get up when nap time is over."

These answers will not satisfy a three-year-old; he needs to know *why* time matters. "It's daytime, but night is coming." "It's time for Daddy to come home." One day when Marcy and her brother were out playing, she looked up at the sky. "When the clouds are out it's day. You can't see them at night. When the clouds are out, I don't have to go to bed."

Time, as with other new concepts, acquires meaning as it relates to a child's life. The child experiences the same time span differently in various circumstances. "In fifteen minutes, we'll go to the store" is likely to feel like an endless fifteen minutes. But "In fifteen minutes, you'll have to go to bed" seems far too short.

Minnie was sliding down the slide, over and over. Mrs. Lee warned her, "Minnie, in just fifteen minutes we have to leave. I have to go home and fix dinner. Daddy may already be there." When the time came, Minnie ignored her. "It's fifteen minutes now, no more" Mrs. Lee said, interrupting Minnie's next trip up the slide. "Now!" Minnie acted as if she were wounded and fell to the ground, screaming. Mrs. Lee was in a quandary. Give in to her, or make her live up to the warnings? Of course, the latter seems more appropriate. Minnie couldn't be expected to want to give in, but Mrs. Lee had given her plenty of preparation. Now it was time to go. Minnie was just learning about limits on time. Time also means that one event stops and another begins. Change is challenging for any three-year-old. Although preparation helps in handling transitions, they won't necessarily be smooth.

When a child is three, time goes by a subjective internal clock that is so much more compelling than the clocks on walls that are mysterious and undecipherable. When Minnie and her dad were walking in the woods, Minnie shouted with excitement: "Look! A crocus!" "Did you know that today is the first day of spring?" Minnie looked up at her father intently and asked, "Is tomorrow the first day of summer?" Inner time—less bound by the world around her—expands and contracts with the feeling of the moment. Outer time is still so long, so short, so hard to understand.

Eventually time—so difficult for a three-year-old to measure—will tell when separations must be anticipated, and when they will be over. A separation can seem to last forever, but a sense of time and of its importance will soon help. Billy's mother worked part-time, and everyone expected Billy to cry when his mother had to leave him at daycare. He did. At first. But then he came upon an idea that helped him to accept it. One morning, he asked his mother (he was trying to keep from crying in front of her), "What day is this?" "It's Tuesday, Billy." "No, I mean is it a work day or a home day?" "You mean for me?" He nodded. "It's a work day." "When will it be a home day?" "Tomorrow." "Oh." Billy was learning to measure time the way a three-year-old is able to, that is, according to when the important events in his life occur. Losing his mother was a little easier when he knew he could anticipate the separations and count on the reunions.

Learning about *space* surfaces when a child is three or three and a half. "Mommy went away. But she's coming back." Can the three-year-old picture where she went? "Daddy is at his office. It's in another building—way away from here." "Mommy went to get books at the library." It is hard to know what images this conjures up for a three-year-old.

Space is organized around what is within a child's reach, or is too high, what is within his sight, or around the corner. Space contains an implication of action on his part. "Where do you sleep?" "In my bedroom, silly." "But where is that?" "Next to Mommy and Daddy's room." "Where is that?" "I walk down the hall. I walk past their door. Then there's mine. If you go to the bathroom, you went too far." He visualizes his door by picturing himself walking to it. Activity and space are closely tied—a child needs to move to learn about space; then he can name the places and relations in space he has come to know through his activity.

The use of language to explore ideas also shapes a three-year-old's sense of space. Over, under, above, below, inside, outside, and especially "too high" are words he comes to understand. "The toy is under the table." "Can you put it on top of the table?" "Sure." "When you do, does the toy change?" "Now I can see it." "Is it a different toy?" "No, but now I want to play with it."

A three-year-old also uses language to plan how he will use his body, where he will put his body in space so that he will arrive at the place he has decided to go. Watch a three-year-old silently say, "Up, up, up" as he climbs up a slide. We take for granted the thoughts, and the words that go with them, that guide our movements in space towards our goals. A three-year-old can't yet.

A young child's active exploration of space thus helps him learn about object permanence, causality, and planning out his body's movements. "If I go behind this wall, I know you'll still be here on the other side." "If I close this door, I won't be able to see into that room anymore." "If I want to pull this door open towards me, I'd better move my body out of the way first." All that a child learns through these spatial investigations will lead him to find his way around and discover his place in the world.

Moral Development

Empathy

What does the world look like to a boy like Billy? He is half the size of the adults around him. He must look up to everyone else and struggle to be like them. He has to begin to give up on his own impulses so that he fits their expectations. He can learn by imitation or by trying things out. His antennae are out. He must also learn about the meaning of his actions—a big step.

Because Billy finds most of his world mysterious, he must either shut it out (ignore it) or be unsettled by his lack of understanding. He searches to explain what he can through references to himself because he can't yet imagine the world through someone else's eyes. He knows his own perspective—what he sees, hears, feels, what he can do—so he must rely on this. His endless questions, "Why, Mommy?" "What's that, Daddy?" "When can we go and *do* something?" seem to his parents more like space-fillers than a search for answers. Billy wants to explore and to find the answers *himself*. His parents' answers are only partly satisfying. His own quest is so much more exhilarating.

The big slide, his current quest, is "too high." Any slide will catch Billy's attention, but this one, the one here right now, carries an extra meaning for him. "It's too high for *me*." He is beginning to use judgment to size up his world, to decide what is useful or dangerous for him. A child throwing sand reminds Billy of another time when a child threw sand at him hard and made his skin sting. It hurt, hence it needs to be avoided. He can remember and compare: "That slide is different. This child is doing the same thing."

Mrs. Stone had warned Billy always to ride on the swings with the protective bar on them "so you won't fall out." He always heeded her warning at "their" playground. But one day when they went to another playground, Billy rushed to climb up on a regular swing—no bar. "Billy, only the barred swings!" He looked surprised and sad. "At this playground, too?" Billy must now learn to

generalize from one setting to another, from one prohibition to another. A three-year-old must live with so many of them. But Billy
is learning that he can size up each new experience against previous ones, and he can judge for differences, for danger, for pleasure.

This same memory for past events helps a child learn what is
right and what is wrong. He uses his parents' past reactions as a
guide. But can he generalize these from one experience to the other?

Billy pulled a plastic shovel out of another little boy's hands, in
plain view of both children's mothers. "Give that back!" said Mrs.
Stone. "But it's mine." A wish becomes reality. The other boy
started to cry. "No it's not," said Mrs. Stone. "I saw you take it away
from him." "I took it from him 'cause I wanted it. It's mine." Billy's
disarming honesty told his mother that he didn't know enough to be
deceitful. Should she discipline him and set the stage for lying in
the future? Or should she let him find his own remorse? Billy was
too excited about the shovel to be able to take in the other child's
feelings. He would be ready when he began to care more about the
friend than the shovel.

While playing with peers, the three-year-old begins to be aware
of wanting them as "friends." Empathy with others is beginning. He
now knows he needs them. A three-year-old is just beginning to
want to please other children so that he can keep them nearby. He
knows his peers have feelings and that he must respect those feelings if he is to win friendship.

Billy played in the sand pile next to some new-found friends. Together, they built a sandcastle; Billy wanted to adorn it with a red-
and-yellow cup that belonged to a child nearby. He watched her
dump sand in and out with the cup. He waited until the child was
distracted. Carefully, he slid across the sandbox and stole it out
from under her. Looking guilty, he hid the cup under his shirt and
snaked his way back to his own perch. The victimized child turned
back to find her cup for digging again. When she realized it was
gone, she dissolved in tears. "Where's it gone? Where's my cup?"
When she looked around the sandbox for it, Billy hid it again. Seeing her misery, he pulled it out to hand it to her. "Here it is. I found
it." The child looked at him gratefully. He looked back to smile at
her. He turned to his mother who had been watching: "It's hers,
Mommy—not mine." Mrs. Smith relaxed, recognizing that Billy
was developing a conscience.

Billy looked as if he were aware of the achievement. He'd mastered a strong impulse. This step toward moral development may seem small to an outside observer. But to a parent, it is a major accomplishment. Those around Billy can soon rely upon him. He can begin to understand that his world encompasses the needs and feelings of others, not just his own. He is now becoming aware that he can affect others.

Still Billy thinks about his world mostly as it affects him. He evaluates people and things as they relate to him. When they reach out to play with him, he likes them. He is the center of his world and he understands that world through his own experience. He can't really know yet about the world beyond his immediate experience, beyond the grasp of his senses. But he is filled with excitement about the world beyond and lunges ahead to discover it.

Aggression:
Fighting
and Biting

A renewed surge of aggressive feelings surfaces in the third year. As opposed to the tantrums of the second year, this aggression is directed more at others. It can be upsetting to everyone – to parents, and to the child. It carries with it a price: the price is in the anguish that the child's own aggression stirs up in her. Fears and nightmares, though more elaborate in another year, are an expression of this anguish. Aggression and the fears that result are a touchpoint of the third year. How can a parent help a child face her own aggressive feelings with less fear, in preparation for the eventual task of mastering them?

Minnie was pushing aside another little girl to get to the snack table at her child care center. She shoved her forcefully. The girl fell and hit her head on a block. A bruise soon resulted. Mrs. Thompson had seen it all happen. She panicked and rushed to comfort the victim and to apply a cold cloth to the bruise. The girl was screaming, "I hate her!" This reminded Mrs. Thompson of Minnie's responsibility. She handed the hurt child to a helper, and gathered Minnie up. Minnie was stiff and looked away. But as Mrs. Thompson talked, Minnie began to listen. "Minnie, I know you're sorry and maybe the child you pushed knows it, too. But you've got to get yourself ready to say you're sorry to her. And only when you can really mean it." Then Minnie looked at Mrs. Thompson anxiously and blurted out, "I'm sorry." And she was.

Mrs. Thompson's comfort to the aggressor offered Minnie a chance to feel sorry in safety—instead of being overwhelmed by her loss of control. When a child is overwhelmed, she must defend herself—by being unresponsive to the other child and to herself. Mrs. Thompson's approach allowed Minnie to face her own fear of losing control and to feel sorry about consequences of her acts. She can apologize, and she sees that it helps.

Even as she was shoving the other child so hard that she fell, Minnie's awareness of her own role was evident in her eyes and her face. Was she sorry? Of course. But she needed time to recognize it. Her fear of losing control pushed her into even more relentless activity. Minnie needed comfort as much as the child she had attacked. The comfort shouldn't be an acceptance of what she's done. The purpose is to reassure Minnie that she is no longer out of control and to give her hope. Great care must be taken to encourage her—not, of course, to repeat what she's done, but to believe that she will learn to control herself.

A child who is repeatedly left alone at such times is at risk of feeling that she is indeed bad, and of acting on it. A caregiver's question must be: Is the child ready to handle her own guilty reactions? Or will she have to turn away from this experience to protect herself? The child needs to be aware of her actions and their consequences, but if she's overwhelmed, she will not learn. Instead, she will be forced to protect herself against the pain of feeling guilty and frightened by deciding that she really is "bad." This is when "bad behavior" takes hold, to be repeated over and over again, as a child comes to believe that she *is* always "bad." The goal is to help her recognize her guilty feelings and her power to stop herself. In the meantime, she will need help in holding on to the hope that she can succeed.

Biting and hitting may be left-over behavior. In the first year, all children go through a period of biting their caregivers. Then, in the second year, a toddler bites a friend. Both mothers are horrified. The bitten child screams. Everyone rushes to her. The biter is surprised, overwhelmed, maybe even a little fascinated by the response and how overwrought everyone is. There is little chance of learning control from such an episode. Violent reactions from parents will only add to this behavior.

Any impulsive behavior such as biting or hurting is frightening to the child. She doesn't know how to stop. She repeats it over and over as if she were trying to find out why it produces such a powerful response. Biting, scratching, and hitting all start out as normal exploratory behaviors. When adults overreact or disregard the behavior, the child will repeat the behavior as if to say, "I'm out of control. Help me!"

One strategy is to introduce a technique to the child on which she can fall back when she has an urge to bite: "What about grabbing for your lovey when you're upset?" One mother of an elderly (three-year-old) biter gave her a rubber dog bone to dangle around her neck. When she felt the need, she resorted to it.

Billy had just hit a little girl in diapers sitting in the sand box." Mrs. Stone heard her wail. "Did you hit her?" "I sure did. She made me real mad." "Why did you do that? You hurt her." "I wanted to." Billy's mother was stunned at Billy's naive honesty. Should she punish him? Would punishment make him cover up in the future? He needs his mother's discipline, but to overwhelm him now might only dampen his feeling of responsibility: "Mommy's so mean. It's her fault I hit that girl." Should she let Billy find his own remorse? This is the source of future morality—but it will not come for another year or so. Now, limits are necessary. Billy has indicated that he needs them.

Frantic responses are not likely to help. Limits must be firm and consistent. After such an episode, a parent's response should be definite and effective in stopping the child. A time out, or holding, is one way of doing this. The look on a parent's face and the tone of her voice must be unequivocal—this is the source of information for learning. Helping the child find words for the feelings she has put into action can help her the next time. But deserting her at such a time is not helpful. Instead, it helps to pick her up and comfort her. Remind her how frightening it was to lose control. "I'm sorry and you are sorry." Tell her you'll set limits for her until she can achieve them for herself. Reassure her that she will learn how to stop herself. Point out an example from someone she cares about. Use yourself. When she sees you, her parent, about to lose control, but catch-

ing yourself, let her know what you are doing. Children learn most about self-control from modeling on their parents' behavior.

The current dispute over strictness versus permissiveness misses the point. A child needs limits *and* nurturance; neither one alone is sufficient for a child to grow. At three, a child may not be ready to take in, to remember, and to know when to expect the limits. She may need reminders from one time to the next. Little by little, a parent's patient repetition will help her to take them in, and make them her own.

Discipline Discipline means teaching. It is not the same as punishment and shouldn't be confused with it. Discipline is aimed at an important goal—self-discipline. Stopping the child is important, but it's not enough: the goal is to teach the child to stop herself. Setting limits on one's behavior, learning to control one's wishes and impulses is a lifelong job. A child who recognizes and can act on her own limits is already a secure child. One who can't stop herself is likely to be anxious, demanding, hungry for someone to say "Stop! That's enough!"

In the third year, to discipline effectively, a parent calmly but consistently breaks the child's cycle of being out of control. Holding, rocking, and removing her from the too-exciting situation may accomplish this, as may ignoring her or isolating her briefly until she has calmed down. Then, quickly pick her up to reassure her: "I'm sorry, I have to stop you—until you can stop yourself. Every time you do this, I will stop you." Consistency and a calm approach are difficult for parents to achieve, but they are an important goal. Discipline that succeeds creates its own reward. A child who has been successfully disciplined looks up at a parent gratefully, as if to say, "It's a good thing someone knows how to stop me!"

Striking a child, in or out of anger, is not respectful; it conveys the message that the parent, too, is out of control. It forces a child to repress her own anger, but out of fear—there is no mastery in this. It says to her, "I'm bigger than you so I can control you (for now)." Physical punishment conveys the message that violence is a way to settle things. In our violent society, it is no longer permissible to convey that message to our children.

Some of today's parents were brought up in families in which parents were excessively permissive, trying not to discipline their children. They felt that this was the way for children to take responsibility and find the controls for themselves. But three-year-olds can't do it. At the end of the day, one can expect a three-year-old in such a family to be climbing the walls. Coming over for dinner means sharing the meal with a wild, uncontrolled child. A child without limits will charge about, whine, throw food until exhausted. I have seen such a child finally lie down in the center of the room, thumb in mouth, eyes glazed over. Any attempt to comfort him only elicits screams: "No! No! No!" It can be a nightmare.

Long before this situation arises, a parent in control will say, "No! This has gone far enough! It's your bedtime and you are showing us all how you need help getting yourself to relax for bed." A "spoiled" child is desperate—desperately searching for understanding, and for structure. Such a child knows she hasn't the capacity for self-control. Her anxiety rises when she can't rouse controls in those around her. The most serious aspect of this ineffective parenting is that the child never has a chance to learn how to control her own frustration. Teaching controls and skills for putting up with frustration is a major gift to a child.

Some parents feel they must react against their own upbringing. Perhaps they grew up in families with rigidly high expectations. Too much was asked of them, so they ask too little of their children. Neither extreme works. When a parent says "No!", the child often needs to find out whether she *really* means it. An inconsistent or weak response will invite another try. An overwhelming punishment will leave a child focused on the hurt and the resentment, with no interest in the lesson to be learned, and no motivation to do better next time. A parent is walking a tightrope.

Minnie was always a handful at the market. As she and her mother paraded through the different sections, Minnie would reach for everything. Until now, Mrs. Lee hadn't realized how much easier it had been to keep her confined to the shopping cart when she was younger. Now, she'd pull things off shelves and ignore her mother's desperate pleas to leave them alone. Once, she dropped a box of rice with a loud *splat* all over the floor. When Mrs. Lee tried to stop her, Minnie ran away, disappearing around the corner. The manager of the store brought her back, and looked disapprovingly at Mrs. Lee. By the time she finished shopping, she was exhausted, worn out by the anger she was harboring against Minnie. At the checkout counter, when Minnie began to tease and to run off again, Mrs. Lee resorted to the candies. "Minnie, if you'll just stay with me long enough, I'll buy you some candy." Minnie looked at the candy to size it up. Then she ran off again. Mrs. Lee was desperate.

Mrs. Lee knew that her discipline was tentative. Neither she nor Minnie took it seriously. Why was she so tentative? Did she hesitate because she feared that she might unleash her anger at Minnie, not just about today, but for all the times Minnie had left her feeling pushed away and ineffective? Other considerations hamper Minnie's mother in her quest for discipline. Something is uneasy in her relationship with Minnie.

Later that day, Minnie was playing ball with her father. Because they were in the house, they were using a soft cotton ball filled with fluff. In her excitement, Minnie pitched the ball too high. It went over her father's head into the forbidden living room. The ball hit her mother's favorite porcelain figurine. The figure fell, disintegrating into pieces. Mr. Lee was stunned. Minnie looked shaken. She ran away to hide, screaming, "It's Daddy's fault. He did it. I didn't break it." Mr. Lee was immobilized. He knew it was as much his fault as Minnie's, but why couldn't she face her role in the disaster? When Mrs. Lee rushed into the room and saw her lovely figurine in pieces, she collapsed into a chair weeping. Mr. Lee felt compelled to discipline Minnie. She'd hidden in the laundry, and by the time Mr. Lee had found her, his anger had built up. He pulled her out from behind the washing machine and started to spank her.

Then memories of his own childhood came back to him. He'd hated the spankings his parents had given him. He'd sworn he'd never hurt his own children. Minnie winced as she sensed his anger and his near loss of control. Mr. Lee melted and took Minnie in his arms. "I'm sorry, Minnie. We did it together—and I was about to blame it all on you. It's not fair, is it?" Mrs. Lee felt hurt. "You and Minnie are always in trouble. I can't trust either one of you! First you leave me to take Minnie to do the grocery shopping when you know how hard that is for me, and for her. Then you can't even discipline Minnie when she needs it. You just leave it to me!" Although it was as much his fault as Minnie's this time, he knew that what Mrs. Lee said was true. He couldn't bring himself to be a disciplinarian. His own childhood always returned to make him cringe.

Among the most important resources for parents are the experiences they can draw upon from their own childhoods. One of the most painful challenges, though, is to avoid being driven, unwittingly, by the past. It's difficult to teach discipline when "ghosts" from a parent's own "nursery" make him feel, for the moment, more like a child himself: either longing to retreat from the responsibility of teaching or fearing that he may be unable to hold back on hitting.

Discipline is perhaps the most difficult task for many parents. It reminds them too much of their own upbringing. Parents, for example, who have been abused themselves as children may have a difficult time with their attempts to give up on abusive punishment. They may never have learned alternatives to violence from their own parents.

"Time out," isolation, containing the child in your arms, and confining her to her room are all effective, immediate responses to out-of-control behavior—the child's, and the parent's. But these responses need to be followed quickly by the parent's assuring the

child that she can rely on herself to regain control and face what she has done. Next, a parent can offer the child a chance to apologize, to repair the damage, and to feel forgiven. I do not believe that spanking offers a solution. Children learn little from a spanking, except to be hurt and angry.

Temper
Tantrums Billy wanted so much to be like his stepfather. One day he tackled Mr. Stone's computer to try to find his favorite computer game. He'd watched his stepfather set the computer game up the night before, so he felt competent to imitate him. It didn't work. He tried out different keys as he thought he'd seen his stepfather do. When his mother finally found him, Billy was in a state. Not only was he furious but he was attacking the computer. His mother was thunderstruck. What had Billy done to his stepfather's precious documents? "I wanted to do it! Like Daddy!" She called Mr. Stone, who rushed home to size up the damage. Fortunately, the documents could be recovered. But what was to be done about Billy?

Mr. Stone knew he had to take Billy's desire to imitate him on the computer into account. But of course Billy needed discipline; he must understand what he'd done. Mr. Stone realized that he had to lock up his computer; he would bring it out only when he was there to use it with Billy. At the same time, he wanted Billy to learn a lesson from this. By now, Billy was having a full-blown tantrum. Frightened of what he'd done, and anticipating his stepfather's anger, he threw himself on the ground to thrash.

Mr. Stone sat it out. When Billy was finally through screaming, he looked up to be sure his stepfather was still there. Mr. Stone said quietly, "Billy, I have to stop you. You know it wasn't your toy. It's my valuable computer. I want to be sure you'll never touch it again when I'm not here." For a moment, Billy began to giggle with relief. "What are you laughing about? Don't you realize how serious this is?" Then Billy broke down and began to sob. He did know how serious it was, and was having trouble facing it. He huddled on the floor, devastated. Mr. Stone sat still for a while. After a long, long time, it seemed, he gathered Billy up in his arms. "I know you were trying to do what we did last night, but it's far too complicated. You can't do all the things I do yet, even though you want to. Someday you will—but I know that doesn't help you right now. How can I be sure you'll never wreck up my computer again?" Mr. Stone needn't have worried. His quiet approach was much more effective than a violent one. Billy never forgot his lesson.

Later, Billy's stepfather used the computer to help Billy understand himself. He showed Billy how to turn on the computer game, then sat back and watched. Billy tried the sequence, failed, became frustrated. "Show me again, Daddy." Two more times and Billy had it. Billy learned the value of mastering a task by mastering his frustration. His stepfather had the fun and the reassurance of watching Billy's mind back at work. He also had the opportunity to help Billy tolerate his frustration and to learn how to calm himself down. Mr. Stone's own calm through it all was a real asset to them both. If he had added his own frustration to Billy's, there would have been too much tension to handle. It would have interfered with Billy's chance, and the magical feeling of "I did it myself."

Parents, like Mr. Stone, who are away all day and who are likely to be overloaded themselves, may find it difficult to let a child learn on his own. It may be hard for them to put up with a child's frustration. Showing him and letting him see how much he can do on his own can be much harder than stepping in to do it for the child. Having been away all day, a father might prefer to be the "good guy" and to fix problems right away.

On Saturday, Billy went to the grocery store with his stepfather. Billy picked out cans and boxes of foods under his stepfather's guidance for quite a while. At last, though, he wore out and began to throw in choices of his own. Mr. Stone was annoyed. "Billy, I'll either have to pay for all those or put yours back on the shelves." Since Billy had grabbed boxes of sugared cereal and a can of soft drink that Mr. Stone would never have chosen, it wasn't difficult for him to sort them out.

Billy began to whimper at the checkout counter: "I want some candy." "Billy, you can't have candy and you know it." Billy lay down on the floor in a temper tantrum. "I want it! I want it!" Mr. Stone felt helpless. Everyone looked at him as if to say, "Can't you handle that child?" He felt like smothering him or smashing him. Billy sensed his stepfather's anger. It made him feel even worse. "Daddy, Daddy, I want candy! I need it!" What could Mr. Stone do?

Mr. Stone could walk away from Billy, which would certainly have stopped the tantrum. But he was in the middle of the checkout line and in a hurry, and Billy knew it. Another parent came up to commiserate. "Why do they always have to sell candy right in front of the checkout counters?" As Mr. Stone's anger subsided, Billy calmed down too. The crisis was past. But as they left the cash register behind, Mr. Stone overheard the bagger mutter, "What a spoiled little brat!"

When it was all over, Billy was embarrassed. He giggled. "I'm silly, Daddy." He began to cavort around the parking lot, embarrassed, dancing and singing, "Hee hee hee!" Mr. Stone knew that Billy was losing control again, but so was he. He grabbed Billy's arm, then picked him up brusquely. Billy's fearful expression made him stop. He cuddled Billy. "It's so hard to go shopping, isn't it? It's so boring. Should we stop now and go home, or can we go to another store?" Billy, mollified, said, "I'll stop, Daddy. I'm sorry." And he did. He held his stepfather's hand, proud of his new inner controls.

Mr. Stone's sensitive sharing of Billy's frustration was a way to help Billy understand himself. It also provided Billy with an opportunity to break the cycle and stop himself. If Mr. Stone had blown up at Billy, he would have distracted Billy from his own responsibility, and the cycle would have continued. Three-year-olds are hungry for firm, dependable limits as long as a bit of loving goes with them. The need for discipline (teaching) and firm limits is always there at three. The loving not only keeps the child from turning away from the limits but also helps him feel comfortable enough about them to be ready to make them his own.

In the third year, parents begin to hold their children to external standards and expectations. Mr. Stone knew that Billy was fed up. He could have tolerated his "out of control" behavior, and did, until he saw the other customers' faces. He wanted to protect Billy from such reactions, but he also wanted to protect himself. Billy needs to handle his own frustration, and, at three, fortunately he is ready to learn. Mr. Stone's approach, holding Billy to calm him down, explaining to him what he'd just been through, and modeling for Billy as he calmed himself, is an effective one. When it works, everyone feels satisfied.

When parents can wait out a child's temper tantrum or their own immediate over-reactions, then gather up the disintegrating child to help him regain control, the child will have learned about handling himself in the future. After a brief period of isolation or a "time out," a parent can pick up the now-quieted child and say, "I'm sorry, but you just can't do that. Every time you do, I shall have to stop you—until you can stop yourself." If parents avoid frightening the child further, by restraining their own blow-ups and helping him calm himself, he stands a far better chance of facing his own role in what he has done. A parent's blow-up is only a distraction from this crucial challenge. Don't overdo the lesson to be learned. Leave room for the child. The goal for discipline is self-control. It takes years—often a lifetime.

Discipline Guidelines

Because parents of three-year-olds must expect more frustration as their child grows and faces the increasing expectations of the culture around her, here are a few guidelines in helping a child learn where she has transgressed without leaving her feeling deserted:

- A parent's first task in discipline is to survive the breakdown in behavior, then reassure the child that you will be there to stop her until she can stop herself. Ask yourself what she is likely to have learned from this episode.
- Develop techniques such as hugging and containing the child, soothing maneuvers, time out, or isolation as ways both of containing the child and giving her a chance to pull herself together. Limit-setting in this way is reassuring.
- Intervene before the child is overwhelmed. Knowing when takes time for a parent to learn. Take stock of the stresses (transitions, frustration, overstimulation), and of the child's nonverbal behavior that occurs repeatedly before the blow-ups.
- Frustration is a healthy force for learning as long as the child is given opportunities to master the frustration. When she succeeds at last after a period of frustration, a child is more likely to feel, "I did it myself."
- Tolerating frustration is a major achievement for a child. It is difficult for a parent to watch a frustrated child; it sets off the parent's own frustration, which the child is likely to feel and respond to. You need to be prepared for setbacks and slow progress. Stay focused on the end result—self-discipline.

You can't avoid mistakes in discipline. Temper tantrums may result, but they aren't the end of the world. Both you and your child will learn from them. Parents are often amazed by how forgiving their children can be, by how many more chances there are.

Relationships: Building a Family

The New Baby: Parents' Issues

Billy's mother had taken Billy to his doctor for a two-and-a-half-year-old checkup. Every time Billy bent over to let himself down to the ground, he'd let out a little grunt. At first the doctor wondered whether Billy was sore from constipation (no, he wasn't tender in his abdomen) or had a sore hip or back. None of these proved to be the reason for the child's grunts. Finally, the doctor hit upon an explanation. Halfway through the exam, she asked Mrs. Stone, "Are you pregnant?" "No. Billy's just two and I want to wait until he's four or five before having another baby. Why did you ask?" "I just wondered," replied the doctor.

When Mrs. Stone discovered a few days later that she was indeed pregnant, she called the pediatrician, who said, "Well, Billy knew before you did. I guess you don't need to announce that you're pregnant to him." Billy had been imitating his mother! So intimate are their shared feelings that Billy knew his mother was different, even if it was only just beginning. He'd begun to imitate her behavior, and Mrs. Stone hadn't even been aware of it.

"When should we tell our child?" parents ask. My answer is "Never don't tell him. He'll know by the change in your behavior. Talk about it as early as you want, but don't emphasize it until close to the end. It's a long wait otherwise." Even a three-year-old wants to know, "How did the baby get in there?" How will he get out? Will he get out like my poops?" Here's a new and important reason to withhold his poops "like Mummy."

Later in his mother's pregnancy, as Billy imitated her walk, stomach sticking out, legs wide apart, arms flopping, everyone laughed. "Look at Billy! He's imitating his mother. But Billy, little boys don't have babies!" Billy sensed disapproval in their humor. Why couldn't he have a baby? What was a baby anyway? Everyone pointed babies out to him these days. They weren't all that interesting. They squirmed, and squealed, and cried, and pooped. After he'd been forced to watch a neighbor's baby, he squiggled around on the floor, squealing. "Billy, get up! You're a big boy now." Nothing he did was likely to please them.

A mother's new pregnancy can be a touchpoint—not just for the child, but also for the parents, who feel they are "abandoning" the first child, and "pushing him to grow up too soon."

Billy will have questions. "Where did the baby come from?" "How did it get inside you?" "Could I get one inside of me?" "How are we going to get it out?" And he will need answers. Always respond to his questions. Never miss the chance to keep communication open. Avoiding his questions now will only make them more awkward and harder for the parent to explain later. Answers can be short, probes whereby parents can sense when the child is satisfied or is ready for more. Billy will surely sense the pride and excitement his parents are feeling.

Before this "baby" was "in there" Billy's parents responded to him every time he made a real bid for their attention. But now he often sensed that his mother was off in a dream world. He began to equate her dreaming and his parents' preoccupation with this baby. None of this was conscious, but Billy felt a slight shove "out of the nest." He treasured every chance to be picked up and hugged even more than before.

Mrs. Stone chanced on him sitting in his chair, sucking his thumb. The sight tore at her heart. She picked him up to love him, but her large belly made her hesitate as she lowered herself to gather him in. Billy sensed that something just wasn't the same.

Being urged to feel his mother's stomach was the worst. She was big and tight. She looked uncomfortable. What was about to happen? Billy's stepfather seemed so concerned about her. "She won't pick me up any more. Will she pop open?" Everyone called him "such a big boy." But he just wanted to be hugged. "Is Mommy sick? She's going to the hospital. Can I go with her?" He wondered who would take care of him.

Why do parents feel uneasy talking about the pregnancy and the new baby? I think every parent anticipates the second child's arrival as if it were a desertion of the first. Mothers in my office who announce, "Guess what! I'm pregnant with my second one" often begin to cry when I ask whether they feel they are deserting the first child. Parents need to acknowledge this feeling before they can openly face their first child's inevitably mixed reactions to the new baby.

"Billy still needs me." Mrs. Stone pulled Billy in tight. Billy was surprised and taken aback. He pulled away forcefully. Mrs. Stone looked at him sadly. "I'll still see to it that he's the center of our universe." He will be—until the new baby comes. Then—despite all intentions to the contrary—as a mother turns toward her new baby, she moves imperceptibly away from her first child. Even during pregnancy, a mother begins to withdraw and to prepare herself.

Mrs. Stone can help prepare Billy by talking to him and emphasizing her need for him. But he may still sense his mother's withdrawal; he will try her out to find out whether she's still his. He may even push her away. A mother is vulnerable at this time to her own guilt at leaving the older child. The child will test this out. I would urge Mrs. Stone to increase her presence with Billy. Be there for him at this time. "You and I can do things together" carries an extra meaning. "We can conquer this separation together." Facing these feelings gives the parents a chance to see that bringing a new baby into the family can also be a gift to an older child.

Once parents can acknowledge the "selfish" feelings they have about wanting a second child, they can be more effective in helping the first child face the birth as an important new event. Their efforts to back up the older child should allow him both to resent and to love the new baby. The goal will be to help him feel that "this is my baby" as well as his parents' baby.

Toward the end of the pregnancy, talking together about what to expect is critical. The big worry for the older child is about separation. "If Mommy has to go to the hospital, is she sick? Will she stay there? Will she come home?" Underlying this question always is: "Who will stay with me?" This is a time to listen for questions.

A Potty-Training Problem

The Stones had waited until Billy was two to help him with his toilet training. They believed they'd left it up to him, that they'd done everything "correctly." When they began, he was two and he had demonstrated his readiness with three important cognitive advances: He could say "no" if he didn't want to go; he was ready to sit down and to imitate others around him; and he had even discovered the concept of putting things where they belonged. Sometimes he would even pick up his small toys when he had finished playing and put them in the basket in his room. Mrs. Stone was amazed at her two-year-old's sense of order and recognition of adult expectations around him. She wondered, "Have I pushed him too hard? He was so bright and so eager to please us." But perhaps she knew intuitively that these accomplishments were signs that he was ready.

She had followed the steps she'd read about:

1. She bought him a potty chair of his own and told him that it was his. Billy had been so proud. He sat on it. He put his trucks in it. He put his teddy bear on it. He parroted his

mother, reassuring his teddy bear: "Someday you'll sit on it like we do."

2. Mrs. Stone took him once a day, fully dressed, to sit on his potty while she sat on hers. He leaned up against her as she read him a part of *Mr. Bear Goes to the Potty*. He soon got bored, however, and ran off. But the next day, he was ready and willing to sit and be read to while he sat on his potty.

3. After a week of sitting on the pot with his clothes on, Billy seemed ready to sit there without them. Each day, his mother said, "This is to show you what Mommy and Daddy have to do to go to the potty for poops and pee-pee." He seemed ready. One day, he grunted as he sat there. No production.

4. The third week, she took Billy with his dirty diaper to the potty and dropped the diaper in. He said, "Mommy, don't spoil my potty!" She said, "But Billy, this is where we want you to put your poop some day. Someday you can even wee into the potty." "No! No! It's for my teddy bear." "It's for you, too. See, this one is mine and Daddy's. This one is for you. Your bear can use it, too." Billy: "But suppose his poops smell bad like mine?" "Poops are supposed to smell bad. That's why we use a potty. Someday, you can go on it by yourself." Billy's face lit up. "Just like Bear. Just like Daddy and Uncle John and Mommy. Would you rather use ours?" Billy looked at the huge toilet seat. He wanted to climb up on it. But he looked down at the full toilet bowl with a certain amount of horror. "I might fall in!" He tried to put one leg into the water. His mother jumped to stop him. "You'd have to sit facing it. It's too big for you now. Your seat is just the right size for you. Try it." He looked at the two choices. He looked at her. "OK. I'll try it."

5. Two weeks later, Mrs. Stone dared to try Billy on the potty when he was undressed again. She put his potty seat in the play room, to remind him. "Billy, can I come in to remind you to try it?" He nodded. When she came in the first time, he sat down to urinate on his potty seat; his urine splashed on the floor around the potty and on the seat, but a little bit went in the potty. "Wipe it up, Mom! Wipe it up!" He looked frantic. She wiped up the spilled urine, but she saved the potty with its few drops of urine for his stepfather to see. All three of them

admired Billy's production. Next time Billy went, his stepfather said, "Billy, hold your pee-pee down and it will go into
the pot. It makes such a great noise when you hit the pot!"
Billy looked down to concentrate, trying out the suggestion.
When he held his penis and aimed at the plastic bottom, Billy
was thrilled with the sound he could make. He performed each
time with glee and pride. When he finally produced a bowel
movement for the potty, it was cause for celebration. But he
looked down at it. "Mommy, Mommy, wipe it up! It's dirtying
my potty!" Mrs. Stone started to dump Billy's poop into the
toilet to flush it away. "Not there! It'll get lost!" She saw his
anxiety. She held back. She comforted him. She asked him,
"Billy, this is yours. What do you want me to do with it?"
"Leave it alone. I'll cover it." He grabbed toilet paper and covered the poop. "It smells." "That's right, Billy, let's wash our
hands." With great sensitivity, she left the bowel movement
until Billy lost interest and ran off to play with his toys. When
his attention was diverted, Mrs. Stone could flush his movement away. Billy came back a few minutes later. He rewarded
his mother's sensitivity by looking at her full in the face after
he had noted the empty pot. She realized how concerned he'd
been over losing part of himself, his bowel movement. After
the first few days, he was less concerned about the disposal of
his poops. He washed his hands each time. He didn't even ask
where his poops went, but Mrs. Stone knew the question was
on his mind. She discussed what she should tell him with her
husband. Mr. Stone looked surprised and confused. "I guess
we can tell him that this is where all of us send our poops.
That's where they all go." "Where?" "Ugh. I guess to the poop
dump." "How will a two-year-old ever understand anything
like that?" "I don't know. How do we understand it, either?
Just don't be too uncertain. He's worried. We can reassure him
that it's everybody's concern."

6. As he approached three, Billy's toilet learning seemed complete during the day. He talked about his accomplishment at
school. He asked his friends, "Are you?" All of them answered, "Yeah," even though only about half had completed
this daytime training.

Billy's day time toilet training had been so easy that it surprised the Stones when, toward the end of his mother's pregnancy, he stopped using the toilet. All had seemed so seamlessly rewarding when Billy was two. Why should he go backwards now that he's three? Could it be the baby? Could it be his beginning daycare? Had Billy been exposed to a traumatic event? All these questions ran through his parents' heads. Billy was as upset as they were. "Mommy, Mommy, I'm wet." This happened a few times, but most upsetting was that he was withholding his bowel movements.

A few days passed before Mrs. Stone realized that they were all in a predicament. The poops were being held hostage. She called Billy's doctor. "What do I do?" "Give him prune juice two times a day, and even a laxative if he keeps this up." After a few doses of prune juice, Billy produced a hard stool. It hurt him. He sat on his potty and turned red with his straining. He whimpered. At one point, he jumped off his potty chair and ran around the room. "No poops! No poops!" He looked tortured. He lay down on the floor, his legs together, and pulled them up. As he strained with his body, his mother could see that he was holding on to his bowel movements. She tried again to relieve her son's agony. "Just sit on the toilet. That will help you."

Billy was indeed worried about his mother and the awaited baby. And he was angry. Even before they all talked about Mrs. Stone's pregnancy, Billy had begun to withhold his bowel movements when he sensed his mother pulling away from him. He wasn't necessarily conscious of holding back his poops, but when he did, his belly got big. Billy had felt his mother subtly withdrawing into her pregnancy. Being just like her was his way of holding on to her.

The anxiety around the house now centered on Billy and his poops, not the pregnancy. "Can't you go, just for Mommy? You know you're uncomfortable." No one seemed to understand what made him worried about his poops and why he needed to hold on to them. This was a touchpoint—Billy was trying to deal with all the excitement and anxiety of his mother's pregnancy. His need to regress in an area he'd just mastered was to be expected. Just when Billy's parents were worrying about how they'd manage with a new baby, Billy was pushing them to face how much *he* would still need from them. His parents' tensions, and their anger with this regression, reinforced his anxiety. Billy was crying out for their understanding and help.

In her anxiety, Mrs. Stone called Billy's doctor again. "Will he be absorbing toxins this way? Should I give him an enema?" "No, I don't think so. Many boys when they get trained begin to withhold their bowel movements. It's almost as if they were saying, 'I want to be in complete control.' The only danger is that he'll hold back until his hard bowel movement hurts him when it does come. Then, you'll have a compounded problem. The hurt sphincter feels a bowel movement coming. It cramps up. If it gets hurt again, Billy can begin to withhold for an even longer time—out of fear."

"What should I do?" "First of all, apologize to him. Let him know he's in control. Say to him that you're sorry you've been involved. Potty training is his issue, you know." "But I haven't been. I just remind him now every two hours or so to go and try. I've never punished him. He did all of this on his own." "Many children who catch on to the idea of putting their bowel movements and urine where everyone else does and who learned this from a relaxed training schedule such as yours still need to prove that they are in control. They do this by holding back on their bowel movements. They can't prove it to themselves (or others) any other way. It's time to say, 'You decide. I'm out of it. If you want to wear a diaper at nap time or night, you can use it for your poops. You can go when you want to.' " Mrs. Stone had known all this for a long time. But her pregnancy, and Billy's reaction to it, made it hard for her to apply what she knew.

She wanted to defend herself. "But I haven't interfered. I've been relaxed! He must just be imagining that I push him!" Mrs. Stone and parents like her can hardly believe that a child is so sensitive about being trained that he over-interprets almost any utterance from a parent as interference. He wants so much for the success to be "his," not someone else's.

The doctor sensed Mrs. Stone's defensiveness about Billy's holding back. "One more warning. For now, please don't flush his bowel movements away until he's lost interest in them. He may feel he's losing part of his body."

"But he looks as if he loves to flush them, and even to see them go," she replied. "He even said to me in the bathtub yesterday as we let the water out, 'See Mommy? See that water go down? If my poops were here they would go, too.' "

"Maybe he looks as if he loved it," Billy's doctor offered, "but many children are conflicted about seeing them go. After all, remember that children see a poop as part of themselves, and watching it go away means a loss forever to them."

"Should I mention when it's time for him to go? Won't he try?"

"Absolutely not. Stay out of it completely now. Just leave it to him and tell him you will leave it up to him. I'll bet the problem will clear up when he's ready to take back control."

It did. Within a week, Billy was proudly using his diaper for bowel movements. He was proud of how big he'd made them. Indeed, he didn't want to give his poops up right away. After the second week, when a bowel movement no longer hurt, all was well. He was back on the potty in a month. He was so proud. (See "Toilet Learning Problems Revisited" in Part II.)

The New Baby: A Sibling Adjusts

When little Abby and her parents came home from the hospital, Billy was with them. The Stones had done everything they could think of to help him make an easy adjustment to his baby sister. He'd visited his mother in the hospital. His grandmother had come over to be with him and his stepfather. His stepfather had made himself as available to Billy as he could. He kept saying to Billy, "I'm all yours," and he had been. They'd had fun together. They'd found a closeness that each of them valued. They needed each other.

For the times when he would be less available, Mr. Stone had bought Billy a toy panda, one which he could feed, and which would wet and need diapering. The panda had a prerecorded whimper that Billy could turn on whenever he wanted to. The toy was a huge success. Billy now dared to ask his questions. He'd "lost" his own father; now it seemed as if he'd lost his mother.

"Why is Mommy gone with the new baby?" "She needed to get the baby out of her stomach, so we could have her here to play with her. She'll be *your* sister." "What's a sister?" "It's someone whom you can love and grow up with. And she'll love you, too." "But I don't want her. I want Mommy back." "You will have her back. We all want her. I know you miss Mommy. She will be back in a day or so. We'll go get her together." Billy's eyes were downcast. His body sagged. No one ever listened to him any more. He just didn't want this baby.

Billy mourned his mother's absence. He sat by her chair and sucked his thumb and fingered his blanket. His grandmother came over to him. "Billy, you miss your Mommy, don't you?" "Maybe she won't come back." "Oh Billy, she will. And she misses you, too. Let me hold you and rock you. Choose your favorite story that you read with your Mommy. We'll read it together." Billy went to find a book. First he first picked up *Good Night, Moon.* Then, as if he had thought better of it, he shoved that book back and picked up a book at random for his grandmother to read. While they rocked and read, Billy's eyes stared off into the distance. He hadn't dared bring out his mother's "best" book. It was too painful a reminder.

When the time came to go to the hospital to get the new baby, Billy's stepfather said, "It's time for us to go get Abby and your mom." Billy disappeared. He ran to his bed, crawled under it, and curled up, his thumb in his mouth. Mr. Stone: "Billy come out. It's time to go!" No answer. His grandmother tried: "Billy, your mom will be waiting. She'll be so eager to see you. You can bring Panda, too." No answer. No one understood how much it hurt Billy to have been deserted and replaced. Finally, Mr. Stone pulled his stepson out by one leg, forced him screaming into his snowsuit, and dragged him kicking to the car. "Billy, I'm sick of this! You ought to be glad to get your mother home."

Billy felt little and alone while the nurses dressed "his" baby and his mother pulled herself together. Everyone clustered around the baby. "Isn't she cute?" He didn't think so. She looked so little and pudgy and squirmy. She never even looked at Billy. She just squawked. He had thought she might be his "sister" as they'd said. A sister should want to play with you and look at you and talk to you. She didn't. He felt rejected by her and he didn't like her from the first moment he saw her. Everyone wanted him to love her. The nurses in the hospital hovered around and said, "Isn't she sweet? She's *your* sister and you'll love her someday." When was "someday"?

Billy retreated to a corner of the room with his panda. *He* could make this panda do everything. He could make him cry—and make him stop, too. He could do whatever he wanted to the panda without everyone closing in on him. The panda was his own, and already he felt a warmth and a closeness for the panda that he didn't feel for Abby. The adults almost forgot him when they started for home. He was crouched in the corner to stay out of the way. Mr. and Mrs. Stone started out the door with the baby. Then they turned to find him. "Billy, come on. Let's go home now." Billy felt sad. He flung himself on the floor as if he were going to have a tantrum. His step-father turned away wearily. Billy jumped up and followed them down the hall. He saw his mother's hand dangling at her side. He reached up to grasp it. Mrs. Stone looked down at him. "Billy, I've missed you. I'm so glad you came to get me. I hope you'll like Abby. She'll be so proud of you. Little sisters are always proud of big brothers like you." Billy looked appeased, but he felt the pressure in that remark. Everyone wanted him to grow up!

When they arrived home, everyone forgot him again. They rushed into the baby's room. They cuddled, they cooed, they made silly noises. Grandma was as bad as his parents. But he still had his panda, and he tried to turn to it. He "oohed" and "gooed" a couple of times to the panda, but he felt pretty empty inside—and lonely. Finally his stepfather came out of "that" room to find him. By now, he felt like hiding; he'd retreated to his own bed and curled up beside the panda. When Mr. Stone tried to pick him up, he let out a wail and tried to struggle away into a corner.

"Oh Billy, please don't be so negative right now. We all love you, but we've got to get the baby settled." His stepfather's voice was too matter-of-fact. He'd deserted Billy, too. What could Billy do but curl up and hope? He certainly never expected to be forgotten. His mother hadn't even looked at him after they arrived home. His grandmother finally came in and sat on his bed and comforted him, and he felt better. "Billy, I want to read your book with you." And she didn't mention the baby *or* growing up!

When Billy saw Abby nursing, he wanted to try to do it, too. "Big boys don't drink mommies' milk," Mr. Stone said nervously. "I don't want to be a big boy like Daddy. I want to be a baby." He leaned up against his mother. He sucked loudly like Abby, but he had nothing in his mouth. His parents laughed. "Do you want to try to suck on my breast, Billy?" He put his mouth up to her nipple. Nothing happened. He began to suck the way he did on his thumb. Her nipple stood up in his mouth and he felt this sweet, sweet, taste. He jerked away. "Yucky," he said, and turned to his thumb. After that, he watched Abby but he didn't want to try nursing again. His mother cuddled him to her. "Billy, it's good to hold you again." He moaned a little bit as he snuggled into the space between his mother's arm and chest.

His parents and his grandmother paid a lot of attention to him after that. They hugged him a lot. They let him help when they diapered Abby. They let him fetch her diapers. When he began to wet again, they even let him wear diapers "like Abby." He heard his mother say, "Oh, I hope Billy won't go back to holding on to his BMs!" But he didn't really need the diapers. He wet a few times without them. But because his parents now respected this as *his* struggle, he soon found he was back in control. He felt like the big boy they all wanted him to be. He still needed diapers at night, but that didn't seem to bother anyone.

Now, when his mother was busy feeding Abby, Billy tried a new way to handle it. He pulled back and turned to his stepfather. One morning, when his mother was still in bed feeding the baby, Billy slipped into his stepfather's shoes and stomped out the front door. He sat on the stoop and talked about all the things he would do when he was "big like Daddy."

Billy was trying hard to give up his role as the baby in the family. His reward, sometimes exciting, and sometimes not enough, would be to be "big like Daddy." "Being like Daddy or Mommy" is a way of feeling close to them when they are busy and seem far away. The adjustment to a sibling creates a touchpoint for a three-year-old. No child ever *wants* to *learn* to share. No child wants to learn to share her parents, nor to give over her special role as the baby in the family. But the older child in a family must learn. He is bound to feel abandoned. The lessons about sharing taught through the arrival of a new sibling are difficult and painful, but necessary, and ultimately invaluable.

Every parent dreams of making it possible for the older child to succeed in "loving the new one." It is so important to parents because of their own grief at "turning away" from the first child to nurture the next. A second-time parent feels guilty about the new baby's invasion of the family. The parent must face separation, and his or her guilt at choosing to have another child. Parents wonder whether they and the older child can do it. And yet, they must. Can they parent two—or three? They must face having to spread themselves too thin. Can they save time and energy for the older child?

Preparation for the mother's departure for labor and delivery is very important. Introduce the older child to the expected substitutes: his father, his grandmother, his aunt. Assure him that he's not being abandoned, that it's a temporary separation. Use the phone to help him; make him cards to give his mother and the new baby; and let him visit the hospital.

When the baby arrives, give the older child a new doll or a stuffed animal to love and to nurture while the parents attend to their new baby. As soon as possible, let him help with diapering; let him take part in feeding a water bottle, in holding, in rocking. Introduce the idea that he can be a nurturer, too. But let him turn away on his own, and expect resentment as normal.

Every day, perhaps while the baby naps or at the older child's bedtime, a parent can plan for time alone with the older child to fall back on old rituals or to make new ones. It helps to plan special times together at least weekly. Talk about these times with joy and conviction in between times. During these times, concentrate on the child. Listen and watch. Watch for the behavior that is his language.

Include the older child in the care of the new baby, without forcing him into more responsibility than he is ready for. Praise him when he does help out, but accept his disinterest or resentment of the baby when he expresses it. Encourage him as he identifies with you and with your caring for the baby. He may experience your caring for him vicariously when you are caring for the new baby. But respect the older child's need to be cared for directly by you, even when you must attend to the baby.

When Abby started to crawl at around eight or nine months, Billy began to act up again. His sister's new ability to get around, to make everyone squeal when she pulled up to a table or crept up to a light plug constituted another touchpoint. Billy began to take Abby's toys away from her. He'd leave them out of reach so his mother had to come to save her. When she learned to creep, he'd stand in front of her so she couldn't move. "Billy, you're in Abby's way!" or "Don't take her toys away from her. Play with your own toys." He discovered that tormenting his sister was a sure way to get his mother off the phone, or away from her computer. Somehow, his behavior felt good to him. Maybe he even liked his parents to feel upset, just as he felt when he suffered Abby's invasions. He felt excited and even powerful. But he sensed the anger in his mother's voice even before she displayed it. It was as if he *had* to get his mother angry, as if he *had* to make Abby cry. It was as if he had to become an aggressive, loud little boy so that he could more easily face the challenges of "growing up."

Billy needed to find out how to handle this invasion into his world. Everyone treated Abby's new mobility as if it were some sort of miracle. The "oohs" and "ahs" that she elicited reminded him of all the approval he used to get. No one took Billy's side any longer. His grandmother had gone home. His stepfather turned to Abby and said "how cute she was" when he came home. He no longer came home early. Mrs. Stone seemed angry with Billy most of the time. "Billy, don't touch that! Don't leave things around. Abby might hurt herself. If you take one more toy away from her, you're going into time out for good and all!" The little boy felt deserted. He ached.

To help the aching older child, a parent can deflect some of the attention his way by allowing him to help entertain the baby. The older child can be proud of himself for amusing his sister. When he wanted to play with Abby, Billy learned to pitch his voice higher. He squeaks out, "Hi Abby! Let's play!" Abby is ready to play with Billy at any time. When he imitates their mother's voice, Abby prepares for more nurturing. She softens and begins to be more baby-like. He pats her head, offers his sister her bottle. He croons to her. Soon, however, he loses interest in that kind of play. He starts to be jerkier, rougher in play. Abby changes, too. She becomes more guarded, more ready to defend herself. She recognizes the old Billy.

Everyone in the family was aware of Billy's need to regress and to tease. But how far should they let him go? He spent a lot of time teasing Abby and provoking his mother. She was a wreck by the end of the day. When Mr. Stone came home, she'd turn to him and say, "He's yours! Take over—I can't stand him any longer." Billy would look up at his stepfather for a glimmer of approval. Not there. "Billy, why do you have to make life so tough for everyone? We know you're feeling jealous of Abby, but it just makes us angry with you when you keep teasing your mother and Abby." Billy wanted to ask, "What's 'jealous'?" but all he felt was empty and lonely. No one listened to his side. He wanted to please people as much as they wanted him to—but it always turned sour. He couldn't help it.

Sibling rivalry is a tangle of positive and negative feelings. A new sibling's arrival is bound to present one or even a series of touch-points for the older child; these are times for regression and reorganization. An older child will eventually regress, even if he does not do so at first. Often, it happens at the time of a spurt in the baby's development—when the baby's touchpoint makes her more attractive to everyone—at four to five months when she's outgoing, at seven to eight months as she crawls, at a year when she begins to get into the older child's toys and encroaches on his territory. The older child usually regresses to a former stage of development: talking in an immature way, regressing in toilet training, waking more often at night, eating less and struggling at mealtimes, demanding discipline at special times. Expect this behavior. The older child is (1) regressing to gather necessary energy for making the transition; (2) trying out his identification with the intrusive baby with baby talk and baby behavior; (3) attempting to shift some of his parents' energy back to him; (4) communicating to parents the costs to him of assuming new responsibilities, renouncing old roles, and sharing his parents with another child. This behavior is guaranteed to have an effect on parents and make them worry about their own role in producing it.

Parents must put aside these guilty feelings that lead them to offer pat reassurances to the older child. Stop and listen to the child's questions and concerns, and let him know that you welcome them. Answer them simply, but realistically. Don't expect too much—it will be years before he realizes that by having another child you have given him a new relationship that is just as important as his relationship with you. Even so, when parents understand and value all that siblings can give each other, they find it easier to offer hope and encouragement while accepting the older child's negative feelings.

Try not to take regressive behavior too personally or too urgently. See it as necessary to the readjustment. Support the child by understanding his suffering. Although the older child must be supervised with the baby, try to stay out of their relationship. Sibling rivalry and sibling caring are two sides of the same coin—if siblings can develop a relationship without a parent's intrusion. The chance to learn how to cope with the loss of a unique relationship with parents may be the most vulnerable gift a parent can give an older child.

*Turning from
One Parent
to the Other*

Minnie's father went to the playground after his softball game. His team had won and he was flushed with success. He was jovial and ready for Minnie's driving activity. When Mr. Lee entered the playground, his daughter catapulted toward him. Not looking him in the face, not calling out to him, she just charged him. Proudly, he swung her up in the air. They'd both moved on from the broken-figurine catastrophe. Mrs. Lee could tell he'd won his softball game. "You can watch Minnie now. I'm a nervous wreck. Look at that slide! She dangles at the top!" Mr. Lee hugged his daughter. "Aren't you a brave girl! Just look at that slide. It's too high for me!" As soon as he had uttered his praise, she rushed back to the slide. Her haste made her clumsy. Her foot slipped through two rungs. A third rung pounded on her groin. She winced briefly and her father started toward her. But Minnie ignored the pain and continued to climb up the tall slide. At the top, she stood up straight. She looked ahead as far as she could see, but her bravado drove her mother crazy. Her father looked on with pride. Her mother held her breath until Minnie sat down.

Minnie's drive to achieve lends a kind of insensitivity to pain. Pain is one way the environment says, "Take it easy—you've not paid enough attention." There is a parallel between Minnie's lack of attention to messages from others and her relative insensitivity to her own internal messages. She can ignore them. This is fine as long as the pain isn't signaling real danger. Her father's encouragement helped promote her recklessness.

Minnie is at the mercy of praise, as is every child at this age. She thrives on it and draws courage from it. Too much praise either overwhelms the child by creating a kind of dependency or loses its significance altogether. "Mommy always says I'm a good girl." Praise needs to be saved for important achievements so that it carries its full significance and encourages further growth. Praise can be a powerful guide to what is acceptable and what isn't; however, it can also take away the child's own motivation, her ability to make her own decisions.

Although Minnie appeared to pay little attention to her father's presence, it was easy for observers to see that it cranked up her activity. Now, she wanted him to play ball with her. She could throw with accuracy if her dad stood close. She hadn't yet mastered the job of catching, but Mr. Lee tried to show her how to put her hands together and to wait for the ball. That didn't work very often. Minnie wanted her father to participate with her on every structure on the playground. She begged him to join her on the seesaw. He eagerly complied. He felt like a kid again. He went up, she went down. He went up, she hit the ground. As they played, he added to the excitement by banging his end of the seesaw down. Minnie laughed. He added some surprises to the rocking game by banging his end first too soon, the next time too late. He stayed down. She stayed up. She giggled each time. He stopped her in the middle of a swing up. She laughed loudly. He loved her responsiveness. Every time, he'd try a new surprise. She laughed out loud, and he laughed with her. They reveled in each other's company. Neither of them paid attention to how excluded Mrs. Lee must have felt.

Tim's father also arrived at the playground to relieve his wife. Mrs. McCormick got up quickly, and Tim clung to her even harder. He was like a baby monkey clinging to his mother's fur. She tried to pry him off to hand him over to his father.

His clinging became a kind of clawing. He tried to resort to his trusty thumb-sucking but found that meant letting go with one hand. He quickly returned to his clinging, burying his head in his mother' shoulder.

Mr. McCormick was embarrassed by this show of dependency in front of other parents. He made a brief stab at trying to get Tim's attention. "Timmy! I came to be with you. I want to play with you. Won't you come to me?" No response. His father dropped his arms to his sides in resignation. Was Mrs. McCormick holding Tim a bit tighter? Had she encouraged him to cling to her? There was no overt evidence of it.

Tim may sense that the more he clings, the less likely his mother will be to give him up. Perhaps she holds him in a way that says, "I don't want to give you up. You need me." Meanwhile, Tim's father feels shut out and helpless; he is bound to generate unspoken resentment for Tim and his mother. When both parents care about a child, they are going to compete for that child; this is all a part of caring deeply. Mr. McCormick might easily think to himself, "If she gave him to me, he wouldn't be such a wimp." Tim's clinging increases his parents' tension. They are likely to take it out on each other. But Tim may be paying an even greater price—the chance to learn about his male identity, the chance for independence from his mother's hovering.

Independence and Separation

Childcare

Perhaps the most severe stress on parents of young children today is the struggle to find optimal, yet affordable childcare. Tim's mother had to go back to work because the family needed both parents' incomes. Tim's father was under too much stress. Mrs. McCormick felt she needed to get away from being "just a mother" at home. At times, she worried about losing her sanity. She loved being with Tim and watching his observant, inquisitive mind at work. But after three years of watching and waiting—and worrying about him—she needed the company of adults. She needed to get back to work—for herself as well as for the extra money.

But as she thought about returning to work, Mrs. McCormick looked at Tim with new worries. Was he going to be okay? Would his caregivers understand him? Would he grieve? She began to realize the extent of her own anxiety and even her own grief in giving him up to someone else. She tried to prepare herself. All parents must go through this when they give up a child to the care of others.

She looked around to find the perfect place for Tim. She looked to friends and to books for guidance. She examined each childcare site for dangers, for cleanliness, for ratios of adults to children. (See "Childcare" in Part II) She tried to gauge the atmosphere of the center from the behavior of the children. Did the caregivers like them? Did they get down on the children's level to play and to communicate? Were the children happy and interested? Did the center have a curriculum that led to a child's learning? But each time, she found herself coming back to her main question: "Would they like Tim?" Tim seemed to be unusual compared to other three-year-olds. She looked over each caregiver for sensitivity and an ability to relate to the shy children in each class. Many of the centers were plainly oriented toward outgoing children who fit in and who managed for themselves. She'd no idea how Tim would manage, and even less faith in whether he could.

When she finally made her choice, Mrs. McCormick could face her husband again. He'd been scornful of how long it took her. When she'd decided on a childcare center, she took her husband over to see it. "Do you think he'll make it here?" she asked him. Mr. McCormick answered quickly, "It'll be good for him. He's got to become a regular kid. We've spoiled him." But inside, he, too, felt queasy. Would these caregivers be able to like Tim? All along, Tim's parents had worried about whether to choose a caregiver in the home or center-based daycare. But they just couldn't afford a caregiver at home; anyone they could afford was likely to be untrained, a real gamble and too risky. Center-based care might also push Tim harder to be like other children. Both parents dreamed day and night of this possibility.

When it was time to take Tim to the childcare center, Mrs. McCormick felt almost immobilized by a sense of foreboding. She kept telling her son over and over that she'd always come to get him. His eyes would deepen as he looked at her. His serious face made her heart skip beats. She realized that she could hardly bear to make the separation from him. When she took him that morning, her voice was so choked up that she didn't dare say good-bye to her husband or to Tim's brother. Tim sat quietly, almost stoically, in his car seat. Not a word, not a movement from him. He seemed to sense her grief and to respect it. But, his immobility frightened Mrs. McCormick. What if he couldn't make it at the center? Was she doing him irreparable harm in leaving him? He seemed so vulnerable.

As they entered the childcare center, Tim stiffened, but walked along beside her. Mrs. McCormick clutched his little hand. She felt a tear gather in each eye. The childcare teacher, Mrs. Thompson, came up to greet them. "Welcome! Hi, Tim. I hope you'll like it here!" Tim's withdrawal, his averted gaze, his lack of contact with her, all registered with Mrs. Thompson. She stopped chatting and waited for Mrs. McCormick to make the next move. Mrs. McCormick said, "I guess I'd better sit here for a while until Tim gets used to it." "Please do." For three days, Tim and Mrs. McCormick clung to each other and watched the other children play. Finally, Mrs. Thompson said, "Why not leave Tim here for an hour or so? You go. He and I can sit here and watch the children." She thought, "Maybe he'll loosen up if his mother leaves him." Mrs. McCormick told Tim several times that she was leaving. No word, no movement, no response from him. When she finally left, she couldn't really leave. She hid herself around the corner, waiting for Tim to demand that she return. No word, no movement. He sat stoically where she'd left him. Mrs. Thompson tried several maneuvers to encourage him to play with the other children. The children came up to woo him. No word, no movement. Finally, in desperation, Mrs. Thompson went off to work with the others. Tim remained quiet, immobile. After a while, the other children got used to Tim's unresponsiveness; he sat in one corner, watching. The other children played around him, essentially ignoring him. Now and then, one child would make another try. "Come play with us." But they sensed that Tim would rather watch and be left alone. No word, no movement from Tim.

When his mother came back after an hour, Tim was still sitting where she'd left him. He looked at her without a word. Mrs. Thompson assured Tim's mother that he'd been happy, but he'd never moved. She didn't know how to reach him, she said. Mrs. McCormick said that this was par for the course with Tim. Mrs.

Thompson assured her that many children need a parent to stay with them for the first week at least.

To Mrs. McCormick's surprise and gratification, as soon as they had left the center to go home, Tim opened up in the car. He told his mother about the two children who'd had a fight; he told her about the little girl who'd played house and had fed her dolls; he told her about the boy who'd climbed the jungle gym and stood there yelling for help to get down. As he talked, his face brightened, he became animated. Mrs. McCormick realized that Tim had lived all these episodes from a distance. He'd participated by watching. She couldn't wait to tell Mrs. Thompson, to reassure her, just as she felt reassured.

For Mrs. McCormick, this seemed a first step toward "normalcy" for Tim. His responsiveness to what he'd watched was a sign that he'd managed without her. A sign of failure would have been too much for her. She needed his reassurance that she could leave him at daycare.

Separation in the morning is always a hurdle when children first go to childcare. Many children fall apart. They moan and cry each day. When they have a teacher with whom they have a relationship, that can help. But the separation is still likely to be fraught and painful. This protest is healthy for the child but not easy for the parent. All parents must steel themselves to leave after a teary good-bye. If they need reassurance, they can wait and watch from around the corner. Most children seem to pull themselves together. They accept the caregivers' bid for comfort. Eventually, they turn to relationships with the other children to fill up the loss of the parent. Children do indeed learn social skills and learn to enjoy their peers as they make such an adjustment.

Minnie's parents had also looked into all the guidelines for high-quality childcare before deciding to leave Minnie. They had looked for safety precautions, nutritional food, and health protocols (did the caregivers wash their hands between diaper care for each

child?). They had looked for an optimal ratio of adults to toddlers (not more than four children to one adult) and for caregivers who had experience with toddlers. Such a center cost twice that of centers that were less well equipped. They realized that the cost would be almost prohibitive for more than one child at a time. It certainly affected the Lees' decision about having more children.

Mrs. Lee had not returned to work until Minnie was a year old. At that time, she had felt a terrible burden of guilt every time she had to leave Minnie. She knew that Minnie would not be easy for caregivers. Her accidents had proved that. She felt that Minnie was detached in making social connections and she feared that leaving her might make her more remote. Any mother wonders whether caregivers will like her child "as she is" and will foster her optimal growth. Minnie's impersonality could be a problem.

Mrs. Lee watched to see how the teacher interviewed Minnie and related to her. At first, the Lees had thought it silly that a one-year-old should be interviewed for a slot in a childcare center, but afterwards they were grateful for the interview. Mrs. Lee saw the head teacher get down on the floor to Minnie's level. She tried to talk as she looked into Minnie's face. It didn't work. Minnie became more agitated and active. Mrs. Lee became anxious. Was Minnie really a difficult child? She could see a slight frown cross Mrs. Thompson's face as this question arose in her mind, too. Then Mrs. Thompson sat still, turning slightly away from Minnie. She gave up quickly on her attempt to make direct contact. Instead, she took a toy doll and constructed a block edifice for the doll to climb on, singing quietly to herself as she built. Then she moved the doll and said, "Now she wants to walk, and to stand on the blocks. She wants to climb and be a very big girl." As soon as Mrs. Thompson reduced her social attempts and put the safety of the toys between them, Minnie began to pay attention. As Mrs. Thompson talked, Minnie's interest quickened. She moved in and sat next to Mrs. Thompson. Mrs. Thompson pushed a few blocks over to Minnie, but said nothing. Minnie tried to build onto the house. Soon the two were in play together. Minnie's interest never waned. At the end of fifteen minutes, of play, Mrs. Thompson said, "I think I now understand Minnie and I think she understands me. We can make it with each other and that's what I wanted to know. She is active, and she doesn't like intrusive social overtures, but she can immerse herself in a task. She can relate to someone like me, as long as I let her take the lead. I like Minnie and I think she'll like me. I think we'll get along just fine." Mrs. Lee was almost in tears, she was so grateful. It was a relief to see someone in authority struggling to understand Minnie the way Mrs. Thompson did. She felt that Mrs. Thompson could help her understand Minnie better.

Now that Minnie was three, she and her mother battled over getting dressed nearly every morning. Unless Mrs. Lee had laid out all her daughter's clothes in advance, Minnie was liable to dart from one place to another as her mother stopped to choose underwear, socks, pants, shirt. She'd turn her back, Minnie was gone. When Mrs. Lee had located socks and shoes, Minnie would be gone again. Overalls had to be buttoned on the run because Minnie never stopped moving. Shoes came last. Because they could be secured with Velcro straps, Minnie loved to take them off, put them on, take them off again. All through breakfast, the tearing sound of Velcro drowned out the snap, crackle, and pop of cereal. Minnie defied her mother at each mealtime. Especially at breakfast, she dawdled, she whined, she got up and down, she fiddled with her shoes. It seemed obvious to Mrs. Lee that she wanted to delay the inevitable leaving. But she didn't feel she was particularly important to Minnie. How she longed for signs of tenderness.

Minnie had found that she could undress herself on the way to school while her mother was driving. She would arrive at school completely nude. Mrs. Lee was overwhelmed with shame. Although the teachers laughingly said, "Just give us her clothes. We'll dress her. She won't tease us this way," Mrs. Lee was too embarrassed to continue. Mr. Lee took over the drive to childcare. With him, Minnie didn't undress herself. She and her father talked and giggled all the way to school. He told her absurd stories; she laughed and added a sentence or two. "The cow jumped over the whole world and landed upside down!" Minnie chortled, "Her milk fell out of her!" Laughter.

By the time they arrived at school, they'd had so much fun that Minnie was hard to extract from the car seat. She kicked her father as he tried to unbuckle her. He tickled her back. They skipped into the center.

When Minnie arrived, her teacher, Mrs. Thompson, said, "Look who's here! Minnie and her dad! Welcome." Mrs. Thompson let Mr. Lee take off Minnie's jacket and boots. He made a game out of it. "Take off your jacket, but not your shirt. Take off your boots, but leave your feet attached."

Minnie rushed into the room, already full of children. Several greeted her, and Mr. Lee stopped to watch. He was fascinated to see Minnie take a leadership role with her peers. She skipped, she danced, she led them up to the jungle gym. "Minnie! Minnie!" He was thrilled. He couldn't tear himself away. He glanced at his watch: time for work. He ignored it.

Mrs. Thompson said, "It's circle time now!"

All the children stopped what they were doing, as if by common consent. They climbed off the jungle gym. They collided with each other to find their places in a circle. Circle time was the highlight of the new day. They sat around in a circle. "Clap, clap, clap!" "Welcome, Takiesha! Welcome, Aaron! Welcome, Rosa!" Round the circle, each one sitting up straight when his or her name was called. "Now let's sing our morning song!" "We're glad to be here! We all missed you last night!" As the children sang, trilling their contributions enthusiastically, they reached out for each other and held hands. The atmosphere was charged with warm feelings. Each child beamed. Minnie crinkled with a smile at her father, who still couldn't tear himself away.

Mrs. Thompson said, "Now, everyone tell something exciting! One at a time!" Aaron told about his new guinea pig named Woodrow. "He let me hug him. He squirted all over me!" Everyone giggled. This was a reminder of how recent their own achievements were. Some of them reached for their own underpants to feel whether they were still dry.

"Minnie, tell us about your excitement!" "Well, my daddy brought me to school. He didn't leave!" Mr. Lee beamed. Every child looked in Mr. Lee's direction. What an excitement his presence added. But it also reminded the children of their own homes and of the fathers they'd left.

Mrs. Thompson sensed this and rushed to keep going. "Carlos, you're next!"

Childcare had been a success from the first. Mr. and Mrs. Lee felt confident that Minnie was in good hands. They participated in every parents' event out of real gratitude. Mrs. Lee used each of Minnie's teachers to try to understand Minnie better, and to expiate her feeling that she was not on her daughter's "wavelength." Although there had been many ups and downs, things had gone well.

One day recently, Minnie had fallen apart at the center just before it was time to go home. When Mrs. Lee arrived to pick her up, Minnie flew into a rage. She flung herself to the floor thrashing and moaning. When Mrs. Lee attempted to gather her up, Minnie kicked at her mother's face. Mrs. Lee was mortified by this outburst of rage. "Is she this mad at me for leaving her?" she wondered to herself. The incident revived all her worries. How much harder these guilty feelings made it for her to stand up to Minnie's temper tantrum, and to disengage. The assistant teacher added fuel to the flame: "I just don't understand it. Minnie never acts like this with us." What a blow! Of course Minnie never acts like this with her—the caregiver never makes up for a parent's absence. What no working parent is adequately prepared for is the disintegration of the child that occurs as the parent walks in the door at the end of the day. Parents who have to leave their children all day are afraid that they can't measure up to the caregiver. This was Mrs. Lee's worst nightmare, and Minnie seemed to be proving it true by her behavior. But the assistant's remark is just an example of the competitive gatekeeping between caregiver and parent, and Mrs. Lee will need to be prepared for this.

Minnie's end-of-the-day disintegration at daycare is very common. A child saves up all her frustration, all her overload throughout the day. She saves it until she is within the safety zone her parents provide so that she can let off steam. She saves it for them because these are her deepest, most important feelings. She is saying, "Thank goodness you're here. I can trust you with my deepest feelings and all my miseries." Mrs. Lee needed to hear this and to understand what was happening. Instead, she felt torn and guilty for leaving Minnie. She wondered what kind of environment Minnie experienced all day. "Did they punish her and break her spirit? Will she learn from this experience, or am I dooming her to a lesser life for leaving her? My mother was always at home for me."

Foreboding is bound to arise in every parent's mind; it reflects the grieving that all parents must experience when they share a child with another caregiver. To face the pain of sharing her child, Mrs. Lee needs ways of coping with her feelings.

These are the universal defenses a parent can use to handle this grief:

1. Denial—denying that it matters either to her or to the child, trying to convince herself that it's not that important.
2. Projection—projecting all the good parenting onto the caregiver and feeling nothing but guilt for herself—*or* the opposite: blaming everything that happens on the caregiver.
3. Detachment—an emotional distancing, a need to feel less involved with the child; not caring because it hurts too much to care.

These are universal defenses, and to some degree they are necessary in dealing with a painful separation. When they interfere with the trust that is necessary between parent and caregiver, however, they need to be brought out in the open and shared. Otherwise, it's all too easy to feel resentful of your child's teacher and caregiver. "Gatekeeping" and a stress-filled relationship could be the result.

Marcy's mother returned to work early. She felt too much unspoken pressure at work to forgo the full three months of unpaid leave. Marcy was only two months old. Mrs. Jackson worried for months ahead, even during her pregnancy, about leaving her child with someone else. Her older boy had experienced such difficulty when she'd returned to work—there were times when she felt she'd lost him and worried whether she'd ever get him back.

Now, Marcy needed a caregiver so that Mrs. Jackson could work full-time without having to worry. She chose what she judged to be a well-run childcare center. But the Jacksons soon found out what we all know: that the pay for childcare workers is so inadequate that the turnover of caregivers is a major problem. In one year, Marcy had four different caregivers! How could a baby adjust to so many different people? Each time, Marcy showed the stresses of change at home. She slept fitfullly, she ate poorly, she sucked her thumb more. The Jacksons felt she was more clingy and hungry for them each time she had a new caregiver. But Marcy was resilient. Each time she snapped back within a few weeks. She became her old cheerful, outgoing self after each episode. She seemed to develop wonderful social skills as she grew. At each period of stranger awareness, at eight, twelve, and eighteen months, she sailed through with some distress but no real disintegration. She seemed to learn to turn to her peers for comfort. Whenever she had a new caregiver, Marcy wanted more play time with the other children in her class. Mrs. Jackson noticed this and arranged play dates after work.

For Mrs. Jackson, another worry had been, "Do they really like black children, or are they just welcoming on the surface? I need to know that they won't take out their feelings on Marcy when I'm gone." The Jacksons had looked for a racially and ethnically diverse childcare center. Now, at three, Marcy seemed content and had a wide choice of friends. Mrs. Jackson took it as a sign that they had made the right choice from the start.

Still, Mrs. Jackson continued to wonder what Marcy's days were like. She needed to experience it for herself. Instead of imposing rigid visiting hours for parents, this center had always welcomed parents at any time. It is not a good sign if a childcare center does not have flexible visiting times. But parents should recognize that their presence can be disruptive for children who are working at being without their parents. Children demonstrate this by the longing they show toward any parent. Separation and independence may be their biggest challenge at such a time.

Mrs. Jackson visited the childcare center, but felt ambivalent about still harboring such distrust. She was shown to Marcy's room and was able to watch her daughter through a one-way glass. Marcy was proudly leading two other children around in a marching game. When her companions tried to stop, Marcy said, "No, keep on until I tell you it's time to quit!" "Imperious, isn't she," thought her mother. One child began to crumple. Marcy went over to him and patted him. "John, sorry." Mrs. Jackson was surprised that Marcy was so sympathetic.

Fortified, Mrs. Jackson entered the room. "Mommy! Mommy! You're here!" shouted Marcy. All the other children crowded around her. Marcy said, "It's my mommy! She came to visit." Mrs. Jackson sat in a big chair. Children fought for a place on her lap. Marcy was excluded. Mrs. Jackson realized it when she saw Marcy across the room, sucking on her thumb. "Marcy, come over here. I came to see you!" She looked to the teachers for help in divesting herself of some of the children on her lap.

Mrs. Thompson came over to ask the children to make room for Marcy with her mother. "When there's a parent in the room," she said, "they always treat us as though we weren't here, or were pieces of furniture. Anyone's parent will do; the parent doesn't have to be their own." Mrs. Jackson was struck with the distinctions that children needed to hold on to in such situations. As Mrs. Jackson hugged Marcy to her, and Marcy nestled cozily into her arms, each of the other children looked on with soft, hungry eyes. Many of them resorted to their thumbs. One little boy had a square of blanket pinned to his shirt. He grabbed for it and rubbed it. It was his lovey.

That these children appeared so happy and well-adjusted on the one hand, but could show such longing on the other saddened Mrs. Jackson. She found herself wondering once again whether it really was okay to leave them. (See also "Working and Caring" in Part II.)

Preparing for Separation

How can parents cushion their children's adjustment when they return to work? The first job for parents is to face their own feelings of loss. Unless parents can recognize and face their own feelings, they won't be free enough to help the child with hers.

Preparing a child ahead of time is the next step. If a parent can say, "You know, I must leave you at school. You and I will miss each other all day. But the teacher will be there to take care of you. And when I come back at the end of the day, you'll be able to tell me all the fun things you've done." Such preparation gives the child a chance to anticipate the separation.

Next, the parent must be prepared for a child to react; this is likely to be a touchpoint in her development. Regression is likely and it will deepen a parent's vulnerability in leaving her.

The child is bound to sense her mother's anxiety, blurring with and intensifying her own. The behavior one sees on the surface is her attempt to manage this cost of separation. It is bound to be difficult because it is usually the first time a child has to deal with a long period without one of her parents. She must face a caregiver who wants to get close to her—to invade her dependency on her parents. Her reactions—clinging, protesting, regressing at home—are all expressions of her attempts to manage the situation. Her reaction patterns that go with her temperament are likely to intensify with this stress. She may become hypersensitive to stimuli or may withdraw and shut them out, and this can be disturbing. Motor activity may be affected—a child as active as Minnie could become even more active and more insensitive; or a child as quiet as Tim could become even quieter and more immobilized.

Blankets, Loveys, and Thumbs Many children need a transitional object, especially during separation. A child who already has fastened upon a blanket or a thumb is better prepared to fall back on her own resources. Grieving parents might find it hard to watch the child actively replace them with an object. This is a touchpoint in a child's development—learning to become even more independent. Regression and reorganization are necessary both for parents and child. At such a time, a child needs a comforting reminder from home and from the family relationship. Marcy turned to an imaginary friend. "When Mommy goes, let's talk." She'd say this at home and abroad, always when her mother could hear her. Mrs. Jackson winced whenever Marcy talked to her imaginary friend. But Marcy felt safe when she unloaded her sorrows on her friend. "Mommy's always mad. Daddy says don't pay attention."

Billy's blanket took on new importance when he started daycare. He fingered it, he covered his head with it, he sucked on it. It was dirty and smelly, and Mrs. Stone kept wishing she could wash it. One evening as Billy slept, she slipped the blanket out of his hand to take it away and wash it while he was asleep. Later, a piercing scream came from his bedroom. His stepfather rushed in to Billy. "My blankie! My blankie!" Mr. Stone recognized his anguish and rushed to retrieve the blanket from the dryer. He handed it back to Billy, who looked it over carefully to be sure it was his old lovey. His sobs slowed as he examined it. It was a changed lovey. Mr. Stone apologized. "Billy, it *is* your old, dear friend. Mommy thought it needed washing, but it's still the same." Billy looked up at him with sad, cowed eyes, as if to say, "How could you, without asking me?" Mr. Stone said, "I'm sorry we did it at night. We didn't think about how you loved the blanket the way it was. Will you forgive Mommy and me?" He gathered Billy up to hug him. They rocked together for a long time, as Billy's tears subsided. He clutched his dear lovey, fingering the silk border as it if were especially comforting to him. Billy's moans and low-pitched croons to his dear friend, the lovey, were a reminder of how deep was his reliance. At last he fell asleep, still clutching his lovey-blanket.

The next morning when he got out of bed, Billy announced triumphantly, "Mommy tried to steal my blankie, but Daddy saved it." This was a low blow for Mrs. Stone and a double-edged triumph for Billy's stepfather. They would need to repair this rift together.

Recognizing this deepened need for dependency and giving it credit is an important way to support a child through changes and stress. Billy's stepfather respected Billy's need for his lovey. Cuddling Billy alone with the blanket was another way of affirming Billy's own efforts at becoming more independent. Encouraging his wife to do the same helps lessen the gatekeeping that might otherwise intensify between them.

Tim's grandmother had recognized his fragility early on and wanted to help. She thought that a "lovey" for Tim might help him protect himself in overwhelming situations. Tim had been an avid thumb sucker as a baby. He withdrew to his thumb when he was agitated. He sucked loudly, as though his thumb were almost luscious. His eyes rolled up in his head as he sucked his thumb. At first, the McCormicks had not been concerned, but as their son withdrew more and more, they responded by trying to break him of his thumb sucking. When he was nine months old, they wrapped his thumb. They applied bad tasting medicine to it.

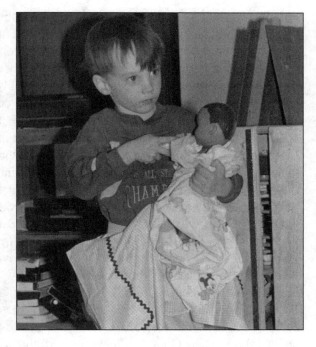

When he rubbed the medicine into his eyes, it caused severe conjunctivitis. Finally, at the grandmother's suggestion, they'd offered Tim a soft blanket to hug. He wadded it into a ball, called it his "baby," and carried it around with him. Often now when he sucked his thumb, and when his parents scolded, he was able to give up his thumb for his "baby." As he tried out each new developmental task—standing, walking, trying out new words and phrases—he needed his "baby" whenever he reached a point of frustration.

Mrs. McCormick found herself resenting Tim's blanket as much as she had his thumb sucking. She wanted him to become more outgoing. She thought his blanket was just a crutch that reinforced his withdrawal. She resented it when he fell apart when he was without it. Often, she'd "forget" his blanket when they went out. He was more fragile without it. He would search around for it, whimpering, "Baby." When she couldn't produce it, he'd sadden, return to his noisy thumb sucking and close his eyes, or bury his head in her shoulder. His color would change, he'd shudder and stiffen. She sensed how upset he was, so she gave in to his dependent behavior. The dirtier and more ragged the blanket became, the more devoted Tim was to it.

Parents may believe that because a child is in school now, she needs to give up a blanket, or a pacifier, or a thumb. This is not the time for such a step. This is a time to accept the need for regression as the child struggles to grow independent. Just as Billy and Tim showed, this is a time for increased dependency—not only on the parents, but on the beloved transitional object that has come to represent them.

A lovey helps a child soothe herself through a traumatic event. One day, Minnie fell down as she rushed to school, skinning her knee. It was a raw-looking wound, but superficial. Mrs. Lee knew the scrape didn't need stitches, but she knew it hurt. She rushed Minnie into the house to wash the knee with soap and water and bandage it. "No! No! No!" Minnie screamed. "But I have to clean and bandage it!" "No! No! Don't touch me! It hurts!" In a stroke of inspiration, Mrs. Lee thought of Minnie's beloved doll, Googie. "Googie fell down too, Minnie. She knows how much your knee hurts. Look, she's crying, too. Can we wash her knee off and put a Band-Aid on it?" Minnie's eyes lit up. "Oh!" She clutched Googie, rocking her back and forth. Mrs. Lee brought the warm, soapy water. As she washed Googie's knee, then Minnie's knee, she sighed with relief. Here was a battle that they'd won together—she and Googie!

Reunions and Rituals

Every parent who must be away all day wants desperately to make up for the lost time. Coming together again must be the expectation. The notion of "quality time" is too easy. It may help a parent feel less guilt, but what a child really needs is a sense of reunion and closeness. Working parents can try to save energy during the day so that they can handle the child's disintegration without falling apart themselves. Then they can pick the child up to love her and reunite the family at the end of the day.

I recommend a big rocking chair. When a working parent comes home at the end of the day, he or she shouldn't disappear into the kitchen to do chores. Save them. The first important job is to reunite as a family and to get close again. As you rock your child, look down into her face. "I missed you all day. How was your day?" "Yuck." "Mine was too, but now we're together." Once the parent senses the child softening in her arms with the rocking, the parent can feel that they are together as a family again. At that point, parents can take the child to the kitchen with them. Even a small child can help in the kitchen; she can put napkins on the table, stir something, and clear (unbreakable) dishes. This may create a lot more work for the parents, but it is important to include child in the daily rituals. She will feel proud and will know she is an important part of the family. She will feel she is participating in the family's work.

Be sure to make times in your day when you give up everything to be there with the child on *her* terms. It is hard to give up your own day, your beeper, your e-mail, your telephone calls, the cares from work that clutter your thoughts. But if you don't, you are passing the message to your child that she comes second. That message is not one you or she can live with. A parent needs the family to come first, as much as the children do.

Other rituals send children the message that "I'm yours now. I miss you when I'm not":

- Morning times can let you get close before you go to work. This means getting up earlier to organize yourself. Give children orange juice in bed before they get up so they feel energized. Use breakfast time to communicate.
- Bedtime reading, rocking, singing songs together become a critical reunion time. Often, the same stories over and over become a reminder that "this is what we always do. We are together, and reading this story is our way."
- Bath time can be a wonderful time for just sitting and watching children play. You are confirming that a child's own rituals are as important to you as they are to her. Her chance at *safe* self-exploration, at questions about her body, the opportunity to share them with you as you sit close by can be powerful.

Facing separations is easier for parent and child when they both know that they can count on getting close again when they are reunited. "Floor time" is Dr. Stanley Greenspan's concept. An adult gets on the floor to play with the child and join her at her level. The child recognizes it immediately. "He's mine, He wants to play with *me*." A busy parent can quickly convey a sense of focusing entirely on the child. Floor time is genuine quality time.

Marcy was playing with her dolls. "This one is the Mommy. She tells me, 'Go to bed!' My Daddy says, 'Not yet.' " Marcy's brother, Amos, watched from his chair in front of the computer. "Sissy play—dolls! Yuck!" Mr. Jackson came into the room and watched Marcy from a distance. Intrigued, he sat down near her, and Marcy sensed he was interested. "Daddy says, 'What a good girl. She can turn somersaults!' " Marcy's doll turned over and over. Marcy gradually moved her dolls nearer her father. "This is the house. They play in the yard. She likes her Daddy to push her." Marcy put the doll on a play swing. Mr. Jackson was seduced. He reached over and pushed the swing. With that, Marcy and her father sang together: "Swing me up and down."

Mr. Jackson was wise not to take over the play or use the chance to try to teach. He watched and made himself available to play. It isn't easy for adults to shed the parental role. It's all too easy to want to teach "lessons" in how to live or to teach skills; but a child feels more in control and more gratified by a parent's willingness to be "hers."

"You be the daddy and I'll be the mommy," said Marcy. "Now, be the baby and cry. No, cry loud." After the initial test of her ability to control her father, Marcy may let him enter the play. "Now, Mommy's gonna put you to bed. Lie down." When Mr. Jackson was flat on the rug, Marcy's impulse was to jump on his stomach. Then she brought out a book to read to him and thus reproduce their nighttime ritual. Play was the time when Marcy's father was hers, when she had him all to herself.

Marcy's mother found it hard to relax in this way. She felt harassed by her job. The commute was terrible, one long traffic jam. Her boss watched to see whether she was on time. Her coworkers were not as friendly as she'd have liked. All this added to the stress of getting going each day. Mrs. Jackson left the breakfast and dressing the children to her husband. One day, Marcy said, "Mummy, I never see you!" Mrs. Jackson responded quickly, "You have me every night—and on weekends." "But I don't see you in the morning." Mrs. Jackson started to defend herself: "I'm in too much of a hurry." But something inside her said, "This is important. I need to listen." When she got Marcy up, there was usually a long argument about what clothes to wear. Marcy dawdled and was always late to the breakfast table. They ended in a fight and Mrs. Jackson thought it was hardly worth it. She'd go to work ready for a battle with her coworkers.

But Marcy's remark caught her attention. Mrs. Jackson decided to change the morning pattern and establish a new set of rituals that would help them all: She set the alarm a half hour earlier so there was less sense of hurry; she laid out Marcy's clothes the night before—only one choice at most; she offered Marcy a glass of orange juice to drink before she got out of bed. Some children may be hypoglycemic (suffer from low blood sugar) first thing in the morning. Giving their sugar a boost before it's needed by activity can settle some of the grouchiness and combativeness. Many children with normal blood sugar also respond to the extra gestures of a drink and a parent's nurturing to start off the day. This brief first moment together may also cut down on the dawdling that goes with getting dressed and is sure to draw a parent in. Next, Mrs. Jackson saw to it that everyone came to breakfast together. At the table, she didn't leave room for choices; they were too hard to handle at that time of day. It was easier to have one kind of cereal, one kind of toast, and everyone either ate it or they didn't. Mrs. Jackson encouraged her family to talk about the day ahead and anticipate what was coming: "You'll be with Billy and Minnie, Marcy. They like you." At the end of the meal, everyone kissed each other good-bye. "We'll see each other this evening."

Another way to make up for the necessary separations is to set up a regular and sacred "date"—one parent to each child; parents need this for themselves as well as for their child. The "date" doesn't have to be long (not more than two hours), but it has to be reliable and predictable. The child can decide on what to do during this time. Talk about it all week: "We don't have enough time together now, but we will have. Remember our date? You can tell *me* what to do for a change."

Value all rituals—daily ones, mealtimes, retrieval at daycare, supper as a family, times when families can be together. Holidays—Christmas, Hanukkah, Thanksgiving, Easter—become more important than ever. They become opportunities for togetherness and also for sharing family values. These are times to bring the extended family together. When both parents work, children need the structure and the expectations of predictable shared experiences more than ever.

Each ritualized moment has a way of invoking all the others that have occurred and that will occur. Multigenerational rituals magnify the child's sense of his own place in the family. A child has a sense of security in his world when he can line himself up next to a parent and a grandparent. We used to go to dinner at my mother-in-law's every Sunday. Everyone complained about "having to give up such a beautiful day" on the way over. But after we had all been to- gether—three generations—each of us felt a sense of peace. My children have never forgotten this ritual occasion. Parents today may want to arrange or revive such rituals and even invent new ones. They can act as anchors in our chaotic world.

Mealtimes

At three, if there is a problem with food left over from the first two years—poor eating and poor weight gain, vomiting after meals, hid- ing food, refusing one food after another—it is time for parents to reevaluate the situation. All these problems suggest a risk of eating problems in the future. A three-year-old may be begging for struc- ture at mealtime. Does the child's behavior indicate that she doesn't feel in control and must use deviant behavior to satisfy her need for her own control? "I will" or "I won't" games or teasing at meal- times are signs that food has lost its importance except as barter. More important, mealtime has lost its significance as a family time for communication and closeness.

A three-year-old has just left the toddler's tortured struggle for independence. She has learned to say "yes" or "no" but has not yet learned when to look for a middle ground. She has just begun to enjoy a sense of being able to make her own choices and deci- sions. She can say "I will" and mean it; this can be heady for her. Each step toward independence is a struggle. Food, clothes, and baths all become involved. To the parent, it can feel like a struggle for power. For the three-year-old, it is a struggle for learning about herself.

Minnie categorically refused vegetables. Mrs. Lee couldn't accept this. She called her mother for support, because she remembered all the fresh vegetables they'd had when she was a child. She could almost taste broccoli in her mouth now. She'd hated it but she'd been taught to eat it. "Broccoli has the most valuable vitamins in it. You'll grow up with beautiful hair and eyes." She was still waiting and hoping for the rewards. Her hair and eyes were okay, but nothing to reward her for all that nasty broccoli. Now, Minnie sneered at Mrs. Lee's broccoli and at all her cajoling. Was it right to push her? Her mother, on the phone, confirmed all Mrs. Lee's determination. "Of course, Minnie should be taught to eat vegetables. Entire cultures live on nothing but vegetables and they're healthy. How can a child exist without them? You always ate them. I saw to that!" Without being aware of it, Mrs. Lee had uncovered a "ghost in her nursery" that made it important to her to push Minnie to eat vegetables.

Food and mealtimes are likely to become an issue for struggles in the third year. Children have made progress with the basics now, and parents' expectations for compliance may increase. A child's refusal to eat is likely to call up her parents' own issues—their obligation to feed their child coupled with their own past experience with food and family. Hence it becomes a critical time to defuse the struggle and turn it into a shared positive experience. Learning to eat with the family—with manners, sitting down, etc.,—is learned from modeling.

1. Mealtimes are times for families to be together. Breakfast and supper are important opportunities for rituals and expectations.
2. No three-year-old child will accept these expectations easily, but they must be seen as important times for learning to live with others and accepting their values. Don't fight over them, but don't reinforce rebellion.
3. If necessary, start to feed a three-year-old before the family dinner so that she can sit and talk at dinner.
4. Do not press food as an issue.
5. Offer small portions—less than the child is likely to want.
6. As soon the child begins to tease, to throw food, to drop it, or to move around the room, her dinner is at an end. Ignore her behavior as she clamors to be the center of attention.
7. Once the child is excused, no one reinforces her by joking or playing with her.

8. Offer no food between meals. No snacking outside of regular times. When meals are over, food is no longer available.
9. Do not talk about or teach manners at the table. Manners and standards are learned by modeling at four or five.
10. Maintain your own standards throughout the meal—*no matter what!*

(See also "Food and Food Problems" in Part II.)

Sleep Problems

Sleep is a separation issue for parents and child. Separation at night can be difficult for all parents who are away during the day. Working parents cannot give up the child at night and she can't let go of her parents. Bedtime and the light waking times during the night become "opportunities" for a parent-child reunion. Sleep is a more serious separation than it may seem.

Tim begged at night for one story after another. At one point, he introduced a need for music at bedtime. His parents gave in. They thought music might be soothing for a light sleeper. They tried classical music. Tim whined. They tried rock and roll. This just seemed to jazz him up, as anyone could have predicted. Finally, they tried Ella Fitzgerald and her love songs. Tim loved them. He'd curl up, thumb in mouth, blanket wadded up into "his baby." But Mr. and Mrs. McCormick found that Tim demanded a change in CD's as soon as one finished. At first, they were compliant. Finally, one night after three changes, Mr. McCormick rebelled. "Why does he need all that music? Can't we just stop after the first CD?" Mrs. McCormick was about to resist. She went back in her mind to the difficulty she'd had in not going to Tim every three or four hours when he was smaller. He'd had a terrible sleep problem for the first year. She had breast fed and rocked her son to sleep in her arms. After gently depositing him in his crib, she would slip out quietly. But every three or four hours, at every light sleep cycle when he roused, cried out, and scrabbled around, she had rushed in to him. She had crooned, rocked, and nursed him back to sleep. Mr. McCormick had stormed, "You didn't do that for Philip. Let him alone." Their tension rose as Tim woke every four hours.

Finally, in desperation, last year Mrs. McCormick had sought help for Tim's sleep problems. He'd been awake and needing her as much as six hours out of the night. She was a sleep-deprived wreck. The specialist pointed out that she'd never helped Tim learn to get himself to sleep. When she put him down, she had become a part of his pattern of getting to sleep. She rocked him to sleep in her arms, worried about his sensitivity. If she put him down before he was asleep, he'd jump and cry out. Every time he came up to a light sleep cycle—every three to four hours—he fell apart and had no pattern to get himself back down that didn't involve his mother. "You need to leave it to him. If it's too hard for you, why not let your husband help him learn to sleep?" This had never occurred to her. She'd been afraid Tim's father would say, "Let him just cry it out." Instead the specialist suggested, "You don't need to desert Tim, but you do need to let him learn that he can put himself back down to sleep. Start when you first put him down. Rock, sing, read to him as your ritual has been. Get him into bed after he's soothed and quiet but before he's asleep. Then sit and pat him down, saying 'You can do it, you can do it.' Give him his lovey and show him his thumb. Let him know these are substitutes for you." Mrs. McCormick winced.

The specialist predicted that the process would take several weeks. It did, but Tim was soon able to make it through the night with only one waking. His mother was grateful. His father was relieved. Tim was proud.

Now as Tim started in daycare, his renewed difficulty in separating and getting himself to sleep at night revived all his parents' earlier fears. Tim seemed even more fragile these days. His mother and father were so attuned to Tim's vulnerabilities that they feared a regression to the earlier sleep problems. This became a new touchpoint.

Tim's parents examined the changes in his life. His mother was working and Tim was just beginning to sense his own and others' need for him to make relationships with his peers. There may also have been other stresses that they hadn't identified, but these were quite enough to bring about the regression at night.

Setting up goals and a firm end to the demands was reassuring to Tim, as they would be to any child. His father said to Tim, "Two CDs are enough. We'll come change it once and pat you down. Meanwhile, you have your thumb and your 'baby.' You take over and get yourself to sleep." Tim needed the reassurance of that kind of firmness. Prolonging his apparent neediness into a family struggle was bound to give the wrong message, and to reinforce his sense of himself as vulnerable.

Three, and Beyond

The three-year-old has just begun to be aware of the ways he can learn about his world—and about himself. At two, he was caught up inside himself, sorting out the difference between "yes" or "no," "will I?" or "won't I?" Now, his turmoil is still there, but he exercises more control over when and why he will show it. He has learned that if he needs attention, he can fling himself down in a deliberate temper tantrum, a contrast to the ones that seemed to come out of nowhere only a year ago. If he wants loving, he can make an appropriate appeal for it—and usually he can get it. He is just beginning to sense how powerful his behavior can be. With this sense of power has come speech; he can shape the world with his language. He shapes himself, too, and that brings a new awareness.

He has begun to learn about time, about space, and about responsibility to others. The latter is in response to the realization that other people matter to him—a lot. He wants to hang on to Mommy and Daddy—often at the same time. His awareness of his gender—and how each parent represents their own—is dawning. He has become aware of his need for still others—siblings, peers—and is beginning to realize that he can affect them. He is beginning to be aware that he can hurt others as well as please them. The most important use of all of this awareness is learning about himself: his gender, his individuality, his competence, and how he feels about his world.

With all this growth, there will be "touchpoints" during the year that include regression and falling apart. No wonder these periods of regression are so dramatic—for parent *and* child. When he can pull himself together, he feels an enormous sense of pride and empowerment. He can affect his world—and he's beginning to know it. Next, his world will teach him about who he is becoming.

2

FOUR YEARS OLD

New Power, New Fears

Halloween Party

A chance to dress up! A chance to play the person you've always wanted to be. Minnie's parents were giving a Halloween party. They asked each child to dress up. Here was a chance for the goblins and superheroes to bring the scary, angry, and competitive feelings that four-year-olds face out into the open. The Lees reassured the other parents, telling them not to worry about a perfect costume. "Find whatever you can at home."

Marcy knew immediately. "I'm going to be Cinderella, a dancer." Her mother had a different point of view. "Cinderella wasn't a dancer. She was a chore girl who helped her stepmother by washing dishes and sweeping the floor, until she met the prince!" "I don't want to be that Cinderella. I want to be the one in a dress and high-heeled shoes. I want to be a beautiful princess." She twirled round and round. Mrs. Jackson tried to slow her down. No use. She found a way to help Marcy "float" in a gauze petticoat and some old red high-heeled shoes. Marcy wanted a crown, so they made a paper one, and glued white rice on it for diamonds. Mrs. Jackson bought some glitter to apply to the crown and to the worn-out red slippers.

Marcy glowed. "I'm the queen! I am so beautiful- the prince will have to marry me!"

Tim was awestruck by the invitation. At first, he refused to go. But with great effort and persistence, his mother wooed him into going. "You'll see your friend Billy there. And I won't leave. I'll stay with you." "But I don't want to go." "But it will be fun to dress up. What do you want to be?" "A spaceman." "What does a spaceman wear?" "A space suit. Everyone knows that! And a helmet with a mask over it to breathe. A suit that doesn't let out any air or let in any sound." Mrs. McCormick felt daunted. Tim wanted to help make the suit, but he was sure it would turn out all wrong. More coaxing and cajoling. Finally, he took his brother's bicycle helmet and taped on a plastic mask. No one could see in, and Tim could barely see out. Mrs. McCormick had to make sure her son could breathe. For a space suit, Tim gathered up a set of coveralls and instructed his mother to tape them up securely with silver tape. Every opening—the collar, every outlet for hands, feet, and head—was securely taped, so no "air" or sound or intrusion could enter. Tim was ready—and securely protected from the world around him.

Minnie dressed as a ballplayer. Her older sister knew a boy who played Little League. She borrowed his uniform for Minnie to wear. Minnie tied her hair up so that it fit beneath the baseball cap. She begged her mother to buy her a pair of cleated shoes. She lost patience trying to make a catcher's mask out of a dish strainer with ear pieces attached. Her father lent Minnie his catcher's mitt. Then she stormed around the house, leaving indentations in the wood floor. She talked her father into a game of catch. She was amazingly competent already—in catching and in throwing. Mr. Lee wanted her to demonstrate her skills at the party. His wife demurred. "We don't want Minnie to be a show-off."

Billy was a pirate. He had several sticks lined up for swords and guns. With his mother's help, he found a bandanna, an airplane sleeping mask—cut in half to make a pirate's eye patch—a scarf of his mother's for a sash, and a pair of baggy shorts from his stepfather. He studied and studied the picture of Captain Hook in his *Peter Pan*. "Pirates are really mean, aren't they? Can't they conquer girls?" Everyone assured him that they were that fierce. He asked his mother to make him a beard. She applied mascara to his cheeks and chin. When he swaggered up to the mirror to see himself, he stopped dead. He looked at himself, cowered, whimpered, and retreated to his mother.

"Not too mean a pirate!" In his fright, he dropped his "sword and gun" and forgot them when he was taken to the party. His mother noticed that he was more subdued than usual when he arrived. Gradually, in front of his friends, his swagger came back, but he refused to look at himself in the mirror again. The other children began to cheer him up, and he seemed to regain his sea legs. He was the center of attention, strikingly handsome as a dashing pirate. His bravado returned.

The party was a great success. Each child lived for a while in his or her own costumed fantasy.

Four-year-olds are involved in so many exciting new developments:

1. Language is now able to keep up with the child's more complex ideas, to lead on into new ones. The feeling of inner excitement gets expressed as an idea and can become a reality. This is matched by the new power over everyone around. When a child can put her own urges across as forcefully as "I want to marry Daddy," everyone becomes immobilized around her. Whatever the response, she will knows her words have touched them deeply. She feels she can control her own universe. She can see now that she matters.

2. There are new emotional satisfactions: a four-year-old can begin to see the rewards of growing up. Her ability to identify with her parents and with those around her gives her the incentive to learn new skills. She can also mirror their ways of handling stress. She can assume their values—or she can deny them forcefully. She isn't just overwhelmed by her negativism, she can turn it off and on. She can even look for a solution of her own. Her responses need no longer be black or white. She is aware that her decisions do matter, even when they must be overridden.

3. This awareness of her own power brings new fears to a four-year-old. She becomes more aware that she's a small child, a small part of a larger world, dependent on her parents or others at critical times. Her new understanding brings an awareness of her limitations.

   A child this age feels pulled between this sense of dependence and a desire to master her world which propels her on-

wards. Play and fantasy are powerful ways to work this out and construct a world that will work for *her*. The child's ability to verbalize and to reason make her fantasies more detailed and elaborate. But these vivid fantasies lead to fears and bad dreams. "I dreamt of a witch in my closet." "I *know* there's no monster in my room, but I feel it."

The monsters and witches that appear at night in her dreams may also represent the strain of facing "new" feelings. Becoming aware of powerful negative and aggressive feelings can be frightening. She will need a parent's help to accept them. To master them, the child also needs to learn, gradually, the difference between feeling an emotion and acting on it.

4. New feelings about being a girl or a boy are also confronting the four-year-old. An awareness of differences between herself and her friends, her parents and other parents, is built on expanding cognitive abilities. New questions and uncertainties will come from these observations.

5. The beginnings of a conscience, the awareness of an ability to decide about right and wrong, carries an increase in responsibility.

All these are new potentials in the small child. All can be exciting as they emerge. But they can be draining to both parents and child. Parents must learn to adjust to the changes, which will affect their own ability to control and protect their child. They need to watch and listen, to gain an understanding of the purposes of these periods of regression in order to see to the other side of the turmoil. Each of these times becomes an opportunity to understand the child's individuality and can bring parents and child closer to one another. New worries need to be balanced by an awareness of the four-year-old's competence. Parents will have their hands full keeping up with these exciting and constantly surprising developments.

Temperament

Individual Differences

When a child has a birthday, there is always a crossover in everyone's mind. Certainly, the child expects to feel different; and adults are likely to increase their expectations, at least subtly. The individual way each four-year-old meets his new prowess may be as important as the age milestone. Each child is different, and the way children greet each developmental step is another instance of "temperament."

When she was three, Minnie seemed made of wires strung together with a constantly whirring motor. She had always been active and passionately involved. Indeed, she'd barely survived. She'd reached for every available bottle of detergent, laundry soap, and liquid Benadryl, testing them when she had the opportunity. She'd investigated the surfaces of every climbable object. Her parents had become as hyperactive as she in an effort to protect her. Now Minnie's constant activity gradually began to become more coordinated. Her activity became smoother and more graceful. She was more fun and less frightening to watch now. She could climb safely and jump to the ground surely. She could almost dribble a basketball. She worked at kicking a football and amazed her athletic father with the deftness of her pitches; he caught himself already dreaming of a future in sports for her. This led to his spending more and more time with her as he attempted to teach her the athletic skills that so intrigued her. Minnie learned easily, and they both loved it.

Minnie often got herself in trouble with other children. Insensitively, she'd barge ahead of them, paying little attention, often even knocking them down. Mrs. Lee let Minnie ride over her—and all those around her. Other parents told her to be firm and to be more of a disciplinarian. Why couldn't she?

Minnie's mother was aware of several reasons why this was so difficult. Minnie had never listened to her (as opposed to her older sister, who had always been easier). Minnie had always been hard to understand. Minnie had looked past her even as a baby when she tried to talk to her. As soon as she'd become mobile, her goal had seemed to "get away." Minnie's "unreachableness" had always made her mother feel inadequate, just as she had often felt during her own childhood. With these feelings came a curious sense of resentment; she resented her feelings as well as Minnie's power to call them up. Minnie's older sister had never done this to Mrs. Lee. It was as if they had fit with each other from the first. She and Minnie hadn't.

Mrs. Lee would say to her friends, "Minnie makes me feel so useless. She doesn't seem to need me. She's so different from her older sister. I feel close to May." Parents of a child who is difficult to understand or who reminds them of their own pasts are likely to experience such feelings. "Is it my fault she's like this? If I can't fit in with her, what use am I as a parent?" The feelings Mrs. Lee has about Minnie are to be expected. A difficult fit calls up a parent's childhood feelings of helplessness, and Minnie calls these up in her mother. "She makes me feel the way my mother did when she criticized me. She always seemed to think that I was hopeless. And my older sister was always the best in sports. I was no good, and whenever I wanted to join in with her, she'd say, 'I don't want her on our team.' Now, Minnie makes me feel like my sister did." When difficulty arises in the parent-child relationship, a parent always feels guilty. This is one of the times when "ghosts from the nursery," as Selma Fraiberg calls them, become attached to feelings about being an "inadequate" parent; ghosts such as these undermine a parent's strengths. Minnie and her mother did not have what Stella Chess and Thomas Alexander call a "goodness of fit." They will have to learn to live with their difficult fit.

In her third year, the whole family's efforts had been aimed at keeping Minnie out of trouble. Her sister resented the constant demands Minnie's activity placed on her parents' attention. Now, at four, Minnie had switched her demands into a new channel. Her speech had become richer. Her drive to explore everything at her fingertips had extended to her entire universe. Now she used language as well as movement for her investigations. As soon as she had her parents' attention, she'd begin asking a long, unrelenting set of questions. "Why is grass green? Where does the dew come from? What makes our clock tick and chime? How does it know when to chime? Why does your face get red when you get angry?"

When her parents tried to give analytic answers to Minnie's questions, they all realized the approach was over her head. It was hard to find the right way to explain things. Sometimes they felt exhausted from Minnie's barrage. They tried hard to think out answers that a four-year-old could understand.

Minnie's apparently insatiable curiosity seemed driven; indeed, she hardly waited for answers. She was holding on to her parents' attention with a mighty grip. She also needed to catalogue out loud all the things that caught her attention—and just about everything did. Her world was an onslaught of undifferentiated information. It seemed clearer now that in all her urgent activity, Minnie had been trying to attend to everything around her at once. She took in too much.

Billy, at four, approached each new thing as if it were to be conquered. Everything intrigued him and he wanted to understand and master everything he encountered. He sailed with enthusiasm into each new and exciting project. He seemed unaware of boundaries. He would start questioning at the top of his voice while others were talking: "Why is this door so hard to open? Is it latched? Come undo it for me." All of this tumbled out. He was almost constantly talking or

questioning. Since his mother also talked a lot, he had had to learn how to break in to her long-winded conversations. But he also seemed to be under his own head of steam. As a result, he often didn't wait for an answer. He seemed more hungry to express the question than to get an answer. He seemed to be shaping his world with his speech. One could hear him assess a new situation: "There are three kids over there. I wonder who they are? Can I play with them? This is a new place. I don't see any toys." Most of this was not directed at anyone, but seemed to be a part of orienting himself and establishing his goals.

Billy could run and kick a ball. He could throw a ball with accuracy. As he moved, his legs and arms were synchronized. This physical ability brought him closer to his stepfather. They played ball at every opportunity—throwing it back and forth, back and forth. Billy couldn't catch it yet, although he held both hands stretched out in front of him as he tried to do so. He did not yet understand the concept of making a nest with his hands and arms. But his stepfather showed unbounded patience for teaching Billy. Mrs. Stone remarked on it: "You'd never have as much patience teaching me as you have with Billy." Billy and his stepfather were a lot alike, which had made it easier for them to fall into the relationship they'd developed.

Billy tried to swagger as he walked, imitating his stepfather. He talked like him. He watched him at the table and imitated him. Most of this behavior was subtle, but Billy was obviously his stepfather's child right now.

All the children in the neighborhood loved Billy. Older children would come to the house and ask for him. "Can Billy come out to play?" When a nine-year-old asked for Billy, Mrs. Stone thought it strange. She watched to see why the older child wanted him. His sparkle, his contagious laughter had attracted the nine-year-old. Even his four-year-old clumsiness was appealing to

older kids. They'd show him off. "Watch Billy throw! He's just a little kid and he's better than you!" Children his own age fairly worshiped him. He was already a leader in his own group, where he dominated the scene. "Do this! Do that! You'll like it if you try it!" "Where did Billy get it?" was his parents' constant refrain. No one could resist their charming little boy.

Billy was aware of this charm. With his curly hair and inquisitive face, Billy would boldly enter a crowd of adults with "Hi! I'm Billy." He didn't need to strut or bully. He was too self-assured for that. He was spoiled by adulation and attention. When his mother asked him to do a chore, he might say, "Let Abby do it." Mrs. Stone was aware that she needed to be more emphatic and demanding with her son. Her pliancy often made her feel guilty. Sometimes she worried that she was too hard on him, but most of the time she knew he needed the discipline. Her discipline was often uneven, however, because she was so amused and proud of Billy's spirit and charm. She envied both traits in him.

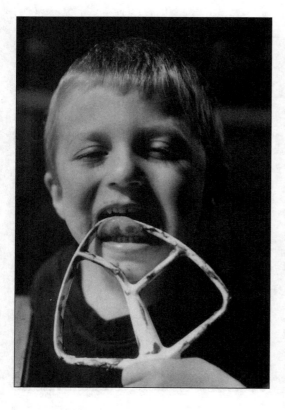

By the end of each day, however, Billy's mother was exhausted. "Billy, leave me alone!" When Mr. Stone arrived home from work, she pleaded, "Take him off my back. I have to cook dinner!" As soon as Billy and his stepfather began to enjoy each other's company again, however, Mrs. Stone wanted Billy back. She hadn't yet become aware of how much she relied on her son's presence to keep her going. The baby was demanding and even rewarding, but Billy was always exciting.

Billy was learning to use language to get himself under control. When he was becoming too angry or too excited, he'd say to himself, "I'm going to hit her, she makes me so mad!" By putting this thought into words, Billy was looking around for an adult's help. Speech was important to him not only in expressing himself, but also in understanding himself. His mother had been trying to teach him to "use your words, not your actions." He tried. When he was about to start a battle with a peer, he'd say, "You make me mad. I want to hit you." The other child would draw back and give up meekly.

Tim at four was still a quiet, thoughtful little boy. He had been sedentary from the first, and he approached each new step cautiously. He watched his noisy older brother constantly. He became so absorbed that he jumped at each new sound or new change in

Philip's behavior. He never seemed to become immune to Philip's raucous way of life and seemed to retreat when Philip came too close. Though not chronologically behind, Tim had delayed walking for several months after he was physically able. His parents were aware that he had acquired the ability to stand, to balance himself by holding on to furniture, to cruise around a table. But he always sat down when Philip approached, as if he knew that his newfound abilities were no match for Philip's.

Tim's parents felt that their son had been slower and more deliberate with each new acquisition because of Philip. Although watching Philip made him hunger to learn about each step, his apprehensions about the daring required held him back. Tim's parents had adjusted instinctively to his sensitivity without having openly acknowledged to themselves the ways he seemed different. They had to approach him slowly, cuddle and rock him before feeding or going to bed at nap time or at night. He still startled easily. He had come as such a surprise after Philip, who was just the opposite. Tim was easy as long as one respected his sensitivity, but it cost him a great deal. Each day seemed to be followed by disintegration. When he fell apart, his screaming was unapproachable. No one had realized that he used it as a protection against any more stimulation.

In his second year, Tim put words together quickly. At safe times when he was alone with a parent, he was eager to express himself. His parents were delighted when he could name and point to his nose and ears, and count to ten. His intellect seemed to be just fine—and that reassured the McCormicks. They hadn't realized how anxious they'd been about his development.

Tim's third year had been, in some ways, too easy. His parents worried about his quiet, studious way of accepting the world around him. He watched. He sat. He dared to try a few new things, but he clung most of the time. He appeared to be waiting. They needed his pediatrician to reassure them constantly that Tim was developing "normally."

Philip's friends had learned to avoid Tim. Adults tried to approach him briefly, then gave up trying to talk to him. But his big, round eyes never seemed to miss anything. If one approached him quietly, he was responsive and wanted to talk. "Why do Daddy and Mommy go to work? Why does Daddy lose his temper? Why does Grandma look so wrinkled in the face? Does she draw on her face? Her eyes have markings around them, and her mouth has a lot of red paint on it. Why?" If one approached him loudly or too quickly, he withdrew. He turned his head to one side and sucked his thumb.

At home, Tim was freer. He explored, he found quiet games to play. He loved the computer. He had learned to open it up and to find games on it. He was trying to read from it, sounding out his own name spelled on the screen. He could even draw a few letters. Tim seemed hungry for learning opportunities and Mr. McCormick was eager for this kind of communication with him. Every day, when he came home, he and Tim sat for half an hour in front of the computer, testing Tim's skills. Mrs. McCormick warned her husband, "You're just playing into Tim's need to be alone and out of touch. How is the computer going to help him learn about other kids?"

His parents tried not to worry about how isolated Tim still seemed at daycare. Most of the other children avoided him because he was so quiet. Now that he was four, his mother finally listened to a friend's advice. "He's just shy. Find him a shy friend. Let them play together a lot. That way, he'll learn how to deal with other children." The friend was right: Entering a group as two shy people is a lot easier than entering it alone. Mrs. McCormick listened, surprised that she hadn't thought of it herself. She found a child at the school who seemed as overwhelmed as Tim. Getting them together three times a week became a ritual that both children looked forward to. The two sat and talked like grownups. They talked about all the other children at school. They'd not missed anything. Observation was their way of participating. After a few visits together, one child would lead the other into more activities from school. They drew pictures. They sang songs. They danced "Ring Around the Rosie."

Mrs. McCormick had no idea that Tim could already skip on one foot. He did—all for Lizzy, his shy friend. They became more and more adventurous—as long as they were together and alone. In school, they reverted to their shy stances. One of the teachers played on their developing relationship when she asked them to lead the two lines that formed each morning. Watching each other carefully, they stood straight, heads shyly cocked toward each other, then hesitantly led the lines into the schoolroom. From then on, Lizzy and Tim were tentatively accepted as part of the group. They had grown from this experience, but their temperaments had not changed. Their sensitivity and shyness persisted. They could not really become as outgoing as others in the class. But they had demonstrated their

capacity to compensate for their sensitivity and to master its cost to them as they entered the group. Their mothers felt a sense of triumph and relief.

When you try to change a child's temperament, you can't. But in trying to do so, you say to the child, "I don't like you the way you are." Shyness is considered a deficit in our society. A shy child is likely to be considered a loser. Shyness hits deep in parents, calling up all of the inhibitions from their own childhoods. Many of these children's parents were shy children themselves. Their feelings about their own shy child may blur with their memories of their own childhoods. More ghosts in the nursery. The parents may begin to worry about the child's future. Will he make it in society? These fears often make it harder for parents to respond to the shy child's needs.

Parents are influenced, often more than they realize, by whatever inevitable pain lingers from their own childhoods. They want to protect their child from the hurts that they remember. But instead of trying to change the child's temperament, a parent's best role might be to accept the child's sensitivity and help him find ways to adapt to it, to use it to his advantage. Showing awareness of the child's feelings, and approval of his efforts to reach out *and* to pull back into self-protection, can be therapeutic. Although Tim's guardedness protected his high sensitivity, he could participate visually long before he could let himself participate actively. Valuing his use of observation, and his own pace, were critical. Valuing his caution was important, too. Understanding his special way of taking in his world was affirming for him and could lead him to insight about himself.

My advice to parents is to accept the child's temperament as much as possible. At the point where he loses control, or his behavior is otherwise unacceptable, it may be necessary for the parent to step in. Otherwise, your willingness to acknowledge his distress and to support him may help him the most. "I understand how hard it is for you to feel comfortable with other kids. They are awfully rough and loud, aren't they? Maybe we can find ways to help—you and I together. It's great how you keep an eye on everyone. Lizzy probably feels the way you do. I did, too, when I was little, but then I found friends who liked the same things I did."

Learning Self-control

When a child is out of control, understanding what we call "state regulation" helps a parent react constructively. States from deep sleep to watchful alertness to fussy, uncontrolled crying all serve a purpose. But a child must learn to manage these;—he must sustain one state when conducive to his needs and shift to another if not. At the far ends of this spectrum of states (deep sleep on the one hand; crying, tantrums, or unfocused activity on the other), the environment—and learning—are shut out. A child's ability to pull himself out of those states varies with his temperament. Parents are most concerned with their child's capacity to maintain the attention needed for him to listen and learn. But they are also profoundly affected by how well a child can console or calm himself. Most children need their parents to help them with this, but they vary in the ways they take in and use the comforting their parents offer.

Each of the four children in this book has a different set of equipment to deal with. These different temperamental qualities appear in the early weeks of life. The baby's first job is to learn ways to manage his internal reactions (heart rate, respiration, motor reflex activity) so that he can master the biggest job: that of maintaining awake and sleep states throughout the day. As babies become more and more competent, they learn to control interfering startles and movements and to maintain a longer and longer quiet state of attention. In this state, babies are able to recognize cues from their environment—the mother's face, her voice, her smell, her attitudes. As children mature, alert states in which they learn about their world become more and more important. These are the child's windows into adapting to his world. Intense activity and a short attention span can make this difficult. Extreme hypersensitivity can also pull a child out of a learning, interactive state. All children have the job of managing these interfering temperamental qualities as they learn to adapt and enter the world. Without an understanding of states and temperament, parents can easily submerge a child with overwhelming, ineffective pressure. This can set up a vicious cycle of guilt and ineffectiveness, leading to a destructive self-image. Understanding the mechanisms of each child's temperament is thus a vital job for every parent.

When Minnie built up to a peak of demands, her besieged parents had to learn how to bring her down to earth. Sometimes they tried to sit down with her to discuss what she wanted. If they turned their complete attention to her, it sometimes worked. When she was very active, they'd often gather her up to cuddle her in their arms in a rocking chair. This could be magical. But, at times, it seemed as if there were a motor inside Minnie, complete with its own buildup over which she had little control. She would begin to whirl around in constant motor activity, racing from one part of the house to another as if she were internally driven. Finally, after either a verbal barrage or a frenzy of activity, she'd collapse in misery. As she wept and squirmed on the floor, no one could reach her. She'd cry out in anguish. Her parents felt that they had lost contact with their daughter. Her loss of control was so painful that they wondered whether

she was hyperactive or even manic. The behavior frightened them and it frightened her.

Gradually, Minnie's parents learned ways to help her calm down. She needed sensitive handling. Mrs. Lee became aware that she should approach Minnie in advance and lead her gradually into a change. "In fifteen minutes, we are going to the store." "In ten minutes, we have to leave. Can you begin to gather up your coat and your bear or whatever you want to take?" "In five minutes, we need to go.

Let's sit together and plan what we'll do." If Mrs. Lee could coach Minnie to calm herself down, the child would gradually gain control of her over-active state, and the transition would be smoother. Minnie found it very difficult to make changes; controlling her excitement and her need to be active was a difficult job for her.

Billy was always ready for battle. He was so intense that Mrs. Stone could have spent most of the day correcting him, but her words rolled off his back. When she began to harangue him, his eyes glazed. He had learned to ignore her. This, of course, made her even more frantic. She tried to break through: "Billy, are you listening to me?" "Uh-huh." "What did I say?" "Nothing." "Billy, you haven't even been listening." To an onlooker, it might have been obvious that she would have done better to save up her disapproval. When she sat down quietly with Billy, he changed. As they sat there together, without talking, Billy became attentive. What was about to happen? His eyes and face lit up with interest. "Billy, what can we do when you get out of hand like that?" "Time out, Mom." "But you don't pay any attention to me in time out."

Mrs. Stone had been missing the point of time out. Billy had gotten it. Time out breaks the cycle of build up; it gives the child time to gain control—and to realize it. Then he can listen and even hear you when you say, "Billy, every time you do this, I have to stop you until you can stop yourself."

When Billy had been disciplined successfully, he was almost grateful. His eyes sparkled. When he was corrected he began to regain the energy he'd lost. He fairly danced away from a successful interchange with his mother. When Mr. Stone needed to discipline Billy, however, it was an entirely different affair. One disappointed look from his stepfather was enough. Billy was so eager to please Mr. Stone that a mere furrowing of his stepfather's brow was all it took.

When Tim was barraged by too many sights or sounds, when he was exposed to a new group of exciting people, when he was expected to live up to new occasions or to important expectations, he would retreat into a daze. Withdrawal was Tim's way of losing control. If he could, he'd run into his room and shut the door. If he was in a public place, he withdrew physically and emotionally. In a crowded room, he would sit down or hide in a corner; his eyes glazed over, his face grew blank. At times, he wrung his hands, or even pulled his hair. The episodes frightened his parents, and they worried about autistic behavior. Tim seemed unreachable—to them and to himself. Fortunately, they learned ways to help their son handle the stressful situations that overwhelmed him; they knew they must teach him ways to cope with noise and activity before he went to 'real' school.

Like Minnie's parents, they discovered that preparing their son ahead of time for a demanding new situation helped Tim's behavior. They found that he relaxed a little when they encouraged him to rely on his own strategy of staying back and watching carefully. Staying close by him to protect him from too many overwhelming stimuli also helped. Praising him when he managed his way through a situation eventually helped Tim recognize his sensitivities and how he had compensated for them. His parents knew they couldn't help him by gathering him up or by scolding him. They also were realizing that their own anxiety just added to his withdrawn state. Briefly they wondered about seeking help for him. But it was hard for them to face.

Tim's shyness was his response to a hypersensitive nervous system. Many children like Tim are all too easily overwhelmed. Every touch, every sound, every direct approach is twice as overwhelming to them as it is to a less sensitive child. All their energy goes into learning how to guard themselves from overwhelming stimuli. Research with premature babies and other fragile infants has shown us that, as newborns, such children can tolerate either touch, or sound, or being picked up, or being looked in the face. But only one at time. After they take in one modality and adjust physiologically, they can then take two, three and finally four kinds of sensory input at once. But it costs them a lot. Their nervous systems are likely to be overwhelmed unless they can set up defenses. Shyness helps to limit the amount and number of stimuli such a child must face.

There are many such hypersensitive children, not all of whom are born fragile or premature. We think this may represent an immaturity of the nervous system that will often mature in time, or a temporary disorganization that an understanding environment can eventually help to organize. But the immediate responses such a child uses as he hides behind his shyness may disturb his parents; understanding these defenses and helping him find other ways to cope over time is a major challenge for these parents.

Each child deals with a stressful environment in his own way. An important feature of individual temperament is the child's particular way of "tuning in" or "tuning out" to buffer the sensations and demands that surround him. All children must learn to adjust to their sensitivities, and to control the motor or sensory disruption that follows an overload of stimulation. Parents can offer their understanding of how their child's state of mind and his particular sensitivities affect his capacity to deal with overload. If explosions can be predicted, children can learn how to keep them under control. It may help to keep a chart: —(1) what it's like when things are going well; (2) what kind of behavior precedes a blow-up; (3) what characterizes a blow-up; and (4) what does he need from others to pull himself together? What does he contribute himself? How does the child behave afterwards?

Tim's version of a blow-up is withdrawal. He has had to deal with a hypersensitive nervous system. With an impulsive, motorically driven child such as Minnie, overload turns into aggressive behavior. Despite these differences, each of these children demonstrates a parallel pattern: vulnerability, stimulation overload, and *kapow!* After the blow up, whether it is a tantrum or withdrawal, the child shows an apparent reorganization and the ability to face the stressful environment again.

When such a chart can be made, you can see the pattern of the child's behavior. Eventually, the behavior in (2), just before the blow up, can be explained to the child to give him the chance to cut off the peak.

Tim's tendency to withdraw and his shyness can be seen as his ways of being in control of the overwhelming aspects of his world. His 'crutches'—the thumb, the blanket—are useful ways he finds to control his reactions to this sensitivity. Tim is showing an increasing capacity to manage stimuli. For example, at three, he had been overwhelmed at the playground. Retreating to his mother's shoulder, he had mustered enough organization to peep out and watch the other children. As he watched, his mother sensed his in-

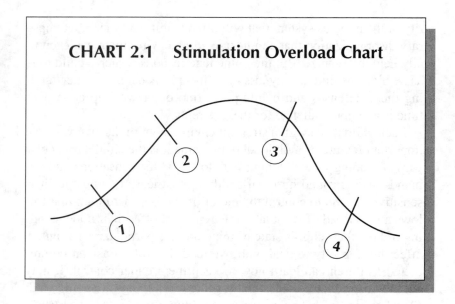

CHART 2.1   Stimulation Overload Chart

terest in the activity and his hunger to participate. At the point where Tim can watch the other children, and even model himself on them, he will be able to open up gradually. It may take time, and that is difficult for Mrs. McCormick. For parents of retiring children like Tim (or "wild" ones, like Minnie), it can be hard to wait for the reassurance that a child's growing up is likely to bring.

Parents will learn that each child is more vulnerable to losing control when in a particular state of mind (anxious, frightened, frustrated) or a particular physiologic state (hungry, cold, tired, and so forth). The child can learn to gain control over these states before he blows up by using what comes naturally, resources based on his temperament—but he may need parental prompting and support. A parent's contribution needs to be accompanied by respect, patience, and the understanding that change will occur over time. It's not easy for a child to change his patterns. If you enlist the child to find his own ways to control his behavior you communicate three messages: that you respect his temperament; that he can look at his behavior with you without shame; and that he can share responsibility for his actions. Parents feel less desperate when they realize that they have a way to intervene. The child feels better about himself when he discovers that he can master his own difficulties.

The job of learning how to manage one's own temperament is life-long. Parents who accept and value their child's temperament profit by the kind of predictability that this understanding brings to each developmental change. They can use their awareness of the child's temperament to understand difficult behavior rather than seeing it as intentionally disturbing. If they can face the ghosts of vulnerability from their own childhoods, they are less likely to overreact to their child's vulnerable behavior, less likely to reinforce it by hovering or applying pressure to change. If parents can accomplish this, they can look forward to reinforcing three important assets in their child—self-awareness, self-accept-ance, and self-esteem.

A Setback Becomes an Opportunity

Because Marcy had turned four, everyone became newly aware of the changes in her. Her face was slightly longer, more mature. Less baby fat, her mother realized. Her eyes seemed warier. She seemed to be more thoughtful. She wondered about everything: "What makes the clouds stay up in the sky?" "Why do my nails grow?"

Marcy was growing up. But after the excitement of her birthday party, Marcy wet her bed, the first time in over a year. Her toilet training had been easy: it had been on her own time. She had stopped wetting at night almost a year ago. She'd even asked not to wear diapers at night, "so I can go to the potty if I need to." When Marcy wet her bed this time, her mother was worried. So was Marcy. "I'm a big girl now. I'm four years old. I don't want to wet like a baby. Why did I do it?"

The next day she was grumpy. She cried easily. Her mother won-dered what was behind her fragility, but hoped it would pass. That night, Marcy wet again. She crept into her parents' room, whimper-ing, "I couldn't help it!" She was so upset that they let her sleep with them. They tried to downplay the whole incident. Marcy rolled and tossed all night. No one slept soundly. In the morning, Marcy was upset again. Her parents had hoped the problem would go away, but now they had to face it. She told her mother that she had dreamed bad dreams, that a mean monster had frightened her and had made her wet her bed. Marcy seemed to need her parents to take her wetting more seriously. Mrs. Jackson tried to reassure Marcy that there were no such monsters. Marcy wept. She felt deserted by her parents' limited concern.

Two hours later, Marcy came to find her mother. Her brown curls were dancing, her eyes bright. "I know what we can do, Mommy. Get me some big diapers. Ones for kids who have to wet at night and can't wake up." Mrs. Jackson was shocked. But she was also impressed with Marcy's determination to solve her problem. They went to the store together. Marcy chose her own diapers. Proudly, she displayed them at the dinner table to her father and her older brother. Her brother, Amos, giggled. Marcy's face reddened as she realized that he was laughing at her. "They'll help me." Mrs. Jackson's stern look quelled her brother's laughing. She wondered whether he was being "meaner" than sibling rivalry entitled him to be.

At bedtime, Marcy seemed particularly worried. She asked for the diapers. She patted them appreciatively. She seemed more clingy than usual. After her bedtime story, she asked her father to help her look for monsters left over from the night before. Mr. Jackson looked in all the closets, and under the bed—no monsters. Marcy snuggled down with both parents in attendance. She asked for the old frayed blanket to wrap up her beloved Missy, the doll she'd turned to when the blanket and her thumb were not enough. Because she'd given up the blanket several months before, her parents had to search for it. When they gave it to her, she wrapped Missy up in it. "Don't worry, Missy. You won't wet the bed tonight." She tugged on her diapers as if they were already a comfort. She slept soundly.

Mrs. Jackson was anxious to check on her daughter in the morning. Marcy marched triumphantly out of her room. "They worked!" "Oh, Marcy, aren't you proud?" "They did it, Mommy. They helped me grow up to four," Marcy said, holding out four fingers, her thumb folded behind her hand.

At first, Mrs. Jackson had been unsure about the idea of letting Marcy rely on the diapers each night, but she was reassured by Marcy's pride. She seemed confident enough, now, to face her backslide. Like any parents, the Jacksons would have preferred to ignore Marcy's initial wetting. At first, they thought it would pass, but Marcy was too upset to ignore it. "Why did she wet? Why did it happen right after her birthday? Marcy surely wasn't going to get into a problem with this, was she?" The Jacksons had been having enough trouble with Amos lately; it was hard to face more in Marcy, who'd been so easy. The danger would have been for them to ignore the wetting problem for as long as it would let them, and then to push Marcy too hard, beyond her capacity to regain her old control. That kind of insensitive pressure could have created a problem for them all. Instead, the Jacksons listened to Marcy and allowed her to find a solution of her own.

The bedwetting didn't recur. Marcy's pride in herself was affirmed. Each night for two weeks, she and her father checked on the monsters, but they didn't come back. Marcy seemed secure enough to give up her diapers a few weeks later. As Marcy's mother tried to reconstruct the events, she became aware of the expectations that had built up around her birthday. Marcy wanted to grow up so badly. She wanted to live up to her older brother. She counted on four to be a turning point for her. Her parents did too. But they hadn't left room for her equally understandable need to regress, to be like a baby again. The "accidents" were a kind of protest against her own and her parents' expectations. By finding a symbol of comfort (the diapers) and by allowing herself to fall back on the frayed blanket and her other "loveys," she gave herself the strength to face this step, enormous for her. She reached back for what had worked before. She enlisted her parents' support to face the "monsters." These achievements were a thrilling example of the many elaborate resources that Marcy had at her disposal to face the task that had at first overwhelmed her: becoming a four-year-old!

Parents faced with a setback in their child's development may react in one of three ways. Denial of the problem leaves the entire responsibility to the child. When a child's struggle is reminiscent of sensitive moments in a parent's own past, a parent may overreact. Parents may need to ask why the child's difficulty is stirring up so much reaction in them as parents before they can respond sensitively to the child's needs. Touchpoints are precisely those events in a child's development that touch parents deeply, opening up feelings which may be hard to face, hard to keep from acting on impulsively. The third, and most productive approach is to ask, "Why now?" and "What does this setback mean to my child?"

There are many achievements which are thrilling and over-whelming for a four-year-old. The child's rapid intellectual growth and his increasingly intricate use of language to express himself marks an enormous step for him and for his parents. He becomes more aware of his effect on those around him. He wonders more deeply, has more elaborate fantasies. He is just beginning to become aware that there is a much larger world beyond the one within his grasp. At the same time, he is more able to find his own solutions to life's puzzles, or at least he can dream up possibilities. The magical power that Marcy was able to invest in those diapers helped her to free herself from the responsibility of being four, a pressure that had temporarily overwhelmed her. Her need to fall back on the safety of earlier patterns marks how much the child's push toward a major step in development may demand of her. Exciting developmental steps, or touchpoints, are always stressful and demanding. The child's ability to fall back so that he can gather the necessary energy to take a demanding step forward has always impressed me with its effectiveness.

When a child finds his own solution, he will be able to face other stresses with an assurance that he can look for and find such solu-tions. If Marcy's parents hadn't found a way to respect her idea, she would have never recognized her own strength. Instinctively, she knew how to reach back for what worked before so that she could face new challenges. Marcy was so clear in her behavior that she lit-erally led her parents to the solution.

The cognitive area—of language, and with it, the ability to for-mulate and verbalize his increasingly complex ideas—gives a four-year-old power. Marcy could see that her solution worked—both for her and for those around her. She could talk back to her older brother. Marcy's new interest in the rewards of growing up pushed her to identify with her parents. Her pride in her own solution helped balance her dawning realization that she must be dependent on her parents at critical times.

Learning

*Magical Thinking:
Making Room
for the Real*

Billy's magical thinking invaded everything. When he went to his doctor for his checkup and she undressed him, his penis became erect. He proudly said, "Look how my penis is. It's because I eat all my vegetables." The pediatrician said, "Is that how it works?" "Yup! Someday it's going to be bigger than this whole world." Wishing can make it seem true.

Billy had a pet hamster. The hamster, named "Afraid," loved Billy and would immediately leave the exercycle when he came up to the cage. Billy had learned to handle Afraid gently, let him crawl on his shoulders and arms. Billy had been taught to close the doors to his room in case Afraid got loose; this kept his mother from worrying about Afraid's escaping. One day, Billy was holding Afraid. When Billy jumped at a loud noise and accidentally squeezed Afraid too hard, the hamster bit him. Billy was inconsolable. "He bit me on my finger! It hurts! Could he bite my finger off? Why did he bite me?" Underneath Billy's reaction was the loss of trust he had placed in Afraid. At this age, Billy was just becoming aware of how his behavior may have caused Afraid to bite. But his overreaction to the little bit of pain was also an expectable part of Billy's growing awareness of his body, and the seemingly limitless ideas he had at his disposal to explain what might be happening to him.

A four-year-old on the West Coast asked me to write a book for children. When I demurred, saying that I wouldn't know what to write, he said, "I can tell you what to write. Write about why I go to the doctor." He paused and looked at me seriously. "What do doctors look for? Are you just looking for my badness?" The child delivered this last statement cautiously, and I realized for the first time why children are so vulnerable during a check-up visit to the doctor. No pain, no intrusive examination could match the child's fears and fantasies of what a doctor might find. Among these fears is often children's own concern about a doctor's "uncovering badness." This explained to me why preparing children of this age with reassurance may not work. If there is "something wrong," magical thinking leads them to believe that it is their fault. They know they are susceptible to making mistakes, and at this age are becoming all too aware of feeling responsible when they err.

Marcy tries hard to control her world in her head. When she can't get her way, her face darkens. She withdraws into a silent, thoughtful state. She becomes almost motionless as she begins to think things out. In this state, she can dream of her own world and manage to make it fit what she wants. One day, she said, "Amos broke the glass, Mummy." Her mother wanted to believe her, but she knew better. Amos had not even been at home. "Marcy, you know he didn't. Why do you lie to me?" "But I wish Amos had broken it." Her mother's concern subsided dramatically, for she was accustomed to Marcy's use of wishful thinking to explain transgressions.

Once, Marcy lost her doll. She cried and flung herself down to have a temper tantrum, sure that her mother would then find the doll for her. When her mother walked away and said wearily, "This time you find it. I have other things to do," Marcy knew she was beaten. She was never good at finding things, and she knew that, too. So she enlisted her older brother. Amos found the doll after a search. Marcy marched into the kitchen, carrying her doll triumphantly. "I found . . . we found . . . Amos found my doll!" Reality was brought to bear on the wish. Marcy was no longer at the root of everything. She was beginning to recognize the causal roles that others play.

Billy awoke on the morning of his long-awaited fourth birthday. His parents went to his bedroom and sang "Happy Birthday" to him. When he broke down weeping, they were shocked. "But, Billy, this is your birthday! Why are you sad?" He looked up at them with soulful eyes. "I wanted to skip being four and to pop into being a daddy." He paused and looked down. "I'm still just a little boy."

The sadness of his wrecked dream tore at his parents' hearts. No matter how much they tried to console Billy, his birthday was heavy with disappointment. His party and presents cheered him up through the afternoon. At bedtime, they all discussed Billy's sadness about not being able to wish himself into being a daddy. They tried to reason. "No one gets all he wishes for, Billy." "But I wished so *hard.*"

"But if you popped into being a daddy, you'd miss all your friends. They'd still be little boys and girls. They'd miss you, too." At that, Billy brightened. "Then I couldn't have a birthday party." He hesitated for a moment, then said "But daddies have birthday parties." "Yes, but only with other daddies and mommies. They don't have little boys and girls their age to play with. Remember how much fun you had teasing Afraid this afternoon? And you chased Céline all over the yard. Daddies don't get to play like that." Billy looked thoughtful. He curled up with his beloved teddy and his tattered blanket. As he settled down to cuddle his loveys, he looked up at his parents as if to say, "I guess it's going to have to be okay."

Though resignation was beginning to sink in, Billy couldn't quite give up his dreams. It was painful for his parents to watch, for it took them back in time to the dreams and wishes they had relinquished. All parents wish they could protect their children from disillusionment. Billy struggled to accept their efforts to substitute a reality for his dreams. But facing reality required strategies for facing the limits of his powers and coping with sadness that were still beyond him.

The day after his birthday, Billy said, "Mommy, I want a piece of cake." She replied, "But you can't have it. You've already had one piece." "But I deserve it." "Why?" "Because I want it so badly." When he didn't get it, he sprawled on the floor to have a rip-roaring temper tantrum. His mother was furious until she realized that her son's capacity to master frustration was overwhelmed. She could see that he was trying to wish himself magically into being gratified. As the tantrum resolved itself, he said plaintively, "I do wish I could have it *so* much" After he had calmed down, she was able to hold him and say, "I'm sorry, Billy, but just wanting something a lot doesn't make it happen." He looked up at her, "But why not?" Why, indeed?

We all wish we could give our children everything they wish for. We all wish we could spare them the turmoil of growing up, of relinquishing their wishful dreams. Since we cannot, what *can* we do? Outbursts and tantrums are a child's passionate efforts to make the world her own. If parents make fun of her or in any way put her down, they are saying, "It's not your world after all." By acknowledging her frustration and sadness at giving up her wishes, a parent is sharing the sadness with her. This way, the child does not feel alone, and she can be given the respect she deserves as she faces the

struggle. She is learning to live in reality. If she can do this, she joins our world. If she doesn't, she'll have a worse time. She needs her parents' help.

A child's struggle to hang on to her dream can lead to behavior that she has outgrown. She needs to pull back, to fall apart, to reorganize. This regression will give her the force to regroup and to face the necessity of accepting a more reasonable approach. If parents can understand the importance of this struggle, they can help a child live in a world that forces her to give up many of her wishes. She will eventually be able to understand the reasons why she can't shape her world entirely as she wishes.

A four-year-old is more ready intellectually to understand reality. Temper tantrums are different at this age because a child is cognitively ready for more than a simple yes or no. A parent can explain why something cannot be done. Tantrums are a struggle against harsh reality rather than the "Will I?" or "Won't I?" struggles of temper tantrums in a two- or three-year-old. This is a touchpoint at four: the child balks at what her new cognitive skills force her to face about herself and her world. It is also a touchpoint for parents as they face their new role. No longer will they simply provide for all their child's needs, but they must also help her forego the wants that cannot be satisfied.

Cops and Robbers, Witches and Queens

What are the purposes of the magical thinking that fills up the dreams of four-year-olds? A child is learning to face her own world. She needs to dream and to wish for a world in which she, not her parents, is in control. Magical thinking is a thrust toward independence at an increasingly thoughtful level.

When you watch a child play, you will notice that she mimics adult behaviors she has seen. But she twists them to serve her purposes, to fulfill her dreams. Play becomes a world in which she can try out magical solutions. At this age, a child seeks solutions to intolerable feelings of frustration, of love, of anger, to forbidden extra pieces of cake, to being able to control her world, to not being just like the adults around her. When the game ends, she must face the reality of the adult world around her.

Billy watched the policemen who came when the neighbor's alarm went off. One policeman spoke to Billy, squatting down to acknowledge him. "What are you going to be when you grow up?" Billy was silent, his eyes wide open in awe. "Would you like to be a policeman? Come on—climb up in the squad car with me." Billy was completely won over. "My daddy's a policeman—like you. He catches robbers, too." He looked quietly at his mother, who averted her eyes. "He flies around in airplanes looking for robbers. When he sees one, he chases after him." "So he's a real policeman, is he? Would you like to try the siren?" Billy was thrilled. He cringed at first at the siren's loudness, then he straightened up. "I'm a real policeman, aren't I?" The policeman said, "You can pretend to be one right now. And when you're grown up, you can become a real one and ride with me and sound the siren." Billy was carried away with new dreams. From then on, he bragged to everyone he met, "I'm a policeman and I get to blow the siren." After a few days, he began to enlarge on his dream. "I caught a hundred robbers. I blew the horn every time so little kids would look." A few days later: "I grew up. I married Mommy and we flew in an airplane." A few days later: "Mommy and I looked for robbers. We put them in jail." A few days later: "I'm as big as Daddy and he wants to be a policeman like me. I'm a hundred years old!"

A four-year-old's world is full of fantasy. Magical thinking has offered explanations for all sorts of mysteries—how the last piece of cake disappeared, and many others. Although a four-year-old is beginning to know better, she still plays out the wishes in her fantasy life. Fantasy protects her dreams, her wishes, her ability to relate to the future. But she's having to give up exploring her could-be world so that she can accept reality around her. As wonderful as becoming aware of herself and her influence over others may be, such awareness limits her dreaming about being more powerful than she really is. A four-year-old is bound to totter back and forth, between how the world is, and how she dreams it should be. The kind of playful representation that Billy began to develop in his second and third year—making a doll into a fireman that could ride on a fire engine, playing with a dinosaur that could climb over the dinner table, ruining everyone else's dinner—is leading him to a fuller life.

Imaginary Friends

Billy is never alone. An imaginary friend called Buddy can talk to him in the car when he's bored. Buddy helps him deal with Daddy when he's mad. Billy can transfer his own "badnesses" to Buddy. "Buddy was trying to steal your computer 'cause he loves it so much. I told him the police would come get him and put him in jail. But he didn't listen." Billy needs to be ready to face his stepfather's anger with what he calls a lie. "I know you broke my computer again. I told you not to play with it. Why do you lie to me about Buddy?" The sudden loss of trust in his four-year-old represents a potential touchpoint for Billy's stepfather; either he could overreact or he could recognize it as a predictable step in Billy's development. Maybe he could even enjoy the candor and the magic

behind Billy's "lie." At four years, Billy has entered a phase of magical thinking that gives him a new kind of power. Billy can imagine
Buddy as the bad one. Billy can be the good one. He can scold
Buddy: "You broke my dad's computer. He told us not to play with
it. Why do you lie to me?" As Buddy collapses under this disapproval, Billy can pick him up and love him: "I know you didn't
mean to break it. You just meant to play with it like my daddy."

What does his stepfather's disapproval do to Billy's lying? It
drives it underground for the time being. Billy continues to construct situations in which Buddy plays an all-powerful role. But for
now he avoids sharing these with his stern, disappointed stepfather.
But Billy's magical thinking is too important to him. He has few
other defenses to fall back on at four. The defenses he does have,
such as denial or avoidance, work only at the expense of hiding
from reality. It hurts him too much to face his disappointment in
himself for having wrecked his stepfather's computer. His stepfa-

ther sensed this and tried to repair Billy's feelings; later, he said to Billy, "Poor old Buddy. He must hate it when I jump on you. I just wanted Buddy to be more careful next time and to leave my computer alone until he learns about it."

His mother welcomed Billy's new dream world, and smiled at his tales about Buddy's exploits. "Buddy played with my friends today. He was the biggest, the fastest of all. He won every race we had." Billy had come in next to last in the nursery school races. He was a sturdy, determined, but awkward runner. Buddy was agile and quick—all the things Billy dreamed of being. Think what an incentive to Billy this companion has become.

Unfortunately, only a first child is allowed to be open about imaginary friends. A second or third child may have them, but a sibling will laugh at them and send them underground. This is probably why most younger siblings never talk about their adventures with their imaginary friends.

Imagine the pleasures of making up anyone you wish and becoming that person temporarily. To be able to carry around your trusted friend, always ready to stand up for you, to encourage you, to fly away with you! Wishes are fulfilled, anxieties made tangible. When others enter this world, they bring it to reality, and the magic is threatened. I urge parents to value these fantasies in their children, but not to invade them by making them too explicit. Fantasies need to remain fantasies.

Marcy had two imaginary friends, Happen Orter and Guessus. Guessus was the Queen, and Happen Orter, the Witch. If her parents tried to delve much farther, she'd clam up. She didn't really want her parents in her private world. They confronted her (and her imaginary friends) with too much reality. "How did Guessus get all dressed up for the party? What did she wear?" Marcy's face would darken as she tried to answer these mundane questions. They felt like an unwelcome challenge. She hadn't really wanted to pin her ideas down. Finally, she'd answer, "In a grand cloak of diamonds—like Mommy's ring!" She'd watch their faces to see how far they would go with her. She realized that her parents' participation in her fantasy held her to the earth. Parents must tread lightly when entering this magical world with their child. It is magical and wonderful for an adult to contemplate—but it needs to be respected as a private world for the child.

Adults play into this magical world with such customs as the tooth fairy or Santa Claus or the Easter Bunny. Are we trying to participate, or are we confirming the importance of magical thinking? Parents ask me when they should attempt to "tell" their child that there is no Santa Claus. My answer is, "Never." Don't we all want to believe? Do we really need to tell them? Don't they know already? They will let you know when they can tell the difference between what can be known and what they want to believe. My six-year-old grandson collected his twelve Easter eggs and said, "Where are the rest?" His parents said sternly, "That's all there are." He said plaintively, "There should be more. I'm an only child!" This was his way of saying that he already "knew" about the Easter Bunny and its limitations. He was testing his parents' willingness to share their reality with him. They didn't need to "tell" him about the Easter Bunny. If they had understood his underlying question, they would have enjoyed his exploration of their position. A child's ability to play with magical thinking is often confusing for adults. We had to give it up long ago. Watching our children go through letting it go makes us wonder whether we are depriving them of something when we fail to shield them from reality.

Make-believe Billy's days were made up of changing from one costume into another. When he put a bandanna around his face, he became a robber. "Stick 'em up" said he in a low growling voice. If you didn't comply, his fingers were in your ribs. "I said, stick 'em up and I meant it. You're dead!" An old cape of his grandma's and a pair of glasses turned him into a vampire. "Where did you learn about vampires?" "From TV." "What is a vampire?" "They fly around and they land on people. If you cry, you're in deep trouble. If you fight back, they fly away." This followed an episode at preschool of standing up to a bully and fighting him.

Many of Billy's costumes were superheroes. "Who is the strongest? Who is the fastest? I can shoot you down so hard you can't get up." One day, Billy wanted to try on nail polish "like Mommy." When his mother let him try it on, he looked at it approvingly. "Don't tell Daddy." Mrs. Stone wondered where his awareness of "girl" things had come from.

Billy's seven-year-old cousin, Tom, came over to play. They dressed up in capes, hats, and masks. They were pirates on an ocean, ready to sink any ship in sight. In the yard, they found sticks for swords to joust with, but Tom was much more adept. After a while, it was obvious that swordplay with each other wouldn't do. So they dueled in the air with an imaginary swordsman. "We are trying to save Abby from the other pirates." One-year-old Abby was terrified. She toddled off screaming from these two madmen. "Abby, if you don't let us save you, we won't ever play with you again." Abby calmed down, looked at them seriously. Billy and Tom threw themselves on the couch and rocked away on the cushions. "It's a boat rocking on the water. We've escaped the other pirates and we have Abby safe." Abby, now rocked on the couch, looked peacefully at these big strong boys.

Minnie's parents gave her a guinea pig for Christmas because they thought she might warm up to a small animal. It wasn't long before Minnie's mother felt that Minnie talked more to Agula than to her. Agula became the target for Minnie's play and her dreams. More than once, her mother spied Minnie flying around the house with Agula, mumbling to her that "we can fly to the moon together." One day, Minnie dropped the guinea pig. After that, the frightened animal cowered in the corner of her cage whenever Minnie came up. Minnie's mother gave Minnie a stern lecture about being gentle with animals. Then Minnie crept back to the cage and said, "Bad Agula, the no-good aster-naut."

Marcy was fascinated with babies. She and her mother went to visit her aunt, who had delivered a baby two weeks ago. Marcy watched everything the baby did. "Look at his legs move. He has hands and fingers just like us!" She wanted to hold the baby. She sat down in a chair and let the baby be handed to her. She sat motionless and entranced for thirty minutes, as if she sensed how fragile the baby might be. When the baby's diaper was changed,

Marcy's eyes were glued to the process. She asked about his
"weenie." She seemed especially aware of and inquisitive about
where his urine and stools came from. "Is that where he wees? I
wish I could watch it—just once! Can't I, Mommy? Look at his
poop. It's so gloppy. Is that the same as mine? Does it come out
of his tummy—or do boys' poopies come out their weenies?"
"Can I have a baby like him?" For the next few weeks, Marcy
pushed out her stomach as she walked around. She dreamt of
having a baby. She dressed up her dolls. She diapered them. She
put them to her chest and fed them. She talked in a high-
pitched, gentle voice to each of them. She wished so hard that
it might come true, and worked to find an acceptable form for
the wish that was still there: to be a baby again. She could easily
fall apart if anyone devalued her efforts. "You can't have a baby
until you grow up." Marcy's wishful thinking was too important
to her.

Fairy tales have always been a way for parents and children to share this wonderful world of magic. The themes of a child's life at this time—angry feelings, differences between boys and girls, wishing to be a baby or a spouse or a parent—are all addressed in fairy tales. Cinderella and the prince, the wicked stepsisters and stepmother—they echo the underlying fantasies that all children share. When parents read these tales to their four-, five-, and six-year-olds, they, too, indulge in the fantasies, the horror, the deeper feelings reflected in these tales. The conflict-less story lines, the soft and cuddly characters of many contemporary stories can't get at these deeper feelings, while action-packed videotapes overpower the imaginations of children this age.

Cinderella can become a princess instead of the drudge who *must* help her parents. Cinderella's wicked stepmother can be the darker side of a child's own mother. Or, she can be the damaged mother whom Cinderella hopes her father will reject. Cinderella can then become the triumphant female who overcomes all her competitors. The wicked stepsisters represent all the problems of siblings and their rivalry. The Cinderella story makes it safe both to hate and to compete with them. Ambivalent or seemingly contradictory feelings are universal, but they are confusing and hard to reconcile. As she triumphs as a princess, Cinderella can even forgive her stepsisters and give them princes of their own. What a world opens up for a child who shares this story with her parents! It is important for us as parents to share such stories, but it is also important that we allow children to savor them in their own way—and with respectful privacy. We could so easily take away the safety when we make the themes of children's stories too explicit. With the protection of make-believe, a child can dare to dream.

Cops and robbers. Witches and queens. The good child and the bad. In fantasy and play, these can be reconciled.

Curiosity About Differences

As four-year-olds become more aware of their influence on the world, they become more aware of differences between themselves and others. As they play together and become more familiar, they will begin to comment, "Why is your hair curly?" "Why is my skin dark?" "Will it wash off?" Similar questions and comments are typical of four-year-olds learning about each other and about differences. The curious questioning reveals the worries that come with this new recognition of differences. A four-year-old will wish that her difference makes her more powerful, but she will also fear that it weakens her.

Minnie's older sister, May, had a strawberry-colored birthmark on her cheek. Other children wanted to feel it, to see whether it would wipe off. One of Minnie's friends said, "Did she get it from tomato sauce?" All Minnie's friends were awestruck with it. They even teased Minnie about it. "Did you put it on your sister? Is it because you're Asian? Why don't you go in while she's asleep and wipe it off?" One child said, "It's ugly. I don't want to play with her. Do I have to go to Minnie's house?" From all these remarks, Minnie began to become aware of her sister as "different." She had always looked up to May and had even been afraid of or resented her quiet strength. As the reactions built up from her friends, a change came over Minnie. She began to protect her sister. She'd retort, "She's my sister and she's beautiful. That mark won't go away, but it doesn't matter. She doesn't mind it if you don't talk about it." Or, "You're mean. You deserve one on your face. You make my sister feel bad." She began to nurture her sister in ways that she'd never thought of before. She'd walk with her to school. She'd wince when another child approached. She'd anticipate their questions by changing the subject. Mrs. Lee was amazed by the change in Minnie. She'd never seemed to care about others. Now, she seemed to be taking a motherly role with her older sister. Not that it worked. May was all too aware of Minnie's concern and of what it meant in relation to her birthmark. She became more aggressive to Minnie. She even tried to avoid her. No love was lost between them.

Minnie couldn't handle all the questions about May's birthmark and their ethnicity. One day, when Minnie and her father were on an excursion together, she quietly asked, "Daddy, if May has a red birthmark because she's part Asian, where is yours? Will I get one?" Her father was stunned. He hadn't been prepared for this kind of association. "Who said it was because she's part Asian?" "All my friends." "Well, they're wrong. It hasn't anything to do with being part Korean. May is beautiful, like you. And like me, you have olive skin. I'm proud to be Korean. I'm proud of you. I hope you can be proud, too." Minnie looked at him, a bit overwhelmed by his emphatic reaction. Being different wasn't anything a child of Minnie's age could be proud of. She wanted too much to be like everyone else. Why wasn't her sister like everyone else? Was it because of her sister's "badness"? Her mother had always said that Minnie was "too" active, "too" everything bad. Minnie was afraid now that if she didn't pay attention and try harder, she'd get a birthmark, too.

When Billy saw a child in a wheelchair, he grabbed his mother's hand. Squeezing it tightly, as if he were afraid, he said, "Why can't that boy walk?" His mother tried to quiet him, for he had blurted out his question in a loud voice. "I don't know," she said softly, "but don't embarrass him. He may feel very badly about not being able to walk." Billy stopped, his eyes glued to the crippled child. As he looked toward the wheelchair, his mother sensed his fear and his fascination. "He's about your age. Won't you go and speak to him? He might feel better if you could be his friend." Billy broke into loud sobs. "No! No! No!" His mother was embarrassed and rushed Billy away. Billy kept looking back at the now-crying child in the wheelchair.

Mrs. Stone sat down and pulled Billy onto her lap. She couldn't understand why he was so upset. "Billy, what in the world is the matter?" "I don't want to," Billy wailed. "I don't want to talk to him!" "You don't have to, but you must control yourself. You embarrassed me, and you have surely upset that poor child in the wheelchair. He's just a little boy like you." "What did he do?" "Do? I don't know what you mean." "Why did his legs stop working?" "I don't know, Billy. Did he scare you?" He sobbed loudly and nodded a vigorously yes. "Well, it won't happen to you." Not reassured, Billy murmured, "What if I can't walk?" What Billy couldn't express was how much he identified with the other child, how frightened he was to think that he was vulnerable to just such retaliation for being "bad." He worried about the possibility of being punished in this way. At this age, Billy's cause-and-effect magical thinking led him to see a disability as the inevitable result of a guilty act. To Billy, it seemed that "contagion" from such a disability was too likely. He referred everything around him to himself—a four-year-old starts with himself to understand others.

Billy's mother wanted to push him to overcome these feelings. "Go over and say hello. He'd love to run and play the way you do. He wants to know someone like you even if he can't be like you. Can't you make him feel better?" Billy shook his head, sadly. "No, no, no." He wasn't ready to master these fears; it was just too much to expect of him. Mrs. Stone realized she'd pushed him too hard.

Disabilities in other people frighten (yet fascinate) children of this age. Damage to others' bodies remind them of their own fears. "He has a broken leg. Will I get one?" "She has a mark on her face. Its ugly. Will I get one from spilling juice?" They think in such concrete ways that any guilty act is likely to generate fears of disabilities. Hence, the first job of a parent is to help the child see the disability as belonging to the other person, not to her. Assure her that she won't become disabled by contagion or from bad behavior. At the same time, parents can encourage understanding and empathy in the child, even at this age. If a child is too reluctant, however, don't be surprised and don't push. [See "Differences" in Part II.]

Gender Differences

In her book, *The Magic Years*, Selma Fraiberg, writes of the young child's approach to her world and marvels at her skills as a scientist, as an explorer. Now that she can compare, contrast, and make categories, she brings her investigational skills to bear on the differences that she is beginning to notice around her.

This opportunity to identify with each parent provides children with behavior, feelings, defenses, and self-images that go towards the long process of sorting out their sexuality. Of course they will strut and imitate male behavior. Of course they will want to dress up in their mother's high-heeled shoes and scarves. Of course they will steal her jewelry to wear, her lipstick, her blush. Halloween and other dress-up times serve a major purpose for this kind of exploration. Parents find it easier to accept this when they understand what's behind it.

What happens when a child imitates the behavior and dress of the opposite sex? I have had many letters from parents (and grandparents) who are worried because their son wants to play with dolls. "He wants to wear his mother's underclothes. He struts around with all sorts of feminine gestures. Should we worry about his being gay?" Worrying won't do any good. Children learn about their sexual orientation at their own pace. Whatever their sexuality eventually turns out to be, you cannot change it, and it will need your acceptance. Most often, though, dress-up behavior at this age is short-lived and has little bearing on eventual sexual orientation or gender identity.

Because many four-year-old children go through a period of sorting out gender, I would recommend that parents "play along" with it. This means supporting the child in his or her exploration of herself. This acceptance could be compared to accepting fantasy life in other areas. "Look at you with lipstick and rouge! Mom's shoes are pretty big for you. How do you suppose she can run in them?"

When parents write to me to say that their boys are trying out "feminine" behavior, they point out that if the boys are teased or corrected, their faces fall. The boys don't understand why they can't play with dolls. When boys are allowed to play with dolls, they become warm, cozy—imitating the way their parents care for them. These parents realize that this is the way boys learn nurturing behaviors. To one anxious father, I was able to point out that his son was learning to nurture and to be a gentle, caring individual just like his father. If the child identified only with his father's tough side, mightn't the child miss this warm side of his father? This seemed to allay his father's fears.

If a father is worried about his son's masculinity, the father's concern can be a signal for him to play a more active role in his child's life. He can plan more times together, more chances for a father to approve of and admire his son. They can do the sort of things that they both enjoy. If a boy is shy about sports, don't push him. Let him learn at his own pace and with his own style. A regular chance to try out his skills, safely unpressured, can make all the difference. My four-year-old grandson hit a tennis ball at last—one out of twenty. He said, "Wow! Now I'm a tennis star!" He's been hitting them off and on ever since. Meanwhile, we dream together of how he will be a star soon.

Already at this age, forces are at work that tend to drive a child toward gender-specific behavior. The parents' unconscious and conscious pressure is a major force—regardless of their ideas about men's and women's roles. "You look so pretty when you walk that way," or, "Aren't you great, standing up at the potty just like your dad." As the need to separate from and become independent of these two important caregivers increases, a child turns to other models—siblings, older playmates, even to an important adult, such as a supplementary caregiver. He imitates, he absorbs, he plays at becoming that admired adult. Gender-specific play is a major part of a four-year-old's day. Children in groups shun the other sex because they are trying to keep their focus.

One current view, supported by Carol Gilligan and William Pollock, maintains that parents pressure boys to suppress their nurturing and dependent feelings prematurely, but at the same time they reward aggressive feelings. This view holds that boys are pushed to make an early separation from their mothers and turn instead to their fathers. Nightmares and fears are seen as the price they pay for their new aggressive feelings.

Girls, according to this view, are raised with a different set of expectations. They are allowed to model and to identify with their primary caregivers, usually their mothers, for a longer time. Their nurturing behavior heightens. Their gentle play is valued. But what happens in today's society when women are also expected to be more competitive, more self-expressive? Will girls, too, then have to pay a different price? Or if girls play out more aggressive feelings, fears and nightmares may begin to surface.

Our values for each sex are changing. We want each sex to be more of a mixture of both roles. We want to raise nurturing males, and we want girls to be competitive and self-assured enough to master two roles: nurturing caregiver at home and successful career woman in the workplace. Doesn't this mean that we had better be more respectful of our children's conflicts, more sensitive and open as they explore gender roles and work out their own identities?

Sexuality

Often, a four-year-old will become more conscious of her father's body. His nudity, his bathroom behavior become a focus in her quest for understanding him. Now is the time to pull back. I can remember my own little girls' feet pounding behind me when I headed for the bathroom. I was embarrassed, but my daughters weren't. They wanted to understand what made my body different from theirs. Their questions were easy to answer when they were four, but the urgency behind this questioning was leading to more difficult questions at five and six. Children learn important attitudes toward sexuality from their parents.

Boys and girls are aware of their differences at four. They have already been sorting out the difference between their genitals and anuses. Now, they are becoming aware that boys and girls are made differently. "How do you know it's a girl?" "By her hair and her clothes." "How else?" With embarrassment, "She hasn't got a pee-pee, she's just got a wee-wee." Four-year-olds are already self-conscious and aware, even naming themselves differently.

Marcy told her mother that boys are silly and babyish. "They are always showing off. They have little 'weenies' that stick out from their bottoms. I saw one peeing on the tree," she told her mother, with more fascination than disdain. Billy surprised his stepfather when he said, "We never play with girls. They're silly. Only boys are okay." Where did he learn such things? No one in his house would consciously say such a thing. But four-year-old boys say these things to each other.

As soon as toddlers are out of diapers, both sexes investigate their sexual apparatus. Having been covered, genitals have become heightened as a focus for exploration. Girls find that exploring themselves can be rewarding. They are likely to insert objects into their vaginas to "find out how deep the opening is." They discover that self-stimulation is exciting. Indeed, masturbatory activity is common in four-year-old girls. What should a parent say? Very little. The child is more likely to feel that she has completed her explorations if she is left to feel that these are her own private discoveries. However, a child who seems absorbed in masturbation for prolonged periods may have some special need for self-soothing. She may need help in learning other ways to calm herself, or she may be letting her parents know that she has been sexually overstimulated and traumatized.

A boy finds quickly that his penis has heightened feelings. Many little boys begin to hold on to their penises while they suck their thumbs. This behavior is both comforting and exciting. Adults react with disapproval which reinforces it. As boys react to a full bladder with an erection, they find that playing with their penises gives them a rather special sensation. By the fourth year, masturbation is almost universal among boys. They need to learn that self-stimulation is best saved for a private place. Parents who recognize the importance of masturbating will not interfere with this behavior or stop it. Prohibition is likely to increase its importance, as it does with thumb sucking or other rewarding behaviors. A parent can divert these activities to a private place without conveying a sense of disapproval.

As children find out about their own genitalia, the urge to explore each other is bound to surface. Parents should be prepared for classic questions: "Why is his wee different? Where has *her* pee-pee gone? What is that sticking out of *his* wee-wee? What's the difference?"

It was 5:00 P.M., the end of the day, and everyone was keyed up. Mrs. Stone got Billy undressed and into a warm bath. As she undressed Abby, she saw that the little girl had had a liquid bowel movement. After she had cleaned Abby up as well as she could, Mrs. Stone wondered briefly whether it was fair to put her daughter in the tub with Billy. Would his bath be contaminated? They always took baths together as a reward at the end of a long day. Mrs. Stone thought of it as a wonderful, relaxing time. She would sit on the floor beside the tub and watch them splash together. The usual dissension was rare at bath time. Abby would be in her "safe seat," which allowed her to kick and squirm, but not to slip and slide in the tub.

Mrs. Stone rinsed Abby off and put her in her seat. Billy looked gratefully at his mother as Abby joined him. "I like Abby." "Oh Billy, what a lovely thing to say." "I do, Mommy." As Abby sat in her chair, her legs splashing in the water, giggles arose from each of them. Billy giggled, Abby imitated. Billy splashed with his hands, Abby followed. He splashed hard, and water hit her in the face. She might have cried, for she jerked away. But she didn't; she chortled out loud. Billy splashed again and again. Water sloshed onto the walls and floor. Mrs. Stone: "That's enough, Billy. Now it's time to wash." He began to wash himself. But then he thought better of it and took the washcloth to Abby's legs, her hands, and he started to wash her bottom. Mrs Stone diverted their play and brought the bath to an end. They'd let her know it was time to stop baths together. She will need to let them know without making them feel ashamed.

"Where do little girls' penises go? Mine isn't going, too, is it?" "Little girls have wee-wees or vaginas. Boys have penises. Your penis will always be there and her vagina will always be there. Later, her babies will come out from there." "But I thought babies came from your stomach, like poops. Your stomach got big when you were having her." "No, your bum is for your poops. The vagina is where babies come from." "How do you get a baby?" "A mommy and daddy love each other. They make love. He puts his penis inside her vagina. A seed from the daddy comes out from his penis into the mommy's vagina, where it finds a little egg. Together the seed and the egg can grow into a baby. The baby comes from mommies and daddies loving each other and wanting to have

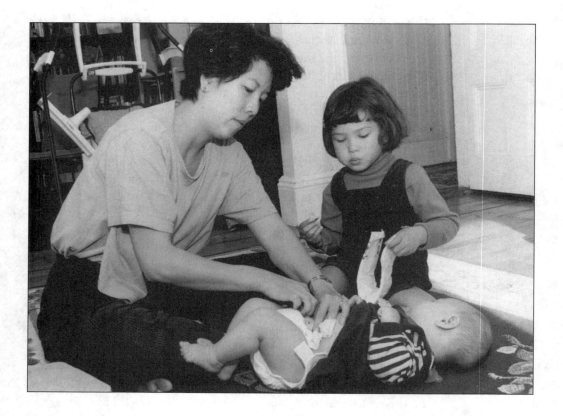

someone like you! Boys and girls are different so they can become daddies and mommies."

"I don't want to be a daddy." He'd heard enough for now, perhaps more than he was ready for. "Someday you will."

As Billy got more excited in his play—washing and splashing himself and Abby, he got an erection. He looked down at it. "Uh-oh, Mommy. I can't move." "Why not, Billy?" "I just can't." Mrs. Stone wondered what to say. Should she comment on it—or not? "That's okay. In a minute it will go down, and you'll be able to move." Mrs. Stone didn't pursue the subject further. More comments could all too easily have reflected an adult approach and adult self-consciousness. Four-year-olds' explorations are part of their own learning about their own bodies, at their own pace.

How should a parent react to Billy's exploratory behavior? It is likely to make any parent self-conscious, even anxious. Suppose you gave an answer that stimulated the child's imagination and led her to have more dreams than she already had? It is always possible, but not likely. In contrast to the information a child absorbs from television programs and the information peers share at this age, your statements are likely to be more reassuring. They can give a child a feeling of safety and calm that counteracts the giggling, guilty quality of her discussions with peers. A major concern about television is that children can come across adult sexual behavior when they are alone, and with no one to share their reactions. These images can be confusing, and over-stimulating. Children have their own questions about their bodies and physical sensations, and don't need the burden of adult preoccupations. Children need to know they can bring their questions to responsive parents who will respect their need to know and their need for limits.

In 1970, Mary Calderone wrote a classic book with Dr. James Ramey, *Talking with Your Child About Sex*. They addressed the sexual questions that children still ask today in the language of children of each age. Some examples: "Why doesn't Daddy have breasts? He has nipples." "What is my belly button for?" "What's this bag under my penis?" "Why is my penis covered with skin? Neil's isn't." "Will I hurt if I stick my finger in my vagina?" "Mommy, why do you wear white things over your wee-wee?" "Can I stand and pee like boys?"

Most of these questions are relatively easy to answer. I urge parents not to get too explanatory or to make their answers more complicated than the child can understand. Watch their eyes and their faces. When you have gone too far, you can tell. And *always* encourage the child to ask her own questions. They might surprise you, but you will share them and keep lines of communication open.

More difficult questions lie ahead. Each one is a precious opportunity, a window into the child's mind, a chance for you to become the confidant she can trust for the future. Shutting her off or even allowing her to sense your discomfort can not only heighten her curiosity, but cut off communication.

If your information is over the child's head, it will not be taken in. But it needs to be honest. The willingness to share information with a child is most important of all. The more open she feels you are to her questions, the more significant the interchange can be. Each family, though, must turn to their own personal and cultural values for help in handling these sensitive issues in ways that are consistent with their beliefs.

A week after the tub episode with Abby, Mrs. Stone urged Billy toward a play date with his older cousin, Tom. Tom was an overpowering, dominating boy, and he usually managed to relegate Billy to a subordinate role. The Stones had noted this at family gatherings. Billy's mother was also aware that the boys liked to disappear to an upstairs bedroom. Once, she had burst in when they were undressed and playing on the bed on top of each other. Each child had been embarrassed. "We're playing doctor," they said quickly.

Playing doctor is an ingenious way for children to explore each other. Every four-year-old remembers his body being examined by the doctor. Every four-year-old asks a friend, "Lie down and I'll test you!" After a few safe explorations of each other, they are usually satisfied. A parent's role is to avoid frightening or shaming the child. This is normal behavior and the more attention that it generates from parents, the more heightened it may become. If a parent gets so upset that she frightens the child, she immediately sets the experience up as more intriguing. The child will feel guilty, but will search for more opportunities to test out the reasons for the "excitement." First of all, I would advise checking with the parents of the other child, so you can agree together on an approach. Then, independently, talk it over with each child. This is normal and self-limited behavior. Hence it needs to be treated as such, not shunned or overemphasized.

"Mommy, Tom makes me undress and show him my pee-pee. He wants to play with it. I don't like it. Do I need to play with him today?" Mrs. Stone reacted to Billy's feeling of being coerced. "No, Billy, you certainly don't." This was different from normal exploration because Billy felt coerced. It was no longer mutual. Billy's mother was right to be concerned and to curb this play. Billy certainly needed her backup, and her support to feel in control of his own body.

If parents overreact with adult sensitivities, they can all too easily cut off opportunities to communicate. Billy needs to be assured that this sensitive part of his body is okay to be proud of and to investigate, but also that he needs to be in charge of it. Billy was able to come to his mother with his new concerns because of the calm, open, and developmentally sensitive way in which she had handled his earlier questions. (See also "Sexuality" in Part II.)

Moral Development

Lies and Fantasy

Marcy's mother went out shopping, leaving Marcy with her father. Marcy stole into her mother's closet and dressed up in her mother's best evening dress and sequined high-heeled shoes. Marcy knew the dress was precious. As she stepped into it, she heard a *rip-p-p-p*. Horrified, she looked down at the dress. She'd torn it. Marcy didn't know what to do. She hesitated briefly, but the spangles on the dress were too enticing. She'd dreamed for so long of becoming the Cinderella princess. She lifted the straps of the dress onto her shoulders. She stepped in front of the floor-length mirror in her mother's room. Now she was the princess. She glided around the room, and tripped on the dress as she pirouetted. The spangles glittered. Marcy envisioned the prince's entrance. She curtsied for him. Another *rip-p-p-p*. But by now, she was caught up in her fantasy. She paid no attention. "Yes, Your Majesty, I *will* marry you."

She heard the gravel rustle in the driveway. Her mother was returning. Marcy hastened out of the dress and shoved it into a corner of the closet, then rushed to meet her mother. "Hello, Marcy, I'm back—what have you been doing?" Mrs. Jackson asked, sensing the guilty expression on Marcy's face. "I was just playing with my dolls, Guessus and Happen Orter." "Well, what has Happen Orter done this time?" "Nothing."

Marcy was silent after this. She was wrestling with her feelings. Should she confess? Should she hide her mishap? Could she lie her way out of it?

Marcy's mother discovered the torn dress that evening when Marcy was in bed. She told Marcy's father. He was so furious that he woke Marcy up and dragged her out of bed. "Marcy, how could you destroy your mother's clothes—and worst of all, not tell us about it?" Marcy was only half awake. She was frightened and guilty—so guilty that she couldn't answer. As her father berated her, Marcy responded with anger. She felt like fighting back. She screamed back at him, "Leave me alone!" He was rigid. "Don't talk to me like that!" Marcy felt anger welling up in her, frightening her.

Marcy's parents did not understand their daughter's angry reaction. After all, she *was* guilty. She should be disciplined. She didn't have the right to be angry. Their inclination was to put on more pressure and more discipline rather than trying to understand Marcy's defensiveness—which came out as anger. Being half asleep and confused, Marcy herself couldn't understand her own reaction and it frightened her. Marcy's parents were confronted with new fears about their daughter. "Is she getting too fresh, too spoiled? Why is *she* angry? We should be, not Marcy." They needed to understand her defensiveness as an initial step toward confronting her own guilty feelings. Yet it might still have been difficult for them; for then the Jacksons had to realize that they were giving up their image of Marcy as innocent. She was more complicated now. This was a touchpoint for both Marcy and her parents.

To help Marcy make this developmental step, her parents could say something like "Marcy, of course you feel responsible and guilty. Maybe we scared you when we wakened you to scold you. But we were disappointed that you had to lie. Now, it's upsetting that you got angry. *We* are angry. You were wrong. And you will have to apologize."

Lying is part of any four-year-old's agenda. When they wish hard for something, when they long for something they can't have, they can't stand the longing. It becomes almost unbearable. A lie can supply the bridge. They lie when there is a passionate wish at stake, or a reality they don't know how to face without their parents' help.

At four years old, the lie is transparent, because it is so clearly related to the child's wish. "The store man gave me this candy." "You know he didn't," said Billy's mother. "You took it off the shelf as we went by. How could you do such a thing? It doesn't belong to you. You're lying, and that's wrong!" Billy's face darkened as he faced this barrage. "I didn't mean to." What didn't he mean to do? He didn't mean to have to face reality with his wish. He didn't mean to be caught. Lying was his way of protecting the wish and of evading the confrontation. When he was confronted, his conscience met him head on. As he began to weep, his mother was able to say, "You know you don't need to lie to me. We'll take the candy back, and you can tell the store man that you are sorry you took his candy." This action will help Billy face the reality of having taken someone's property. It will also help compensate for the guilty feelings he has begun to experience. Guilt is a powerful mechanism. It helps to produce solutions.

Lying needn't be the end of the world at ages four and five. The wishes are so intense, the fantasies so important, and the ways of

facing reality so limited, that all children need to lie. The second lie
("I didn't mean to") helped Billy fend off his guilty feelings. It was
his way of acknowledging his misdeed before he was ready to accept responsibility for it; for this, he needed his mother's offer of a
way to make reparations.

Billy threw a truck at his friend in preschool. The truck hit Sam in
the back of the head and drew blood. The teacher rushed to comfort
and take care of Sam. She was horrified and furious. "Billy, how
could you do such a thing?" Billy: "I didn't do it. She did." His lie
was obvious, because the teacher had witnessed the entire episode.
"Billy, I saw you throw the truck." "No, it was that boy over there."
Billy started sobbing, watching his friend Sam fearfully as if he
himself were wounded. Sam hit back at Billy. Billy looked relieved.
The teacher pushed Billy to "tell the truth." Billy continued to sob,
and retreated into a corner to hide his face. The head teacher sized
up the situation, hugged Billy, and said, "Billy, Sam knows you are
sorry. Could you apologize to him? You are such good friends. He
won't want to feel like you meant to hurt him." Billy's face lit up
slowly. He went over to Sam, who cringed a bit. Billy hugged him
and mumbled, "Sorry, Sam." After a brief hairwash and Band-Aid
ritual, the two boys played happily again.

Billy had been too frightened by his own action to pull himself
together without help. Defense mechanisms and coping strategies
are already developing at age four. But they remain fairly crude,
and sometimes costly. To overcome his terror of being out of control, Billy had denied to himself the reality of what he had done, and
had lied to everyone else. His initial denial and lie had helped him
control his terror and he began to recover. The head teacher's sensitive reaction gave him an opportunity for reentry. At this age, as we
have noted before, the aggressor needs as much comfort as the victim. Only when Billy was reassured could he learn from his trans-
gression. He might learn how to say, "I did it. I threw the truck. But
I didn't mean it to hit and hurt Sam." A caregiving adult must
be aware of a guilty four-year-old's need for comfort and backup.
The child learns from his fear of what he has done, but does so more
effectively if he is supported and understood in the process.
(See also "Honesty" in Part II.)

Most children have stolen candy from a candy store—if not in reality, at least in fantasy. What should parents do about the child who has dared to do it? Transgressions like these can make parents angry, even frighten them. They are faced with giving up their child's innocence. This is a touchpoint. The difference between a child's dreaming and a child's facing reality can be enormous. A child who "gets away" with acting out a forbidden dream is likely to be a worried, frightened child. What will stop him next time? By five and six, he will have developed the morality to know it's not acceptable behavior. At four, he needs to know that even though parents understand his motive and his daydreams, they cannot allow him to steal. "Stealing is something we don't allow. Everyone wishes for things that don't belong to them, but you cannot take someone else's property. You'll have to give back what you have taken."

Facing a four-year-old's guilt is painful, both for the child and for parents. Parents have a difficult task steering clear of overwhelming shame on the one hand, and over-protectively minimizing the wrongdoing on the other. But the lesson a child learns from assuming the responsibility to apologize and make reparations is an important one. You are helping him set up boundaries between wishes and reality. Then, within the safe and acceptable limits imposed by the child's developing conscience, and his parents' consistent responses, the world of magical thinking can still be a wonderful place to explore.

Almost coincident with her fourth birthday, Minnie began waking up at night, crying out in terror. "There's a monster in my room!" First, the monster was under the bed, then he was in her closet. No amount of reassurance calmed Minnie. This kind of awakening was new. She'd always been a good sleeper. She was not a fearful child. She was always in the middle of rough-and-tumble play at preschool. She was always the first to think up games that would spill into chaos. Her parents knew of no disturbing event that might have led to her sudden nighttime fears. She'd watched television, but less than many of her peers. Now her parents were concerned that television might be too much for her, and stopped her watching. Her father began to put her to bed at night. Before the reading ritual, he and Minnie looked under the bed and into the closet together to reassure her that "no monster was there." Minnie protested about being left alone in the dark at night, so her parents installed a night light. It helped, for she was now more docile about going to bed. When they checked on Minnie before they retired, she was curled up in sleep, her hands folded together under her cheek as if she were praying. She looked so peaceful in deep sleep. But every night, at about the same two o'clock time, she woke up screaming. Her parents were completely perplexed.

When her parents finally brought up Minnie's fears at preschool, they were somewhat comforted to hear the other parents' stories. "Marcy is suddenly afraid of dogs. If one barks, she always jumps." "Billy has never been afraid of anything before. Now, he looks out of the front door before he'll go out. When I ask him what he's looking for, he says, 'I want to be sure there aren't any ambulances or fire engines coming.' I say to him, 'Are you afraid they'll run you over? Are you afraid of where they're going?' When I finally got to the root of it, it turned out he's afraid of the loud noises. Why is he suddenly afraid of them? He used to love them." These were the parents of the more outgoing children. Parents of the shy, quieter children reported no such problems at this time. A child's temperament has a great deal to do with the form some of these four-year-old crises take.

Quieter children go through this same crisis, but in a different way. Their fears and fearfulness may be reflected in an increase in shyness. Tim was crying more often, but he was comforted less easily. He refused to go into crowds with his mother. When she took him to the grocery store, he tried to hide beneath her skirt.

What is this new fearful behavior trying to say? What is the trigger for it? Why is it predictable in the fourth year? Just as a child's increasing understanding of the world has led to his awareness of others' feelings, he finds a new recognition of his own. He has a growing concern about right and wrong, good and bad. As a result, his burgeoning angry feelings begin to frighten him. They can often be faced in the daytime, but not at night, when separation is followed by darkness and solitude. These feelings flood the child in the form of fears and nightmares. Anger has been shoved under all along. A baby is taught early to suppress his anger—with waiting for the bottle, with having his toy taken away from him, with having a new baby in the house whom he must love, not hate. Because they have been treated as wicked for so long, anger and aggressive feelings have become more frightening and potent. Now, a four-year-old is telling us that it is time to let him face them and find better ways of dealing with them.

Parents find it difficult to make this connection, for the child has changed so little during the day. Marcy is still her pleasant self; she is always outgoing, cheerful, winning. But underneath this exterior is a surge in her awareness of her aggressive feelings. Billy will be happy to flex his muscles for you. Marcy will stomp her feet to demand attention or to put over a point. Each is saying, "I know I can get what I want if I can be stronger." This is the beginning of self-assertive behavior, with its goal of independence. This is an important stage of development for a child and it deserves our understanding and encouragement. The surge in self-assertion, aggressive feelings, and the child's discomfort with them, constitute a touchpoint for the child and for the parent – as they strain to understand the fears. If parents recognize the nightmares and fears as a child's reaction to these new feelings, they can help the child deal with them. Eventually, the child can also understand them. A parent's goal is to help the child channel these angry feelings. Setting limits on how they are expressed is as important as understanding them, for the child's comfort and feelings of safety.

Billy's mother and stepfather sought ways to help their son channel these "new" feelings of anger. "When you feel like punching your baby sister, how about hitting a punching bag instead? Of course, you want to hit her at times. But you can't, I can't let you hurt her. You can't let yourself. Come and tell me how angry you are. Let's talk about it. Whack away at this punching toy." Knowing that his mother understood and accepted his feelings made it easier for Billy to go to her for help with them.

Excursions with his stepfather gave Billy a chance to learn about "safe" anger. "Daddy, why did you swear at that lady's car? You said a bad word." "She swerved right in front of me. I wanted to hit her car, but I couldn't. It would have been dangerous and stupid. So I swore at her instead. 'Damn' is an okay word when you're mad enough." Billy's eyes and ears took it all in. Why did his mother tell him never to say "damn?" "Mommy says I can't say 'damn.'" "Well, maybe it's wrong sometimes. But there are times when 'damn' is better than other things." Laughing, Billy said, "Damn Abby! Why was she born?" He and his stepfather laughed. That evening, Billy and his dad watched a basketball show. "Billy," said his stepfather, "did you see how that guy stopped himself from hitting back when the other one tried to hit him? Wow! Isn't he a great player!"

Marcy had developed a fear of dogs. Her mother tried to help her with "When he comes up to greet you, Marcy, let me hold you tight. Then, watch me pet him and see how he loves it. Watch his tail wag. He wants to love us and he wants us to love him." Marcy clung tightly. She didn't want to be talked out of her fear. It was symbolic of her inner feelings. Marcy's mother helped her more by understanding her outbursts when she got angry, and by valuing her efforts at self-control: "You really got mad that time. I thought you were going to throw your glass at me. But you didn't, and I still knew how mad you were."

One day Marcy was in a bad mood. She pouted, angry with everything that happened. Her mother was reluctant to be around her. At last, she said, "Marcy, I have to go shopping for groceries. Do you want to come with me or do you want to stay with Daddy? If you do, I don't want to hear any of your moaning and groaning." Marcy dragged her feet to the car, kicking at every rock and pebble. Finally, she slumped into the car. "Put on your seat belt." "No, I won't." "Marcy, no seat belt, no market." Marcy whimpered and made a big deal of putting on her seat belt. At the market, Mrs. Jackson ignored her daughter and soon filled her basket. She was conscious of how irritated she felt by Marcy's foot-dragging. As Mrs. Jackson stepped into line to pay for her groceries, another lady moved in front of her. Mrs. Jackson almost blew up at her. She turned to Marcy: "Did you see that woman get in front of me? Rude people make me so mad!" Marcy: "Why don't you slap her, Mommy?" "I couldn't do that. I might hurt her and then I'd be sorry. I just have to keep it to myself. If I could just say, 'Don't you see I was here first?' maybe she'd realize what she's done. But it doesn't help to get angry." Marcy, impressed, watched her mother's face as her own anger seemed to subside. She perked up to cheer her mother. She had a model of self-restraint to learn from. A child of this age models herself on such episodes. It places a real responsibility on us as parents, doesn't it? My children learned to swear from me as a result of standing in grocery lines.

Tim was eager to play a game on his father's computer. As he shoved in the disk, he heard a snap. Something had gone wrong. Should he tell or let his parents find out? But he retreated from the confrontation with his parents.

When Tim's father came home, he tried to turn on his computer. He soon discovered the disk, which was wedged in the wrong slot. He knew that Tim had been at the machine again. He didn't know whether to discipline him or not—Tim still seemed so shaky so much of the time. He talked to Mrs. McCormick. Together, they decided to let it go. "Should we or shouldn't we? He never seems to learn." They were stymied. They felt as if they were walking on eggshells with Tim.

Discipline becomes a difficult decision with a vulnerable child like Tim. He knew he deserved it. He came into the room when they were discussing their decision. "Dad, I broke your computer." He had learned more than they had given him credit for. Their efforts to teach through discipline had been more effective than they had thought. Mr. McCormick faced his son. "Tim, I'm glad you told me about it. What should we do to help you remember that my computer is too valuable for you to play with without me? I'll fix it, but you must leave it alone in the future."

A fragile child needs the reassurance—as much as any child—that comes with being held responsible for the consequences of his actions, whether he intended the consequences or not. The importance of discipline as a way to help a child feel secure—especially as he faces his new, angry four-year-old-feelings—becomes obvious when it is withheld. A child without discipline is at the mercy of his impulsive behavior. He will be fearful of his own feelings and won't have a chance to respect himself.

Billy woke up with lots of energy. He worked his way through breakfast, teasing his half-awake parents by dropping his cereal piece by piece on the floor. They scolded. Billy became more excited with each new warning. His stepfather finally stormed off to work, thoroughly disgruntled. His mother was still half-dressed. She didn't have to be at work until noon. Billy needed more of a reaction from his mother, and more contact, perhaps, before she left. Is this an inevitable reaction to anticipating the loss of her for the afternoon?

The family's old cat slunk by. Billy hopped off his chair in time to kick out at the animal. He watched his mother out of the corner of his eye as he managed to swipe at Tornado's tail. The cat maneuvered on by, but Mrs. Stone saw Billy's action. "Billy, that was a nasty thing to do to poor old Tornado. He's as sleepy as we are." Billy sensed the indecision in her voice. This time, his eyes narrowed, his face set. He watched his mother out of the corner of his eye as he headed toward Tornado. He yanked on the cat's tail to elicit a loud screech from her. His mother stiffened, looked at him incredulously. She was horrified by what she could only see as his sadism. She felt her anger rising, and she felt another frightening feeling—she didn't like Billy right now. "Where does he get this kind of behavior? Is it my fault? Is he a vicious little boy? What will he do next? How do I stop it?"

This time, she descended on him in rage: "Billy, leave that cat alone!" He felt frightened by her outburst, and he began to feel abandoned by her as her anger displaced her other feelings for him. Tuned in to her completely now, his jaw clenched, his eyes narrowed, he pulled the cat's tail so hard that she levitated off the ground. Then, he paused for his mother's wrath. As she rushed toward him, he dropped Tornado and retreated to his room in fear.

Mrs. Stone was so overwhelmed that her face was red, her breath short, her eyes bulging. She wanted to strangle him. She found herself unable to stop thinking about a "ghost" from her own "past"—a time when she'd been hurt, and paralyzed with fear, an incident she usually tried not to think about. She felt herself being immobilized in that same way now with Billy. It helped her to remember this because it made her stop at this point, sit down and ponder. When she did, her thoughts remobilized her, and her fury abated somewhat. She was helped by trying to figure why a four-year-old could show sadistic behavior. Was there an underlying reason? In any event, this was unacceptable behavior.

As Billy's mother burst into his room, he recoiled in anticipation of the punishment. She sat down with him, holding him firmly in her arms. Tears came to her eyes. Her voice cracked as she said, "Billy, I can't believe what you've just done. You and I know how terrible it is for Tornado. That is absolutely unacceptable. I can't let you ever hurt her again." Billy subsided in her arms. His eyes closed, his face grim. "Mommy, I'm sorry." "Of course you are, Billy. But being sorry is not enough. You just can't do things like that. You can't be cruel to animals. I have to stop you until you are big enough to stop yourself. Why must you take it out on Tornado?" In all likelihood, Billy, at four, won't be able to answer her. But he will know he can be protected from his own impulsive feelings. He can dare to face Tornado again (who is more forgiving than he realizes), because his mother has helped him recognize his responsibility. "Now you must make it up to Tornado. You can brush him to let him feel you like him." Naturally, Tornado ran away. Billy, chagrined, had to approach the cat carefully. As he softly and sadly brushed Tornado's coat, he felt relieved. Now he could count on being able to repair the damage he'd done.

As his mother calmed down, as she felt Billy's relief, she could allow herself to wonder. Just wondering about Billy's behavior gave her a chance to get away from her own memories which were incapacitating her. What made him do it? She may not ever know. Billy may not either. Was he feeling neglected and just needed a passionate reaction? (Had he missed one from his departing stepfather?) Was he dreading the afternoon without his mother? Was it just a bad day, a wave of reaction that can be part of any four-year-old child's day? It helped that Mrs. Stone stopped to reflect on the interference her own feelings were contributing. But it was also vitally important that she not tolerate her son's behavior in any way. Although she empathized with his mood and guilty reaction, it was critical that she set firm, uncompromising limits—until Billy could feel sure enough to find them for himself. Once she had set these limits, they both felt safer. Giving Billy a chance at reparation was another step toward his learning control.

Needless to say, these crises can't happen too often—for either of them. A resolution such as this one must leave parent and child with the feeling that they share common goals and a common understanding. This is the purpose of discipline at this age.

Selma Fraiberg says that a child who is not stopped when he knows he should be feels that he and his behavior don't matter. "My parents don't care enough about me to tell me to stop."

Discipline is teaching. It is forward-looking, it anticipates the future. It is respectful. "I know you can do it. You can learn how to stop yourself and then I won't have to stop you." Punishment is backward looking, and it may not be respectful to the child. "See what you've just done. You are a bad boy! For that you go to your room without supper." In essence, this is saying, "You can't control yourself. Don't do it again in front of me." Such remarks contain an implicit challenge. "Wait till I'm not around to try it again." Billy was more affected by his mother's soothing and carefully timed talk about limits (only when he was ready to listen) than he would have been by a spanking. He would more likely have been rebellious and ready to torment Tornado all over again.

By the fourth year, parents and children have been through important stages together. Whereas a toddler has a temper tantrum to settle his inner turmoil, but is gratified by his mother's response when she picks him up to love him, a four-year-old is frightened by his own tantrum. Not only is he frightened by his loss of control, but he is aware of how upsetting it is to his parents. "I'm sorry, Mommy. I just had to." He's more aware now of how his behavior looks to others.

When a four-year-old knows that he needs attention and uses misbehavior to get it, set up firm limits at the time and stick to them. If you don't, you risk reinforcing the misbehavior. After the crisis, tell him that you suspect he's feeling neglected. "Every time I start talking on the phone, or pay attention to your brother, you seem to lose control. Maybe you feel that I'm not paying enough attention to what you need. I know you hate my talking on the phone. I want to be with you, too, but I can't always be. You can learn to be by yourself when I can't be with you. But how about our having some special times together? We can do something special that you'd like, just the two of us. When you begin to get upset, I'll remind you of our agreement." Talk about the plan occasionally in between, when you are both calm. Four-year-olds can be so clear in their cries for help. Respond as clearly. They are still likely to want to please you. As they get older, that may not be as true. Value it in a four-year-old. "Marcy, you are such a wonderful little girl. I know you are sad when I'm busy with Amos. Let me cuddle you and we both can feel close again."

One powerful way of defusing a child who seems to be in a repetitious pattern of misbehavior is to offer him chances to succeed. Give him alternatives to his behavior at times when he's not in trouble. In the heat of the moment, though, your goal must be to break the cycle. When it's broken, quickly hug him and recount why your "time out" helped. "You were so upset and I was upset. Once you had your time out, we both calmed down. Now we can talk." "But, Mommy, I'm still mad." "Of course you are. Time out helps, but it doesn't tell me what you were upset about." "You won't read to me when I want you to." "You're right. I always seem to pick my own time to read to you, don't I?" The child looks back, surprised. "Why don't we plan times to read? You tell me when, and if I can't do it then, we'll make a 'special time' to do it. That way we can always have reading times." If the child can make any suggestions, try them. If it works, give him credit. If not, ask again. This is a way to offer to share responsibility.

None of these maneuvers will settle all bids for discipline. Parents naturally wish for simple and effective solutions. Every parent feels angry and ineffective after a bad time with a child, but expecting simple solutions is unrealistic. It takes a long time for a child to learn the inner controls that make his aggressive feelings safe. That is a long-term goal, not a short-term one.

One of the most difficult aspects of disciplining your four-year-old may be your own disappointment. "He'd already learned not to do that. Why is he testing me again?" It's all too easy to fall into the trap of seeing his behavior as antagonistic or deliberately testing you. He may need to try limits over and over until he's finally mastered his own controls. Such regressive periods can be touchpoints in which parents will find it helpful to recognize how upset they are. "But he'd already mastered that. He had learned how to hit a punching bag instead of his little brother. Why do we have to go through it all again?" At these times, parents may feel discouraged, as if all their patient discipline has been in vain. It hasn't. The child may even be choosing a safe area—one that he knows you'll react to in a reliable way. In his own disorganization, he may need the reassurance of your reliability. Learning one's own limits is a lifetime job. A small child needs refueling from time to time and will ask for it in this way.

One of the difficult aspects of these regressions may be your wondering, "Is he in more trouble than I've been able to face?

Maybe I've pushed too hard or not enough. Maybe I haven't read his cues and he's really got problems I haven't understood." At such times, you may feel a tug from the ghosts in your own past. Feeling lost about parenting your own children can lead you back to the earliest landmarks you remember. These are likely to be times during your childhood when you were out of control, or misunderstood, or even traumatized. This kind of memory adds a further unsettling dimension to your reaction. You may well put on more heat than the behavior deserves, or you may even feel immobilized. You may react with an ambivalence that unsettles your child.

At times like this, you may need a time out of your own. Perhaps your spouse or a friend or even your mother-in-law can step in to help you become more objective. "You know, that really doesn't deserve quite such a reaction. He's not after his sister to kill her, and he's not just setting himself up in a war with you." At such times, it's important to try almost any way you can devise to pull yourself out of the fray, then try to understand your violent reaction. This is not to say that overreacting is always going to harm the child. Children are amazingly resilient when they are reacting to someone they love and trust. One little boy whom I know once responded to his mother's loss of control this way: "Mummy, I think we'd better discuss this later, when you're not so upset." At the time, it made his mother even angrier, but then she regained control and began to laugh. Her son was right. They did do better later.

We all strive for consistency in our discipline. And yet, every parent I've ever met knows that consistency is an impossibility. We get too angry. But the child learns from our emotions, too. Our feelings about his behavior teach him the importance of his transgressions. I often wonder how much parents are learning about self-discipline at the time they are leading the child to a surer set of self-limits.

Discipline Guidelines Revisited

1. Discipline is teaching, not punishment.
2. The goal is to develop self-control.
3. Children experience guilt and need reparation.
4. Children need a face-saving approach.
5. Every "no" needs a "yes."
6. Parents need to take their own feelings into account.
7. Try to understand the meaning of the behavior.

8. A firm, consistent response to misbehavior shows caring.
9. Share responsibility with the child to find solutions.
10. A loving and understanding approach is powerful.

The Beginnings of Conscience

How does a four-year-old move beyond being "told" what he can and cannot do? How does he move from "you can't do it because I say so" to a real conscience of his own? No matter how often four-year-old Billy is told not to hit his sister or not to tease her as he walks by, he will find subtle ways to achieve his ends. As he passes Abby sitting on the floor, he steps on her little finger. Pure chance! He runs by as Abby is teetering on her feet, preparing to take a step. Abby plops on her bottom. No one seems to notice. Billy does, at some level. When Abby reaches for a toy, Billy takes it. Now, his mother catches his eye and shakes her head. Billy had already begun to realize that all of his advances to Abby were negative. Very quietly, he pushed the toy back to Abby. The toddler reached out for it, brought it to her mouth, smiling and drooling. Billy watched her silently. Was he savoring the subtle satisfaction of giving in to his conscience?

If this was what was happening, it meant that four-year-old Billy could: (1) incorporate reprimands; (2) experience the guilt on his own; (3) summon the ability to transfer that guilt from one act to another—in other words, make the association that these acts carried the same meaning; and (4) be ready to give in. Billy was beginning to realize his own capacity to behave in a way that he felt proud of, with very little help from the outside. He would be able to store and access this experience the next time. It wouldn't happen all at once, but it would come gradually. Watch for the quiet pride in a four-year-old when he succeeds.

Values and the opportunities for a developing conscience begin with parental responses to daily occurrences: "You can't take his toy. How would you feel if he took yours?" "Let's pull out toys you *can* share before your friends come, so you won't be so greedy when they get here. They won't feel very welcome if you snatch everything away from them. After all, it's a strange house and they will be missing their mommies and their things at home." These explanations give a child the chance to have an understanding of the reasons behind sharing and being courteous. They give him a chance to see the consequences of his actions when passions are not running high. This preparation helps him make the shift from a self-centered world to other people's perspectives. The shift will have to wait until he is ready, of course. When he is, success will bring a boost to his self-esteem.

When I was four-years old, my mother assembled a select group of ladies from my small hometown in Texas. She called me in to "show me off." I remember standing in the middle of all of these powdered, bepearled, dressed-up ladies. One of them, to make conversation, said, "And whom do you love the best in all the world?" I blurted out, "Annie May!" Annie May was our dearly beloved African American cook and nursemaid, whom I loved unreservedly. Perhaps my anger with being "shown off" or with the simpering question provoked my reply. But I can still recall my mother's face. It fell completely. Her whole body slumped. Everyone giggled self-consciously, but not she. I had hurt her deeply. I've never allowed myself to blurt out such a hurtful statement again. A bit of conscience dawned that day.

Most values are learned from modeling. A child can model himself on parents' actions and values, on older siblings, or on important friends and relatives. When a child sees his father speak gently and concernedly to a frail elderly person on the street, he learns from it. When someone swerves in front of his car and he swears and says, "I feel like chasing that guy down to chew him out for that," *but* doesn't, a child is watching.

When his parents took Tim to church on a Sunday, getting him dressed up in his best outfit, the preparation for leaving him in Sunday school, and the ceremony ahead all became sources of conflict and resistance. When the family arrived at church, everyone was polite and welcoming. Tim's parents left him cautiously. Mrs. Mc-

Cormick even came back to check on him later. He recognized her concern. After church, they all gathered as a family. Each one was subdued. A few comments were passed among the adults. "He preached too long. But I liked the way he explained the passage from the Bible." Even the criticisms were in subdued, somewhat reverential tones. Adults were showing how they could put up with and even value a rather boring situation. A four-year-old takes all this in.

Parents may feel uncomfortable with the intensity of the child's reliance on them as he models their behavior. Perhaps it places a brake on their freedom of self-expression when they are upset. But it is not one outburst, or even one gesture, that is important. It is the overall pattern of their words and deeds that the child is making part of himself.

The Rewards of Manners

Minnie was learning to say "Hello" and look people in the eye. Very proudly, each morning she greeted her childcare teacher. Each day, her teacher and her mother beamed. The fourth day, however, she rushed right by her teacher to get to the toys and her peers. Her mother felt defeated. But on the fifth day, and from then on, Minnie remembered her manners on her own. It was almost as if the day of failure was an important part of learning.

Her mother was so confident that she stopped reminding Minnie. One Saturday morning at Mrs. Lee's health club, a trainer greeted Minnie and asked her if she wanted to hoist herself up on an exercise bike. "You're so big, your feet almost reach the pedals!" Minnie became mute and shy, and just looked intently at her sneakers. When they left the club, Mrs. Lee said, "Minnie, why weren't you able to answer that nice lady? You do it at school for your teacher every day." Minnie: "But she's not my teacher." Mrs. Lee had expected Minnie to generalize this behavior to other adults. It hadn't occurred to Minnie that all adults must be treated like her teacher, to whom she was devoted. She was still naive about generalizing her behavior. Understanding that it is too early to expect this from Minnie will help Mrs. Lee to be patient when she has to remind Minnie in new situations. Minnie will be more likely to listen.

With a child's growing awareness of how he affects others around him, a new opportunity arises. He is ready to enjoy the positive effects of his behavior. When he says, "Thank you" or "Please," he receives a reward from those around him. Parents have already attempted to set up these patterns. I call them "learn to please Grandma" patterns. In the second year, and certainly by the third, a parent will look the child in the face, and say appealingly, "Now, say 'thank you.' " Or, if she is brave, she may say, "Put out your hand to Mrs. King and say, 'How do you do?' Don't you remember how we practiced this?" The three-year-old's eyes will cloud up. He will drop his arms forcefully at his sides. He is likely to look away, or even to run away. If he is an especially docile child, he may put out his hand. But he will do it with a kind of passivity that covers his negativism. A child's hand can feel like a dead fish at this age, clammy with the negativism that parental instructions invoke. Negativism can be expected, but don't give up. Parents who give up deprive their children of opportunities for recognition in social interactions.

At times, teaching manners is discouraging. You may wonder whether it's working. But watch for a reaction in your four-year-old when someone special arrives. Without parental instruction, he may even put out his hand to the new person. If things fall into place, the person may say, "Aren't you a big boy? What a nice greeting!" Your teaching has finally paid off. You have introduced behavior that he was resisting, but he has taken it in and has even absorbed its purpose. He can now recognize that he receives a reward for his good manners. You have taught him with purely instrumental behavior, such as "Thank you!" "Say hello!" "Put out your hand." He has resisted your pressure, as he should have. But, underneath his resistance, he has absorbed the manners you have been offering him. As long as the manners are yours, for example, "Say 'please' to Grandma," they are only remotely effective—but they are still worth encouraging. Sooner or later, he will "slip up" and use manners on his own. When he does, the adult's pleased reactions become his own reward. He has learned the satisfaction manners can bring, and this is a big step. You may wish he went further on his own, but be patient. He's bound to fail as often as he succeeds. You may feel it's your failure when he does. But if you can accept that he will need reminders for a long time, you can go on providing them without becoming frustrated and undoing the rewards that learning to be polite can bring.

The risk in this kind of teaching must be obvious: if the child is only compliant, only mimicking your instructions, he will not incorporate the behavior and will not feel its rewards. I urge parents to balance the instructions with opportunities for independence. If your child has a favorite uncle, don't warn him ahead of time. Instead, see whether the child will try out these wiles on his own. You may want to prepare the uncle, too. Urge him to be ready to stick out his own hand and to reward your child for any polite response.

Can one prepare a child for events such as this without becoming intrusive? This should be thought out carefully. "Today we are going to Aunt Isabel's for a party. There will be people there who already like you and want to see you. But they don't know how big you've grown. The last time they saw you, you were just talking baby talk. You were still walking like a toddler. Now, you can do grown-up things. Imagine Aunt Isabel's face if you walk up to her, put out your hand, and say, "Hi, Aunt Isabel! I'm glad to see you." Make it sound like fun. Then stop! As a parent, you have planted the seed. If your child can live up to it, it will be a real achievement. If not, you may have to wait for a less charged occasion.

When your teaching does work, don't overwhelm him with praise. If you do, you are taking away his sense that the achievement was his own. Let him experience the reward himself. At most, you can say, "Aunt Isabel was so happy. She is proud of you. So am I." Your goal is to give him opportunities to affect the world around him in a positive way, to realize that what he does matters. (See also "Manners" in Part II.)

Relationships: Building a Family

Helping

When children reach the age of four, this is the time to begin to have regular family meetings. Four may seem young, but if they are introduced early on, they will come to rely on these predictable times for communication. I recommend them once a week. Everyone sits down together. The idea is to give the child the feeling that she's a valued member of the family with clear responsibilities that she can

be proud of. Make a list together of some of the things that can be done around the house by a four-year-old. With help, a child can participate in setting the table, clearing the table, feeding the pets, watering the plants. A child can pick up her toys, hang up her towel, put her dirty laundry in the hamper. Assign one or two chores to each member of the family. Each child may need an adult to be a moral support and a help to her in carrying out her chores. Let the child decide who that person will be. Together, they can accomplish these tasks. Mark them on a big chart, and remember that a four-year-old's chores must be adapted to her capacities. At first, the chores may seem largely symbolic, but that is what matters most at four. It may seem like more work to include a four-year-old in household chores, but this early experience of finding a valued role, of being proud of contributing, builds a foundation for the family's future.

You may decide in the meeting what the rewards are and what the discipline will be if chores go undone. Threats and nagging miss the point. The main goal is not the reward, but being a family: in a family, everyone helps, everyone takes care of each other. Chores need to be seen as a whole family's cooperative effort. In my experience, even children at four are proud to participate.

Even if a child finds reasons to worm her way out of chores, she can still learn. "I'm too tired to pick up my toys." "Then, if I pick them up, they'll go in the closet where you can't play with them." "I'll pick them up. But will you help me?"

Making and Giving

"Let's make Grandma a present she'd like. She'd love something from you." "I don't know anything to make her." "How about a box to keep her paper clips in? You could color the paper first, then I'll help you make the box part." "What colors? I don't know how," Tim whined, and retreated from the idea. "Here's a box that I use on my desk. It's very useful. It's just the right size. Suppose we took a piece of heavy paper that would fold up to be like it. Could you color it?" Tim looked overwhelmed. "I don't know how to color." "You decide what colors. She'll be so thrilled." Resistance continued. "Let's work on it together. I'll do the outside border; you can color the inside. After each color, we'll fold it up to see how it looks before you do the next color. Hey! That's a great swatch of blue you just did!" They folded the box. "Now, it's yellow—even more beautiful." With continual encouragement, and even pushing, Tim and his mother achieved a free-flowing paper that they folded into a box held together with tape at each corner. The tape spool ran out after Tim began to apply tape to the corners over and over "to make sure it won't break." But they made their box!

Grandma was warned. They visited her for the presentation: "We have a present for you. Tim...we...made it together. I hope you like it!" Grandma acted as if the homemade, fragile, stuck-together box was the most delightful and beautiful thing she'd ever seen. Tim looked around at his mother for reassurance. "See. She likes it!" No one could have predicted that he would help his grandmother as she cleared a place for the box. He emptied the wastebasket next to her desk. He sat lovingly in her lap as she filled the box with paper clips. He looked up in her face adoringly, "Mommy and I thought you needed something nice from us to remind you of us."

These apparently small incidents add up. Tim will be readier and more aware of the effect of his next handmade present. Each successful effort leads him closer to this goal of sharing himself with the important people in his life. The opportunity is always there to help the child recognize his effect on others.

Grandparents It was grandparents' day at Marcy's childcare center. She had been itchy for several days. She hadn't slept the night before. No one connected her tension with the coming event. Mrs. Jackson had alerted her parents to Marcy's day at school several weeks before. The grandparents had both arranged their work schedules so that they could be there. No one took it very seriously—except Marcy. It came as a surprise to the Jacksons when Marcy announced that morning, "Is this the day?" "The day for what?" "For Granny and Papa." "Oh! I'd almost forgotten. I'm sure they are coming." "Call them to be sure." "I don't need to, Marcy. They won't forget." "They might," said Marcy quietly.

The childcare center was full. Adults were milling around. Children were showing off. Noise levels reached their peak. Marcy stood at the door, eyes searching, thumb in mouth. She saw them before they saw her. She whirled down the hall. "Granny! Papa! Come quick! Everyone else is here!" She raced with them, holding each one tightly by a hand. She pushed her way through the teeming room to her teacher. "Here they are! Granny and Papa!" Her teacher was welcoming and grateful. "You can see how important you are to her! She talks about you a lot." All through the morning, Marcy kept looking at her grandparents—to be sure they were still there, to greet them with her eyes, to anchor herself in the midst of all the other families.

Only two children had no grandparents. They flinched and fell into subdued activity and quiet responses when they were called upon. Their peers were aware of their sadness. Marcy took her friend, Annie, up to meet her grandparents. "Granny and Papa, this is Annie. Hers didn't come." Granny reached out to hug Annie. Annie withdrew, but looked back at Granny gratefully.

When it was time for a sing-along, the grandparents were supposed to sing with their grandchildren. Marcy watched her silent grandparents through the first verse. She came up and stood beside them. "Sing!" she ordered. They mouthed the words. "That's better." She sang proudly beside them.

Tim's grandmother lived nearby. She loved to have him come to visit, and he loved to visit her. They would sit at her kitchen table, telling each other stories. She sipped a cup of tea. He sipped a glass of cold milk. He was utterly contented as he swung his foot beneath the table while she hummed a song, or told a story. "Tell me the one about Grandfather riding down the river in a canoe, and getting so excited that he tipped it over and had to swim!" Or, "Tell me about the big bird you saw the last time you were at the beach." She looked off in the distance, her eyes focused on a far-away spot. "I was standing at the edge of the water. It lapped around my feet. I was watching a seagull as it flew over the water. Tim, it was so beautiful! Its white wings flapped a few times, then it sailed up and down in the air. It glided over the water in the most elegant way, as if it had nothing else to do. It seemed to be dreaming of being above the world, of being where no one was ever angry, where no one ever fussed about getting dressed, or about what you ate for breakfast. That beautiful white bird seemed above it all. It made me wish I was a bird. Then suddenly, it dropped like a rocket into the ocean. It came up with a fish hanging out of its mouth. How do you suppose it even saw the fish from up there? It sailed over to the beach and gobbled up the fish. I thought, 'Here's a lovely bird, and I thought she just wanted to fly and sail all over the sky. But she didn't. She wanted her lunch!' " Both of them giggled. Tim loved his grandmother's stories best of any—better than the books he was read every night.

Minnie's mother's parents came to visit for Hanukkah. Minnie was aware of how much their visit meant to her parents—she knew already that her mother and father were different, and for most four-year-olds, this mostly meant having different holidays, songs, and special foods. For Minnie, it also meant an extra, unexplained tension. They had been preparing food and candles all day. Every time she wanted her mother to play with her, she'd say, "I have to get ready for Hanukkah. After all, Grandma and Grandpa are coming." Minnie was annoyed and excited. What would they all do together that was so important? She'd been through ritual meals before, but she always forgot them. Now she was old enough to want to take a real part in them. Her mother had taught Minnie the blessings. She was ready. When her grandparents arrived, she remembered her grandmother's smell, her soft lap, and her grandfather's wonderful sense of humor. He loved to tease her. "Minnie, winnie, winner of the dogsled races! You are the fastest girl I know!" She loved all the times she spent with them. Her grandparents were fun, and they made her feel special. She never felt that anyone else was as important to them as she was.

Billy's grandmother had come to help when Abby was born the year before. She came in time to be with Billy when his mother needed to be away. When his mother and father left for the hospital, Billy became immobilized. His face was white, his eyes were blank. He stared off into the distance, as if he were out of contact with what was happening. He was silent. His grandmother said, "Billy, your mommy will come back. I'm here for you until she gets here." She went over to him, but he ran off to hide in his room. She found him on his bed, turned into the wall. Without a word, she sat next to him with her hand on his shoulder. At first, he was stiff and resistant. Gradually, he relaxed and cuddled next to her. After a while, he began to squirm. She relaxed her hold. He got down, and without looking at her, he held her hand and began to show her silently around the house. Later, when she was lost and couldn't find something, he led her to it. They became silent buddies. He'd never forgotten it. Nor had she.

Now, even a year later, whenever his grandmother came to the house, Billy met her quietly at the front door. As if she were his, he'd lead her around to show her his latest treasure. If she approached Abby before he'd completed his tour, he would disappear. He'd retreat to his bed with hurt eyes, his body curled up. She had to repeat the ritual of touching him quietly before he would return to the activity of the family. He was clear in his demand that he'd have to have her first, and she could be everyone else's property afterward. Of course, they both loved this closeness. A precious heritage.

The strength and comfort that grandparents can bring to any family are hard to do without. They can step into emergencies in a confident, reassuring way that no outsider could reproduce. They are reliable and are not interchangeable. They are always familiar at stressful times. From his grandmother, Billy received the ultimate assurance that he mattered, and that he had an anchor whenever he needed it. She'd been there when he was born, too.

Grandparents play a critical role today in building their grandchildren's self-esteem. Many families feel more alone now. Parents are often without the good neighbors and close-knit neighborhoods in which they may have been lucky enough to have been raised. Today, your neighbors are as busy as you are. There's no time to get to know them, to visit them, to rely upon them in times of stress. Grandparents are busy too, and many have lives as full as those of their children. But they are committed. A grandparent can offer the most rewarding kind of nurturing because it is almost all positive. The discipline and daily chores are not a grandparent's job. Grandparents show a child special joys and pleasures. Parents have all the work, day after day. They get caught up in routines and problems. But grandparents can bring relief, treats, and unconditional admiration. This is indeed a special contribution to the child's self-esteem. (See also "Grandparents" in Part II.)

Sibling Rivalry

Abby had proved that she was here to stay. Now that she was safely through year one and on her feet, she had become a more interesting target for Billy. He not only played with her and manipulated her, but he could get a predictable rise out of her. If he took away one of her toys, if he shoved and she collapsed on the floor, if he teased her by offering her something first and then made it disappear, she was sure to protest and cry. Parents were sure to respond. Half the time he got away with it. The other half may have been the best. His parents' faces got red, their bodies tense. They watched, seething. Billy could see that they'd like to smack him, but their consciences were too strong. They took time to size the situation up. He and Abby watched hungrily. Both children knew who would get the scolding. But meanwhile, the drama and the attention had made it all worth it. Billy also now knew about revenge. Sibling rivalry has powerful motives.

In Abby's first year, Billy was more likely to regress, to mimic Abby. Getting up to breast feed came first, then crawling on hands and knees. Then, wetting all over again, "just like Abby." These are common responses. Less expectable for parents is the older child's frustration at being invaded when the younger one becomes mobile. When Abby learned to crawl and walk, Billy's whole world was threatened. Not only was his domain no longer safe, as she went after his toys, but she also began to follow him around. He became the center of her universe. One of her first words will be "Bih-wee." She'll try to do everything he can do. Even his accomplishments, which mark him for being "such a big boy," will no longer be his own. Instead of enjoying the rewards he has earned in the past, he'll lose out to her. "Watch Abby try to imitate Billy. Isn't she cute! And she can almost do it! She's so precious." He won't to be able to steal center stage from her. What can one expect from a child whose whole world is crumbling? Sibling rivalry.

Rivalry becomes a predictable communication between siblings. Of course they are competitive. Of course they tease each other to bring on a crisis. Of course their goal is to involve the nearest parent. Of course a parent is vulnerable. No parent ever feels there is enough of her to go around. When children fight, parents feel implicated.

They worry that they're the reason their children are so hostile, so angry with each other. Maybe, Mrs. Stone wondered, if she did the right thing this time, she could help them toward a loving, caring relationship. Mrs. Stone even wondered whether Billy had witnessed too many of her marital squabbles with her first husband and if this was why he teased Abby so much. But then, Abby provoked many crises, too.

At other times, she remembered her own childhood. She and her younger sister never missed an opportunity to set up a battle. "You'll be the death of me" so often rang in her ears. Her mother always got so involved. "Now, who started it?" Is there ever an answer? They both started it. Both were ready for battle. Any mother who thinks she can "get to the root of who is responsible" may be missing the point. Siblings were made to fight with each other. Rivalry is a healthy, normal part of an important relationship. Caring and competing with each other are two sides of the same coin. One without the other would not be possible. The two together fuel a passionate relationship.

Parents' best course is to stay out of such rivalry. You'll never know who started the battles. When you're involved, you add fuel and excitement—your upset makes it worth all the effort. You become part of a triangle. I would advise, short of real mayhem, that you say, "Look, this is your battle, not mine. Settle it yourselves." This approach is not possible, however, until a baby can fight back. But if there is no adult nearby, older siblings are less apt to tease younger ones. Although there are situations of abuse in troubled families, and accidents happen, too, rarely do older siblings injure younger ones in a serious physical way. They might, though, be more likely to try if there is an adult nearby whose attention they can vie for.

Independence and Separation

Turning from One Parent to the Other

Mrs. Lee called her nurse practitioner about four-year-old Minnie. "Minnie won't even hear me. Every time I speak to her or ask her to do something, she looks down, tosses her head, and walks away. At first, I thought she was having hearing problems. But I can tell she is selectively not listening to me because she can hear her father's car on the gravel in the driveway and I know that's not easy to hear. I get so angry at being ignored that I have to put her on 'time out' over and over. But it just doesn't do any good. When I ask her whether she wants to go with me some- where, she always answers, 'Is Daddy going to be there?' I'm getting sick of it. She fawns all over him. She climbs in his lap as soon as he gets home. He barely greets me before they are off to-

gether. He plays with her hair. He'll bring her presents when he comes home for no particular reason. It's too much!"

The nurse assured Mrs. Lee that Minnie was going through a "normal" phase and that it wouldn't last. "I feel so silly to be this vulnerable," Mrs. Lee said. "Tell me what gets to you." "Well, she behaves as though she's so grown up. I didn't expect her to be as coy as this so early. And, of course, her father plays right into it. He encourages her coy behavior by falling for it. Aren't we mak- ing her grow up too soon?" "I don't think so. I hear this all the time about four-year-old girls." "You do? That's a relief. I even worry that someday she'll be seductive with someone on the street and they'll take her seriously. I haven't warned her yet about how to take care of herself." "I really don't think it's up to her. You have to protect her at this age. But you can feel pretty safe about her coy behavior. She's likely to limit it to her father. Children without fathers at home may behave seductively with others, but not if their father or a strong male presence is available to them. It's a good sign that she feels safe with him and able to be this close. Have you noticed how much she's learning from him?"

Mrs. Lee thought about it for a moment. "You know, I hadn't looked at it that way." She paused. "But it does make me jealous."

Four-year-olds are likely to turn to one parent and ignore the other. They have an amazing capacity to shut out the requests and demands of the ignored parent. The child will brighten and alert when the "preferred" parent arrives, acting as if the other parent were not there. The "rejected" parent is likely to feel helpless and guilty. "What have I done? Why doesn't he listen to me or pay any attention to me?" As the tension builds up, this parent begins to feel jealousy and even anger. This process of turning from one parent to the other is the child's way of taking on those parts of the parents' personality that will become her own—one parent at a time. The child is developing her ability to become independent-from one parent at a time. This can become a touchpoint, a time when both parent and child feel out of touch with each other, and when understanding the child's reasons for this, and a parent's feelings, can help them both.

This touchpoint is particularly painful. It helped Mrs. Lee to remember that Minnie was growing up and establishing herself as a separate person. She was absorbing each parent intensely on her way to combining them into her identity. The child needs this opportunity to model each parent's attitudes and values, even if it sets off emotional conflicts between them. Parents need to remember that the tide will turn. Eventually, Mrs. Lee will become the adored parent and Mr. Lee will be rejected just as heartlessly. During each period, the child absorbs everything he can from the adored parent. He walks like that parent. He uses that parent's inflections. He learns moods, transitions, self-control—and lack of it—from that parent. He absorbs that parent's ways of dealing with aggressive feelings, with religious and ethnic feelings, with all important feelings. He is in tune with that parent. And next month, he will be just as in tune with the other. "Look at his gestures. He even talks like her." But what cannot be observed is even more critical. The child is discovering the values, the vulnerabilities, the coping patterns, the defenses, the passions, and the limits of each parent. He is absorbing personality traits in a way that comes from deep identification. Of course, the child identifies different traits in each parent.

In imitating his parents, the child is even reaching back to their own ghosts. He identifies with reactions that they aren't even aware of any longer. No wonder this behavior can be so painful for the parents. "Why does Daddy get upset when I keep hugging Mommy? He does." Unconsciously, the child is feeling that he wants to be just like his father and able to stir up the same cuddly reactions in his mother.

Even though a parent may feel shoved away at these times, it is critical for that parent to remain available. Had Mrs. Lee deserted Minnie, the four-year-old would have found the situation much too frightening. Mrs. Lee could have offered Minnie special times, but she may have needed to include Mr. Lee as well. It is especially important to maintain the threesome, when possible, as a means of maintaining the balance, especially when a child is as wrapped up in one parent as Minnie was.

Be aware of the potential tension between you and your spouse when your child is turning from one parent to the other. Ask your spouse for a special time with you alone. Your child needs to know that you are close to each other. Such times can present the opportunity for you to discuss your feelings of rejection and how you understand them. Then, when the child turns on one of you, you can both share the experience more openly. Parents sometimes report to me that, as a result of such jealousy, a real emotional distance opens between them. This need not happen if parents discuss their child's behavior openly. It is important to parents and child that he sees you as a united, passionately involved couple which is not threatened by his own involvement with you. He is then freer to identify with you and to see himself as separate in the process. Finding your way through this as a couple can become a cementing process.

Under stress, parents are likely to polarize; when this happens, the child is confused. For the child, falling back on one parent then means risking the loss of the other. Parents understandably fall back on their own upbringings for answers. At such times, parents often learn more about each other's families—things they never knew, things they may never have suspected. But these are times that may help spouses to understand each other better. Their relationship may even deepen as a result of the phase their child is going through. If one parent undermines the other's authority, however, the child will remain confused, driven to cling to one parent while longing for the other. If they are to face this difficult time together, parents will need to be aware of the tensions and discuss them in private.

"I really feel left out when Tim clings to you that way." "I can't push him away. He's so desperate. I can't desert him." "Maybe he needs to realize that I can comfort him, too." When both parents are so vulnerable, it helps when each one talks only about his or her own feelings rather than making comments about the other. Tim needs his father as a balance to the kind of hovering his behavior has called up in Mrs. McCormick. A parent's efforts to provide needed protection for the child can make it harder for him to manage on his own. He begins to see himself as vulnerable. A vicious cycle is set up around his feeling of inadequacy. Tim could already be caught in such a cycle.

*The Need for
Both Parents*

When Minnie turned away from her mother, it revived memories Mrs. Lee had of being rejected by her sisters but it also added to the painful distance which had been increasing in the Lee's marriage. Over the past few years, Mrs. Lee had come to resent the ease and joy with which Minnie and her father related. She felt useless and left out. Mr. Lee had sensed this distancing but hadn't been ready to face it. He felt challenged by Mrs. Lee's demands on him. They had found it very difficult to face the differences in parenting from which each of them had come. They had recently resorted to family therapy in an effort to save their marriage. In therapy, they'd identified the forces which drew them apart, but neither partner was able to overcome the hurt enough to work at mending their relationship.

The children had been feeling their parents' tension. May walked around with head and eyes downcast, not speaking to anyone in the family. Minnie became quiet, too. She was still active, but subdued. She ran into furniture and even into the walls, but she ignored everyone in the family. It was as if she couldn't face the stress between her parents.

When Mr. Lee moved out of the house, the overt tension lessened. But Minnie's face was drawn, sad. She moved more slowly, more determinedly. She asked her mother one morning, "Is Daddy coming back today? I'll be good if he does. I'll try to sit still the way he wants me to." Mrs. Lee realized that Minnie was blaming herself for her parents' separation.

Children in a failing marriage feel responsible. Four-year-olds are already capable of developing their own theories about other people's behavior; usually, they relate it to their own. Any explanation feels better than none at all. When their parents' marriage is strained, children inevitably wonder whether their "badness" has caused the problem. In Minnie's case, she'd overheard her parents' arguments about her behavior and her being so difficult to reach. With Mr. Lee's departure, these memories flooded her with guilt—and responsibility.

When Mr. Lee came back to see the girls, May withdrew from him and went to her room to read a book. Minnie was elated. "Daddy, you're back! I missed you." She climbed into his lap. She clutched his hand as he walked around because she needed to stay in physical contact with him. Mr. Lee naturally responded to this show of his daughter's affection. "May I take Minnie out with me? We can spend the afternoon together." Minnie's heart raced. Mrs. Lee said, "What about May?" But May mumbled, "I don't want to go anyway."

Once Minnie and her father left the house, her mood began to change. She became cranky. In the car, she sat huddled in the backseat away from her dad. She answered his questions in a monotone. "Minnie, what's happened? You seemed so happy to come out with me. Where shall we go?" "I miss Mummy—and May." "But we'll go back to them later." "Mummy may not be there when we come home." "She'll be there." But Minnie's sad mood persisted.

Minnie was demonstrating four of the reactions that children suffer when parents separate: (1) her longing to reunite the family; (2) her fear of loss—if one parent can move out, will the other one abandon her, too? (3) an awareness of her mother's importance, as a balance to the intense relationship Minnie has with her father; (4) and her feeling that she has been responsible for her parents' breakup. It no longer feels as safe to Minnie to devote herself to her father because her mother might not be there when they arrive home.

By the time they returned home, Mr. Lee had realized that both parents were necessary to Minnie. She needed their balance. He sat down with Mrs. Lee and said, "This just didn't work, my being with Minnie alone. She just wasn't happy without you there." Mrs. Lee felt gratified. "But what can we do? Our marriage is over. We can't both be present all the time."

They need to be aware of their children's natural wish to cling together as a family. Losing one parent makes the child vulnerable to the fear of losing the other. Minnie is bound to need her mother now. She may not be able to show it directly, but she will be threatened by separations from her. Mrs. Lee must warn Minnie about each impending separation, however brief. When Mrs. Lee returns, she can remind her daughter each time: "See Minnie, I'm here. I told you I'd be back at three o'clock. Let's look at the clock. What time is it? Three!" Mr. Lee's visits should be just as predictable. The first visits alone might best take place in the home. Minnie's mother could leave her children at home together with their father. Minnie could be gradually weaned from worrying about going out with only one parent. Leaving her mother has an underlying connotation for Minnie: "If I can leave her, she can leave me." This feeling brings back the old ambivalence about separating that a toddler experiences. Minnie's regressing to difficult-to-understand behavior is inevitable at such a stressful time.

Almost coincident with his fourth birthday, Billy began to cling to his mother. He wanted to sit in her lap. He shoved his sister away. Sitting in his mother's lap, he patted her face, stroked her hair. He ignored his stepfather and his sister. Until recently, Billy had run eagerly into Mr. Stone's arms when he came home at night. The little boy would begin to get ready for his stepfather's arrival an hour before. They had roughhoused and teased each other every evening. Now, Billy appeared to have changed. Both parents worried about him, but could see no reason for his behavior. Meanwhile, Billy began to talk and gesture like his mother. He looked adoringly at her as she tended to him. She alone could bathe him at night, read to him at bedtime. One night, she discovered that Billy had been sleeping with her silk pajamas. Both parents were taken aback. When they tried to take the pajamas away, Billy fell apart. His clinging behavior worsened as the time approached for his preschool to start again. He had loved preschool last year; this year, he began to whimper about having to go back. When his mother took him on the first day, Billy insisted on taking her pajamas as his "lovey." Embarrassed, Mrs. Stone explained her son's new behavior to his teacher. The teacher had known Billy the year before and she admired him. She understood and accepted his clinging. She advised Mrs. Stone to plan to stay a while for a few days. Billy would not leave her lap, and he fondled her as he sat there.

Sometimes Billy's mother found herself enjoying her son's way of treating her like a precious jewel. But then she wondered whether she had somehow encouraged him, without even realizing it. At last, Mrs. Stone put her foot down. "Billy, I can't stand this. You're a big boy now, too big for all this." "I love you so much, Mummy." She found his behavior cloying. She began to try to push him off. At first, this only served to increase his clinging.

Mrs. Stone was beginning to be seriously worried as well as embarrassed. Was this just a normal phase in his development—or was there something worrying him that his parents hadn't detected? Mr. Stone needed jogging from his wife to remain available to Billy, despite Billy's apparent rejection of him. That was an absolutely critical part of his "recovery." This episode felt to his parents as though Billy had been ill.

Billy's behavior is an example of how unsettling the child's turning to one parent can be in a family. It seemed as anxiety-producing for him as for his parents. Their upset coupled with his mother's pulling away increased his determination to cling to her. It was almost as if he had to pay homage to her, even to love her clothing. The fact that he had "lost" his father early in life could have added to his fears. His behavior might well have been representative of an unexpressed problem. The key to this behavior's "normality" was that Billy was eventually able to relinquish it. It did seem to represent a phase in his development. However, it would have been easy for this to become a family problem. Billy's stepfather had to remain present, and available.

Could Mrs. Stone have ended Billy's behavior sooner if she had pushed him away more firmly? Perhaps. But it was probably a much-needed developmental phase for him. His stepfather might have wanted to pull away, but that would have been even more upsetting for Mrs. Stone as well as frightening for Billy. The four-year-old needed the triangle for safety. (See also "Divorce" in Part II.)

3

FIVE YEARS OLD

Who I Am Matters

Birthday Party

Today was the day, Billy's long-awaited fifth birthday party! The Stones had been using it as a bribe for weeks. "Billy, if you'll just calm down, we can plan your party." "Billy, if you get so excited and don't obey me, there'll be no party." Billy only half listened. He knew he would have his party.

The birthday fell on a Friday. But he wanted to have his party on Thursday. He was adamant. "Why, Billy?" "I just do." Not a good enough answer. Billy's behavior indicated a kind of evasion. He wouldn't look his mother in the eye. He started kicking at a stone. If she pressed him too hard, he'd be off on some mission, chasing a ball. Because he was so adamant, the Stones gave in and changed the date of the party. On Thursday, the morning of his birthday party, Billy explained at last: "Wow! Today's my fifth birthday party! Then on my real birthday, I'll be six years old!" His drive to grow up was strong. "Why do you want to be six so badly, Billy?" "Because then I'll be the best soccer player in the world."

The Stones festooned the house with crepe paper ribbons, and Billy helped hang them. He was proud that many of them dangled. Abby grabbed one and tried to pull it to the floor. Billy disintegrated in tears. "She's ruined my whole party. I hate her! Get her out of here!" His meltdown and sobbing were heart wrenching, but predictable at such a time. Mrs. Stone tried to soothe him. He kicked out at her. "Leave me alone." Mr. Stone sat down by him, calming him with a low voice. "Billy, stop it. You'll be all miserable for your friends. We can put up the streamers again. Here, help me get up on this chair. I'll tape it high up so Abby can't reach it." Billy watched silently as his stepfather repaired the damage. Just in time for the arrival of his friends, he managed to pull himself together. When his first guests arrived, they could never have guessed at the previous meltdown.

Billy's curls were bobbing. He was charming. "I'm five years old today. I'm a whole hand," he said as he held up all his fingers. It was hard to resist Billy's appeal. Mr. Stone was impressed that Billy's temper tantrum had passed so quickly, and that he was instantly ready for the party.

First to arrive were Tim and his mother. Mrs. McCormick knew that it would be easier for Tim if he was already in place when the others arrived. Mrs. Stone, her friend, had invited them to come a little early.

Billy greeted Tim gallantly: "Hi, Tim. I'm glad you came! You brought your mom. You can sit over here and watch me open presents." Tim looked grateful.

Tim's golden hair framed his sensitive face. His big eyes surveyed the room with a wise look that belied his years. His quiet inactivity had not changed. He was still the watcher in any group. He always looked from one person to another; his face was impassive, his body moving as little as possible. When someone spoke to him, he'd startle slightly. His face would redden, he'd look down and stammer out a "yes."

When Tim's mother had tried to get him ready to go to Billy's birthday party, his eyes took on a wounded look, as if to say, "You just don't understand." He had been happy in front of his computer; he could play computer games for hours on end. But when he realized he was going to Billy's house, he stiffened and seemed to withdraw. His mother, worried about how reclusive Tim still was, had recently consulted her pediatrician: "He's just a shy boy—he'll outgrow it," the doctor reassured her.

Tim and his mother retreated to a couch at the far end of the festive room.

Minnie arrived next, on the run. She always seemed to be leaning forward, her legs trying to catch up with her body. Never tripping or falling, she skipped down the hall. Her pace gave her an appearance of gaiety, making an observer want to smile. Her eyes alert, her head jutting forward as if with determination, her arms akimbo as she propelled herself, Minnie was full of purpose. She rushed into the room, glanced quickly around, and dived at the first thing she saw, a toy truck. Once she'd looked it over—too quickly to digest it—she moved on. From one object to another, her interest always seemed to race ahead of her. Just as she moved leaning forward, she seemed to think leaning forward. She gave herself no time to anticipate, to evaluate, or to digest.

When Marcy arrived, Billy was ebullient. He rushed up to her, yelling, "Marcy, you came!" Marcy was beautiful to watch as she entered the room. She was tall and straight now and had lost her clumsiness. As a result of her ballet lessons, she was graceful and more and more sure of herself. She could carry a glass of milk in one hand, a cookie in the other, and slide gracefully onto a stool. Quite an accomplishment, but neither Marcy nor her parents seemed to notice any longer. Yet the feat required her recently developed balance, coordination, and capacity to plan out what her muscles would do next. Occasionally, she'd knock over the stool, but for the most part she was dependable. Her grace was irresistible as she glided into the birthday party. She greeted Billy exuberantly, cocking her head to one side as if to woo him without even realizing it.

The other children in Billy's kindergarten class arrived one by one, each with a parent in tow. Billy greeted each one warmly, looking for the present each had brought. When he shook hands with the adult, his charm and his glow increased with the size of the present. He used all the manners he'd so laboriously mastered. His parents felt a new anxiety. Was he using his manners to manipulate? His storybook looks and built-in manners could win the world for him. Was he aware of how he used them?

Billy's use of his winning ways was an expression of his social awareness. "If I wish for it, it may happen. If I dream hard for it, it may be more likely. But if I act to carry out the wish by including others, then it will be more likely still."

Billy kept hanging around the front door. His mother wondered about it, because all eight children had arrived. They were ready to start the games. Mrs. Stone uncovered the donkey without a tail, mounted on the backdoor. Then she told the children the rules for pinning the tail on the donkey: "Each of you has to be blindfolded and turned around twice, then you can head for the door to pin the tail on him."

Billy wouldn't budge from his post at the front door. Finally, his mother realized the reason. Billy was waiting for his father to arrive. He had promised to come. Billy's father had been invited to the party and had phoned Billy to say he would be there. Billy was beginning to expect that his father's promise might not be kept. But he couldn't give up hoping. Mr. Stone, his stepfather, sat down in a chair near Billy, trying to distract him. The more he tried, the more determined Billy seemed to become. Mrs. Stone was about to burst, filled with the old anger at her ex-husband, with sadness for Billy's sadness, and the feeling that she had let her child down. She sat on the floor and took Billy onto her lap.

"Billy, let's go along with your party. When your dad comes, he can join in. He loves games. He may not get here on time, but he'll be sad if you aren't having a good time anyway." With this, Billy's eyes grew big and reproachful. "You never think he's coming!" Billy fell apart. He lay on the floor, sobbing in a heap. He rolled over on his back, kicked and pounded his feet on the floor, and roared in a temper tantrum. His parents had learned to do nothing but stay close by at such times; anything else they tried prolonged the tantrum. Mrs. Stone sat by him, waiting for him to subside so that she could comfort him.

Finally, as he calmed down, she pulled him back onto her lap. "Billy, I know how disappointed you are that he's not come yet. But we are all here, and we love you. Your stepdad is sitting here waiting to hug you and wish you a happy birthday. All your friends have come. They want you to join them." Billy gave up his inconsolability with a determined wrench. He looked up at his stepfather as if to say, "You'll have to do." Slowly but doggedly he pulled himself together. He almost crept into the other room. His movements were slower, his face drawn. He slowly joined the others.

All the children had been silent as they watched the drama. As if they knew the anguish Billy was experiencing, they seemed ready to accept him, even to comfort him. Tim moved a bit closer to him. Billy looked at him and smiled gratefully. Minnie had been watching quietly as Billy fell apart. She glanced fleetingly at her mother as if she were touching base with her. She handed Billy her donkey tail. Marcy sailed across the floor and tried to put her arms around Billy. For one brief second, he looked at her gratefully, then he shrugged her off. He was ready.

The room was subdued. Mrs. Stone started her explanations again. "Who dares to be the first?" Minnie's hand shot up. "But I need a new donkey tail." Everyone snickered. The room became alive again.

As the children waited in line for their turns, they played out their eagerness. The boys wrestled with each other. The girls watched; they giggled when a boy screeched as he scrabbled on the floor. Mr. Stone tried to hurry the game along to allay the frustration that was building up. The tails were finally pinned—all over the door. One tail was on the donkey, under his chin. Lizzy, Tim's friend, had come the closest. Her prize was a very fuzzy, cuddly toy puppy. The other children wanted to touch it, to hug it. More than a few wanted to own it. Lizzy was a hero for a while, but for the other five- year-olds, it was very hard to lose. Some clamored for another chance. Others were overcome with the conviction that they'd never, ever win anything.

Two more games—ring-around-the-rosey and London Bridge—stretched the tolerance of the group. The efforts to line the children up, and then to keep them lined up and upright rather than on the floor, were proving too much. Finally, as Mrs. Stone fetched the birthday cake and lit the candles, the children let go. They piled up in a frantic mass. Minnie led the girls. Billy led the boys. Laughing and squirming, they hurled themselves on top of each other. Squeals of frustration were heard from those at the bottom.

When the cake was ready, when the ice cream was doled out and melting, it was time to unclench the wriggling pile of children. Each parent grabbed for a leg or an arm. Disheveled, whimpering, glowing, the children were pulled apart. Tim and Lizzy had not joined in. This kind of physical play was too much for them. But they'd watched hungrily.

Clothes were torn, hair messed up, shirts pulled out of trousers, dresses pulled awry. The party was a success. Ice cream and birthday cake were the peak. By this time, smears of food on best clothes no longer mattered. It was the children's day.

Billy kept watching for his father. Not until after everyone had left could Mrs. Stone telephone her former husband. She called him and paged him to remind him of Billy's big day and how much he had missed his father. "Let me talk to Billy." "Here's your dad. He's called specially to talk to you." "Hi, Dad." "Billy, I'm so sorry to be late getting to wish you a happy birthday. I got caught by an emergency and couldn't get there on time." "Uh-huh." "Will you forgive me, Billy? I'll bring you the present I have for you tomorrow." "Okay." The phone call was over. Billy's shoulders slumped. His limbs were heavy. He lowered himself to the floor in the midst of his birthday presents and looked at each one in turn with sadness and resignation.

Children of divorce pay a terrible price. Under stress, five-year-olds still resort to the view that they are at the center of a world whose ills result from their actions. They inevitably wonder, "Is it my fault?" and "Who will go away next?" No suffering on the part of the adults matches the feelings of despair and emptiness, of rejection, torn loyalties, and undeserved guilt that their children must face. In divorce, parents must put their children's needs first. To do this, some divorcing parents must ask themselves whether they hate their ex-spouses more than they love their children. They need to move past the intensity of their anger with each other and collaborate in raising their children while keeping the rest of their lives separate. It is not easy, and, sadly, not always possible.

Billy's father couldn't possibly imagine the pain that Billy felt when he was abandoned at such a time. But he may learn to understand Billy's feelings if his own guilt does not continue to keep him away when Billy needs him. He can learn from Billy—if his own need to be forgiven does not prevent him from seeing what Billy can show him.

Billy was learning to adjust, and he was doing a good job. But the costs to him were great. Thank goodness for Mrs. Stone's sensitivity to his pain and her ability to share it. She had had to face and master her own.

As Billy sat in the midst of his toys, Abby sensed her brother's quiet sadness. She sidled up to him and sat down beside him. She reached out for a toy. He grabbed her hand. "No Abby! That's mine!" They were back on familiar ground.

As if she knew how powerful she was in diverting him, Abby scrambled to her feet. She grabbed for another toy as if to take it away. Billy went after her. Mrs. Stone watched this episode from a distance with relief. She realized how important Abby had been for Billy. She went to her big rocking chair. "Come here, Billy. I want to cuddle and rock. I want you and Abby in my lap. I want to be our family again." With Billy on one knee and Abby on the other, she rocked and softly sang, "Happy birthday to Billy. We all love you so much. You are the biggest and best six-, I mean five-year-old there is." Mr. Stone abandoned his hunt for the shredded balloon fragments that had flown in all directions and pulled a chair up to sit by them in silence.

Temperament

A Vulnerable Child

With Tim's new kindergarten teacher, Mrs. Sosa, as her confidante, Mrs. McCormick was able to understand Tim better. She'd never experienced this kind of support from Tim's father. It was Mrs. Sosa's acceptance that freed Mrs. McCormick to face Tim's troubles with less anxiety and more pragmatism. She had already begun

to understand Tim's shyness as hypersensitivity. She had overpro-
tected him—without realizing it—as she had responded to his apparent fragility.

His father had been exasperated and worried by Tim's lack of social grace. When he watched other boys of Tim's age, he saw the
kind of bravado and outwardly aggressive behavior that other five-
year-olds displayed. Mr. McCormick noticed that when two boys
met, they either locked themselves in a wrestling embrace and
rolled around on the floor, or they started threatening each other.
They poked, they teased, they shouted. They could maintain loud,
physical responses for an entire afternoon. Mr. McCormick, however, knew that Tim wasn't equal to this. Yet he recognized Tim's
thoughtful alertness. Must his sensitivity always prevent him from
enjoying other boys' noisy play?

Tim's father had seen this shyness in his own younger sister.
She'd been painfully shy, and he'd been called upon to be her pro-
tector throughout their school days. Whenever he was ready to go
out, his parents would stop him: "Take Marguerite with you. She
needs you." When Tim was born, Mr. McCormick thought he saw
the same frightened eyes he'd seen in Marguerite. When he talked to
Tim and Tim winced, it gave him a sense of déjà vu. When he had
picked Tim up as a baby to hold him and talk to him, Tim had
turned away, eyes averted, his tiny face screwed up as if in pain. Mr.
McCormick had felt rejected.

Tim now knew his father's feelings. He felt he was a disappointment. Before his father came home at night, Tim would practice
jumping up and running exuberantly to the door. He studied his
older brother's spontaneity. "Why can't I be like him?" he wondered. He imitated his brother's bold voice. "Hi, Dad." But he
couldn't quite pull it off. If he ran to the door, he was immobilized
when his father entered. If he hung back, he almost shuddered as his
father came up to hug him. He demonstrated his sensitivity in every
way—touch, noise, even vision. When his father looked him
squarely in the face, Tim would avert his own gaze. Needless to say,
everyone who came into contact with Tim took this as rejection, just
as his father did. Most people learned to ignore Tim because his reactions were painful for them, and seemed to be painful for Tim.
Meanwhile, Tim longed to be different. He tried to imitate his
brother. One could see the enormous effort, the strain in his limbs,
as he tried to be like his brother. Quiet, watchful Tim.

Tim's father saw that Tim just could not enter into the fray with his brother. Philip had never been like this. He often tried to push Tim to joust with him. When Philip's efforts failed, Mr. McCormick's exasperation was often almost palpable. Tim could sense how deeply he was disappointing his father.

His mother tried to protect Tim from this. In the process, she unconsciously took over the relationship he might have developed with his father. This is typical of the polarization and struggle parents get into when they want to "change" the personality of a child. Although it started out, in his mother's mind, as a way of protecting Tim, it might not have amounted to that in the child's eyes. He began to respond as if it were a confirmation of his inadequacy.

The difference in how they reacted to Tim's shyness made the two parents disagree about how to handle their son. They criticized each other: "If I could do it my way, he'd be okay." This is gatekeeping. Gatekeeping happens at almost any time when there is tension around a child's behavior. "He wouldn't do that to me," or, "If I could only push him, he'd get going." Parents are likely to become competitive with each other: "All he needs is a firm hand. You're too soft with him. He knows he can manipulate you." The trouble is that such bickering can interfere with presenting a solid front to the child when he needs it. Stress can intensify the competition between parents.

Each parent brings a different set of past experiences to a stressful interaction with a child. Their own ghosts are likely to emerge at such times. If one parent continues to undermine the other's authority, the child becomes confused—driven to cling to one parent, yet longing for the other at the same time.

Without realizing it, Mrs. McCormick hadn't been allowing anyone to approach Tim directly. People felt they had to go through her to get to Tim. Could Tim know this? He tried to please everyone in every way. At meals, he was compliant. He sat, eating, without a struggle. Meanwhile, he watched every move his parents and brother made. He rarely made an error. His manners were perfect. He ate everything. He never spilled anything. He wiped his face on his napkin, not on his sleeve. When his brother had a friend at dinner, the friend said, "Your brother's icky. He's so good." Tim tried too hard.

The "vulnerable child syndrome" begins with a parent's feelings that "since the child is so fragile, I must do everything for him." As a result, the child never becomes frustrated or empowered enough to learn to do things for himself. He views himself as vulnerable and his feeling of inadequacy completes the vicious cycle. For the McCormicks, the first step might have been for Mrs. McCormick to loosen the tie enough so that Mr. McCormick could play a more active role with Tim. A father's relationship with his son automatically loosens the mother's tie.

But Mr. McCormick had pulled away from Tim, and, in a way, from his wife, too. If he can face his own feelings about Tim and the echoes from his past that Tim's withdrawal have brought out, he will be able to play a more vital role for both of them. Mrs. McCormick's hovering might lessen, too, if her husband can begin to shoulder the burden of her worries with her.

A father in Mr. McCormick's situation can share special times with his son, and at the same time discover more about him. He might then develop more respect for the child's personality and his quiet way of approaching the world; the child will surely sense this and profit from it. The self-esteem of a child with Tim's personality is as fragile as his father's acceptance of him. Everything that he and his father find they *can* do together will become a reinforcement for the child's belief that he can master his world.

Maybe Tim's father can find an activity or a sport to share with his fragile son; but he will have to be sensitive enough to back off when the child isn't ready. It's all too easy as a parent to introduce one's own interests rather than find an activity that a child can master.

Tim was most comfortable at school with his favorite playmate, Lizzy. She was a quiet, watchful child, like Tim. They could play along with each other, not demanding, not interacting, but watching each other out of the corner of their eyes. Tim felt warm and good when he was with Lizzy. With others, he felt tense and tight, as if a spring in him might break. He wanted so much to be outgoing, like the other kids.

Tim would longingly watch two five-year-olds who were engaged in active, loud, aggressive play. He knew he couldn't join in. Now that he was able to recognize his differences and compare himself to other children, his difficulties were even harder for him and his parents to accept. His parents couldn't protect him any longer. Mrs. McCormick would try to explain, but she and Tim both knew there was no easy answer. She would have given a lot to be able to protect him from his shyness. Her first step might be to let him

share with her how upset he's feeling and to accept his feelings without making light of them.

But this is very hard for parents. Tim's self-esteem was plummeting in front of his parents' eyes. Their worries about him led to more arguments. The whole family was affected by Tim's failure to make friends with his peers, to get along with the aggressive behavior that is the norm at his age, and Tim knew it.

If parents can accept a shy child as he is, he is more likely to accept himself. Then the real job will be to help him use his precocious self-awareness to learn about others, and to develop social skills as a way of mastering his sensitivity in stressful situations.

A Confident Child

Marcy was a delight to watch. She could climb a tree, jump off a four-foot table without crashing. She could pedal a bicycle with kiddie wheels, and was eager to ride without them. Marcy was a favorite with her peers. They were entranced by her bright eyes, her winning smile, and her warm way of greeting everyone. She loved people, and they responded to her. If there was another child in a crowded room, Marcy would stop to look her over. If she was about Marcy's age, Marcy would sidle slowly to be near her. Then, she'd pick up something to examine with inordinate interest. She'd appear so interested that sooner or later the new child would approach slowly to see what Marcy found so interesting. They'd start to talk and would soon be in play with each other. Then they'd discuss each other's favorite toys and hair color, their pets, their scratches, and their birthmarks, all by way of getting to know each other. Soon, they would be friends.

If there were no children, Marcy seemed to accept the fact that a room might be a wasted experience. She would return to her mother's side and stand by her silently. As she became bored, she'd speak to the person next to them. "Hello, I'm Marcy. I'm five." She would hold up five fingers. This would break the ice and charm the neighbor. Marcy was into a conversation. Mrs. Jackson often wondered why Marcy seemed to need people and conversation as much as she did. In a small way, she felt deserted and would have liked Marcy's company in this crowded room. But Marcy was too hungry for new experiences, new people. Her mother could only look on in awe, proud and a little jealous. She felt left out of Marcy's world.

With all this self-assurance, it did not surprise Mrs. Sosa when Mrs. Jackson told her how Marcy bombarded her with relentless inquiries: "Where was I before I was born?" "In my womb, you were a tiny baby growing there into a big baby." "No, I mean before that." "You were an egg—" "No, Mommy!" stamping her feet. "I mean before I was even an egg." Mrs. Jackson was overwhelmed by such questions. What was Marcy after? Her ability to question and to try to figure herself out was new and overwhelming to them all. Mrs. Jackson had to search for answers.

Her mother tried hard to remember particular episodes from Marcy's childhood—what kind of infant she had been, how she had learned to walk and talk. Marcy would sit, rapt in interest when her mother told these stories. Mrs. Jackson eventually realized that Marcy was trying to find out who she was. When her mother embellished too much, Marcy lost interest. When they talked about real events, the five-year-old was intrigued. "How did I do that? How did I talk? Was I a lot littler then?"

When they passed a baby carriage, Marcy would have to stop. She wanted to look in at the baby to see whether the baby was "really small." "Can I hold him?" "Marcy, we don't even know him." "But I want to." Mrs. Jackson always had to pull Marcy away. Marcy would stamp her feet, begin to weep. At one incident in a market, Mrs. Jackson couldn't pull Marcy away. "I want to touch him. If I can't hold him, can't I touch him?" Embarrassed, Mrs. Jackson tried to move her daughter away. The mother of the baby was stunned and overwhelmed. Marcy fell to the floor, screaming and kicking. "You never let me do what I want to do!" However, when Mrs. Jackson said firmly, "Marcy, get up. You're acting like a baby yourself," Marcy stopped and rose. But Mrs. Jackson could see that Marcy was still determined. Finally, she found a solution. "Marcy, let's go to visit Auntie Emily's baby. You can play with him." Marcy was mollified.

When they arrived, the three-month-old baby was just waking up. Marcy watched every movement. When he put his thumb in his mouth, Marcy squealed with delight. "He can put his fingers in his mouth!" As he gradually roused, he began to suck loudly. "Mommy listen to him! He's sucking!" Marcy's aunt gave the infant to her niece to hold. Marcy was tender and, in a high-pitched voice, said, "Look at you. You are so sweet. Do you like me?" The baby's eyes widened. He began to cry. Marcy looked around, desperate. She wanted to be rid of him. "Take him, Mommy. He doesn't like me!" They tried to reassure her, but Marcy's investigations were over. She was shaken, and Mrs. Jackson wondered how to help her regain her self-confidence. "Marcy, let's sit and watch Aunt Emily with him. He was just hungry. It wasn't you he didn't like. He just wanted to be fed." Aunt Emily put the baby to breast to quiet him. Marcy approached them, inquisitively watching the baby suck on her aunt's breast, noisily sucking, gulping. "This is what girls have breasts for—so we can feed our babies." "Oh." "When you grow up, you'll have breasts so you can feed your baby." "When?" "When you grow up!" "That's a long time, isn't it?" "Probably. But it's good for you to know what mommies can do for their babies." Marcy's eyes were wide and dreamy. She seemed to be thinking and figuring. She was learning to plan ahead.

An Active Child

Minnie was still driven. She loved to kick a soccer ball and could throw a softball with accuracy. She was competitive, and she knew she could win. She appeared to ignore other children. Boys liked her. Girls didn't. She hadn't been able to make friends with the girls in her class. But she bragged, "I'm the only girl the boys want to play with." Her mother found her strutting walk and her preference for boys worrisome. She caught herself wishing that Minnie were more like a little girl, but wasn't sure she had the right to feel that way. Minnie seemed too proud and too much of a showoff, but underneath this bravado, Minnie seemed vulnerable. Mrs. Lee could see that Minnie became more awkward around girls, more brash around boys. Was Minnie's strutting and exhibitionism masking insecurity? Mrs. Lee wanted so much to help Minnie feel better about herself. But she didn't know what to do.

The more Mrs. Lee tried to push Minnie toward being "feminine," the more the five-year-old seemed to resist. She dressed "like a boy." She refused to wear dresses. She wouldn't brush her hair. She wanted it cut short "like a boy."

Mr. Lee was aware of his wife's concern, but he rather liked what he saw in Minnie. Minnie would watch her father. He had returned home. When he talked on the telephone, she'd often pick up her toy phone to imitate his way of holding the phone, of tapping the desk with his fingers, of frowning and laughing while he was on the phone. When he'd play ball with her, she'd try her very best to imitate his pitching arm, the way he caught the ball. She was so competent. Whenever she strutted, he smiled. Whenever she compared herself to a boy, he nodded. He was proud of her difference and her willingness to stand up for it.

Whenever Minnie expressed pride in so-called boylike qualities, Mr. Lee might have said that these could be girls' qualities, too. "Minnie, you're great. But you don't need to be a boy to be great at athletics. Girls can be strong and fast too." Although Minnie was confident in her physical prowess, she was less comfortable with her parents' differing responses. This was something that Mr. and Mrs. Lee needed to discuss.

Threatened by Minnie's lack of femininity, Minnie's mother turned to May with relief. Often, without being aware of it, she compared Minnie to her sister. "May is so easy with her friends." No matter how hard Mrs. Lee tried to keep comparisons to herself, all Minnie was likely to hear was how May pleased her mother and how she didn't. She would feel wounded and even less able to cope, rather than supported. She might also be less likely to try to identify with her mother.

Mrs. Lee also began to see how ill at ease she was with Minnie's constant activity; her hurried approach made Minnie seem insensitive to others around her. Her demands to her parents had changed from "I want it" at four to "I need it. I must have it!" What had changed? She realized that she was afraid Minnie was "spoiled." Her intensity, her demands, her insensitivity to others all added up. She expected to get what she wanted—at any cost.

When Mr. and Mrs. Lee tried to analyze it, they realized that Minnie had never been a docile child. She'd always "led" them. She had always surprised them, for her progress had been so rapid. Instead of waiting for help from them, she'd stood, she'd walked, she'd talked—but without their help. Mrs. Lee looked back over these years to see herself constantly running to keep up with Minnie, breathless. When Minnie wanted something, she had demanded it. It was never a choice in which her mother participated. She felt shoved out and unnecessary.

This behavior reminded Mrs. Lee too much of her own feeling of being left out when she was a child. Mrs. Lee's two older sisters had also been very active. When she had tried to join in with them, they had actively excluded her, "Go find someone else to play with." She had never forgotten the feelings that she was left with. She had hoped that motherhood would help. With May, it did, but Minnie overwhelmed her. She relived the old feelings, the old ghosts, and found herself resenting Minnie and hating herself for feeling that way.

She felt she could not confide any of this to Mr. Lee. He was too charmed by Minnie's physical competence. When he came home, Minnie was always waiting for him to play. After brief hugs, she'd lead him from one activity to another. "Let's play!" was a constant cry. When Mrs. Lee called Minnie, she ignored her mother if her father was in the house. Mrs. Lee would become more and more exasperated. "Minnie, can't you hear me? Come and sit at the table. I just made you a sandwich and some milk." Minnie would frown, pull up her shoulders as if to refuse. Then she'd look at her father. He'd nod for her to pay attention to her mother. If necessary, he'd even add his approval. "Go do what your mother is asking you to do." This extra step before she could get Minnie's approval was maddening to Mrs. Lee.

Mr. Lee pooh-poohed Mrs. Lee's concerns about Minnie's being spoiled: "She just knows what she wants and how to get it." He sensed his wife's discomfort with his closeness with Minnie. He wanted to defend Minnie, and he was sorry not to be able to share his joy in her. Minnie and he clicked, and they both knew it.

Minnie reveled in her father's excitement. She built up to giddiness with him, laughing and giggling all the time. She felt the thrill of showing him how far she could go to keep up with him and of keeping him excited by her. They'd play and play, getting louder and louder. But sometimes, suddenly, giddiness turned to chaos. Minnie would break down in sobs. She moved from high to low in dramatic cycles. Mrs. Lee was left to pick up the pieces, which only frustrated her further.

Mrs. Lee's concerns were bound to affect Minnie. Mr. Lee's approval had given her the beginnings of self-assurance. Yet Mrs. Lee's disappointment added to Minnie's self-doubt. Minnie risked feeling as pushed away as her mother did. Then Minnie would have to hold on more desperately than ever to the qualities her father reinforced in her. But if Mrs. Lee could join Minnie in accepting herself and add her approval, Minnie might begin to grow. If Minnie didn't have to depend on her father alone for approval, she could take in the qualities that her mother offered as well. When she can allow herself to identify with her mother, new behavior will emerge.

Mr. Lee needs to recognize the cost to his wife of Minnie's intense closeness to him, and the cost to Minnie of the tension she feels between her parents. He certainly shouldn't withdraw, but he and Mrs. Lee need to face the gatekeeping. At five, a child needs to be able to identify with each parent. Minnie needs her mother's approval. If Mrs. Lee pulls away when Minnie acts up, each of them is lost to the other. If Minnie and her parents can face what is going on, this touchpoint could become a time when a crisis is followed by growth in the child, and a strengthening of the family's ties. For parents who can see a child's distress and its effect on their interactions, such a touchpoint in the child's development becomes an opportunity for their relationship as well.

Learning

Nightmares and New Fears

Billy was very serious at the breakfast table. He said to his mother, who was eating her pancakes: "I knew I'd have a sister like Abby." "How, Billy?" "We were in your tummy together. We talked to each other all the time." "You and Abby?" "Yeah. We played a game to see who would come out first. I won!" "You played a game?" "Abby wanted to be first. So did I. I won the fingers game. You know that one about paper and stones? I was already smarter than Abby." "But Billy, did you know she'd come next?" "Sure. I already liked her." "What was it like in my tummy?" "It was all warm and cozy. Abby and I liked it." "Was it dark?" "No, it was light. I could see Abby's face, so I knew her." At this point, Billy began to realize he was in over his head, and he tried to change the subject. "I punched you and punched you until I got out." He sidled over to Abby's chair, hugged her hard. She screamed. He moved back to his own chair and resumed his breakfast. Enough cozy talk. Enough confession. But his tenderness for Abby and his possessiveness of her were evident.

In his fantasy play, Billy didn't often feel guilty. But he also didn't often go too far. One day, he wanted to make Abby into a boy to play with. He started cutting off her blonde curls. Fortunately, his aunt came into the room just in time. "Billy, what are you doing?" He stopped abruptly, looked at Abby, and said, "I want her to be a boy." He looked so guilty. He had frozen in his tracks. He tried to hide the scissors. He looked beseechingly at his aunt. "Don't tell Mommy." He had recognized his own guilt and was devastated.

Billy winced when he looked at Abby's hair. He mumbled, "Maybe we can glue it back." But he knew they couldn't. He knew he was out of control and, unfortunately for Billy, he now had to feel responsible.

Around this time Billy developed a recurring nightmare. He woke every night at about 2 A.M. His dreams, as far back as he could remember, were about dinosaurs or "bad men." After the haircut episode with Abby, a witch would occasionally join the fray. Waking, screaming, Billy would rouse his parents, who rushed in to comfort him. He was wide awake and crying. His father would look into the closet with him. His mother would soothe him back to sleep. Nothing stopped his nightmares. Had he played too hard? Had he eaten something?

Billy recognized that this was a dream, but he was still scared. His mother tried to comfort him: "Billy, tell me exactly what you were dreaming and then it won't come back. You can go back to sleep. We are right here. Don't worry." Because nightmares are generated by feelings that children experience but can't handle, persuading a child to tell about the dream can be cathartic for him. It helps to put the dream into words and helps the child master his feelings. Billy's nightmares were like those that most five-year-olds experience; expecting them to go away easily is impractical. The comfort Billy's parents gave their son was exactly what he needed. These nightmares were tied to Billy's new fear of his own drive to "conquer his world." They were frightening to everyone, but they would last only until Billy was more comfortable about some of the feelings he was experiencing.

Nightmares are common, and serve a developmental purpose. They bring a balance to a child's surging aggressive feelings; his fantasies of being the "biggest" and the "strongest" are checked through nightmares. In his bad dreams, he is helpless. His feelings of power-lessness, reflected in nightmares, call the parents in to help; when they respond, he feels safe again. Nightmares and fears balance the new and important aggressive feelings. They seem to be inversely correlated with a five-year old's ability to handle aggressive feel-ings. I urge parents to let up on pressure to be "good" at such a time. A child of five is already working so hard to keep himself in bounds, and is so worried about whether he'll succeed. Consistent limits, though, become even more important now—the child needs to be able to count on these. Bad dreams appear to be an outlet for the two sides of aggressive feelings—the "wished for" and the fear-ful aspects of being aggressive.

Marcy and her mother went to a department store to find a birthday present for Marcy's classmate, Ellen. Mrs. Jackson knew that it was dangerous for them to go to the toy section; she knew that Marcy would want everything. They had discussed this in advance, and Marcy had promised not to be demanding. She skipped ahead of her mother, looking over the selection of toys. The dolls were so attrac-tive that she and her mother decided to buy one for Marcy's class-mate. When Marcy was allowed to hold the doll with "real hair," to cuddle it and to croon to it, she fell apart. "I want one too, Mummy." "Marcy, you promised. This is for Ellen, not you." "Yes, Mummy, but I need one too. You said this was a good store and they wouldn't be too expensive. You can buy me one, too. Use my allowance!" She began to whimper, to cry, and then to build up to a tantrum. Mrs. Jackson was shocked and embarrassed. The sales lady looked at them with unsympathetic disdain. Maybe that was what turned the tide, but Marcy won. The salesperson wrapped up two dolls exactly alike—one for Marcy, one for her friend Ellen. Mrs. Jackson was sulky as they left the store. Marcy was no longer joyous. She knew (and her mother's behavior reminded her) that she'd betrayed her promise. The doll was hers, but undeserved. When Marcy unwrapped it at home, it was no longer as delicious as it had been in the store. Her mother never mentioned it. That was the hardest part of all for Marcy. She wanted and needed to be reprimanded, but she wasn't. Her mother's stony silence lasted through supper; her father put her to bed and read to her.

That night, she cried out several times. At one point, she woke up in terror and crawled into her parents' bed. As she slid in between the sheets, she wept and begged for her mother to hold her. Mrs. Jackson cuddled Marcy to quiet her sobbing. "She scared me! There's a witch in my room. She grew and grew. She got so big that she made me show her our kitchen. She ate all our food. She even slurped! She was *so* big!" Mrs. Jackson tried to reassure her, and to settle her down. She showed her the kitchen and the uneaten food; then she carried Marcy back into her room to sleep. "No! No! Mommy, she's in my closet." Mrs. Jackson opened the door to reassure her. "She's under my bed." Mrs. Jackson looked under Marcy's bed with her. "The witch will eat me, too." As a last resort, the Jacksons let Marcy sleep between them. Marcy fell asleep at last, whimpering and gasping between breaths.

The next day, Marcy refused to look at her new doll; she was even wary of the one they needed to bring to Ellen. She wouldn't touch it. When she handed Ellen her present, Marcy treated it as an object she wanted to be rid of. She had her father place her own on a top shelf; from that moment, she ignored it.

Marcy had her nightmare once more. Mrs. Jackson cuddled her daughter to sleep. Marcy woke up once in terror, but the bad dream had less of a grip on her this time. She went back to sleep after her mother came in to comfort her.

Marcy was frightened when she sensed that she only got the doll at the department store because she had a tantrum. It was scary for Marcy to think that her feelings or desires were powerful enough to make things happen. She also sensed the anger her behavior caused her parents. Her sensitivity to this power was different now. She was more conscious of the angry consequences, more conscious of how her behavior affected others. Sometimes, she felt responsible for her parents' upsets. This time, she knew she was responsible. Marcy's conscience was becoming a force to reckon with. A conscience carries with it responsibility. If she knew better than to have a tantrum to get a doll, why did she do it? Can she learn to master her impulses? There are now moments—after the unacceptable behavior—when she feels guilty and knows she should repress her outbursts; but she has to find new ways to do this.

At five, magical thinking and its power to explain the world are beginning to go underground; it was the three- and four-year-old's attempt to understand why things happened the way they did. Magical thinking carried with it the conviction that "My thoughts and actions determine the world around me. If I wish hard enough, it will happen. If it didn't happen the way I wanted, it was because I hadn't wished it well enough or hard enough." But now Marcy's experience begins to challenge and contradict the conclusions of her magical thinking. These experiences make her aware of the limits of explaining the world as something she has caused through her thoughts. She has found the difference between doing and thinking.

Marcy knows now what a thought is, even if she is not sure where it comes from. She can tell now that a thought is different from an action. She realizes that she must learn how to act on her world to change it. She is becoming more aware of her own role and of her responsibility for her actions. Sometimes, that feels good. Sometimes, it doesn't. But, with it comes a shift, a new perspective: she is beginning now to see how limited her powers are. She is beginning to realize that her actions and her abilities can't always have the effect she wants. The knowledge that "what is right" is not the same as "I want" or "I need" brings with it the frustrating realization that the world is so big, and she is so small.

The responsibility that has come with this newfound self-awareness carries a heavy cost. Marcy can feel torn and guilty, but when her guilt is too much to handle, she will turn to the magical again. At five, she is not so old that thoughts and fears don't still sometimes take on a life all their own.

Boys who are becoming aware of aggressive outbursts demonstrate this cost the most clearly when they fall back on the irrational fears and nightmares of the four-year-old. Boys have a tougher time learning how to handle their aggressive wishes and their competitive feelings. The pressure on them to be "brave" and to conquer the world starts early.

We don't push girls of this age as hard to be competent in handling their fears and their nightmares. Girls are more likely to develop phobias not so different from Marcy's. Maybe at five, the phobias are somewhat less believed in, but they are no less feared. They appear to be an effort to keep angry impulses under control; they are predictable, yet upsetting to parents and child. Fears and phobias constitute a touchpoint: the challenge of facing new feelings and responsibilities and the fears and hesitations that go with them. Understanding the underlying reasons can help a child through them.

Farewell to a Fantasy

"When I grow up to be a princess, I'll wear long, shiny braids, a beautiful shimmery dress with dangles off it, and a crown. No, not a crown. It would just fall off when I wanted to climb a tree." Marcy's combination of fantasy quickly topped off with reality amazed her parents. They were sad to see her wonderful fantasies endangered.

A five-year-old's dreaming and wishing must now struggle to make way for reality. Now, the fantasy of being powerful and strong cannot escape the growing awareness of what the real world demands; this can feel like a loss to a five-year-old. Marcy is beginning to be aware of how small she really is, and she can no longer avoid facing the limitations that go with this realization. When she dreamt as a younger child, the fantasy and the wishful thinking were unfettered by reality; they gave her a chance to construct her own world. Now, she knows all too well that this is not how the world works. She can still dream, but she can no longer lose herself in fantasy quite so thoroughly. At the same time, however, she is beginning to recognize that she can often accomplish her wishes by acting upon them herself. The more she can do, the more she dares to dream, but in a different way. Her dreams now have less to do about escaping from the present and more to do with hoping for the future.

Marcy and Ellen were playing with their dolls. "My doll can become the best dancer in the world." "Mine can become a television star! She knows the president!" "Mine wants to climb up to the stars." "Let's tie this ladder to the chair. Then she can get all the way to heaven." "She may not ever come down. My mommy says that when you go to heaven, you stay there." "Well, let's have her come down before she gets there. Her baby's crying: Come back to me, Mommy." "She hears you. She's coming back." "She's a *good* mommy."

Marcy's increasing sense of her own skills leads her to try out some of her dreams in the real world. Although she is beginning to face her limitations, she is buoyed by the exciting successes of her fifth year. "I can draw my house." "I can write my name." "I can tie my own shoes." "I like dolls. I don't like boys. I like Mrs. Sosa. She's nice to me. She likes me." "What do you want to be when you grow up?"

Marcy's use of wishful thinking hasn't ended yet, however. It still serves a purpose. Marcy left her drawing book at school. "Mommy, someone took my notebook. I stopped to play with my friends on the way home. I put it down, and someone took it." Something tentative alerted Mrs. Jackson. "Marcy, are you sure you didn't just forget it?" "No, Mommy . . . well . . . I guess it wasn't on my mind." At first, Mrs. Jackson was disappointed that Marcy had lied. But then she began to realize that Marcy needed to hide behind the fantasy of making someone else responsible. She could accept this, but she let Marcy know that they both recognized the difference between her tale and reality.

Marcy's father began to play on her ability to dream. After he'd read her a book at night, he'd say, "Now, let's dream about what we'd like to be and where we'd like to go." Marcy would try to please him. "Well, if I had a friend like the one I used to have—do you remember Flagia, Daddy? Remember that Flagia was so beautiful? She wore long, shiny braids and long beautiful dresses. She loved to tell stories and to go off with you in her dreams. She went with you—and Mom—to Disneyland. She went on every ride. You bought her peanuts and ice cream every time she asked you for them. She was so happy." Father: "Where is Flagia now?" Marcy: "Well, she's there in my room. But sometimes she seems silly. She wants everything too much. She can't have candy whenever she wants it. I tell her that it's not good for her, and if she has to be so spoiled, she can't come out of her room." Her father said sadly, "I miss Flagia."

Marcy looked seriously at him as if she were sizing him up for teasing her, for invading her territory, or whether, indeed, he wasn't growing up as fast as she was. She thought he was sad about their dream world ending, too, so she needed to reassure him. "She'll come out someday. Don't be sad. Just not tonight." And with that, she abruptly turned away. The end of a dream world is a touchpoint for the child struggling for new ways to face reality. It is a touchpoint for parents, too, who may almost feel that it is the end of childhood, or at least the end of a certain kind of magic that their child's wonder had revived in them from their own childhoods.

Billy had lost a tooth! At last it fell out, after weeks of wiggling a lower front tooth back and forth. He'd shared the wiggle with his friend Marcy, who pushed the tooth back and forth with fascination and disgust. Billy felt like a hero the day it finally came out. He asked his mother for a paper bag so that he could take it to kindergarten. He walked into the classroom proudly holding the tooth in its plastic bag ahead of him. Several of the others had already lost front teeth and they were not impressed. But Billy's special friends were. They came sidling up to see the tooth and to inspect the gap in the front of his jaw. "It looks bloody. Did it hurt? Will you put it under your pillow for the tooth fairy?" At this strain in everyone's imagination, two of the boys giggled. "There's no such thing as a tooth fairy!" "Oh yeah? Wait 'till to-morrow. I'll show you what she brings me." Billy looked at his critics with soft sad, eyes. "I want her to bring me something," he said quietly to himself.

Billy's family had begun looking for a new house. "What about Billy's bed? Will it have to go now? He's such a big boy—he needs a new bed." Everything in their house was being sized up to see whether it was suitable to move or not. When the real estate agent came to take the Stones to see a new house, Billy rushed out with his tooth. "See! I'm getting so old!" In his hurry to extract the tooth from its plastic bag, he dropped it, and it rolled down the drain. He stood looking down in horror. Where had it gone? Mrs. Ellis, the real estate agent, felt his anguish and responded to it. "Billy, you know what? A fairy came to my house not long ago. She said that so many kids had been losing their teeth and she couldn't keep up with them. She thought she had missed a few. She asked me whether I knew of anyone who'd lost a tooth; I was to give this dollar bill to that child if I did. Here—it's yours!" Billy's face changed to an amazed glow. Mrs. Ellis had understood that it was hard enough for Billy to be losing his old home right now and wanted to protect him from having to lose the tooth fairy, too.

No one wants to give up the myths of childhood. Why should anyone have to give up these wonderful magical beliefs? They have served a purpose. In the case of the tooth fairy, they add a magical reward for the loss of part of a child's body. Losing a tooth is a step toward being the grown-up that each child wants to be. But it is also a loss. Coming at a time when children are bound to be concerned with loss and intactness, this event carries extra significance. "Can I lose part of my body this easily? I want to hang on to everything." Sometimes it may seem to a child that growing up is composed of losses.

Make-believe

Play serves many purposes at five. It offers a way to try out wishful thinking, to learn about one's roles, to learn controls, and to be a friend. Play is an outlet for the new pressures on five-year-olds to grow up, to perform, and to fit in. Play is an opportunity to build self-esteem, and a safe way to express painful or confusing feelings.

Dolls have power at this age. They personify dreams that could come true. Even if they can't, dolls satisfy dreaming for a time. Marcy and her friend played with Barbie dolls for seemingly endless hours. In this way they enlarged their world, each child trying her hardest to outdo the other. Girls are free to fantasize with dolls. Often, boys are not be allowed to dream with them.

When my brother and I were this age, we were not permitted to play with dolls. "Dolls are for girls. You boys should go outside and play." We knew that dolls were taboo, but we were not quite convinced. We captured little bottles out of the medicine cabinets and around the house. We made the tall ones into males, the squat ones into females or "mommies." Tiny bottles became the babies in "our" families. "Our" families never fought—except when all the bottles killed each other! "Our" families let their kids stay up as long as they wanted. "Our" families let their kids have candy or a dessert whether they ate their dinners or not. And on and on. As little boys, we knew we were breaking the rules by playing with dolls, and with the stories we invented. It made our play even more exciting and adventurous. We giggled at each other's ideas. We were never as allied to each other as we were in this forbidden play. We were learning to be nurturing. We had the families we wanted, no matter what the future held for us.

Children of this age express a mixture of fantasy and fears in playing with nonhuman figures. Dinosaurs and aliens, for example, are a safe distance away from reality, and for boys, from dolls. These otherwise unattractive and diminished toys are readily personified into characters in stories that can be spun into a fantasy world, yet they are still close enough to reality to be expressive of a child's inner life.

Billy growled as his Tyrannosaurus chomped everything in sight. When his friend couldn't understand him, the growls became more and more like speech. The speech was always somewhat threatening. The boys made these figures perform all the aggressive behaviors they wanted to try out themselves but didn't quite dare.

Fantasy play was safer than reality. The rules seemed to be different for play with miniature objects, such as the dinosaurs. Mrs. Stone realized that persuading Billy and his friend to sit down and maneuver toy figures with little fingers channeled their energy; it gave them more control than running all over the house, waving sticks as make-believe swords, gave them. It was easier to keep the aggression in bounds. The effort to curb their impulses was not as demanding. The play could get as rough as it needed to be to test their controls. They could make the dinosaurs or dolls attack each other viciously—yet all the victims would eventually be revived. Playing with dinosaurs modulated the intensity of the play—a make-believe explosion hurt less when only the dinosaurs, not the little boys, were involved.

If an adult entered their play, the boys warned him very seriously against stepping over the bounds they'd set. If an adult suggested that the dinosaur might grow up to be real, both boys would shudder and change the game; it was safe only as long as it wasn't brought into reality. Billy and his friend followed unspoken rules about how aggressive their "play" could be, and about "just pretending."

Their physical rough-and-tumble play went beyond these unspoken rules. The possibility of going too far in rough-and-tumble play was always present. A fine line still existed between threats and play. Five-year-old boys may need to be aggressive in their play, but they also need to feel protected from themselves. If no one stopped them from rough play with peers, such play could become frightening indeed. Yet with their dinosaurs and aliens, they could give form to urges that might otherwise get the best of them; and in the process, they were learning to control such urges.

In peer play, Billy and his friends seemed to try each other out. Play was a way to learn rules. When their aggression became too frightening, they'd indicate "enough." Surprisingly, the other player usually respected it. Rarely did one child have to run to an adult for rescue. In this rough-and-tumble play, they were learning about their own inner controls. Each was also learning how to value the other as well as himself.

Billy was working on this. He always wanted to win. He wanted to be better than "anyone else." "When I get bigger, I'm going to be better than Michael Jordan or Tiger Woods." He tried to dress up like his sports heroes and his super heroes. Costumes were absolutely necessary; every day, he wanted a new one to wear. He had assembled about ten—one for fire fighting, one for chasing "bad guys," one for riding on horses, and one cowboy outfit consisting of painfully tight cowboy boots. Any costume was exciting—with it went strutting, a deep voice, threatening words, a stance with legs apart, a gun on the hip. Did all this dreaming help Billy face being "just" five?

Games

At kindergarten, play was just as predictable, and just as productive. Unspoken rules, which many of the children were just beginning to learn, dominated the behavior of the group. Learning the rules for making friends and for belonging to a group was now more important than ever before. Billy gravitated to the boys. Marcy was caught up in the "girls' side" of the playground. Their teacher always started boys and girls out together; she even tried to alternate boys and girls at the beginning of their play period. As soon as she left, most gravitated to same-sex groups, Minnie, reluctantly. Only Tim seemed to prefer the gentler group of girls; but he knew this wasn't acceptable. He kept watching the boys over his shoulder.

Testing out each other's ability to stand up for himself or to give in was a main theme in the boys' group. "Throw me the ball!" "No, our side wants it." "If you don't throw it *now*, we'll come and get it." As they reached the ball, they lined up to kick it. The anarchy of pileups had given way to orderly lines. The popular boys always had the ball kicked to them; the less popular were relegated to one end of the line. When watching a boy as "popular" as Billy, one could see that he puffed out his chest, stood straight, furrowed his brow, and was almost threatening in his stance as he yelled, "Kick it to me or I won't be your friend!" Less assertive boys had already learned about the hierarchy. When they asked for the ball, they bent their heads to one side and were more soliciting.

Tim loved computer games. Mr. McCormick found that he could join Tim and engage him in competition. Because he enjoyed this, he would save up time for Tim in the evening when he came home. Tim's older brother, Philip, felt left out—again. He knew his parents worried about Tim all the time, and he tried not to add to their worries. But he felt jealous when their father began to look forward to the games that Tim and he played. Tim was quick and cagey. He seemed to be able to plan several plays ahead. It was as if all the practicing he'd done had really paid off. At first, Mr. McCormick had let Tim win, thinking he needed to win for his self-image. Then he realized that Tim could beat him anyway, and it came as a surprise. When he put on the pressure to try to win, he could see even better how Tim's mind worked. He was relieved to see that Tim had these skills to build on.

Children with social delays are often gifted in cognitive areas. Which comes first? Does this kind of intelligence demand so much that the child is likely to have less energy to be sociable? Or does a quiet, shy child turn to intellectual pursuits instead of social and shared ones? In Tim's case, it seemed as if the latter might be true. Socializing was so demanding. Tim's sensitivity was too great, his defenses too weak. He preferred to be left alone. The computer was forgiving. It demanded only what he gave it. It took its time and adjusted to his. It asked only that he apply his visual and tactile senses and some dexterity. The biggest reward, and the least recognized, was Tim's feeling that he could master something his father was skilled at and passionate about. No wonder he began to invest himself in it. When he and his father played games, Tim almost became a different child. He showed enthusiasm, even a quiet humor. His father could see a different Tim. Playing together changed their relationship. But now Mr. McCormick would have to draw in Tim's brother, too.

Play and Healing

Play is a child's work. Through play, children grow, learn, and heal. Play can be a powerful way of working out the leftover feelings from a traumatic experience. We use play therapy during a child's hospital stay. A small child can identify her fears, her anxiety about the future, can test her ability to regain mastery over her impaired body. With hospitalization and illness, play can restore a sense of control to a sick child.

I was once called in to evaluate a five-year-old with a chronic disease that tied up his joints, legs, and arms. He was confined to a wheelchair. We were worried because the boy was depressed, refused to eat, slept poorly, and wouldn't cooperate with his medical care. His inactivity was making him more and more crippled. We felt his depression and his sense of hopelessness were becoming as serious as his illness. We rigged up a computer-driven board on which he could press buttons to express himself: "I'm hungry," "I'm thirsty," "Leave me alone," "Push me around," "Rub my butt." He was able to turn each one as loud as he wanted. He began to press the last button, "Rub my butt," at top volume, over and over. He drove his nurses crazy. When they reacted with anger and limits, the little boy's joints began to improve. The child was less depressed. He joked. He crowed at the nurses' upsets. Eventually, he began to recover; he started to walk and to feed himself. His improvement became secure. He had played himself from a serious situation into recovery.

Play is also an outlet for minor problems from day to day. A five-year-old who makes a bed right beside her mother's bed for her doll—who is crying all night "like the new baby in the house"—is already expressing how left out she is feeling. As she organizes these feelings into a story, she is putting them into perspective and readying herself to move on. A child who plays out her feelings is showing adaptiveness and strength. Parents can value play as one of the child's most potent means of expression and growth.

Imaginary Friends

Tim squatted on his haunches, neatly lining up his toy soldiers. Patiently he repositioned them over and over again whenever one fell onto another. He was still shy to ask for a "play date" or to respond to requests from another child. Sometimes he seemed to be moving his lips silently. When one of his parents tried gently to intrude, they became aware that he was talking to his beloved imaginary friend, Alfie. Tim and Alfie had long talks. When anyone asked Tim what their talks were about, he'd reply, "I don't remember." If he expected to have a child over to play, at his mother's insistence, it seemed as if he'd talk it over first with Alfie. These talks helped Tim prepare himself for the ordeal. After his friend went home, Tim seemed to retreat back to Alfie. His mother worried that this imaginary friend was a continuing sign of fragility on Tim's part. But it seemed to help him cope. Tim used Alfie to tell him that everything was okay, no matter what. After a talk with Alfie, Tim was often revived. He seemed to use those times to refuel.

Occasionally, Tim would bring Alfie into the conversation to bolster himself in other ways. Then, and only then could his parents understand his relationship with Alfie. "Alfie told me to put this coat on to keep warm." "You'll be too hot." "Well, I'm going to wear it anyway." Or, "Alfie told me I couldn't play with David today." "Why not?" "He just said I couldn't. No reason." "Well, we're going over to David's house." "No, I have a stomach ache." So obvious was Tim's use of Alfie as a support for what he wanted that his mother was caught. She wasn't sure whether she should push her son beyond Alfie's limits, or whether she should respect Alfie as Tim's way of telling her what was important to him. Why couldn't he be more direct with her? His need for Alfie made her feel shut out.

Mrs. McCormick could see that Tim used Alfie as a protection, but she feared that Alfie wasn't going to help Tim in the long run. Eventually, she realized that Tim's discussions with Alfie would tell her how to proceed when Tim was adapting to something new. Imaginary friends serve many purposes. At this point, Tim needed Alfie. But Mrs. McCormick could find other ways to help Tim, and ways for Tim to help himself. Mrs. McCormick could be open with Tim about some of her worries. For example, in her efforts to persuade Tim to socialize: "Tim, you know I want you to go to David's house. You know you need to learn how to play with other boys. But I guess you are telling me that you think this is too much for you right now. I was really pushing you, but I'm proud of you for standing up for what you need to do. You don't need to go this time. You'll go when you're ready." Respecting Tim when he stands up for himself may be an important way of strengthening such a quiet, shy child. Each decision could be made with this in mind. But Mrs. McCormick does need to insist that Tim learn to consider why he's not ready to make relationships. "I'm not going to make you go right now. We can work together to plan how you can feel less worried about being with other kids." She will need to be patient, but the goal must be clear to both of them.

Mrs. McCormick's own understanding of Tim's extreme sensitivity and how easily his senses or thoughts become overloaded by other, unpredictable people will help him understand himself. Tim needs to recognize what is hard for him and what isn't, so that he doesn't have to feel hopeless about everything. He can learn to spot the warning signs of sensory overload, and what his practical ways of protecting himself are. When he can take charge of his own defenses, he will be on the way to overcoming his fragility. Mrs. McCormick has been able to see that his sensory system can take in only so much information before it shuts down.

Touch, sound, and visual input can all still overload Tim, especially when he's frightened or finds himself in a new situation. If he can absorb one of these at a time, if he can predict and adjust to the input, he can manage. With a known person, he can do this. With a machine or with his toys, he can maintain control. With a noisy and unpredictable child, his senses may become confused and overwhelmed. Internally, this builds up quickly to a crisis. He must ei-

ther close down his senses completely by withdrawing, or disintegrate into a panic, a tantrum, or chaotic, aggressive flailing. The latter is less likely with his temperament; the former, shutting himself off, is his pattern.

I would urge Mrs. McCormick to recognize how this overload builds up for Tim. (See our chart, "Stimulation Overload," in Chapter 2, page 110.) If she can see how this buildup affects Tim's adjustment and mastery of his world, she can help her son watch for what sets him off and what settles him down. How effective it can be for a small child to gain such insight when he's ready for it, and how powerful it makes him feel! This will be the goal for Tim and his parents.

When should a parent worry enough about a child as fragile as Tim to seek help? If Tim were walled in, using repetitive self-stimulating or self-destructive behavior to protect himself, if he weren't beginning to come out already to try to get along with other children, I'd urge them to have him evaluated. A parent's worries serve as a guide, too: If most of a parent's thoughts about a child are anxious ones, it may be time to seek help.

Mrs. McCormick knows she has conveyed her worries to Tim. The contrast with his older brother, Philip, always reminds her of Tim's "problem personality." She wonders whether her worrying has become part of the problem. Does her apprehension confirm Tim's self-image of fragility? Perhaps. If she cannot see and support his strengths, she should seek psychiatric help. She may need it herself to help her handle her own fears for Tim. She is bound to feel fearful and even angry because she can't free Tim from his shy personality. Imaginary friends are a help, but they don't replace peer relationships. School and the necessity to be part of a group is on the horizon.

Billy's imaginary friend, Buddy, had 'come to life' as his dog-eared panda. Buddy was dirty and smelly and spit-laden. He'd been a friend for as long as Abby had been a rival. Buddy had bad dreams these days, too. He wanted Billy to sleep with him "to protect him from those bad men." When Abby had arrived, Billy had turned to Buddy and named him. "He's a he, not like Abby." Buddy could do anything Billy could do. He could climb trees, he could whistle, he could snap his fingers, he was even learning to tie his shoes. Buddy could also find things for Billy. He even found his daddy's rifle; it was on the top shelf of a closet in his parents' bedroom—hidden in a blanket. Billy was very proud of Buddy.

When Buddy told Billy about the rifle, Billy had to climb on a ladder stool to find it. He pulled it down from the shelf. It was too heavy and clattered to the ground with a crashing thud, so loud that his parents dropped their forks at the dinner table and rushed into their bedroom. "Billy, what in the hell are you doing with my rifle! Suppose it had been loaded!" Mr. Stone was stunned. Hiding the weapon hadn't been enough. Billy's only sobbing defense was "Buddy found it. I was just getting it down for him." His father was so horrified at the near catastrophe—and his own responsibility for it—that he picked Billy up to spank him. Mr. Stone was out of control.

Mr. Stone was out of control because he was feeling guilty and panicked by this close call. Guns are exciting to Billy at this age. He needs Buddy to blame for getting the gun down, and this will linger as an exciting goal for the future. Keeping a gun in the home is asking for trouble. Mr. Stone knew this. Was it so important to him that he couldn't part with it for Billy and Abby's sake? In the United States, more children are hurt in their own homes by family guns than by guns outside the home.

Sexuality   Does a biological shift occur between the ages of four and six? Why does a girl intensify her search for her mother's patterns to identify with? Why does a boy turn against his father on the surface and woo his mother in the process, and yet absorb his father's behavior, his moods, his ways of managing emotions? Gender identifications are at a peak at this age. The child's focus on this now forces parents to face the implications behind this behavior and makes it a touchpoint for parents and child.

Marcy had repeatedly asked her mother to set up a "play date" with five-year-old Charlie from her school. Mrs. Jackson knew that Marcy bragged about his being her "boyfriend." When Amos teased her about Charlie, she would get embarrassed and run away. When Mrs. Jackson called Charlie's mother to request the play date, Mrs. Cobb seemed a bit reluctant: "Charlie really doesn't like to play with girls." Mrs. Jackson laughed. "I know. I hate to push him, but I'll take them to a movie to make it fun for both of them. Marcy seems so determined to have him come." Mrs. Cobb: "Well, I do know that Charlie talks about Marcy a lot." They laughed together. "It's pretty early, isn't it? I hope it won't last."

The play date for Charlie and Marcy arrived. Marcy was in a state. She changed her dress twice. She wanted to wear her best shoes. Mrs. Jackson was amused and a bit taken aback when they picked up Charlie because he wanted to sit in the front seat away from Marcy. Nevertheless, they began to chatter together and to giggle; they obviously were having fun. They had a wonderful time. After the movie, Mrs. Jackson took them home for a snack.

As Mrs. Jackson cleaned up, Marcy and Charlie disappeared. After a while, Mrs. Jackson listened carefully to see where their voices were coming from. No sounds. She crept upstairs to Marcy's bedroom. The door was shut. She could hear faint giggles and rustles. Her first instinct was to make a noise to interrupt them. But she felt she had a responsibility she must face. She opened the door to find them half undressed and comparing their bodies. Mrs. Jackson thought she was supposed to do something, but was caught completely off guard. What should she do? Marcy immediately said, "Mommy, we're playing doctor! Charlie is the sick one and I'm fixing him!"

Playing doctor is a common game at this age. It is an understandable although potentially scary way of exploring and sharing each other's bodies—and differences. Five-year-olds are ready to face differences, to make categories, and to think about what characteristics it takes to be the same or different. Such exploration makes adults feel uneasy because it is hard for adults to look beyond their adult view of sexuality to see this from a child's perspective. The child does not think about her body, or about being naked with another child, in the same way that an adult does. This may seem obvious, but it is very hard to remember in the midst of incidents such as the one that Mrs. Jackson was faced with. Children look for concrete experiences such as playing doctor to find out what they do not know. They may play doctor with other children of the same or the opposite sex. What is the same about girls, about boys? What *is* the difference between a girl and a boy, and *why*?

Children of any age may be ready for an explanation of the difference between a penis of the boy (outside) and the vagina of the girl (inside). When they are ready, they will ask questions. A parent needs to go slowly and to listen. Go only as far as the child wants to go. There will be plenty of time ahead. Your role is to set up precedents for comfortable communication.

Parents' anxiety and prohibitive responses can be counterproductive. Children may develop a fascination with behavior that elicits dramatic reactions from their parents. Such games are more likely to be self-limited if they receive limited attention from parents.

Parents can instead indirectly prevent them from becoming a main focus by arranging play activities that don't lend themselves to doctor play; for example, trips to the park, playing ball out in the yard. Games in which a parent participates may need to replace some of the time spent in bedrooms, ostensibly in front of a computer or television screen. Parents should also watch for behavior that goes beyond the age-appropriate mutual exploration between equal peers. (See "Sexuality," in Part II.)

All of this Mrs. Jackson knew. But what should she do now? What was her responsibility to Marcy and, of course, even more frightening, to Charlie? She had to handle her own upset first. After hustling the children downstairs, she decided to call Mrs. Cobb and explain the episode to her. "Will this feel different to her because it's her son, and not a daughter?" she wondered as she dialed the number. Charlie's mother was upset, and she sounded angry at first. But then she, too, began to see and understand the normalcy of the children's behavior. Both mothers wanted time to discuss the incident with their spouses. Their main goal was to set up appropriate boundaries and to open discussion for questions from the two children. Boundaries are critical. When children cross the line, knowing the line is there stops them from going too far.

Parents who make "playing doctor" or questions about bodies into guilt-ridden experiences are likely to shove these questions and curiosity underground. The opportunity to share feelings and to explore the child's natural, healthy questions may be endangered. Talking with parents takes the exciting guilt out of the experience and brings in solid reality. Little or no evidence exists to show that the kind of mutual exploration of each other's bodies that children at this age normally engage in can damage later developmental adjustments. A child will move on as long as adults do not overreact, and as long as the child has not been exploited by other adults or by an older child. Children of this age are interested in sexual differences.

When you can accept the child-like mutual explorations of each other's bodies among five-year-old peers (clearly distinct from adult-like sexual behavior in a child), you will hear the five-year old's questions about themselves and others. You can have calm, open discussions of what is okay, but on their time, not yours. The children may have set it up for you to find out. Your real goal as a parent is to let them know that they can tell you and ask you whatever they need to, and not to say so much as to close them off. The goal can be to share information.

This is the time to discuss openly where the limits are in your family. When you discuss issues such as this, you give children the chance to identify deeply with you and your values; their learning to value their bodies and to take personal responsibility for them is the goal of these discussions. As in any other important area, this will not be accomplished quickly or easily; no one discussion will settle it. Neither will one episode of this kind of mutual exploratory behavior determine a child's future or answer all her questions.

But these issues are difficult for parents. Mrs. Jackson had her own inhibitions, memories of her own past experiences to face and digest before she could see what it was that Marcy was asking for. Any parent is threatened by this kind of sex play in a small child. "Will it go too far? Will it be repeated over and over?" If she can separate her memories from Marcy's needs, then Mrs. Jackson can use this time as an opportunity to face the normalcy of the children's behavior and to keep lines of communication open.

Children of this age ask more and more searching questions; they should be answered directly and honestly. But children also learn about sexuality from their parents' actions in the context of a loving relationship. This is just as important, maybe more so than their parents' answers to their questions. The learning begins early on, and will deepen gradually, over time.

At five, a child's focus on private parts will have much more to do with their use in the bathroom than with sexual love or reproduction. Girls may have explored themselves and wondered what their genitals are like. Boys often have done more exploring of their genitals by this age and have tested their capacity to spray the universe. One five-year-old liked to urinate outside the house and enjoyed spraying the back yard. In school one day, he saved his urine until recess so that he could show off to himself and to whomever he could attract to watch. His teacher caught on to this and tried to stop it. "Urinating and bowel movements should be private. Other kids may be embarrassed by you. I am." This boy needed the teacher's help to understand the importance of privacy: a quiet way to show self-respect and respect for others.

Masturbation is a common result of exploration. The genitals are a highly innervated, sensitive part of the body from early in life. Parents can respond with "Kids do that because it feels nice. It's a private thing to do, so save it for when you are by yourself in your room." Limits should be set on where masturbation is done, rather than on the behavior itself.

Children of this age may already have learned to protect masturbatory activity from important adults if they have learned that it is a no-no at certain times and places. They protect it by "going underground," but it is likely to surface again. I urge parents to be ready for this. Nearly all children masturbate, and they often remember later that they started at this age. Masturbation is part of a child's exploring her body and a natural extension of finding out about the importance of her genitalia. Public displays will pass if they are not reinforced with parental anxiety or negative attention.

Moral Development

Living with Angry Feelings

When Minnie was crossed, she'd say, "I hate you, Mommy. You're a poo-poo Mommy." If she had time, she'd start listing off her mother's "bad traits." "Your breath smells like the dog's." "You poop in your pants." "You're not my mommy." "I wish I could go off somewhere and live with Daddy." She rarely blew up to this extent with her father, but he could see the anger in her when she tried to hold back her feelings. For example, when an elderly lady came to visit, Minnie brazenly refused to shake her hand. "I don't want to. I don't like her face." Mr. Lee was so upset that he wanted to slap her. Holding back his anger, he said, "Minnie, I can't tolerate that kind of behavior. We're going to put you in 'time out' until you realize how rude that was." Minnie followed his directions in silent protest. Her cheeks reddened, her face pouted, her eyes glazed over. As she sat down with a thump, she mumbled to herself. Her father said, "What was that?" She said, "Nothing. You're mean." He realized that they were building up into a bigger and bigger showdown. He walked away without responding. Minnie sat in her chair, breathing deeply, her features taut. She was angry, but she accepted the time out. She had come a long way from three when sometimes it was just too hard. No more testing now of whether her father really meant it or not. No more trying to keep talking in time out as she might have done even a few months ago. She has accepted the need for discipline, and in a way, it was a relief to her to have a simple, direct way of giving up her impulses. Her father could have even seen that she recognized her own need for his help in gaining control of herself.

But when hen time out was over, Minnie's father tried to reason with her too soon. He could see that he was making little impression. When he left her after his five-minute talk, she kicked at the door. He turned around abruptly. "Minnie, what are you doing?" She stopped kicking, but her face and her body did not relax. She pulled out a stuffed doll, grabbed her dull-edged scissors from her bureau, and poked the doll open. When the stuffing began to pour out, she flung the doll across the room. As if she were deeply hurt, she threw herself across the bed. Her father heard the commotion and relented. He came back into her room and tried to comfort her, but she turned away. He noticed the cut-up doll, and it made him angry. "Why did you have to cut up your doll?" No answer. "Minnie, just because I scolded you, you took it out on your doll, didn't you?" No answer. Mr. Lee was furious and a bit frightened. What should he do? This was a time when he felt obliged to see that Minnie understood how angry he was. He felt as if he needed to continue to push his point. All of us feel frightened by such behavior and its reflection on us as parents. He must be feeling, "It's now or never. I certainly can't let her grow up so spoiled." Strong feelings such as his can't be hidden. It may be better that he express them, though he could use some time to cool off first.

Mr. Lee was really torn up about Minnie's inability to empathize with the older lady. His disappointment in her made a deep impression. Her need to please him is at a peak. Her vulnerability shows in this extreme overreaction. His pushing will work only when she's ready. But with a child like Minnie, it *is* necessary to remind her of others' needs in a social situation.

Mr. Lee would be wise to let up. He has made his point, but Minnie is still so distraught that she can't yet be reasoned with. She's also likely to feel so ashamed that she'll have a hard time acknowledging what she's done. If her father can help her save face first, she can learn from what has happened. After she's pulled herself together and has the feeling she's gotten herself under control, he could sit down with her. He could hug her and let her know that he hasn't deserted her. She might need to run around to work off her hurt. How can he know when she's ready to talk it out? He could ask her. When she is, he could talk about it with her. This way, he is giving her back some feeling of choice and responsibility. She knows by now that she's behaved insensitively. As parents, we all feel that such lack of consideration is inappropriate at any time.

How do you know when a battle is important and when it's not? Watch the child's face. His face will become tense. He watches you carefully. Even his body is tense and almost motionless, as he teases or provokes. The tension between you builds up. Then, you know it's a time to settle the tension-laden issue. Hold him, or sit down with him. "You know this is too much. You've got to stop. I know you can do it. If you need me to, I'll help." Watch his face. He'll subside and even look a bit grateful. He also may get more defiant, more agitated. That's the time to keep your own calm. "I'm waiting for you to show me you can get yourself under control." "I am." "I don't think so. I know you can do it, even if you need a little help right now." You can see the look of satisfaction on the child's face as the episode ends. You have modeled self-control for him, given back to him the controls he needs, and he knows it.

Minnie's manners will improve. She will learn most from such incidents if she's not completely overwhelmed with remorse. In addition, she will learn by modeling on those around her. When her parents and sister model sensitivity to others, she'll learn from them, too. Each incident, if handled quietly, can be an opportunity for pointing out the reasons for sensitivity and respect for others. Mr. Lee has asked Minnie to take responsibility for her actions, for her remorse, and for the reconciliation.

The complication for Mr. Lee is that he feels his daughter's "badness" is his fault. In a shaky marriage, both parents feel that any deviant behavior is due to the tension in the family. One of the dangers might be that a parent pushes a child too hard, trying to make her feel better, in order to reassure himself that the child hasn't been affected by the adults' problems. But how could Minnie not be? That would take more insensitivity than Minnie's! The other danger is that discipline goes out the window; but discipline is even more important at such a time. Letting up on discipline leaves everyone without boundaries.

From Self-awareness to Empathy

At five, a child becomes aware of the effect of his actions not simply on the responses of others, but on their feelings, too. This is the origin of responsibility, and a prerequisite for conscience. A five-year-old child becomes aware of where he must stop himself. He will cling to a more literal and inflexible version of right and wrong than an older child does. He is just beginning to understand these concepts, and knows that his ability to rein in his own urges is still tenuous. He has little room for ambiguity.

The child now sets up inhibitions in the face of powerful longings; fears and nightmares accompany the process. New concerns about why there must be war, why there are people who have no homes, will also emerge, and the five-year old may struggle mightily with the injustices that adults have failed to address. The battle cry is now "That's not fair." The five-year-old passion for fairy tales is readily explained by his need to delineate clearly the "bad" from the "good," and to be reassured that the former will be punished, the latter rewarded. The complex feelings that are roused as he faces his effect on others—his own "badness" and capacity for "good"—are tumultuous. His conscience is emerging, a remarkable achievement at any age.

Finding that he can influence peers and teachers by his behavior changes the way he views himself and others. Empathy follows when a child has a good enough self-image. At five, the child is beginning to know who "me" is, and this is changing his position in the world. The process is both exciting and demanding.

The five-year-old's developing capacity to think of himself as unique, as possessing distinct characteristics, is accompanied by a realization that other people may think about him in this way. "My teacher likes me." If he can't fit in, he knows this now. Because he can think in categories and make comparisons, he can no longer be protected from an awareness of being perceived as different. He has no choice but to try to make sense of the way other people perceive him, even though his means to understand this is limited. Already Minnie may say, "People don't like me. They think I'm too pushy." Or she may know this and not say it because she has to avoid facing what bothers her rather than allowing herself to be overwhelmed by the feelings that facing it will bring.

At five, Marcy is becoming aware of and proud of who she is. Knowing who she is means that she can say "I don't like boys" and "I really like red." It means asserting what she knows about who she is. "Mummy, I can't stand lima beans." She expects important people to know who she is, too. "Mummy, you know I hate lima beans. You know I'll throw up if you make me eat them." Marcy is defining herself.

Establishing her preferences is one way of defining herself and her personality. Marcy's parents have learned from her older brother not to run headlong into this: "Try the lima beans just this once"; or, "Try wearing your green dress, not that red one. You've had it on all week." We are ignoring this powerful thrust toward autonomy when we ride over a five-year-old's just-expressed preference. A five-year-old establishes preferences as a form of self-definition, a very important developmental effort. In the meantime, parents can reassure themselves with "Tomorrow, it will change." It helps to pull back just enough to weigh when to let up the pressure, to take advantage of opportunities to honor the child's preferences. Flavors and colors are among the harmless choices that you can leave up to the child; this helps to balance out all the times a parent must make choices for the five-year-old. A parent who finds it necessary to "control" a five-year-old in all these choices ignores the five-year-old's efforts to stand up for himself.

At first, Marcy asserted herself defiantly. She may have to be surprisingly insistent now because it is clear to her—at least intermittently—that, along with all the new things she can do, there are still so many more that she can't do. Her defiance can become frightening for her. Since she now has some sense of her impact on others, she is vulnerable to new feelings of remorse. It makes sense for Marcy's assertive clamorings to be followed by backsliding and confusion. As in other touchpoints, this disorganization, the brashness and the fears, accompanies growth and reorganization. It is a time for parents to choose their battles with care.

A child's own feelings dominated his world at two and three. At four, he was just beginning to see that other people are at stake. He saw that other people were different. By five, he begins to realize that events occur independently of his wishes and feelings. He is curious. He wonders how. He needs to know why. He possesses a natural drive to make sense out of the complexity of experiences that magical thinking can no longer account for. A child's deepening self-esteem frees him to try to explain these mysteries. He begins, for example, to look for what others might feel. It begins to matter to him how he makes them feel and what they might feel about him. Empathy is nearby. Conscience is coming.

Jerome Kagan, in his book *Three Seductive Ideas*, asserts that humans are motivated to do right and are basically moral: "The human capacity for a moral motive and its associated emotions demand that five unique (to humans) abilities coalesce: (1) to infer the thoughts and feelings of others, 2) to be self-aware, (3) to apply categories of good and bad to events and to self, (4) to reflect on past actions, and (5) to know that a particular action could have been suppressed." All these abilities are present in the five-year-old.

Discipline

With Marcy's new ability to plan and to dream came a new kind of determination. Mrs. Jackson wondered why Marcy was so persistent in challenging her. Was she spoiled? Even as her parents retreated in the face of her demands, they comforted themselves with the fact that she seemed more focused and realistic. At five, Marcy was beginning to face her own limitations, and those of her world; she could no longer readily retreat from such realizations. She still needed to work harder to tolerate her own frustration, but now she was more available to her mother's limits and could stop her tantrums when she needed to.

In kindergarten, Marcy pushed Mrs. Sosa very hard. She wanted to read. She wanted to learn how to write her name. Her mother reported the same incessant demands at home. When Mrs. Jackson wasn't responsive, Marcy would insist on doing something with her all the time. Her mother couldn't always give in, nor was she sure that she should. Marcy couldn't accept that; she wanted her mother always to be at her beck and call. Mrs. Jackson realized that Marcy seemed to be searching for something. She also realized that limits would be critical to Marcy's new independence. But she wondered how to set them without damping her exuberance. Mrs. Jackson turned to Mrs. Sosa for guidance and advice.

Mrs. Sosa was reassuring. "Marcy is a strong-minded little girl. She wants what she wants when she wants it. But when you're determined, she knows it. She is sensitive to your limit setting and is letting you know that she needs it now more than ever. This is a time when you and your husband need to go over your expectations for her—in private. Once the two of you have agreed, you won't be as likely to be caught off guard, and it will be easier to stick to your guns."

"Why is this so much harder now?"

"Because Marcy is growing up. She knows a lot more now about right and wrong, about your rules and expectations. She has become so competent at so many things. But all these accomplishments can leave her feeling—at least at times—more aware than ever of all the things a five-year-old can't do." Mrs. Sosa pointed out that Marcy knows more now about the consequences of her actions, how she might get hurt, and what she can and can't have. A four-year-old puts a towel over his shoulders and becomes Superman for an afternoon. Maybe he even thinks he can fly. This is harder for a five-year-old to believe. Now Marcy can't escape facing her frustration. This may be why Marcy is demanding her mother's presence so insistently right now.

Marcy watched other people carefully to gauge their reactions. The things she herself felt—excitement, delight, frustration, disappointment—these she could name. As she noticed how other people were feeling, and as she brought her new understanding of herself to the task of understanding them, she could begin to express how they might be feeling, too. "When I don't hug Grandma, I make her sad. So I hug her." Or, "When I tease my baby cousin, he cries. I can either tease him and make him cry, or I can leave him alone." Such choices become conscious now.

Marcy's empathy was a sign of healthy self-esteem. A child who has a sure sense of her self can afford to care about others. When other children responded to Marcy, they sensed this self-assuredness. She seemed already to be a leader.

Stealing,
Lying

Minnie had hidden her mother's valuable necklace. She had cleverly put it under all her crayons in a cookie tin. While her distraught mother was searching everywhere and scolding each member of the family for not being able to help her find it, Minnie was silent. In her own mind, silence was not equivalent to lying. (She had been reprimanded far too often for her imaginative lies.) Mrs. Lee asked her directly, "Minnie, do you know where my necklace is?" Minnie: "I saw it in your drawer yesterday." Mrs. Lee's frantic emptying of her drawer did not lead to a confession from Minnie, who managed to find a reason to leave the room. Mrs. Lee gave the necklace up as lost. But then she wondered, "Why would Minnie have been in my drawer?" She didn't want to believe that Minnie had taken it.

The next day, Mrs. Lee's beautiful new sweater disappeared. This was too much. Mrs. Lee's search turned it up in Minnie's closet, hidden under a heap of clothes. She was so shocked that she broke into tears. "Minnie, where is my necklace? You must have that, too! I can't believe you are a thief and a liar." She tried to stop herself before she went too far. "Your father and I will have to decide on your punishment. I'm too angry to begin to think about what it should be right now."

Minnie returned the necklace, holding it lovingly as she did so. She held her head high. She didn't grovel. She showed little remorse for her mother's scolding. Her mother and father were worried that this was evidence of a serious problem in their daughter. Mrs. Lee confided in a friend whose five-year-old was in Minnie's kindergarten class. "Guess what Minnie has done! She not only stole my necklace, but she hid my new sweater in her closet. She must have known I'd find it. The worst part is that she didn't even look as though she felt bad about stealing when I caught her."

To her surprise, her friend said, "Oh, my Lily has done that, too. In fact, a couple of times. When I called my pediatrician, she just tossed it off. She said that a lot of little girls steal from their mothers at this age, and a lot of boys from their fathers. She told me it had to do with trying to identify with us. I found that when I sat down and talked to Lily, she seemed relieved, although she couldn't say it. She said my things looked so pretty on me that she wanted to be like me. When she tried them on, they made her feel so little, but she was hoping that when she grows up, they'll fit her. So she kept them until I found them."

"What did your doctor say about punishment?" Mrs. Lee asked her friend. "She said I shouldn't make it so severe that Lily would feel devastated. She suggested that I talk to her, listen to her, let her know that it wasn't right to take other people's things, no matter what. But I should also let her know that I understood why she so wanted to grow up. Then her pediatrician suggested that I buy Lily some fake jewelry and some dress-up clothes. I did. She hasn't taken anything since!"

Stealing from a parent can be attributed to a powerful urge to make available a part of the parent that feels unavailable to the child. The feeling may be real or imagined. Perhaps there was also some desperation in stealing that came from being more aware of the ways Minnie could not—or could not yet—be like her mother. A five-year-old's behavior may tell a parent that giving up four-year-old fantasies is painful. At four, Minnie had the ability to control her world, in fantasy, at least. She could be just like her mother if she wanted to; all she had to do was wish. But a five-year-old can no longer fully believe in wishful thinking. Also, the power a four-year-old imagines he has to bring about all his wishes is now frightening. At five, it can be a relief, as much as a loss, to let it go. Minnie's task now is to face how far she is from being just like her mother and to begin the hard work of knowing right from wrong.

Giving way to the urge to transgress carries with it an expensive set of guilty feelings. Parental support, in the form of firm limits, helps a child face reality and learn to deal with his impulses. Knowing what is tolerated and what is not becomes a source of security to the child. I have always been amazed at the relief in a child's face when a parent says, "You simply cannot do this. I'm here to stop you." Parents may be frightened and immobilized. They may overreact so that the five-year-old is too frightened to share his reasons. Or, they may avoid the responsibility to set limits on the behavior. The latter

course leaves the child anxious, aware of his own inability to control this kind of behavior.

For any parent, stealing is a shock. They are bound to wonder who their child is becoming. When they react too violently, there is little chance for them or for the child to make the connection between the act and the motives behind it. They must reprimand the child, but an overreaction might intensify the child's withdrawal into dishonest attempts to save face. Parents who react to their child's behavior without looking for the reason behind it may be missing an opportunity to understand the child. They run the risk of fixing lying and stealing as a pattern.

In small doses, guilt is a necessary and inevitable part of learning to care about right and wrong; in large doses, it may take on a life of its own and distract the child from the job of giving up the unacceptable behavior. A rigid approach can all too easily make a child defensive and reinforce his need to cover his tracks. Parents can say instead, "I want to understand what made you feel you had to do this, but I can't let you do it. If we can talk it out, we can find ways together to help you control yourself." With this approach, a

parent needn't be afraid of reinforcing the behavior. The opportunity for the child to channel this into a budding conscience increases. I always wonder whether adults without a conscience haven't been ignored or misunderstood at this critical touchpoint. Parents should prepare for such a cry for help at this age and be ready to meet it calmly and firmly. (See also "Honesty," in Part II.)

Relationships: Building a Family

Helping

Five is a time for new responsibilities, and a recognition that the child can take a bigger role in the house and can be proud of it.

Marcy could help set the table at night. If urged, she could help take off the dishes and place them in the sink for washing. She was old enough to help. She often looked up to her older brother. If he resented helping, she did too. Family discussions often included the chores to be done. Both Mr. and Mrs. Jackson were working, so most of the household chores were left to the weekends. Trying to sort all of them out was a two-hour ordeal. Both children entered into the "game" and were willing. Each one of the family chose a chore in sequence. If you chose it, you had to have "consequences" attached to it if you didn't do it. Marcy was usually willing to help with the dishes and with cooking. Her parents had learned to cajole her with patience, and persistence.

Should a parent use an allowance as a reward? Probably not, because it won't work for long, and it can feel like a bribe. It's not the way a child is likely to develop altruism—caring about others. A five-year-old might be ready to start receiving an allowance—but for other reasons. If she is already swapping toys and trinkets with friends, she may be saying that she's ready for the new capacities an allowance can help build: counting, planning, saving up, putting away and protecting precious belongings. At this age, it helps a child begin to learn about her "own" money and the responsibility of it. But an allowance should not be allowed to interfere with the more personal satisfaction a child has in knowing that what she does to help in her house matters for its own sake.

Self-esteem and Praise

As a sense of herself develops in a five-year-old, it can go either way. Either she can develop a sense of self-esteem and self-confidence or she can form a low opinion of herself and her ability to master challenging tasks. Some children develop a mixture: high self-confidence in some areas, low in others. Some children appear to be sure of themselves, but it turns out that they are only as sure as their most recent success. A low sense of self-esteem sets up a self-fulfilling prophecy. A five-year-old who is unsure of herself and afraid of failure is all too likely to approach a task with apprehension. She may even avoid the task by making up transparent excuses. If she makes a try at the task, she sets herself up to fail and prove her self-doubts.

Minnie's facade of being "the best" is a not-so-subtle coping mechanism. A strong facade like hers may be a kind of bravado that covers up negative feelings about herself. In her case, her brash exterior is all too easily uncovered; she needs consistent support and praise to fuel her drive and her passion. These are invaluable assets, and they are already a part of who she is. These qualities can be valued without reinforcing her dependence on being the "best."

Marcy could never live up to her older brother; at least in her mind, he was always better at everything. Praise might not ring true for her unless her parents could seek ways of responding to her individuality. "What a nice way to put the breakfast tray together! You made it look so pretty." Or, "You work so hard to do what Amos does. He is able to do it one way because he's older. But you don't have to do it his way. You have your own special ways."

Five years is an important time for parents to reassess their child's self-image. The increasing awareness of themselves and their effect on others predisposes five-year-olds to this kind of self-evaluation. It can be a fragile time. Parental attitudes, reactions, or behavior with the child that conveys acceptance and encouragement will help the child believe in her potential as she contends with a new awareness of who she is, including her limitations. Respecting the child's attempts to save face and salvage self-esteem, especially since fantasies are being punctured at this age, is important too.

The most important tasks to recognize and praise are the simple day-to-day ones: "Marcy, you picked up your nightdress and put it in the closet!" "Minnie, you stopped playing long enough to come to the table when all the rest of us have come!" "Tim, I'm proud of you. You looked at Mrs. Martin's eyes when she spoke to you." Such simple tasks as dressing and learning to tie shoes become opportunities to enhance the child's positive feelings about herself. Each time parents recognize a small step, they reinforce the child's own recognition of the mastery involved.

Observing the steps that a child has taken to accomplish a task is a sure way of backing up her achievement. "I saw how you figured out that computer game. You watched for a long time. Then, when you thought you understood it, you tried it. It didn't work, but you didn't give up. Instead of rushing ahead, you watched again. On the next try, you got it! You had it all in your head." In describing the steps you saw, you are making them more consciously available for the child. In the process, she will re-live her success. She can see the steps she took toward the achievement; it has been hers, not yours. She can sense your pride, but she can also match it with her own. Eventually, the child will find her own satisfaction in what she accomplishes without depending on a parent to cheer her on.

Overpraising is a danger. When several of us studied African child development, we were struck with the low-key approval that mothers in a Western Kenya village offered their children. The five-year-olds we met there were already assuming adult tasks. They were not only competent but were proud of their ability to nurture their siblings, to cook a meal, to help in the fields for long periods. Yet we saw little evidence of adult recognition. The children were expected to perform these tasks and fulfilling them carried its own inner reward. Encouragement can come in the form of unspoken positive expectations.

As we watched the younger children, we saw them learn by modeling on an older child or by carefully observing an adult. For example, a three-year-old girl would stand and watch her mother build a fire for cooking. Other kids, playing outside, called to her, but she appeared not to hear. At one point, the child picked up fallen twigs and fed them into the fire. No apparent response from her mother, nor did the child look for one. Her actions seemed to be their own reward. At five, her sister was eager and able to build the fire herself. Where does this kind of willingness to fulfill tasks come from?

We compared these children in Kenya with a group from Cambridge, Massachusetts. We observed similar age-appropriate tasks. Mothers in the United States would lay out a task, step by step, and suggest that the child take the first step. The child would reluctantly try it. When she did, her mother said exuberantly, "You did it! Aren't you great? Now, do this or this." If she was lucky, her five-year-old might take the next step. "Wonderful! You are just great. Now, do this or this or this." We realized from the study how much we as parents in the United States rely on positive reinforcement techniques and how we use them to dominate our children's behavior. Too much praise risks diminishing the child's own realization that "I did it! I did it myself!" The inner desire to perform a task may be the most powerful motivating force of all. Without a balance between parental encouragement and internal satisfaction, our children may become overdependent on praise and less able to discover their own drive.

Since this study, I have become aware of the virtue of a middle ground. "Tim, I noticed that you made an effort to say 'hello.' Did you see her face? She loved it." Reinforce the child for her motivation. A low-keyed approval may be even more powerful than an exuberant one; it carries with it a sense of your having expected the child to be competent. The overly exuberant one says, "I'm amazed at you. I didn't expect it." Either it sounds almost condescending or it controls rather than supports the child's inner motivation.

*Turning from
One Parent to
the Other*

The attempt on the part of the child to absorb and to identify with each parent, one at a time, intensifies in the fifth year. A parent may unwittingly play a role in reinforcing these shifts—for example, by encouraging a closeness that leaves the other parent out—or may allow these shifts to follow their course.

Tim was strapped into his booster seat in the back of the car. He'd been at kindergarten all day and was tired. He was sucking his thumb. He'd found the silk label on his sweater and was rubbing it with his left hand. Dreamily, he looked off into the distance. His mother was driving. Suddenly, she stopped abruptly to avoid hitting a bicyclist. "Damn him. He crossed right in front of me!" This jolted Tim to react and he mumbled around his thumb. Mrs. McCormick said, "Stop sucking your thumb, Tim! You know I can't understand you when you have it in your mouth!" A playful look crossed Tim's face. "I was just thinking. Could I marry you?" His mother was dumfounded. "What did you say?" "I said I want to marry you and leave Daddy at home with Philip." "Whatever made you think of such a thing?" Whatever, indeed? Tim may have been trying to distract his mother from her upset reaction. This might also reflect the concern he felt when she lost her temper. His question certainly worked, and Tim may even have known it would. "Of course we can't marry each other. I'm already married to Daddy and I love him." "But he doesn't love me." "Of course he does." "Uh-uh," as he shook his head in the negative. The dreamy thumb sucking resumed, this time a bit more noisily.

Mrs. McCormick began to think of all the times Tim clung to her. She thought of the times he refused to let his dad dress him or feed him. He even winced sometimes when Mr. McCormick tried to attend to him. If his father asked Tim to go out with him, Tim would first look at his mother as if to say, "Do I have to?" He'd refuse if he could. His jokes and laughter were certainly saved for her, and she let him know how much she appreciated them. She realized how close they were, and how she'd played into it. She loved this closeness, but now she began to feel guilty. "Have I brought this on?" Of course. She knew the answer. Tim really needed his father as a model and she was aware of that, but she had such a difficult time letting Tim be closer to him.

Was Tim pushing his mother to re-examine their closeness? Perhaps. He needs more of his father, and he may know that, too. He knows he isn't as comfortable with his father as he is with his mother. He may even long for closeness with his father that would open new doors. Tim is becoming aware of where he stands with his peers. He wants to be more like other boys his age, and he doesn't know how to be. He may even hope to learn from his father.

As part of their quest to find out who they are, and who they aren't, five-year-olds must turn to the same-sex parent. Until now, Tim has been attached to his mother. But now there's a danger; if he likes her too much, he may have to face how left out his father feels. Yet he knows he needs his father because he senses the pressure not to be too much like his mother. He needs to be like his dad, even to *be* him. His need drives him to watch, watch, watch. He sops up everything about his father, and he will be gratified when he can turn to him.

For a little girl it's a different process. First, girls aren't pressed to distance themselves from their mothers. It's okay to be like her and to be close. Everyone says, "You look like your mother. Your gestures are the same, your way of taking care of everyone is the same. You are surely your mother's child." Yet girls need closeness with their fathers.

Marcy was ready for bed. She'd put on a flouncey set of pajamas. The fluffy curl at the neck of the top flattered Marcy; she imagined she looked like a princess. "Can Daddy please put me to bed?" Mrs. Jackson: "He's downstairs. I was going to read you a story." "I don't want you. I want Daddy." Mrs. Jackson felt shoved aside, but she called her husband. "Marcy wants you to put her to bed." He ran up the stairs, two at a time. "I'd love to."

Marcy was triumphant. When her father came into her room, she had him tuck her in several times. "Not here. The sheets are all messy. Move me over here." He lay down beside her to read. She snuggled closer. Unconsciously, so did he. As Marcy lay next to him, she said, "Your beard is so scratchy!" Abruptly, she jumped to another thought. "Can we go somewhere?" "Where do you want to go?" "Disneyland." "Well, maybe we all can go." "No, I mean just you and me. Mommy needs to stay here with Amos." "Marcy, I can't leave them—you know that!" "But I want you to." "I'd love to go, but for all of us to go." "Then we couldn't be married. Not with everyone else around all the time." "That's right. I'm already married to Mommy." "But why couldn't we just leave her out? She's always getting angry anyway." Exploring these dangerous territories generates raw feelings between a parent and child; their sense of how close they are at such times can be uncomfortable. For some parents, the intense longing the child expresses stirs up a confusion of feeling that may need to be understood.

For single-parent families, the child's needs are similar, and sometimes heightened. One five-year-old we know lives alone with his mother. His father visits, and his divorced parents have made friends with each other. Yet he still needs to say at times, "Mummy, I want to marry you. Couldn't we leave Daddy and the grandparents and go off together?" This seems to be such a deep-seated need that it makes me wonder what a five-year-old's notion of having one parent to herself really is. I certainly can't believe that it is about sexual feelings in the way that adults think about them. For the child, other aspects of the wished-for relationship are more important: having a parent all of one's own, being dominant enough to control her or him, being rid of outsiders—such as siblings, far-away daddies, grandparents, people on the phone.

All children want their parents totally, and must face the frustration of having less than they want. At four and five, a child also wants to be "like" each parent. At times, it is the same sex parent. At other times, as with Marcy, the child needs to explore what it would be like to have the parent of the other sex all to herself—and to be like him. Children in single-parent families work to find and take in other adults to make the balance. Adults can shy away or exploit this need in a child, or they can follow a child's lead.

In the fifth year, getting close to one parent in favor of the other is bound to occur in unmistakable episodes. The "other" parent feels excluded. For four-year-olds, it's a playful make-believe of filling one parent's shoes and having the other all to themselves. At five, it can seem more "serious," even solemn. Now the child is more aware of the feelings she's engendering. She even becomes aware of the discomfort in each parent.

Parents can become uncomfortable and even a little embarrassed by these wiles. The child gets more reaction than she anticipates. When she sits in Daddy's lap, she knows her mother will move closer. Her father will look uneasy, but at the same time he enjoys the closeness and is flattered to be chosen.

Marcy is aware that being close to Daddy calls up special feelings in her. When she teases him, she gets a thrill. When her mother gets angry, Marcy feels a sense of triumph, but also of discomfort. She needs a better solution than getting close to Daddy at the expense of closeness to Mommy. She senses her mother's feelings, and feels the need to become identified with her mother, to become more like her. Only then can she feel safe with the feelings she has for her father.

Parents and Gender Roles

A father yearns for the closeness to cuddle and be wooed by his female toddler. By four and five, this mutual pursuit of intimacy carries with it an acceptance and immediate reinforcement that is less likely to occur between a father and son. They are more comfortable teasing, poking, play-fighting. A father, even unwittingly, pushes his son to become more active, more independent, more competitive. Marcy's father would hold her in a cuddled position, crooning to her from time to time, while he would throw a ball out for his son to catch. He'd tease the son by throwing the ball so far that the boy had to run far away to catch it.

A mother, too, develops very different styles of reacting to a son and a daughter by the time they are five. She may have meant to treat them the same way, but she will inevitably recognize the impossibility of doing so. Mrs. Jackson knew she treated her daughter and son differently. Whenever Marcy was in trouble, she'd run to her mother. If her father tried to reprimand her, she'd reach back for her mother. They each responded differently to her. Mrs. Jackson realized that Marcy and Amos had different relationships with each parent. When Marcy's older brother fell down and looked to his mother for consolation, she urged him to "be brave." "Here let me kiss it. Now go on playing. Be a big boy." When Marcy fell, Mrs. Jackson held her close. When Mrs. Jackson dressed or used makeup, Marcy was there imitating her. When Marcy made a gentle, sensitive remark, her mother's whole body would soften, her eyes turning approvingly toward Marcy. The same remark from Amos would meet with an unintentionally quizzical glance that was hardly reinforcing. When Amos sat on his mother's lap, she would pat him or jostle him. She hugged him, but not the way she cuddled Marcy.

Mrs. Jackson wanted more flexible gender roles for her children's generation. But it was only natural that she brought the patterns of her own childhood to her interactions with her children. It was only natural that she responded to and reinforced inherent differences. By the time a child is five, these differences are evident, and the influences on the child are both spoken and unspoken.

Separation and Independence

Standing Up to Teasing

Parents are no longer the only source of self-esteem for five-year-olds. Outside influences can easily endanger it at this age. This is also a time when parents are less able to protect children from such negative influences on self-esteem as racism, sexism, and class prejudice which are all around us. Five-year-olds tease each other about any differences they notice. We cannot protect our children from negative influences all the time, but sometimes we can and must. When a child is five, however, this will be at the expense of the child's belief that he can learn to protect himself. Maybe the best we can do for him is not to try to shield him but to share his pain. Even if he can't adequately protect himself yet, he needs help in holding on to hope that someday he will.

One of the boys in his kindergarten class began to tease Billy. "Come on Billy! You're a sissy! You don't like to fight. Fight me."

Billy looked at the boy to see whether he really meant it. He did. Billy wasn't a fighter. He didn't know how to fight and he knew it. He tried to divert his bullying friend. "You're teasing me and I don't like it." "See, you're a sissy. You don't want to fight." Billy tried to gather his courage. He put up his fists; he wished for his sword. At last he got up the courage to put his arms around the boy to wrestle. When the bully threw Billy to the ground, he began to cry. That just fueled the aggressor, who then pinned Billy more firmly to the ground.

Billy was devastated. The bounce went out of his gait. His head hung. He couldn't like himself. In fact, he was being harder on himself than he was toward the other child -who'd already forgotten all about their tussle. Mr. and Mrs. Stone couldn't understand it. They noticed that Billy winced when his buddies engaged in aggressive play. He now avoided play that had been a sure thing before. They saw that their son cowered rather than led. What should they do?

Billy had seemed to be sure of himself until now. He had always been cheerful in almost every situation. He was a leader at school. When he ran into an obstructive peer, he'd work to win him over. Billy's sensitivity toward others was a mark of his self-esteem. His "hunger" for relationships with his peers was another major asset: Billy was truly gregarious. He showed little competitiveness to interfere with his sociability. But when he failed, when someone rejected him, his parents could see how fragile his sense of himself still was.

This was a time for Mr. and Mrs. Stone to listen to how badly their son felt and then to let him know he'd been heard, and to back him up in all sorts of ways. When he nurtured Abby, let him know it. If Billy's father played a major role now, he would add another dimension to Mr. Stone's efforts. On their excursions, he could help Billy uncover the hurt he'd felt. The hurt had been the result of his not being accepted, of his being unable to win over the aggressor. The teasing had made him feel vulnerable in a way he'd not been used to. It was time for his father and stepfather to reinforce him for all the skills he did possess—whistling, finger snapping, tying shoes, and swimming without his water wings. Then, with Billy's permission and cooperation, his father (and stepfather) could begin to help Billy build skills in self-defense.

No one likes the fact that our world is one in which children must know how to defend themselves, to be aggressive when necessary. But it is. This may be a time when a new set of skills, such as karate, aikido, wrestling, or any new physical prowess, can help. These activities have a symbolic value as well. With these skills, Billy would learn about fair play and the abuse of power. A child who knows his worth, who is confident that he deserves to protect himself and can do so should not have to use violence to prove it to himself or anyone else.

Five is an age when children tease each other, when they tend to search for any vulnerability and try to magnify it. Rather than trying to minimize the hurt when the child comes home in tears, a parent can acknowledge the child's suffering. "It's very hard, isn't it? I remember at your age how I felt when they teased me. I wanted to fight, I was so angry. But I knew they'd beat me. I wanted to stay home forever. But I couldn't. I realized that everyone gets teased. It's just a matter of who can take it and who can't. I had to learn how to take it because I'm the same as you." "But I hate them. They're so mean. They make me cry." "But you know that crying is just what they want." "I know." "Can you think of a way to tease back?" "It wouldn't help. They'd go on teasing me." "Probably. But can't you see that by letting it get to you you're giving them exactly what they want? And that's only going to encourage them to keep on teasing." As a parent, you are able to listen to your child and to share the anguish of learning how to adapt to a relentless world. Maybe you and he can find strategies for coping, for self-protection; or maybe not. But at least he knows that he can come to you with his pain, and that when he shares it with you his load will be lighter.

Belonging to Kindergarten

Many children have already had years of interaction with each other in childcare—but peers play a new role now. As more complex thinking patterns develop, five-year-olds want to practice and explore them with each other. "Let's play school" is a universal game in which children use their new capacity to make comparisons and to apply general principles to new situations. How does real school work? Does it work the same way as home? At home, a sure way to get approval is to say, "Mommy, can I help set the table? Can I help you?" Kindergarten has its own rules, roles, and routines. Kindergarten is marked by bids for the teacher's permission. "What shall I draw? How much marker do I use?" "Teach me" underlies this. Five-year-olds are ready for rules—and for directions.

Following rules is a proud part of a five-year-old kindergartner's day. He knows the routines. Each day should be alike in its structure. Children count on each other to follow the structure. On one day, a few children might be out of sorts and unable to follow rules. Rules can feel like a heavy weight—or even a criticism—at times like these, even though they may be more necessary than ever. The other children organize those who can't comply. Being part of the organized structure is important in itself. The leaders in the group want to see to it that the group conforms. Children are learning structure and the expectations of "real school." It surprises adults to see how much rules matter to children of five.

Are they leaving something behind, losing forever a certain innocence, a more magical world, when they take on these rules for themselves? As children struggle to meet the new requirements, they are showing us the cost as they stretch to fit in. Parents, too, may feel torn between protecting the child's earlier freedom from conformism on the one hand and helping the child accept the necessity of yielding to rules for the sake of the group—and its ultimate rewards—on the other. A touchpoint emerges here in the changes that come with adjusting to kindergarten; often there is struggle and turmoil before the step is taken.

Marcy was proud of her role in school. Mrs. Sosa liked her. She liked Marcy's outgoing smile and her eagerness to lead the others into the activities the teachers set out. Marcy would call out, "Tommy, get back in line! We're marching"; or "Come on, Alice, sit in a ring. It's time for show-and-tell. You'll like it. Don't worry." She almost seemed too directive at times, like teacher's little helper. But Mrs. Sosa realized that Marcy loved the structure of school, the chance to identify herself with her teachers. She loved their approval, and she liked being a leader.

When art time came along, each child worried about his production. By watching closely, one could see children comparing their drawings to those of the children near them. Not only were they more critical of their own productions but they were aware of who was best. When Mrs. Sosa asked them to critique their own drawings, they were amazingly good at it. Minnie would say, "I can't really draw a face. Marcy can. She makes nice eyes and hair. I wish I could. Maybe if I watch her enough, I can do it sometime. Look! My face is all yucky. I'm no good at it." A five-year-old is already aware of his skills in relation to others and is becoming self-critical. Most disturbing to adults, they see things as black or white. "I'm no good at it," from Minnie would automatically draw a reassurance from Mrs. Sosa or her mother. "Oh, Minnie, you are. Look at the ears you drew. And five fingers! That's a real achievement." But Minnie would feel the praise was hollow. She has set her goals high. You are either very good—or you're not. Nothing in between.

When Mrs. Sosa sat the five-year-olds down to read to them, they fidgeted, they bumped each other, they picked at each other. Then, when she started to read, they became absorbed. If she read an old familiar story, they mouthed the words. Many of them could recite it with her—and they did. If she asked for cooperation, they all joined in at the right times. When she asked them to read the words, many were able to read some of the simple words. Although they were able to read a few words in a sentence, most were unable to track a whole sentence. Mrs. Sosa would point to one word after another to lead them across the page. She watched to see who could settle in, focus, join the group, hold back on his impulses, and ignore distractions long enough to follow along. These qualities, as well as the children's negotiations with their peers, would help Mrs. Sosa decide who would be ready to move on to first grade and who might profit from another year of kindergarten.

A few children were in the classroom clamoring for "more to do." The student teacher, Miss Pierce, was with them, and as they built up to a louder and louder pitch, she seemed overwhelmed. As a last resort, she handed out sheets of paper and crayons.

When Marcy took the red crayon in her left hand, her fingers closed around it clumsily. She realized that she couldn't manipulate the crayon with this hand. She transferred it to the right hand and crouched on the floor to draw. Intently, she drew a head, eyes, mouth, and even a nose. She mumbled "crooked" when she drew the nose. With Miss Pierce's encouragement, she drew stick lines for a body, legs, arms, fingers, and feet. "Marcy, you're a real artist!" Marcy was encouraged and finished her picture way ahead of the other children. Proudly, she held it up to be admired.

Miss Pierce said, "Now, Marcy, name your picture so that we will all know who it is." Marcy winced. She closed one eye and held the crayon awkwardly again, all her fingers clenched around it. "Miss Pierce, tell me what to write." "Anything you want." "Marcy, I can't read that," Miss Pierce said rather disdainfully when Marcy had finished. Marcy had reversed several letters and spelled the word "gurl." Billy was sitting next to Marcy. He sensed Marcy's feelings as she collapsed. He shot up his hand. "I know what she wrote. It says 'girl'!" Marcy revived. She nodded vigorously and looked at Willie with gratitude and admiration.

Marcy and Billy had demonstrated the many accomplishments observable in a five-year-old child:

1. Eagerness to capture all the elements of a person the child can visualize.
2. Dependence on the positive reinforcement of the teacher's praise.
3. Retreat into clumsiness when the child is faced with a new skill such as writing letters.
4. Instead of naming a friend or a loved one, a child may use a simple term such as "girl."
5. The reversal of letters so characteristic of this age, as is phonetic spelling.
6. The ability to read another child's reversals and the attempt to rescue a peer from an adult's scorn and pressure to correct reversals. This can be seen as demonstrative of a strong self-image and the altruism that develops when a child has self-esteem.

Writing was an exciting activity. Tim could print almost anything dictated to him—one word at a time. His capacity to sound out a word and write it was advanced. The other children knew this and were in awe of it. Marcy: "Let Tim write on the board. He knows how. I'm always wrong." When Marcy drew an *F,* it came out backwards. She recognized the mistake when it was pointed out to her, but she couldn't correct it in advance. Afterwards, she'd say, "I'm no good at letters. I always get them wrong." Mrs. Sosa assured her mother that these reversals were common and would correct themselves in time. It was obvious that Marcy wanted to correct them herself. Adding pressure to correct them was unnecessary and would only make her feel worse about herself. Mrs. Sosa assured Marcy: "Lots of times you print your letters properly, Marcy. I think it just makes you scared when you make a mistake. Everyone does. That's what schools like ours are for. So you can make mistakes, then learn how to correct them. See what you just did. You wrote 'Marcy' without a single mistake!"

When Tim was asked to stand up and figure out a solution to a problem in a story about a cow, he was speechless and embarrassed.

The other children sensed his embarrassment. They encouraged him. "Don't be shy, Timmy. You're the smartest. You can do it." Tim would figure out a problem by talking through each stage of his thinking:

> *The cow was in the field.*
> *Someone had to go catch him.*
> *But one wouldn't be enough 'cause he'd*
> *   run away.*
> *Two people would go.*
> *Finally, the cow would move.*
> *If they weren't careful, he'd move the*
> *   wrong way.*
> *If they finally got him going, he'd go*
> *   through the gate.*
> *Then, he'd be in his pen.*
> *Then, you could milk him.*

The other children would hang on every word as they nodded their approval. When Tim finally found the solution and got "him" in to be milked, they were all relieved. They all felt a sense of accomplishment together.

For these five-year-olds in kindergarten, a sense of belonging and of responsibility for each other were recurrent and dominant themes. These children cared about each other and where they fit with each other. They were ready for "real school."

4

SIX YEARS OLD

Entering the Real World

The First Day of First Grade

The schoolyard was buzzing. Parents' cars were parked for blocks. Lines of first-grade children and parents formed outside the school entrance. Older children had to press by them to get to their classes. Some were scornful of the "babies entering first grade." A few were tenderly nurturing, leaning down from their increased height to say hello to the excited first-graders. Older siblings, such as Tim's brother, Philip, tried to ignore their families. Philip raced ahead to his classroom without a good-bye to his mother, as if he were embarrassed by the way she and Tim clung together.

Tim held tightly onto his mother's hand, often cradling it with both of his. His eyes were huge as he watched everyone around him. He jumped or cringed slightly with each new sound. The noise and confusion were overwhelming for Tim, who had no choice but to take it all in.

May and Minnie came next in line. May was reluctant to leave her mother's side. Minnie demonstrated her independence by running off, and May had to retrieve her twice. Mrs. Lee's calls went unheeded. Minnie raced to the swings. May called after her, "Minnie! Come with me. It's time for you to go to real school like me." Minnie seemed to stop her activity at the word "real." She rejoined her mother and sister in line. Mrs. Lee was already exhausted.

On the way to school, Marcy gasped, "Mommy, we didn't get any flowers to bring to Mrs. Simmons. I wanted to bring her a present for the first day." She and her mother turned around. They chose eight roses from their garden for her new teacher. When they arrived at school, they found that others had also brought offerings. Marcy thought her roses paled when she saw the florist's bouquets. But Mrs. Simmons was grateful. "Oh, Marcy, I am flattered. Your roses will make us all feel as if we were sitting in your garden for class today. Thank you."

Mrs. Jackson lingered at the entrance to the classroom. Should she stay—or should she go? With Marcy's brother, there'd been no choice. He'd been so anxious that she knew she was needed. She'd stayed late for several days. But with Marcy, she wasn't sure. She leaned down to whisper to Marcy. As if she anticipated the question, Marcy said, "You can go, Mommy. I'm okay." Mrs. Jackson felt both pride and sorrow. She glanced around at the other parents who were staying because they felt needed. Just as many seemed to be rushing off to their jobs. Mrs. Jackson felt a hollowness. One of the other parents who were leaving fell into step beside her. "I hate having to leave my Jamie. I know he doesn't need me. Mrs. Simmons has already won him over. But somehow I still wanted to stay." Mrs. Jackson sighed and agreed wholeheartedly.

Billy could hardly sleep the night before. He was out of bed over and over. "I need some water." "I need to go pee-pee." "Please one last kiss good night." "You're making so much noise talking that I can't sleep." Finally, his mother found a solution. She lay down on Billy's bed beside him. They exchanged a few quiet sentences. "You are just so excited, aren't you?" "Uh-huh." "Do you think it will be very different from kindergarten?" "Uh-huh." "In what way, Billy?" "Just grown-er up." Soon, he had relaxed and fallen asleep.

The next morning, he was up and around very early. "What will you wear?" "All my school clothes." "But we got you several things." "The sneakers and the long pants are all I need." "Which shirt?" "I don't care. But I want my school sneakers. Everyone will have them."

He ran from front door to back door in anticipation of the "time to leave." He was so excited that two-year-old Abby picked up on it.

She was fretful. She threw her food. She smeared her hair with her oatmeal mush. She had a tantrum. The excitement of Billy's big day was a lot for her to handle, and Billy sensed it. "Abby's as excited as me. Do we have to take her to *my* school? The other kids don't all have babies." Mrs. Stone saw the worry and the excitement, and thought he might need some time alone with his parents. She said, "You know, I think for the first day of school it would be nice for just you and me and Daddy to go. I don't think Abby will mind if we drop her off at daycare a little early today." Billy's face glowed. "Abby can see my new school when she's big enough. Maybe one day when her hair has no cereal in it."

Billy skipped to school. Skipping was a recent accomplishment that had already become automatic in moments of excitement. He loved the exhilarating feeling it gave him. His mother sensed that this was part of the glow of the first day of school. He'd skip out ahead, and skip back to her as she walked more slowly. When they met Tim at the corner, Billy grabbed him by the shoulders and jumped up and down. "We're going to be together. We're school-mates." His mother was moved by the simple and straightforward way he offered his friendship. Mrs. McCormick said, "Timmy adores Billy. He said, 'Guess what, Mommy. Today I'm going to see Billy in my class. He's my best friend.' I can't tell you how glad it makes me to know that Billy will be in Timmy's class." Billy skipped ahead, pulling Timmy along behind him toward school.

At the main door, the crowds of returning children made it particularly difficult for Billy and Mr. and Mrs. Stone to stay together. Billy shot out ahead of them. Then, he stopped, suddenly realizing he'd left them behind. When they caught up to him, Mrs. Stone asked, "Were you scared you were lost?" "No. I thought you were lost. Do you know the way to my class?"

Mrs. Simmons stood at the door to the classroom and greeted each new arrival. Billy exuberantly rushed up to her, clasped her legs in a bear hug. When she instinctively stiffened, he let go. Quizzically, he looked up into her face. Her warm smile reassured him. Just as instinctively, she responded to Billy's sensitivity.

"Billy, I'm *so* glad to see you!" "Me, too. My mommy and daddy came, too! Without Abby." Mrs. Simmons: "This is indeed a special occasion. Maybe your mom and dad will stay for a while and watch us start our class." Billy looked at his parents seriously as if to sort out whether they should stay or not. When they agreed, Billy danced around. "You can see my whole room!" Mrs. Simmons said, "Everyone's cubby is marked with their name. Can you recognize yours, Billy?" "Oh, yes, I can read lots of things."

Billy found his name quickly and stowed his school things with more care than his parents were accustomed to. Taking his parents by the hand, he led them over to a clutch of other parents. He announced to them all, "I'm Billy. And this is my mommy and daddy!" After depositing his parents in their chairs, he took off. He ran from one child to another, greeting each one joyously. Several of the boys he hugged. No girls. He treated the girls with more distance than before.

The schoolroom bustled with activity and gaiety. Each child who knew another screeched out his or her name and rushed over. The whole room rocked with excitement. Billy yelled at his friends, finally finding Timmy again in one corner of the room, as if he were trying to retreat. Billy's face lit up. He danced over to Tim, reaching out as if to hug him. Timmy withdrew slightly. Billy sensed this, but wasn't ready to give up. As he began to greet Tim, he quickly dropped his voice, as if he recognized how easily Tim might be overwhelmed. He almost whispered, but he leaned his bright face toward Tim. Tim withdrew a bit, but as Billy whispered, "Timmy, we're in the same class! We can be friends," Tim's face brightened and his whole body relaxed. He was able to say, "Oh! Good, Billy." He turned to his mother to ask her to hand him his beloved blanket, which he wanted to share with Billy. But it was too late. As he turned back, Billy had skipped away to other friends.

No matter how much experience a child has had—in daycare, in preschool, and in kindergarten—first grade is a major step. Many elementary schools even physically separate their kindergartens so that there truly is a new threshold to cross into first grade. In the child's mind, it is the big step of entering "real school" where all the older children are. "Now I'm really growing up." All the dreams of being like them are coming true. "Maybe now I can become part of that world, and learn all the rules. Maybe now I can talk, read, and laugh about everything that they do. Maybe now I can understand the big kids and they will understand me. Now I'm a big kid too!"

For parents, too, first grade is a milepost, a beginning. Their child is entering the "real world." She will be labeled. She will be assessed. She will be exposed to influences over which parents have little control. A teacher becomes a powerful presence in new ways in the child's life. Beyond the teacher's task of nurturing cognitive growth, he or she will be able to influence the emotional development and values of the child. Her teacher will become the ultimate authority on a variety of matters, which had previously been just between parent and child. "Mrs. Simmons says that if you yell too much, you'll get a sore throat!" Your child is no longer just yours. She belongs to the world in a new way. Will that world like her? Will it see her lovely traits and talents—or just her weaknesses? Parents' feelings of having to share their child, of giving her up to others, deepen with first grade.

This is a touchpoint. There is bound to be the regression that accompanies any major step. During the preschool years, the child has been showing a passionate hunger for learning. Knowing this, parents sense how important it will be for her to enter a world where learning is the whole purpose. She may sense their worries: Will she learn to read? Will she make friends? Will the teacher like her? When she regresses during this step, when she pays the price by becoming exhausted and disintegrated at home, parents can be ready to expect it. Nevertheless, it is one more reminder of how they must share her with the larger world, and how hard she will work to belong.

First grade and "real school" are a rite of passage in our society. Even though preschool and kindergarten have been loaded with learning curricula, there is a change in expectations with first grade. Everyone assumes that children must now learn to work. Play is no longer enough. Even though parents have recognized their child's hunger for learning and the fact that she is proud to be big enough for "real work," they wonder "Is she ready?" They can no longer protect her from the expectations of others, nor can they do for her what she needs to do by herself. They are bound to fear the threat of a teacher's label, but at the same time they fervently hope that the teacher will recognize their child's special gifts. To handle these feelings, a first-grade teacher needs to be warm, hopeful, encouraging, and accepting. At this crucial time, teachers must balance their relationship with each child with sensitivity to each parent's feelings.

One of the most serious blows to American education has been the loss of parent involvement. Many parents, for various reasons, in-

cluding increasing work pressures, have stepped back from their children's education. Schools—willingly or not—now often find themselves educating children without a strong partnership with parents. From that distance, parents are left feeling guilty and empty-handed.

When a school seems to say, "Leave it to us," this accentuates a parent's reluctance to "interfere" or to appear too "hovering." Parents know that "too much" involvement isn't in the child's interest. Busy teachers—whose expertise and commitment must be respected by parents if their children are to be successfully educated—can become overburdened with excessive parental involvement, with a feeling of being watched critically. Yet children do need to feel that their parents care and also support their teachers. Schools need to define roles for parental involvement, and create opportunities for parents and teachers to collaborate; otherwise, only the most confident, experienced parents are likely to participate.

There is a deeper, and often unconscious, reason why parents and teachers may not communicate easily: gatekeeping. Gatekeeping occurs between two parents, but is also an inevitable and natural reaction on the part of parents and teachers. All adults who care about a child are in competition for that child. Unless parents and teachers can understand the competitive feelings, and unless they recognize and value each others' efforts, competition can turn into an interfering dynamic. Jealous competition is not necessary. All these adults are striving for the same end: the child's optimal development. However, each adult is likely to blame the other for any deviation in the child's behavior. No child is perfect. No parent is perfect. No teacher is perfect. Intense caring, which can lead to pressure and then to regression in the child's behavior, can easily be seen as a threat coming from the other party. Parents and teachers who value each others' efforts can move past competition for the child's sake. Teachers who value the passion in parents can enlist them to support the school and the child. If parents and teachers can speak freely about their feelings of commitment and competition, they can better serve the child's interests.

Parent-teacher associations may have lost some of their vigor today, but they were founded on a wonderful concept: teamwork between parents and teachers is surely the most important support a child can have. Children respond to parents' excitement about their learning. It is critical that parents be involved in their children's education, to show that education is a priority for them. Parents can work closely with schools to monitor how things are going, stimulate student effort, and help out where needed and appropriate. Children whose parents are involved in their schools will perform better academically, participate more in extracurricular activities, and have fewer behavioral problems. For all these reasons, involved parents need and deserve recognition from schools. Encouragement of parental involvement is particularly important for parents who may feel uncomfortable because of a lack of facility with the English language, or because their own schooling was limited. A common complaint of grade-school teachers today is that they are too often deserted. They must play the roles of social worker and child psychiatrist as well as teacher. Naturally, they feel overwhelmed because they are untrained for the additional roles. It is time for parents and teachers to work in mutually supportive ways—in the child's best interest. I urge parents to try hard to develop a relationship with their child's first-grade teacher, and with every teacher thereafter. Having a teacher over for dinner to meet the family, or taking her a simple present from time to time are among the ways to express appreciation.

Parents who feel guilty when they work long hours and leave care to others may rationalize their guilt by overestimating their children's readiness for independence. Staying involved in a child's school sends an important message to the child, and to the teachers. Understanding the dynamic of gatekeeping and the pressures that

overwhelm teachers with responsibility, will help parents participate thoughtfully in their child's education.

Temperament

An Active Child

Minnie was in a constant state of frenzy about going to "real"
school. She had been especially difficult lately. She fell apart easily.
She had temper tantrums similar to those of her three-year-old days.
They left her parents just as exhausted as they had been at that time.
Her clamoring demands for attention struck them as manipulative,
but these demands were also new. She'd never shown so much interest in a response from them before. They both recognized her increased need for them and felt drained. But her new questions intrigued them. Did Minnie really want to know everything, or was it
her bid to find her way to center stage? Her sister, May, thought the
latter, but her parents were less sure.

I think Minnie was desperately trying to switch her insatiable curiosity from the motor sphere into the world of ideas. She now wanted not just to explore but to "know" why and how. She needed her parents' attention to her questions as reassurance that she could make the shift that some children make earlier, and that others, less wrapped up in motor activity, barely need to make at all. She was also becoming more aware of herself, including her aggressive feelings and the hurts she suffered from others. With this came a realization of her own vulnerability. She needed her parents' acceptance to feel secure as she discovered new dangers and risks. "Could the sky really fall on me?" She still needs her magical thinking to help ask these questions, but she needs reassurance that the reality is not so fearful.

During this time, she found it hard to sleep. If Mrs. Lee heard her and got up to check, Minnie would apologize. "Mommy, I just couldn't sleep. I had bad dreams." Mrs. Lee would put her back to bed and rub her back to comfort her. On one occasion, she even began to sing a bedtime lullaby. Then she worried that she and Minnie were regressing to an earlier stage. But Minnie loved it. Her muscles relaxed. Her face softened. The worried expression was replaced by a mesmerized look of pleasure. Mrs. Lee felt relieved and wondered why she didn't do this more often. Why hadn't she recognized that Minnie needed more of her right now? Maybe she'd reacted too strongly, pulled back too far when Minnie sought her father first. She and Minnie both felt as though they were being given another chance at something they'd missed with all Minnie's new achievements. Mrs. Lee realized that she need not worry about Minnie's regressing right now. It was part of growing up.

This newly revealed sensitivity in a child who had been so intense and so driving that she barely seemed to notice anyone around her made for a period of real readjustment for her parents. They no longer recognized Minnie as the child they'd known. Her sensitivity made her more appealing to them, but it also unsettled them. Minnie felt unsettled by the changes too. She, and they, would have to reorganize as she began to use her growing cognitive skills and let up on her customary motor activity.

Minnie was changing, but she was still Minnie. She fumbled. She dropped things. She squirmed at the table. She challenged more than she cooperated. Yet her face had changed. Mrs. Lee noticed that she looked older. She was still her bubbly self when she was out in public, but, at home, she was more serious, more thoughtful, even preoccupied.

Mrs. Lee was reassured when she saw that Minnie could put on such a good face and pull herself together when they were with others. She could see that this was Minnie's way of preparing herself for a big new step. Minnie saw first grade as a major social opportunity: "I will have a whole room full of friends." Her eyes glowed when she heard from other children about the recesses and the sports. She was already a Saturday soccer team star. She'd watched the games on the playground—soccer, dodge ball, baseball—through the fence for a long time. She loved challenges, and she knew school would be full of them.

For Minnie, so full of unbridled energy, fitting into the routines of school will be difficult. In class, she will have to sit still, conform to lines of marching children, and take directions about every activity, usually paced to accommodate other, slower children's needs. She will have to obey rules she hasn't heard of before. She will not be able to think of "me first." Too many others will have demands that must be met as well.

Mrs. Lee had visited the school and introduced herself to Mrs. Simmons. She felt an urge to warn the teacher that she'd always found Minnie a handful, even a difficult child, and to share her confusion about how Minnie was changing. At this early point in the school year, most parents concentrate on defending their child against the new teacher's scrutiny because they want the teacher to like their child. Mrs. Lee was caught between wanting Mrs. Simmons to know as much about Minnie as possible, and worrying about labeling Minnie in her eyes before Minnie had a chance to show her strong points. Mrs. Lee longed for an ally, perhaps more than she realized.

As a result, when she and Mrs. Simmons had their talk, she blurted out such things as, "Minnie's so self-centered. She never listens. She never has. Even as a baby, I couldn't understand her. I sort of knew where I stood with her, though. Minnie was in control of me from the first." Mrs. Simmons detected a plea for help in Mrs. Lee's confessions, but she wasn't sure how to interpret it. Was this a mother who was overwhelmed, or who basically rejected this child she described? Was Minnie going to be as difficult as her mother predicted? Mrs. Simmons found she was already protective of Minnie before she met her. She felt critical of Mrs. Lee. She knew Minnie was probably active and tense. Was she spoiled, or was she wired to an overactive engine?

Identifying Hyperactivity

Mrs. Simmons had taught many children like Minnie before. She both dreaded and felt challenged by Mrs. Lee's description of Minnie's behavior. Such children certainly took time away from the others. She wondered whether Minnie was hyperactive. If children were truly hyperactive, driven and insensitive, they were difficult to teach. But if Minnie was sensitive to others, yet active and tense, Mrs. Simmons wouldn't be daunted. She'd faced other such children and had won them over so that she could work successfully with them. She was eager to meet Minnie.

When Minnie entered the room in her usual whirl, Mrs. Simmons noted the lean-forward gait, the propulsion behind her activity. She watched for jerkiness of her limbs, for any unsteadiness or shakiness, for overshooting as she reached for a toy. These are called "soft neurological signs" and may accompany the behavior of driven, hyperactive children. (Mrs. Simmons had become some-thing of an expert on the signs of hyperactivity because one of her own children, now grown, had been hyperactive.) If these signs are present, they suggest an immaturity in the central nervous system characteristic of a truly attentionally disordered hyperactive (ADHD) child. (See "Attention Deficit Hyperactivity Disorder," in Part II.)

If you clap your hands, a child with ADHD will automatically re-spond to the sound. Continue to clap and he might continue to re-spond. Any sudden bright light would demand a response. Hyperac-tive children are at the mercy of visual, auditory, tactile stimuli. They can't maintain attention because external stimuli can't be shut out. The accompanying, almost constant activity may be the child's way of managing sensory overload; or it may be independent and reflect a poorly organized, all-too-easily-stimulated motor nervous system that must keep moving. Which was the case with Minnie? An attuned observer, Mrs. Simmons would be able to make the dis-tinction.

Minnie, however, had neither problem. She was active, but she could take in everything around her. She could pay attention to other children—and to the adults around her—even if she often didn't. She was no longer as driven as she'd been a year or so ago. The wound-up and wired quality she'd displayed at four was less pervasive now, and more under her control. She was easily caught up by activity around her and all too easily fell in with it, but it usu-ally seemed to serve a "fun" purpose. In contrast to an attentionally disordered child, she could shut out such distractions to concentrate on a task.

Mrs. Simmons tested this by giving her a puzzle to complete; then she clapped her hands. Not even a blink from Minnie. As a fur-ther test, Mrs. Simmons talked loudly to another child. Minnie never looked up. Mrs. Simmons moved around the table noisily, but Minnie concentrated on the puzzle through it all. Minnie had shown her ability to control sensory overload, behavior that was not typical of a truly hypersensitive, hyperactive child. Reassuringly, there was no evidence of unsteadiness or imprecise movements of Minnie's hands or legs. Bursting with energy, she ran into things, but she could avoid them if she was concentrating. Minnie's activity had a heedless quality, one of "I want to get there—no matter what."

*Calming an
Active Child*

Mrs. Simmons knew how to begin working with Minnie. First, she must woo her; then she could enlist Minnie's help in pacing the other children. "Minnie, you can do everything so well. But when you go so fast, everyone else gets confused and tries to keep up with you. You could help the other kids in the class if you would concentrate on slowing down. Will you try? I'll tell you what. Try to imitate the slower way I walk and do things." Minnie was so taken with Mrs. Simmons' appreciation of her that she tried to do anything her teacher asked—including slowing down. Wanting to please is a powerful motivator. Even with plenty of motivation, though, Minnie couldn't always rein in her high energy when she needed to.

Sitting at her desk, Minnie was still in motion. She was always slipping out of her chair, kicking the desk with her feet, fingering her clothes, her face, her hands. When she was allowed to move around, her face lit up. She giggled, teased, appealed to other children to join her. She shot up her hand at every question. At any slip, she giggled loudly. Her intensity affected the whole class.

Minnie was by no means the only active child in the classroom. First grade is a busy place. Many six-year-old children learn "on their feet." Schools find it hard to meet the need for periods of high activity and exercise as demands increase and resources dwindle. Children eventually need to learn how to channel their gross motor energy; those who are not yet ready and are pushed too far too soon, however, may be lost if we cannot meet them half way.

Minnie's energy and demands often distracted Mrs. Simmons and left her exhausted. She needed time to think about the other children as well. Minnie was not the only needy child.

An ideal classroom presents ways to help children channel energy into constructive pursuits. In the chapter on four-year-olds, we described the buildup and discharge of tension in an active child. As children build up to a peak of frustration and of agitation, they can find opportunities to turn inward and to master the peak. Minnie may need to gain insight into the means within her to control herself. As she builds up to frenzied activity, can she become aware of her strong impulse to move around? Can she prevent herself from disrupting the rest of the class? Can she find a way of channeling her energy—drawing a picture, doodling, practicing her letters?

There are times when only activity will work. Can she put up her hand to go to the bathroom? If she can, Mrs. Simmons could comment on her attempt—"Minnie, I'm glad you asked instead of jumping up." Periodically, Minnie could be sent out on an errand or given a task—to take the attendance book to the principal's office, to sharpen pencils for the class, or to hand papers out. Mrs. Simmons might then look for an opportunity to point out to Minnie how these activities helped her settle down. Minnie would begin to see the value of these outlets. She needs to understand herself and to develop techniques for mastering her need for activity.

The pride and approval of adults are a critical mirror to a child's success. However, these can be overpowering and can feel like pressure for a child as active as Minnie. Minnie's goal should be to recognize success in herself. Eventually, she will need to be less reliant on others' praise and instead be able to find approval within herself. These are major achievements—too much for a six-year-old to master, but important long-term goals. First grade is the time to start.

The relationship between Minnie and her teacher is the first step toward success. Fortunately, Mrs. Simmons liked Minnie and Minnie knew this. A child as active and driving as Minnie is often not a favorite. Minnie wears her mother out. She has learned to expect negative reactions from people around her. When she finds understanding in someone, she knows it. She will do all she can to please Mrs. Simmons.

What will happen when Mrs. Simmons loses her patience? She's bound to get burnt out in her attempts to help Minnie. Without meaning to, Minnie may push her too far. She may even test to see whether Mrs. Simmons can accept her, failures and all. At such times, a busy teacher may feel exasperated and ready to give up. However, these times of failure can also be the very opportunities needed to help Minnie gain control.

If Mrs. Simmons could say, "Minnie, you work so hard to keep yourself under control. It must be discouraging when it doesn't work out. I wish I could be of more help. Let's think up some things to do that you can remember when you need them. If you need me to, I can remind you about them. Can you feel these times when you get so excited you can't sit still? What shall we call these times?" Minnie looked away and shrugged: "I feel like I'm on an escalator. I don't know how to get off it. Maybe it won't stop." Mrs. Simmons responded: "Wonderful. Let's call it 'the escalator of trouble.' Could you turn to me and say, 'Now, Mrs. Simmons, I'm on the escalator'? You and I will know what you mean. Let's figure out what you should do when you start feeling that way. Any ideas?"

Minnie looked eager but confused. Mrs. Simmons continued, "What if we agree on something like 'Minnie, it's time to go over to the reading area with a book.' That won't be a punishment. It will be a way for you to get off the escalator. You just say, 'Mrs. Simmons, I've got to go look at my book now.' " Whenever these agreed-upon techniques work, Mrs. Simmons should give Minnie a lot of credit.

When they don't work, Mrs. Simmons and Minnie will have to face the problems. Investing too much in the solutions puts pressure on the child. Setbacks are bound to happen. They could even devastate both the child and the teacher, but they needn't. It would help both to know in advance that their techniques may fail from time to time. When they don't work, I would suggest that Minnie and Mrs. Simmons sit down together to discuss and share their disappointment.

"Now, Minnie, you see what we are trying to do. What shall we try now? I'd like to follow your suggestions." If Minnie can come up with some responsible ideas, it will be a milestone. She will be attempting to understand and master her own loss of control.

First grade offers children a new understanding of their behavior. Many children in first grade are trying hard to manage their exuberance in order to sit still and pay attention for long periods. A child as active as Minnie can feel like a threat to her classmates as they struggle with their own controls. Her peers could exclude her if she can't learn how to settle down when she needs to. But one of the advantages of first grade is that the teacher understands the child in a different, often more objective way than the parents have been able to.

Mrs. Lee needs to be brought into this effort to help Minnie understand and control her temperament. So does Mr. Lee. Mrs. Simmons needs their help. It will be critical for the Lees to understand the goals set by Mrs. Simmons. But because this is a long-term project and a difficult one, too much pressure at home can also backfire. Although Minnie requires consistent expectations at home and at school, she may feel that everyone is suddenly ganging up on her. When they see Minnie attempting to divert her energy into reading, learning, or just sitting and talking, they can let her know that they can see how hard she's trying. This will be a time for picking battles selectively. There will be times when Minnie just needs to fall apart. There will be a lot of tough calls: Minnie's parents and Mrs. Simmons will need to learn to share with each other their questions and their mistakes. If teacher and parents can use each other for support when they discuss their frustrations, it will be easier for them to reinforce Minnie's efforts.

The pitfall to be avoided here is that Minnie could all too easily get the feeling that no one likes her the way she is. Everyone wants to change her. The fragile new quality to her activity—less driven, more open to others—could easily shut down if the pressure to change leaves her feeling inadequate and unaccepted. These new expectations should be accompanied by attention to Minnie's feelings about herself. Other outlets must be provided, too, such as opportunities for her to excel, to demonstrate her value to her peers in sports and at recess. "Minnie, here's your chance! You've been sitting so still and quiet. It's recess time now! Kick that ball as hard as you can!"

A Vulnerable Child

Tim was as quiet as ever. The only way his parents could tell that he was anticipating school was by watching his face. At the mention of school, his face became attentive, his eyes lit up. It was as if he were trying to understand how important this step might be for him. He wanted so much to learn. Whenever he could find an appropriate book, he'd curl up in a corner. There, he'd sound out the letters, putting them together in an effort to read them as words. His mother noticed that she'd spend part of every morning showing him how to put letters into a word. Such elisions as T and H were roadblocks, but Tim was so eager that he'd soon mastered them. When his father read to him at night, he was engrossed. He'd ask his dad to slow up, and to let him read part of the page. Then, he'd labor over the first few words. Rather quickly, he'd gather steam, and before the book was finished, he'd be able to read it more easily. Within weeks of starting these reading efforts, his parents saw the progress. Tim could read more and more easily each day. The delight he felt matched their feelings about him.

Whenever they met, Mrs. McCormick and Mrs. Stone compared notes about their boys. Because Billy and Tim were in the same class, Mrs. McCormick wanted them to be friends, and she sometimes invited Billy over to play. Billy rushed to the house, his face alight. As usual, he was eager and outgoing. When he saw Tim, he said, "Hi, Tim!" Tim paled, but his eyes opened wide with pleasure at seeing his friend. Billy couldn't have known that his exuberant greeting was almost too much for Tim, but he quieted down instinctively. He moved more slowly as he approached Tim.

Tim looked at this easygoing, charming boy. Quietly, he said, "I can read. Can you?" Billy couldn't, but he wanted to. It was the perfect ploy. Tim picked out *Good Night, Moon*. Billy was familiar with it. His stepfather had read it to him night after night. The boys sat next to each other. Word by word, letter by letter, Tim led Billy through the book. Billy followed along in awe. Tim repeated the letters. They played with sounds. Tim showed Billy how to sound out, then construct word after word. They giggled together. Finally, Billy tired of reading and wanted to play. "Tim, let's play a game. What do you know?" Tim showed Billy his card games. From time to time, the two mothers looked in. Everything was so peaceful that they felt no rush to end the visit. When Billy and Tim had to part, they parted as friends.

Tim was as ready for school as he could possibly be. He was even perceptive about his fears. "I'll bet they sit me in a chair in the corner so the other kids can look me over." "Why?" said his mother. "'Cause I'm so quiet." "But Billy thinks you're great. The other kids will, too, if you let them." "I don't know how to play with them." "Tim, if you can become friends with Billy, you can become friends with other kids, too." "Billy's different. He knows me." It was true. The boys understood each other. Whenever Tim and Billy got together, they fell back into the relationship they'd built. First, Billy would ask Tim to help him with his reading and writing. Then, when Tim was involved and relaxed, Billy talked him into a game. First, a card game. Then, a giggle game. Sometimes even a running game. The predictability was important to Tim.

The McCormicks were surprised by Tim's ability to relate to Billy. Mrs. McCormick knew now that she'd thought of Tim as too shy, too slow—bound to be ridiculed by his peers. Billy's acceptance and his step-by-step approach to his relationship with Tim had opened Tim to him. Mrs. McCormick was stunned that this could be possible.

Billy took Tim over to Mrs. Simmons to introduce him. "This is Tim. He's shy. He's my friend." "Billy, show him your desk so he'll know where to find you. Then you can take him around to meet everyone. You are such a good friend." Tim nodded vigorously. He felt safe and cared for.

Tim's quiet approach stood out in class. He didn't even squirm. He didn't have to move about. He watched and waited. When Mrs. Simmons started teaching, his face lit up. He had been wary at first. But he was ready to succeed in first grade, and little by little he began to sense that he would.

His mother was able to help him achieve this shift without directly confronting him. A shy child is all too aware of how unacceptable to others his personality is. Had his mother pressed him to change, or confronted him with overwhelming situations, the likelihood would be that Tim would have failed, or might have withdrawn even more.

Without undue pressure, Tim had a chance of making it in his own way. Because he was bright and eager to learn, school was an important outlet for his own unique strengths. If his socialization could be carefully paced and his school successes continue, his self-esteem would grow. Tim could become surer of himself and of his ability to master social situations.

A Child Who Copes

Marcy was going to school! She couldn't quite believe it. On her sixth birthday, she had jumped up and down: "I'm old enough! Finally, I get to go to real school!" Her face glowed. Her whole body was bouncing with excitement. "I'm big now." Marcy sensed that first grade was a real step toward being grown up. She is no longer a "baby" in her own or others' minds. Everyone around Marcy will have been waiting for her to enter first grade. Even her older brother will have a new respect for her.

Marcy's mother had always felt sure that Marcy would make it. She had little concern about this outgoing child. Marcy seemed on top of the world. She had the capacity to carry people along with her. When she talked about any obstacle, she seemed to be proud of her ability to surmount it. Mrs. Jackson had worried about her older brother and his adjustment, but Marcy seemed invincible. Worries about Marcy were always easily fended off.

When Marcy arrived at school the first day, she charged ahead. Her mother had introduced Marcy to her new teacher the week before. Mrs. Simmons was well known for her warmth and friendliness; she and Marcy were soul mates from the first. Mrs. Simmons told Marcy that she'd heard about how much of a leader she was from her kindergarten teacher. She asked her where she liked to sit—which desk and in which part of the room. Marcy chose a desk in the front. Mrs. Simmons said, "I like your choice, Marcy. That way I know you'll be right near by. And when I need your help, I'll know you'll be right there." Marcy was already in love.

When Marcy came home that day, she raved, "I like school! I like Mrs. Simmons! I like my class! All my friends are there!" Mr. and

Mrs. Jackson were delighted. They, too, felt welcomed. They both went to the parents' meeting, anticipating it as a chance to participate in Marcy's joyful experience. They were so proud of Marcy.

*An Outgoing
Child*

Billy's idea of school was "more." More children, more times to be with them, more chances to learn to read and write. He thrived on other children. He looked forward to more sports. Over the summer, he'd learned to float, then he'd learned to put his face under water. Finally, with a great flourish, he had learned to swim. "Dad, guess what? I picked up my feet while I was paddling with my arms. It worked!" Soon, his dog paddle gave him more and more courage. He was indeed afloat. By the last week of August, he had the courage to enter the end-of-the-summer race. He tied for last place, but he barely noticed. He was wet and out of breath, and excited. The cheering and encouragement of the crowd captivated him completely. "I love being in races."

Softball had been the same. Billy threw with an accuracy that was astounding for a six-year-old. Catching had been more difficult. He seemed to expect the ball would plop into his mitt because he wanted it to so badly. He missed the ball as often as he caught it. His main accomplishment had been to bat the ball. He hit it over and over when he was playing at home with his stepfather, who stood a few feet away and tirelessly lobbed the big ball at his son's bat. When Billy was on the field in Little Little League, he missed the ball consistently. Once though, he hit a beautiful zinger, but he forgot to run. He was still standing at home base and admiring his hit when the outfielder picked it up to throw him out at first base. Despite the boos, Billy was full of pride: "Did you see how far I hit that ball?" The next game was an improvement. He nicked the ball toward the third baseman, who fumbled. Billy hesitated for a moment before charging to first base. There, he was so enthralled with his accomplishment that he had to be prodded to run to second base. Eventually, he had his chance to run in for a score. But after the game, when the other team was receiving congratulations, he remarked, "I didn't like this game. We lost. Last week, we won. That was my favorite."

For Billy, school meant more of all his favorite activities. He could hardly wait. When his mother took him to town to "buy clothes for school," it added to his anticipation. "These sneakers can be just for sports in school. No other times. I'll take them off when I get home. These pencils and paper will be just for my school. You need special things for school." He was full of the excitement of learning. Every evening, he'd sit with one of his parents. "Want to hear me read? Can I show you again?" He expressed his desire to be ready in the repeated demonstrations of bits of reading, writing, and arithmetic. But these were more than bits—Billy had begun to understand the purposes such accomplishments serve. Kindergarten had helped.

Billy ceremoniously anticipated his visit to the doctor for a pre-September checkup. His visit to Dr. Angela was a triumph: "She looked me all over. She didn't find anything wrong. I even showed her my muscles. And guess what? I didn't even cry when she used a needle for my blood test. Abby yelled her head off—like a baby. Not me!" He wanted to wear the plastic ring Dr. Angela had given him to school, but he lost it a few days after it stopped seeming so precious to him.

He was working so hard to be "ready." When he went for his "school haircut," the barber was impressed by Billy. He sat very still in the barber's chair. He'd been squiggly every time before. When he was four, he'd cried as he watched hunks of his hair pile up on the floor. This time, he confidently asked the barber, "Do you know how to give school haircuts? I'm going to first grade." When he'd finished, the barber said, "Billy, you look older already!" Indeed, he did. The short haircut, the loss of his bangs, the serious intentness on his face made him look older. Mr. Stone felt a twinge of sadness. Billy was growing up so quickly.

When they got home, Billy scuttled towards his mother, yelling, "My hair is really fuzzy now!" She quietly agreed, and looked at her husband. Mr. Stone saw the same realization in her eyes that he had experienced. They both knew that the feeling of loss they shared—although it might not be quite the same for a step-parent—needed to stay between them. Billy mostly needed to feel their pride and excitement at his growing up, their confidence in his becoming able to be more grown-up. Yet, if he needed them to, they could also understand an occasional pause in his usual full-steam-ahead approach. They could understand that he might feel a little sad and scared every now and then about not being so little anymore, about becoming a big boy, headed for school.

Gender differences in first grade are unmistakable. The girls were able to save their energies for recess. But even then, they played with consideration for each other and for those around them. Not the boys, who seemed never to stop moving. They wriggled in their chairs. On a bench, they tipped until they tipped it over. On the floor, they splatted out—all four extremities extended, taking as much room as possible. They twisted and turned, over and over, into each other's spaces. Mrs. Simmons was careful to arrange them in a wide circle on the floor. At the outset, they looked like spokes of a wheel, but almost immediately, they were entangled with each other. They flopped about, they poked, they growled, they threatened. At recess, they chased, tripped each other, and found objects to kick and throw. They took Mrs. Simmons' admonitions seriously—for a moment. Then, the energy overflowed again. Competitive play predominated—although it seemed as much aimed at contact and mutual recognition as at measuring up.

The girls tended to gather in the front of the room. They were less in motion, although they, too, teased each other. They stood straighter than the boys and gathered in groups of four or five. But friends easily stood out because they linked arms or hung on to each other. Although they were very aware of the boys' activity, the girls tried to shut it out by turning their backs on the tangled mass in the back of the room. They giggled and acted as if they were gossiping. Putting one hand over her mouth, Marcy very quietly whispered a secret to her friend. Everyone else crowded in to hear it. "What did she say?" The "secret" went the rounds—nothing important, and completely distorted by the time it had been shared. The goal seemed more of bringing everyone together than of any real intrigue.

As they stood, they played clapping games. The more coordinated girls joined together, the others watched. They used these games to tease and compete in their own way:

> *The space goes eenie meenie op-sa-keenie*
> *Ooo aaa oo be-lee-nie*
> *Ah-chie kah-chee*

Li-ver-a-chee
Say the magic word
A peach, a plum,
A half a stick of chewing gum
And if you want the other half
This is what you have to say:
"Amen, amen,
A-man-diego, San Diego
Hocus pocus
Lemon nokus
Siss siss siss koom bah
Rah rah rah boo boo boo."
Criss cross, apple sauce
Do me a favor and get lost.
While you're at it drop dead.
Either that or lose your head.
Banging on a trash can,
I can you can nobody else can.
Sitting on a bench, nothing to do,
Along comes a fat lady
Goochey goochey goo."

(The children tickle each other.)

The girls quickly learned several of these clapping games, some serving other purposes:

Bubble gum, bubble gum, in a dish.
How many pieces do you wish?
One? Two? Three? Four? Five? . . .

or

Tell me the name of your sweetheart.
Does it begin with an A? B? C? D? E? . . .

or

Teddy bear, teddy bear, turn around.
Teddy bear, teddy bear, touch the ground.
Teddy bear, teddy bear, go upstairs.

Teddy bear, teddy bear, say your prayers.
Teddy bear, teddy bear, turn off the light.
Teddy bear, teddy bear, say good night.
    Good night.

With these rhymes, letters and numbers are made ever more fa-miliar. The girls are then able to distance themselves from the toys they associate with their younger selves.

The school did not encourage gender separation; the children seemed to set it up instinctively. Perhaps there had been other situa-tions over the years where it had been suggested, even unwittingly. Now the children were clustered in gender-specific groups. Parents seemed surprised by this separation; they even made suggestions about more mixing. One mother urged her daughter: "Look, there's Jason, your friend. Go say hello to him." No response. The gender-specific behavior was too important in making new friends. It was as if the children were finding themselves and their places through each other. Mrs. Simmons did not seem at all surprised by this.

Even gregarious Billy, although aware of the girls, wasn't drawn to them. Some of the girls clustered in one part of the room with the doll house and the fish tank. One of the mothers laughed at how lit-tle difference her feminist child-rearing strategies had made.

The boys' activity built up to a peak, but Mrs. Simmons expected this. She assigned drawing to the quieter children, mostly girls: "Draw me a picture of your first day in school." To the boisterous ones, she initially assigned active tasks and gradually followed them with more settled ones. "You four boys get the chairs from over there. Make a circle with them. Then go get my chalkboard. Can you carry it by yourselves? Good for you. You're so strong. Put it at the head of the class for me. Then, find me some chalk to write with. I'll write each person's name on the board so we'll all know who everyone is."

Despite recent efforts to rid ourselves of gender-specific behavior and to mesh boys and girls together, the children themselves seem to initiate gender-based segregation. The children's behavior might have been slightly different before they gathered into a group. But once in that group and in a novel situation, the two sexes separated by themselves. The social skills called upon were different. With boys, there were struggles, competition, testing. The girls tended to socialize in more sedentary groups, predictably mannered, though not always kind. They were aware of each other—sensitive to each other's cues; they used the giggles and the gossip as a way of knowing each other. The boys and the girls sought the comfort and predictability of their own sex. Even Tim, who had begun to soften with Billy's outreach, was hooked on the boys' behavior. He couldn't join them actively, but he certainly watched them with longing. He probably knew where Billy was and what he was doing at any time.

For such an experienced person as Mrs. Simmons, all this was predictable. She knew that the girls would be ready to conform to the school rules. Sitting in their desks, being ready to come back in after recess—all this was easy for most of the girls in the class. So far, the boys seemed to be leaving the girls alone. But Mrs. Simmons knew that teasing and provoking were never far away. She'd always wondered whether the girls didn't bring on the teasing themselves. As a girl walked by a boy, she'd be tempted to tickle him or to step on his foot, or just to give him a sidelong look.

Mrs. Simmons was convinced that it was easier to conduct a big class by giving in to the separation of girls from boys. There was so much to lose, though. Girls learned from boys, and vice versa. It was both exciting and challenging to face the differences of six-year-old boys and girls as the year began. Her main problem was that the boys demanded and received most of her attention. Was it her bias? Or was it just that teaching boys to socialize simply required more effort on her part? These differences do not begin in first grade, or even at three, but during the first year of life. But Mrs. Simmons had learned that such behavior smooths out over the first grade year.

At the least opportunity, the boys would chase each other around the room, weaving around the desks as they went. When they started shouting at each other, Mrs. Simmons's firm warning quieted them immediately. But then they would shove each other, and wrestle. A few boys, including Tim, were standing watching the others. But mostly, the boys joined in, teasing, chortling, laughing out loud. Their gaiety was contagious. Everyone watched them as they kept the room in seething volcanic activity. Mothers of boys loved it and smirked appreciatively. They clustered with each other as if their children had set the stage for their friendships. As mothers and fathers of girls watched these rowdy struggles, they tried to hide their quiet disapproval.

Reading and Writing

Despite the seething activity, Mrs. Simmons found it relatively easy to persuade her first-graders to conform to the rules of school. The psychoanalyst Erik Erikson called this the "age of industry," for children of six are not only ready but absolutely need to start working. They are hungry for knowledge, and to acquire it, most are eager to learn to read.

Distractions are always a force to be reckoned with, of course. Mrs. Simmons spent a great deal of time the first weeks establishing rules and constructive outlets for exuberance. Helping her first-graders to recognize and respect each other's needs was an important part of her curriculum. Gradually, the children learned to handle themselves and to work as a group, although sometimes this required a direct appeal: "This has gone far enough. Come sit by me." The culprit liked the direct attention and containment. With a sheepish expression, she would come to sit by Mrs. Simmons, but then she would turn to look adoringly up at her face.

Billy's enthusiasm overflowed when the class turned to learning. His hand shot up whenever Mrs. Simmons asked a question. He often answered the question appropriately. But just as often, he couldn't. "I just *want* to answer it."

Billy began to invent words. He'd say, "What does this word mean?" as he wrote a made-up word. "Nothing that I can see, Billy." "Well, show me how to make a word. Show me 'cat' and 'dog.'" Mrs. Simmons would spell out C-A-T. "But why is dog different? They're both just animals." "Billy, just as you have a special name, spelled a special way, so does everything else. A cat and a dog aren't the same things, so they aren't spelled the same way. If you wrote, 'See that dog' and it was really a cat, I wouldn't understand you, would I?" Billy's face grew serious, his eyes full of wonder at the power, and mystery, of words.

Tim was already the best reader in his class. Billy would watch him with envy. How did he do it? Billy would take the book that Tim had read from. He would look at the pictures and make up or mimic the stories that Tim had read. But his hunger to make the reading "pop out" of the book already outweighed any temptation to fabricate a story.

When Mrs. Simmons introduced phonics—sounding out the letters—Billy was ready. He discovered that he could look at letters and words everywhere and sound them. When he found a familiar sound, it was like finding an old friend. He began to sound out every sign he passed on the street. On Sesame Street, he'd see a word, hear it, and put it together. Soon, he began to conquer the association between consonants and vowels. He asked Tim to help him. Tim was thrilled. He could listen to Billy's sounding out as often as Billy would trust him.

Mr. and Mrs. Stone were impressed. Billy learned so well and so quickly. Within weeks, he was beginning to read whole words. Soon Billy was able -with great effort, and falteringly- to read sentences. Now he also wanted to be able to inflect sentences from the print, to make the words flow the way Tim could. He sensed the power this accomplishment gave Tim, and he admired it.

Mrs. Stone had always read to Billy every evening. Mr. Stone also saw reading time as his special chance to cuddle with Billy at bedtime. The closeness that Billy thrived on had long been wrapped up with reading. In the Stone household, books and reading had always been important. Now Billy's parents could see how important it had become for Billy to show them what he could do with his own books.

Their nightly reading times became longer, and Billy led them. He'd sound out a word until he got it. Then, he'd proudly say it over and over. "Now, what does it mean, Daddy?" When his stepfather explained it to him, Billy was almost awestruck. He'd sit with mouth open, listening and digesting. After the explanation, he'd repeat the word proudly, following it with his father's explanation. Mr. Stone could see the pride and power in Billy's new skill. The impetus behind it was impressive to his parents. In three months, Billy had learned to sound out words from text. Sometimes he put letters together in comical ways. Sometimes 'talked' still came out as 'tall ked', and words such as "might" and "could" remained baffling, if not downright intimidating.

Writing was just as riveting. Squeezing his pencil with enthusiasm, Billy clutched it with his whole hand at first. When he saw that he couldn't produce the letters he longed for, he watched Tim, who was more adept. Tim held his pencil with his three first fingers; he shifted it from one hand to the other as he tried to compose a word. When he was frustrated by not knowing the next letter, he'd shift the pencil to his left hand. As if the shift freed his thinking, the next letter would appear. Billy tried three fingers, but it felt clumsy; he began holding the pencil with thumb and third finger. This worked.

Over the year, Billy and Tim both graduated to the usual way of writing—holding the pencil with thumb and forefinger and anchoring it with the middle finger. Just as gradually, Tim gave up his less effective shifting from one hand to the other. Efficiency was a powerful shaper of manual writing skill. One day, Billy brought home a frayed piece of paper on which he had written "BILLY STONE GOES TO SCHOOL" with the *S* written backwards twice. Billy was very proud of his writing and hadn't noticed the mistakes. His parents gushed over his accomplishment, but made no comment about the letter reversals. They were confident that the *S* would straighten out over time.

*From
Support to
Self-motivation*

I have been concerned with the pressure on parents today to "teach" their children in the first few years. From the very beginning, parents feel the burden of raising children who can survive in our ever more competitive world. Well-meaning advice may lead parents to overstimulate their children so much that they never learn to stimulate themselves and reap their own rewards. How many mothers now have been led to believe that they must talk incessantly to their toddlers—leaving the child without a chance to think her own thoughts? The pressures of our increasingly intense world push parents away from the balance they'd otherwise come to on their own. The kind of pressured learning that results may not allow motivation which will last.

Because Tim had wanted so desperately to learn to read, he took the initiative and found his own techniques. Maybe these would be at odds with Mrs. Simmons' methods of teaching. But in all likelihood, Tim's hunger for learning would carry over.

Mrs. McCormick had put a lot of thought and effort into preparing Tim to handle first grade. Although getting Tim ready to tackle school hadn't been easy, it had helped her to stop worrying and to prevent her worries from influencing Tim. Her stroke of genius (and good fortune) had been to find him a friend who was responsive enough to help him. It is easier to face a group situation with a peer as an ally. Tim has also come a long way toward handling his own sensitivity in the demanding environment of first grade. He can now be helped to recognize his special strengths. Because he is bright and eager to learn, school can bring him many rewards. If the pressure on him to socialize is gradual and his school successes continue, Tim will become surer of himself and of his ability to master social situations. His motivation can continue to come from within.

A Learning Disability

Marcy's parents rarely worried about her chances of making it—or if they did, they worried about the world she would have to make it in. What a shock it was, when, in March, Mrs. Simmons asked the Jacksons to stop in for a talk with her. With a serious face, the teacher said, "Have you noticed anything unusual about how Marcy tries to read?" She paused when she saw how tense these parents had become. "Marcy's having some trouble. I've been wanting to share with you my concern about whether she has a learning disability. Even though there are wide variations in children's rates of learning, I am concerned about her. She is so competent in every other way that it really surprised me. And it makes me want to find out more and help her now." The Jacksons were shocked. They'd never noticed any difficulty with Marcy. When they read to her, she was responsive. She'd always seemed so bright.

"We have never suspected such a thing before," Mr. Jackson said. Mrs. Simmons continued, "It was Marcy's own distress that started me thinking about this. Marcy is so bright that she is able to cover it up. She can put a brave face on anything. But it is such a struggle for her to recognize letters, and it is so hard for her to make them into words. She even tries to fake sentences. I just don't want her to give up. We can have her evaluated and find out how to help her learn in a way that works for her."

The Jacksons were caught between skepticism and feeling overwhelmed. Mrs. Jackson felt angry that she was being confronted with this, and at the same time bitter because no one had alerted them to Marcy's difficulty until now. Mr. Jackson felt guilty for not having figured it out himself. Although they wanted to deny there was a problem, they realized that helping their daughter now would prevent future difficulties.

That night, Marcy and her father retreated to the bedroom for her nightly story. Whenever Mr. Jackson let Marcy choose a book, she always picked *Cinderella*. This was her favorite; she and her father had shared it together for years. Marcy would read along with her father. She knew what was coming on the next page without looking. This time, Mr. Jackson chose a new book for Marcy, a simple one, but one she hadn't seen before. He said, "Marcy, now that you're in school, maybe we could read together the way we read *Cinderella*." He read to her, stopping from time to time to point out pictures of the animals. He asked her to identify the words below the animal. He said, "Don't worry. You don't have to read the whole word. Read the first letter and sound it out. Then look at the picture. Together they'll help you get it." That worked for pictures of several familiar animals. But as Marcy grew tenser and tenser, Mr. Jackson realized how painful it was for her to face the failure she anticipated when she couldn't read the words. She would try in several ways to deflect him. She'd turn to a squirrel picture and make up a story: "That animal climbs trees. Her tail twitches as she walks. When she's worried, she makes chattering noises. She loves acorns and other nuts. Oh, that's right, it begins with an *S*. It's a squirrel!" Mr. Jackson saw the extent to which Marcy had to go to avoid a simple request to sound out an unfamiliar word.

The next day, Mrs. Simmons asked Marcy to come to the blackboard—an unusual request, for Mrs. Simmons respected Marcy's feelings. But on that occasion it would have been too obvious if she didn't call upon Marcy because everyone else had come up to the board. Mrs. Simmons tried hard to include her without embarrassing her. As Marcy walked up, she stumbled. She reddened; she dropped the chalk. She looked to her best friend for courage. Mrs. Simmons: "Marcy, draw us a picture of your favorite animal." Marcy began to draw a dog. "And write the name of the animal under it, or you could make up a name for your pet." Marcy drew a presentable dog; then she faltered. She tried to write *D,* and then *O,* but she blanked. She couldn't think of the third letter. Some of the boys giggled. Marcy's friend whispered loudly, "*G.*" But Marcy couldn't go on. She squirmed; she tried to retreat to her desk. She was immobilized. Mrs. Simmons realized how difficult this process was for her. She said, "Marcy, you can ask anyone in the class to come up and name your dog. That's a beautiful drawing. Not everyone can draw that well. Not everyone can remember letters and how to draw them." Marcy's avoidance was typical of the behavior that a child develops as a defense against this kind of failure. Memorizing *Cinderella*. Describing the squirrel instead of reading its name. No wonder a child in trouble becomes devious or manipulative to protect against facing the giggles of her classmates or the sense of failure she must feel.

Now, as they reflected, Mr. and Mrs. Jackson realized that Marcy had been hesitating more and more often before she would participate in their reading rituals each evening. They'd always read to her at the end of the day. She had loved it. They had loved it. It was a time to cuddle, to communicate with each other. Now the Jacksons realized that Marcy had always been able to memorize her books quickly. She had then been able to "read" them from memory as they read to her. When she couldn't remember a story, she used an ingenious technique for diverting their attention from her difficulty: she would make up stories so that they would all forget what they'd been reading.

Her parents now understood how much Marcy had felt she needed to hide her trouble with letters and how hard it would have been for her to ask for their help. Armed with the new insight from Mrs. Simmons, Mr. and Mrs. Jackson began to pick up clues that coincided with the teacher's diagnosis. Each evening Marcy chose the same books. If they branched out, she began to show anxiety and would stammer and search for ways out of her dilemma. They could see that it cost their daughter a lot. When she failed, she was miserable. When they caught her in the act of covering up, or of diverting them from proposed tasks, they could see that her face would redden, her hands would clasp, her whole body would tense. Pointing out the problem to her only made her feel trapped. She'd been able to construct such effective defenses that they hadn't seen the toll her troubles were taking on her. But blowing her cover, they realized, wouldn't work.

Marcy probably could have gone on managing to cover up her difficulties in learning for awhile. It took considerable sensitivity for Mrs. Simmons to see that Marcy was trying so hard, but wasn't able to master these learning situations with the ease that fit her personality. Mrs. Simmons must have seen the subtle anguish that this child demonstrated when she was confronted with a task she couldn't master easily. She was astute enough to realize that Marcy's personality was so easy and so fluid that this discomfort didn't fit in.

Her reluctance in class meant more than it would have in a more stubborn or difficult child. Mrs. Simmons had had the same experience with other learning-disabled children. What Mrs. Simmons did for Marcy was timely and wonderful: she identified this remediable disability before it began to erode Marcy's self-image.

One of the most serious aspects of a learning disability is that children who try and can't figure out why their trials fail begin to lose faith in themselves. In my early years in pediatrics, this was not understood and I saw children fail in school year after year. We tended to give them negative labels by calling them lazy or resistant. The children labeled themselves, too; they saw themselves as failures even before we did. By the third or fourth grade, these labels were fixed. The pathway to learning was doubly impaired—by their disability, but even more by their hopelessness and impaired self-image.

This loss of inner security shows in all sorts of ways. Children who feel this way can become the "bad" kids in the class, the show-offs, the bullies. Or they retire into their shells and sit patiently in the classroom, staring ahead. When they are called on for an answer, they startle, redden, flutter with their hands and feet. They may also make trouble, to distract the teacher and the class, so that their "dumbness" might not be noticed. They become so uncomfortable that a sympathetic teacher learns not to call upon them. She will try to ignore them, until the end of the year, when the fact that they hadn't been able to learn can no longer be ignored. In busy schools, such children can be passed on from year to year, labeled as "dumb" or "uncooperative." Many schools now do a better job than this, but we still have a long way to go to provide the kind of flexibility in teaching that children with learning disabilities need to flourish in a classroom. Marcy's self-esteem can be spared, and she can learn—if her parents are ready to act.

Today, we have techniques for identifying the various kinds of impairments in learning. If the disability can be specifically identified, these children can learn to use their stronger abilities to compensate. Testing can sort out the blocks so that they can be addressed before a child's self-esteem is damaged to the point where it interferes with other kinds of learning. Many schools and special clinics retain psychologists who use testing materials to find out strategies that each child can use to learn. Some children can learn from a computer program when they haven't been able to learn from a person. Confronted with an assignment, these children put out their antennae. The expense of performing at another's timing is, in large measure, part of the problem. This can be overcome with a computer or a personal tutor who can honor the child's timing. If Marcy's parents can seek and find the appropriate answers to Marcy's disability, she may be spared the roadblocks to her future education: the disability itself, and the self-image or motivational problem.

The Jacksons were ready to do something. They now sensed that their ebullient Marcy was becoming more and more discouraged as the school year progressed. They hadn't picked up on what was bothering her and they felt guilty about this. Why hadn't they sensed she was having trouble? As they discussed it together, the Jacksons saw that their own denial and reluctance to face difficulties had been responsible. They'd not wanted to face any difficulties in her. They now wondered about her future. Could they find a solution to Marcy's difficulties? When she was feeling blue, everyone in the family felt it. Mrs. Jackson realized what a burden she had placed on her six-year-old. She half expected her to nurture them all.

Now the Jacksons wanted to push Marcy to confront her disability and overcome it. "If you'll only let Mrs. Simmons help you, she knows how." They began to hover. Every time Marcy had a task, or had to face any homework, they would ask, "Do you want us to help, Marcy?" Her face would darken; she would turn away. She showed them clearly that their hovering was undermining her self-confidence. She would lash back—"I understand my homework.

I'm supposed to do it myself. Leave me alone." Hovering by parents carries the implication that a child isn't capable of doing a task herself. If she can face the struggle and explore the solutions herself, she will find a very important prize at the end: "I did it myself!" Marcy will need this as she faces her learning disability. Her response, "I understand it. I can do it" is a way to give herself time. Her own pace needs to be respected.

Marcy's parents now need to seek out a talented, caring specialist who can help Marcy to find her own way of compensating. Because her day is so full, Mrs. Simmons may not be able to find enough time to devote to Marcy.

Parents are likely to be dogged by their impatience and their desire to get it all straightened out. Their most important role may be to pull back, to relieve the pressure that the child senses from their disappointment. Once they find appropriate help, and if they can stand by and turn the task over to the child, they are showing her respect. "You can do it. And when you need us, we are here to help." Then, when she asks for help, she asks from strength. She will still need her parents' help—to offer ways around the block in her learning and to support her when she becomes impatient or can't get started on a task she expects to fail at.

What if she shows signs of being overwhelmed, or is reluctant to work on her disability? This isn't laziness. What might look like laziness is an indication that she feels hopeless. When it looks as though she's not even trying it may be that she doesn't know how to face her failure to understand. Parents and teacher alike should find indirect ways to build up her self-image first: "Look at your beautiful drawings!" "You are such a terrific swimmer."

None of this means leaving a child alone with her disability. Children know when something is the matter. So many children are tested for learning disabilities without being told why or what has been diagnosed. Left alone without information, they can only fear the worst—"There's something really wrong with me, I'm no good." Find words to describe the problem that are honest, yet hopeful: "I can tell it is hard for you to learn the way we've shown you, but we can help you find your own way to learn, one that will work for you." Experts can help a child identify her "islands of competence," as psychologist Robert Brooks calls areas of strength. Children can use these to provide an "alternate route" around a learning "block."

Challenge and Opportunity Marcy was proud of having learned to ride her two-wheel bicycle with its kiddie wheels. She could almost keep up with Amos, and she proudly followed her brother as he raced down the sidewalk in front of their house. Amos loved to screech to a halt. He exulted in the skid of the tires on the sidewalk and the crunch of the gravel he kicked up. One day when Marcy tried to stop the way he did, she turned over in spite of the protective kiddie wheels. As she hit the street, she scraped her knee and her cheek. She fell apart. Screaming, she finally attracted her brother's attention. He rushed back to her and leaned down from his bike to try to comfort her. He had to dismount, but in the process, he turned his own bike over and fell to the ground beside Marcy. As they lay on the sidewalk next to each other, they began to giggle. Comforted by Amos' tragedy, Marcy forgot her wounds. When their mother came rushing out to help them, she found the two huddled together. She took Marcy upstairs to wash the scrapes with soapy water. This reminded Marcy of her painful wounds, so she started crying again. Amos came in to hold her hand for the cleansing. She quieted. Her brother's tenderness was more important than the pain. Mrs. Jackson realized she didn't have to worry about his "meanness"—of course he would be mean sometimes—it went with the tenderness.

After this, Marcy refused to try her bike again. Mrs. Jackson tried to push her. "No, Mommy! I don't know how. I'll get hurt." Her father tried, offering to run along beside her. "No, Daddy! I won't ride it again." They were uncertain whether they should push her. After all, bike riding is a critical skill for a six-year-old. But she'd obviously been frightened by her accident. What should they do? Pressure her or let her work it out? All parents face dilemmas like this.

Several weeks later, Marcy gave in. Her friends were all riding. She got back on her bike and all went well. Marcy then became determined to give up the training wheels. Her brother's confidence as he rode was such a model for her to imitate. Marcy enlisted Mr. Jackson to help her. After she had regained her courage, he began to carry out his program. At the end of each day, he raised the kiddie wheels ever so slightly. Each adjustment pushed her to learn to balance herself anew. As she teetered along the sidewalk, Mr. Jackson realized that he'd better let her learn on a grassy and more forgiving

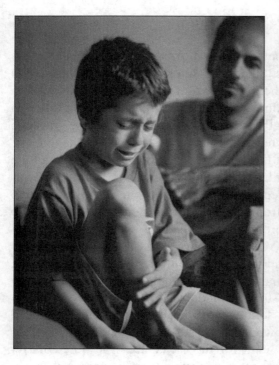
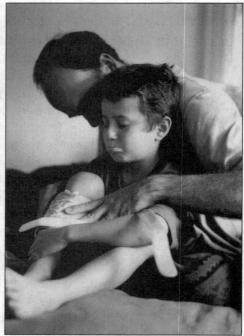

surface. He ran alongside her, steadying her. She tried over and over. Each time her father raised the training wheels, she'd tip and have to stop. So frustrating! She'd wait every afternoon until Mr. Jackson came home from work: "Now, Daddy! It's time to try without the baby wheels." She'd sit astride her bike, watching enviously as Amos showed off down the street.

When Marcy finally took off without the kiddie wheels, Mr. Jackson ran beside her and tried to keep up. She left him behind. As she swayed back and forth, his heart was in his mouth. She kept going, unable to stop at the main street. He shouted to her, "Marcy! Marcy! Stop! Fall off! Don't go out in the street!" She heard him, but was too frightened to fall off; instead, she headed for a neighbor's lawn and fell off safely. "Marcy, that was ingenious! I'm proud of you. You stopped yourself." Practicing reverse pedaling to stop became the next big job.

A month later, Marcy was managing well. She could balance. She could stop. She was proud. The family's efforts had been worth it. Her parents were relieved. They remembered their pride when Marcy began to walk. Learning to ride a bike was reminiscent of

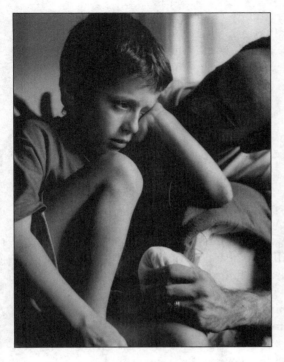

early achievements, of early touch-points.

It helped Marcy to remember other obstacles that had daunted her until she'd mastered them—with her own hard work and the family help she could count on. Marcy's learning disability is one example of many stumbles that parents and children must face together. Parents' encouragement and their respect for the child's autonomy and proud adaptations are essential if she is to mobilize her own resources. Anyone who ever learned to ride a bike as a child can easily remember the sensation of triumph and freedom that came with the first solo ride. For Marcy, and for children like her, this accomplishment is even more important.

The Costs of Learning

The Stones could see the excitement of learning building up in Billy. They found it thrilling to watch, but it cost Billy a great deal. The price of this passionate investment came out at home. Billy was itchy, difficult. He could no longer bear to be told what to do. He hated being crossed and he would throw himself on the couch or floor when reprimanded. Eventually though, he seemed to feel relieved by the simple, clear, and unwavering limits he was familiar with. When they were imposed—with time outs to quiet himself in his room—he seemed grateful for the help in settling down, although he might not have been able to admit it. When his parents withheld a reward he'd failed to earn, he seemed to understand. Billy demonstrated that limits were important to him; their predictability made him feel safe. Even as he protested, Mr. and Mrs. Stone knew they were helping him build the controls he could use by himself in the future.

Billy was no longer as nurturant of Abby. "She's bugging me! Take her away!" Abby waited outside his room where he would sometimes shut himself away. When he finally emerged, she was so hungry she wanted to cling. Obviously overloaded from his day at school, Billy wanted time of his own. He would literally run away from Abby, but she always followed him, screaming. He'd rush back to his room, hands over his ears, slamming the door to shut her out. When Mrs. Stone tried to stop him, or to urge him to let Abby play with him, he glowered, his body tensed; he seemed to know he was close to breaking down. Without realizing it, Billy was defending himself—and Abby—from his response to her advances.

If his parents could recognize this responsible behavior, now would be the time for them to encourage and praise Billy for not lashing out at his sister. He was exhausted. He was taking a step toward the necessary understanding of his own limits by protecting himself—and her—by pulling away. Billy's parents' recognition of this would encourage his attempts to handle himself in trying circumstances. For Billy was a passionate six-year-old, and he was paying a price for all he was accomplishing.

Around this time, Billy began bringing "bad" words home. His parents were shocked at first. Then Mr. Stone recalled that he had done just the same thing at Billy's age. "It's one way of showing off for the other kids. All the kids do this," he explained. Mrs. Stone, however, was upset by such language: "I'm just not going to put up with that kind of talk. I don't want Billy to have a dirty mouth." "Then you talk to him about it," countered Mr. Stone. "I'd rather explain to him about how he's trying to live up to the other kids who talk that way." Mrs. Stone agreed that this was better.

When his stepfather talked to him, he could see the relief in the boy's face. Billy had indeed been trying to keep up with the other boys—but he was also excited by the "dirty" talk. He saw the tension his "dirty" words created at home. He sensed his mother's disapproval. Even after the talk with Mr. Stone, when he was tired and out of sorts, he would use a "bad" word to incite a response from her. Mrs. Stone tried to see this as a way of testing her—not to be tolerated, but not the same as a personal attack.

At this age, children are still intrigued with smutty talk. "Butt"— even "underwear"—incite raucous laughs. "Shit" and "ass" may even elicit a brief, reverent silence. "Poop," "pee-pee," and worse—all are tried out in front of parents; it is a six-year-old's way of learning about the power and meaning of the words. But this will not happen as much as it did a year or so before. A six-year-old is more aware of the effects such talk has on others. Sometimes she will want to learn about her parents' reaction to a new word, or to test others around her. But her sensitivity to others is kicking in.

When they are alone, six-year-olds practice their entire repertoire. "Butt-head." "You like to look at your poop." "You pee outside." And, if it can be found out, "You pee in your bed." Scatological words are saved for times when one six-year-old is trying to get the best of another, or is teasing mercilessly. Girls may be more private about this kind of talk; they collect in a gaggle to gossip and tease. Their purpose of sharing dirty talk may be to find out who is friends with whom.

Where do the words come from? Other kids, older kids on the playground, older siblings, even parents. Here's a jump-rope rhyme first-graders may learn from older peers at the playground:

Ronald MacDonald had a biscuit
Ronald MacDonald had a biscuit
Ooo chi chi hua hua—a biscuit.
I had a boyfriend—a biscuit
He was the sweetest—a biscuit
Like a cherry pie—a biscuit.
La choo choo, la choo choo,
La choo choo bang bang.
Now watch me now watch me now watch me do
*   my thang.*
I said a popcorn cherry pie
Bang bang
Do my thang
Laddie daddie shake my body
Tooty fruit shake my booty.
Uhh-I'm going down
Uhh-into the ground
Uhh-I'm coming up
Uhh-to kick your butt
Uhh-she pushed me down
Uhh-into the ground
Uhh-I'm coming up

Uhh-to kick your butt
Oops-I'm sorry
I thought you knew karate.

Children are more likely to pay attention to words used by the people around them than to the additional adult-generated sources: television, movies, radio, and Internet sites.

Birds and
Bees Again

This is an age when there is likely to be less sharing with parents about sexual questions than there was at five. But when Mr. Stone let on that he understood Billy's need to use smutty language, it was as if Billy had been waiting to explode. The boys of his age had obviously been sharing theories with each other. It drew them close, into an exciting secret circle, in which Billy could also feel—at times—an uncomfortable distance from his parents. His stepfather's understanding bridged the gap.

"Daddy, how do you make babies?"

"It happens when a man and a women are in love with each other. Sometimes, when they can be private, they hug and kiss and feel how much they love each other, and then the man puts his penis in his wife's vagina. His penis gets hard [Billy nodded here because he knew about that] and lets out his sperm into the woman's vagina. The sperm find their way to her egg inside her uterus. The sperm and egg join and grow into a baby."

Billy was nodding vigorously. "I know all that. But what if the lady goes pee while they're doing it. Where do the sperms go then?" Children take in only what they are ready for, what speaks to their perspective, their concerns. Mr. Stone explained that urine comes from a different place.

"Why does my penis get hard?"

"When you touch it, and it feels nice, your penis gets hard."

"Is it bad to do that?" "No, it isn't bad. It's normal. Everyone touches this part of their body at times."

"Do girls?" "Yes, their sex organs are sensitive, like yours."

"But they don't look the same. Did theirs fall off? One of my friends said they did."

"No, Billy, girls were always like that. Their sex organs are inside and are for growing babies. Ours are on the outside, for giving the seeds to grow the babies. We are just different from the very first. It's more interesting that way, isn't it?"

Billy knows he's not ready to act on any of this now. The time when he will be seems very far away to him. A parent may worry that answers to questions like these may be over-stimulating. The child's reactions—what he says, what he doesn't say—are a parent's guide. A parent who faces these questions with a child is joining him in his wondering about the world. The child understands that some answers go beyond his range of understanding and his range of action, but he seems to be looking for his parents to participate in his questions about this part of life, just like any other part of life.

Masturbation is always a question in children's minds. It should go without saying that this is true for girls as well as for boys. If parents wade in by asking about it, the questions are likely to go underground. If the parents can wait until the six-year-old asks, they can adjust the answers to the child's own concerns. Why do children feel that masturbating is harmful or punishable? Perhaps because parents haven't entirely gotten over feeling that way themselves. Despite our distance from the Victorian era, we still haven't completely escaped from the feeling that masturbation is wrong in some way. A parent's role may be to reassure the child while emphasizing the private, special nature of this act.

During his conversation with his stepfather, Billy had not seemed embarrassed. But when they had finished, he began to get red. When he returned to the rest of the family, his stepfather could see how serious he was. Billy watched his mother and his baby sister with renewed interest. For this six-year-old, the smutty words had been covering up important questions. It may be easier to tease with words than it is to ask deeper questions and listen to their answers. Mr. Stone had answered Billy's questions but he'd also prepared him for communication later on. He realized that beneath Billy's smutty words deeper issues were at stake.

Mr. Stone felt closer to Billy after this episode, and was learning about another way Billy needed him. He recognized that Billy needed time with him in order to bring up, digest, and come back to topics like this. A child counts on continuity to share this kind of intimacy with a parent.

Moral Development

Aggression and Self-control

Sports at school are a safety valve for the pent-up emotions and energy that accumulate while sitting in a classroom. When first-graders are let out at recess, they are likely to burst with noisy activity. After running around the schoolyard, they return panting and ready for more controlled sports and activities. Girls of this age often need the physical activity, too, but they are more easily contained. They may use their energy to giggle, tease, or gossip with each other. Their gossip can often contain aggressive ideas; but they, too, are safely couched Aggression is beginning to be more readily contained at this age. Nightmares and fears aren't as predominant as they have been; fantasies are less wild and unrestrained. A six-year-old has a clear sense of the difference between make-believe and reality. He is also beginning to know the difference between wishful thinking and what may really happen.

Whenever recess came, the boys in Mrs. Simmons class literally poured out of the room. They tripped each other. They stepped on each other's feet. They bounced into each other. If one fell down, all the others fell on top of him. Tim, however, waited until all the others were outside. Then he gingerly sidled out and sat on the outside steps, book in hand. He never looked at the book. He watched the other boys as they tumbled about or kicked a ball in "organized" athletics.

Their exuberance was contagious. Everyone wanted either to play or to watch. The girls watched out of the corners of their eyes as they hovered in groups. Tim watched. As one boy was picked on by two other classmates, he left the group grumbling and downcast. As if needing a scapegoat, he walked up to Tim. He grabbed Tim's book and threw it in the air. He started to tease Tim and then to hit him. Billy caught on to this almost immediately. He ran up to them. "Steve, leave Tim alone! You'll hurt him! Mrs. Simmons will get you." "She won't find out unless you or Tim tattle. You can't stop me." "Yes, I can. Tim's my friend. So leave him alone." The boy slunk away, rejected again. Tim looked at Billy with gratitude, but no words.

Cheating   Tim's patience and persistence with the computer was impressive. He could sit in front of the screen for hours at a time. Many other boys of his age would be too restless. Tim used it as a refuge. The computer was responsive to his demands. He could dream on a computer, making up stories and fantasies. When he played on a computer at school, other children were drawn in.

Timmy loved quiet games. He would listen to instructions and watch carefully to see what came next. He seemed to catch on to the rules of each game very quickly—but he loved to win. When he did, his eyes flashed, his face lit up with joy, and he cried out with pleasure. When his parents played with him, they were overjoyed by his interest and his capacity to learn so quickly. But soon, Tim learned to cheat. At first, his parents overlooked it: "He just hasn't learned the rules yet. He's only six." When they corrected him, he broke down in tears. He stomped off, refusing to play, refusing to listen.

His parents were so intimidated by this behavior that they started to ignore his cheating. At first, they rationalized it, thinking it was necessary for his self-image. But Tim was on the verge of understanding right from wrong, and he knew he was cheating. He knew the rules, but enlarged on them by inventing new rules. He knew what he was doing to others.

The McCormicks realized that they had to do something to prevent the cheating from becoming a pattern. What if he could never learn to play fairly?

Tim's need to win at these games was typical of a six-year-old's fervor. Any way he could win seemed worth it. But he was no longer as joyful when he won. He was developing a conscience—his wary eyes showed that. Mr. McCormick was the first to confront this change. "Tim, you aren't really playing with me. You are just making sure that you win. I don't find that any fun, and I'm not sure you do, either." "I want to win, Daddy. You win too much." "But you don't really win that way. Cheating isn't winning. It's just cheating. If you cheat, I don't want to play with you any longer. Don't your friends want to quit when you cheat?" Tim was silent. "Other kids won't like you when you cheat." "I can't help it, Daddy. I want to win so badly."

"When we play a game, I can tell you what I do and why, then maybe you can learn from me how I win." Mr. McCormick watched Tim wince as he spoke. Tim felt hopeless about ever living up to his father. Maybe all the measuring up was driving the cheating. Mr.

McCormick tried again. "You can learn to play without cheating. But first we need to figure out how to help you stand it when you can tell you're about to lose."

In this way, Tim's father was able to offer both understanding and limits. Mr. McCormick was giving Tim a chance to learn. He had heard the longing in Tim's voice for success with his peers. He knew that now Tim could tell right from wrong.

Before a child can understand a game, he will play fast and loose with the rules. Then comes a time when he wants to practice the game over and over to learn the limits. But, at some point, understanding the game and playing it may not be enough: he wants to win so much, he cheats. Parents can tell when a child is ready to follow rules by watching his eyes and his face. They reveal his provocative attempt to test the limits. After he's been caught and reprimanded, his relief may even show through.

Now was a time for other outlets for Tim. He needed other toys that more directly addressed his need to win, to test out new, assertive feelings. Aggressive toys, such as action figures, would give him a chance to identify and overcome his feelings. Certain games gave Tim a sense of power. Now was a time for his father to play a critical role in his life because Tim was asking for that kind of involvement. The big step of developing a conscience was there but, equally important right now for Tim, was self-confidence. The cheating worried his parents, but it also meant that he was daring to come out of his shell. This was a touchpoint for Tim, and an opportunity for his parents to support these fragile new capacities for competitiveness, frustration, overcoming barriers, and adapting himself to the dangerous role of being a winner. These are big steps at the age of six.

Tim was learning how to defend himself from his feelings of inadequacy. He could turn inward and turn to his computer or to other ways of retreating from pressure to be just like other boys. He wasn't like them, and couldn't be. But he could learn to excel in areas that would bring gratification. This would take a lot of backing up from his parents. They needed to participate with him, to admire his skills. Many parents would want to push him to "be like every other boy." That would only undermine Tim, who already wished it for himself. Instead, supporting him for his ability to use the computer imaginatively, to excel in card games, to do well in school, could achieve the goals they are all after.

Along with his increasing awareness of others' feelings was Tim's emerging ability to be aware of his own. "I don't like playing outside at recess. The other kids don't want me with them, and it makes me feel bad. I'd rather do things inside." Becoming aware of one's own feelings and being able to express them as succinctly as this is a step toward managing the inevitable slights from peers. Understanding and accepting one's temperament helps a child learn self-protection. At six, creating adequate defenses is a necessary step toward preserving one's own self-esteem. Cheating is a poor substitute.

Why Is It Tattling If I Was Supposed to Tell You?

Mrs. Simmons had asked the class to write a story. She had given them an idea about a child whose puppy had run away from home and how another child who was bedridden had adopted the puppy. The sick child fell in love with the puppy. What should the first child do? Several of the girls banded together to compare their stories, and to help each other with them. Mrs. Simmons had expressly asked them to do this assignment alone. They were cheating when they compared each others' stories, and they knew they were.

Minnie overheard them and probably felt excluded. Minnie went to Mrs. Simmons: "Those three girls are putting all their ideas together. They aren't doing the assignment by themselves." Mrs. Simmons' reply was, "Minnie, I'm glad you feel you can come to me. But how do you think those girls will feel about you if they know you've been tattling on them? For that's what you've done." "What is tattling?" "It's telling on someone to get them in trouble." "I don't want to get them in trouble. I just wanted you to know about it." "Thank you, Minnie. But I think you need to be aware of what it might mean to them if you tattled on them." Mrs. Simmons was emphasizing the importance of social relationships at this age—an important step for Minnie.

Minnie was confused. Why had Mrs. Simmons deserted her? Why was it wrong to tell the truth? At home, the rule of exposing a mistake was valued, and so was truthfulness. At first, Minnie was deflated. She was also angry with Mrs. Simmons for letting her down. She realized she was trying to win Mrs. Simmons over. But she also began to realize that Mrs. Simmons might have been right about Minnie's desire to get the girls into trouble. She was jealous, and Mrs. Simmons was trying to tell her that this wasn't a positive way to handle jealousy.

When should a child "tell" and when is it "tattling"?

This is a major challenge to the inflexible notions of right and wrong of the six-year-old. At home, Mrs. Lee could help her daughter consider the gray zone between black and white, even if Minnie would not be ready to find her own way there for quite some time. When Minnie reported an infringement by her sister, Mrs. Lee could say, "Minnie, do you need me to interfere in this? Couldn't you handle it with your sister without me? I think you are trying to get your sister into trouble. That's tattling, Minnie." It will be a long time before Minnie understands the motives underlying her behavior, and even then the struggles with a sibling are bound to persist.

Stealing

Billy came home from Tim's house with two dinosaurs. His mother said, "Oh, Billy, those are new, aren't they? Did Tim give them to you, or did you buy them?" Billy's silence and his downcast eyes gave Mrs. Stone her answer. "Billy, those dinosaurs aren't yours. Where did you get them?" "Tim gave them to me." "Are you sure?" "No." "Thank you, Billy, for being truthful. It would be a lot worse if you hid them and lied about it. That would be stealing. Now, what shall we do about these dinosaurs?" Billy looked at the toys sadly. He put them up to his face lovingly. "I guess I need to take them back." "Yes, you do. But I am sure Tim would be happy to let you borrow them. How about calling him and saying you've got them. Can you play with them tonight and take them back tomorrow?" "Then he'll know I took them. Maybe I should just slip them back tomorrow." "You probably could. He probably wouldn't have missed them yet. But that wouldn't be honest. I know it's hard, but if you call him, it will be brave. He'll forgive you. And you'll feel much, much better. Stealing isn't something anyone feels good about."

Mrs. Stone has given Billy a chance to think about right and wrong, and to make reparations. In doing so, she has allowed her son to learn an important lesson: Even if you can get away with stealing, it isn't acceptable. This is a lesson in moral reasoning, and a step toward self-discipline.

*Learning
About Right
and Wrong
from Siblings*

Siblings teach each other about doing unto others as you would have done unto you, about picking on someone your own size, about right and wrong. But the number of children per family is decreasing, and extended families are disappearing. Hence, many six-year-olds never have a younger sibling or cousin, never have a chance to learn lessons in the same ways that earlier generations learned them. An innovative program in Philadelphia called Educating Children for Parenting introduced babies into first-grade classes. Very early, the six-year-olds were shown the concept of the baby as another human being. They saw how difficult it is to care for a dependent person and how exciting it could be to see a baby master a new step towards independence.

The children not only valued the baby and his development but related the baby's changes to their own development. Many of the first-graders regressed; they sucked their thumbs, they wanted to try a bottle and a pacifier, they wet their pants. Such predictable regression should not have disturbed anyone because it nearly always happens when a new baby joins a family. In this case, however, parents complained to the teacher: "She hasn't sucked her thumb in ages. Now you've taught her to do it all over again. Suppose she won't stop this time?" But this type of regression is a part of learning to care about the baby by identifying with what the baby might be feeling—the beginning of caring about doing right and recognizing wrong.

Billy had started to swing from nurturing and protecting two-year-old Abby to pushing her aside as he walked by her. She was constantly demanding his attention. She was intrusive, always calling, "Billy, Billy!" Although he ignored her most of the time, he eventually reached his boiling point. Either he walked out of the room, slamming the door behind him, or he confronted his sister, taking whatever she had in her hand. She would scream; he would turn his back. He would smirk slightly as he flaunted the toy he had taken, and Abby would scream even louder. Mrs. Stone: "Billy, what are you doing to Abby?" Billy would try to run from the room. Fever-pitched screams from Abby. When Billy cringed but hung on to the toy, he almost demonstrated to his mother the source of their trouble. She sensed the conflict: "Billy, give Abby back her toy."

Then Billy would throw the toy at Abby, hitting her in the face. More screams. Triumphant smiles from Billy. Mrs. Stone, angrier now: "Why do you have to tease her whenever I leave the room? Can't you and Abby ever play together peacefully?"

The answer is yes and no. When nothing is to be lost, Billy and Abby play together. But when Billy's frustration or boredom mount, his need to cause a reaction in his sister combines with his need to let off steam. If he wants a reaction from his mother as well, he must push Abby into a more violent protest.

Abby's protest serves two purposes—it rids Billy of some of his own overload (Abby takes it on) and it creates exciting chaos around him. Both of these are a way of ventilating *and* controlling his own feelings. He can watch them played out for him with relative safety.

At six, a child can be seen to evaluate a situation and decide whether he can act upon it or not. Billy could have decided to give Abby back her toy. He could rationalize his defeat by saying to himself, "I'm bigger and stronger than she is. I can always find something else to tease her about." He feels the difference between her age and abilities and his own.

Nurturing feelings can arise to help him give up his urge to tease her. If they were alone and she was unprotected, it is likely that he would have taken care of her rather than tease her. Involving his mother raises the ante. Sibling rivalry rarely escalates to a dangerous level unless an adult is nearby. The triangle that results makes a fight worthwhile. In Billy's case, his use of Abby seemed to be heightened beyond their sibling relationship to one in which she became an outlet for his own feelings. She could turn his need to blow up into a "safer" incident. "Abby is crying. I made her. I'm sorry." Maybe it is too hard for him to say, "I feel like crying, too."

A Child Who Copes

Marcy was subdued. Her recent learning disability diagnosis had stunned everyone in the family. Everyone took it seriously, and her brother even treated her with a new kind of courtesy. This scared Marcy. When she tried to tease him, he reacted with such gentleness that she couldn't accustom herself to it. Her parents were worried. They kept dodging any discussion with her. She'd known that Mrs. Simmons had arranged a meeting with them. She'd known it was about her. She had suspected that something was wrong. But she equated it with what she thought of as her "badness."

Sometimes when she couldn't please people, she'd resort to her "badness." She'd act up, show off, become silly. Everyone would admonish her: "Marcy, you don't need to be the center of attention." Now she would catch her mother looking at her in a new, suspicious way. When it was at a time when she hadn't been acting up, she felt even more scrutinized. What was her mother looking for? She knew there was something in the air, but what?

Marcy had learned to contain her feelings, but now it seemed more difficult. When she felt sad, she showed her sadness. When she was angry, she felt compelled to take her anger out on someone. She felt as if something scary was happening to her. She didn't know whether she could control herself any longer.

When her big brother put her dinner plate down hard in front of her, she jumped. The plate looked cracked. She knew she'd be blamed. Then she noticed that the food on her plate wasn't what she liked. She began to cry. She picked up the plate as if to smash it down on the table "like he had." She almost threw it on the floor. Her mother looked at her disapprovingly. That look saved Marcy. She caught herself in time. She was shaking inside and wondering, "What's wrong with me?"

Marcy was used to being able to control her feelings. Threats to her self-control alarmed her. The mastery she'd gained was temporarily undermined by her problems in school and the tension they caused in her and around her. Her feelings of being out of control were not new, but Marcy's awareness of them shows a new maturity. Her awareness of her difficulty in controlling herself will help her to watch for these reactions so that she can manage them before they get out of hand. The fact that she could use the warning in her mother's look as a prohibition is already a sign of how receptive she is to cues that help her handle her strong feelings.

At six, the awareness of consequences from one's aggression is growing. With this comes the effort at self-control, the goal of all previous discipline. A parent's efforts to instill in a child that "someday you can control it yourself" are now ready to pay off. Marcy did control herself. Her parents would be wise to commend her efforts.

When Marcy and her parents have recovered from the shock of learning about her disability and what it might mean to Marcy, her self-esteem and her ability to use controls over her impulses will recover. Marcy will regress as she gathers steam to face the testing and the help that will be offered her for her learning difficulties. Marcy's wonderful sense of herself as a competent person has been shaken by the family's disappointment. It is time for her parents to resolve their own feelings, and to help her with hers. Marcy's volatility is related to her fears and worries about herself.

Building Relationships: Making Friends

First-Grade Friendships

First-grade friends can offer a refuge from sibling struggles. When you observe a six-year-old as she leaves a group, you will notice that a friend will sometimes walk beside her and unconsciously imitate her movements, her gestures, her speech rhythms. Friendships are forming. There will be triangles—excluding one friend for another. Belonging has become important, and it is heightened by knowledge that someone else is "out." When feelings are hurt, it is surprising to see how little the two excluders notice. Inconsistent as it might seem, though, nurturing behavior is surfacing at the same time as the competitive, selfish kind; yet nurturing feelings may be embarrassing enough to a child of this age to require the cover of teasing and backbiting.

Marcy and Lila were discussing Marcy's new dressed-up doll. "She's so beautiful. Look at her earrings and necklace. She's wearing them at home to take care of her baby." Not to be outdone, Lila spouted, "Mine doesn't. She likes to get all undressed. She's concentrating on her baby. If she's too dressed up, the baby might think she has to go to work." "Oh." Marcy hesitated a moment to prepare her comeback. "Well, mine never leaves her baby at all. She loves her so much."

One day, Billy was invited for a play date with Lila. The crowd giggled about their being in love. Billy never consented to another such date. He had discovered that he had broken an unspoken rule, and

he wanted to fit in. His excuse was that Lila made him be a daddy at her house: "She wants to play with her Barbie dolls." Billy played with Ken dolls during the play date when he and Lila played "families" or "getting married." But he felt uncomfortable. Tim tried to be reassuring: "It's okay to play with girls." Billy protested: "No. It's no fun. Boys can be policemen, firefighters, whatever we want. We can shoot and use our hoses to put out fires. Girls can't."

When Billy played fireman with the other boys, they jumped off the jungle gym. If one boy climbed high to jump, another climbed higher. Each boy added to the other's feats, escalating the goals. As they imitated and endorsed each other, their actions set up the silent code for group membership. Finally, one boy would fall too hard, or scrape his face. He'd fall apart with violent crying. This time, the others would gather around him, frightened and sympathetic. Their fragility showed at a moment like this. Trying so hard to outdo or to live up to each other carried its price: when anything went wrong, they'd all fall apart. This time, all the participants shared in the child's pain and blow-up. They didn't tease him for being a sissy. This kind of play helps children discover the limits of competition and of their own prowess. At the same time, they learn about empathy. Such incidents can go either way. The next time, the group might just as readily turn against the wounded one and taunt him for being the "cry baby" while all too aware of their own vulnerability.

The boys' caring behavior, like their teasing, carries over into the classroom. There, they are just as likely to support each other openly and silently as they are to compare and compete. If one watches carefully, the boys will all be alert as one of them is asked to perform. If he answers a question right, they will nod slightly, their faces will brighten almost imperceptibly. Billy is a favorite of many boys, and it is easy to see how much they support him. Tim is not as popular, but even he receives approval when he is able to generate a bright answer to Mrs. Simmons's questions. Being bright and eager to learn will certainly help Tim with his peers in the long run, especially if he can share these strengths, as he does with Billy, rather than isolate himself further.

Tim and Billy were becoming better friends. When Billy wanted to practice reading or writing, he continued to go to Tim's desk for reassurance. Tim felt important to another child for the first time, and it gave him the courage to open up. At recess, he found he didn't dread the times when he had to be "out" and, at least peripherally, part of the gang. He didn't play on the playground as "they" did, but he watched, admired, and even laughed when they did. Billy always tried to persuade Tim to play, but he had also learned when to let up. That made Tim feel good, for if Billy liked him well enough to ask him to play, it meant that Billy believed he could do it. Preoccupied with his own timidity and fears, Tim could not have sensed how much effort his hero Billy's successes required.

A Parent's Role in Children's Relationships

One day, Billy came home after school exhausted and touchy. He was working hard at being like his new friends, being part of their group. He felt he had to shut out his parents now and then, when his longing to be close to them seemed at odds with being a big boy, like the other boys. "What did you do today in school, Billy?" "Nothing."

A parent is likely to feel excluded. "Can't you remember anything?" "Nope." If pushed, Billy was likely to retreat to his room or become aggressive with Abby or the cat. Such behavior speaks of how costly the day has been for him. He has been working hard all day to learn about himself in relation to other children, as well as to read and write. Mrs. Stone had better wait and give Billy time to rest and refuel, to get reorganized. His news of the day will come out when he is ready. If he can't share his feelings immediately, he will do so eventually. Protections such as temporarily avoiding conversation about the things he is threatened by are necessary, especially at a time of so much learning and change.

Another reason for this new, apparent distance is that the emotional energy that was available for identifying with parents in the fourth and fifth years is now becoming a force for identifying with peers. Just as they have turned from one parent to another, children now push and pull with friends to see how much their friendships can tolerate. This behavior is often painful for children whose peers don't accept them. It's so hard to be different. Tim's sensitivity and Minnie's bossiness become deep sources of pain when the other children are working to be like everyone else. When children are six, their struggles to learn how to get along with others need more empathy from adults than ever.

Children who are learning to cope with the uniqueness of their needs and gifts may be excluded by peer groups. Can their parents protect them? They are likely to try: "You're just as great as they are" rings in Tim's ears over and over. But he doesn't feel that way; he knows he is different, but doesn't know why. He knows his shy, retiring behavior marks him in others' eyes, too. At a time when the other boys are working so hard to be just like every other boy, Tim's retiring sensitivity makes them uneasy. The boys are all trying so hard to be part of the group, to mask their own fears of being different.

For a child who isn't successful, the work of trying to be like everyone else can be exhausting. "Why am I different? What can I do? Will I always be no good?" Can parents protect their child from feelings of exclusion? Not very likely. When parents approach the problem, the child will wince perceptibly. She is in pain, and they see it. Although they cannot share the pain with her, they can gradually acknowledge it; in this way, the child will feel their support even though she will not be able to tell them so. They can let her know that they are available and open to her feelings. They can wait for her to express her loneliness. I urge that parents allow the child to lead them, to find a time when feelings can be shared.

When she is ready, Minnie might say, "The boys hate me. They don't want me on their teams anymore." A parent might minimize the situation. "They don't hate you. They're just jealous—especially of good athletes like you." But Minnie may feel that this doesn't ring true, that her parents were "just" trying to reassure her. She might feel that her parents haven't really taken in what she's saying, that she's lost their support. But she will give her parents more chances to understand.

"I think it's just me. They say I'm too loud and that I tell them what to do all the time." "That's probably true, Minnie," said her father. "But, on the other hand, I don't think you could make them take you in right now, whatever you did." Minnie broke into tears. "It makes me want to give up sports." "Minnie, you could do that. But you would be giving in to them if you do. You have choices. You don't have to see yourself the same way they see you. You can decide that there are things you like about you, even the things that bug them." Minnie sat down next to her father and leaned her head against his shoulder. "It's true they won't let you be on their teams because you're a girl. But what about using all your energy and your anger to become the best girl athlete in the class?" Minnie looked skeptical. "They'd really hate me if I could beat them at their own sports."

One day, Marcy came home from school in tears. "Minnie doesn't like me. She plays with Lila all the time. When I go up to them, they just turn their backs on me. Nobody likes me." The teasing often gets worse in later years, but even in first grade, insults can be surprisingly cruel.

"I don't like you. You have dark skin and curly hair. I like Lila better." What can a parent do to help? We'd all like to shake up the other kids and say, "Cut it out. Everyone is different." Six is a time when conformist reactions to ethnic and temperamental diversity peak. The forces to identify, to "be alike," and to belong, are so strong at six that children throw up barriers against perceived differences. Any parent feels protective and wants to defend her child from being left out—but it may not be possible.

This is a time for parents to face their own vulnerability first. When Marcy comes home in a demoralized state, Mrs. Jackson needs to hear Marcy's anguish without adding her own. "Of course it hurts when your friends turn against you. But you know that everyone teases everyone else."

"But why does she always have to pick on me?" "She might be interested in you, Marcy. Maybe even jealous. She wouldn't tease you if she hadn't noticed you. It's okay to tease her back. You may be different from her, but she's different from us, too. It just depends on your point of view. But don't tease her about her differences just because she treated you that way. Everyone has something different. Wouldn't it be boring if we were all the same? You are fine just the way you are. So stand up for yourself. I know it's not easy. I had to go through it at your age, too, and I still remember the way it felt." If Mrs. Jackson can handle her own vulnerability, her own protective anger, she will be able to help Marcy put her classmates' behavior into perspective.

"Marcy, you don't need to show them how much it hurts when they tease you. That'll only encourage them. Save it for me. And you don't have to agree with them when they say something mean about you. You can decide for yourself what you think about yourself."

Independence and Separation

"Just a Few Days"

Mr. Stone had to go away on one of his business trips. This was a bad time for separation; Billy was as hungry for more contact as his stepfather was. He talked it out with Billy. "I really hate to go away right now. I want to be with you more. How about our making a videotape together—a silly part and a serious part—so that you can play it while I'm gone?" Billy nodded thoughtfully. His stepfather made him a calendar with the dates of his trip marked. Billy could check off each day that Mr. Stone was away, so as to have a more realistic idea of time and of waiting. But Mr. Stone still needed to understand that for a six-year-old, a day is a very long time. If possible, he should phone Billy every day.

When Mr. Stone returns, he could remind Billy about the times they had planned; but he must be sure to live up to these promises. He could tell Billy how much he missed him. It makes a child feel important when a parent levels about missing him.

Mr. Stone's departure will still be painful. But Billy will learn about coping. A child must learn to face and live with his own painful feelings. We can't protect children from inevitable losses, nor should we.

*Do Guinea
Pigs Go to
Heaven?*

Minnie's guinea pig died. The animal had been brought into the family when Minnie was four, and the novelty had long since worn off. Minnie named her guinea pig Agula and had been thrilled with her at first. She'd let her pet out to run around the house. The guinea pig rarely dirtied the floor. When she did, Minnie was excited and immediately wiped it up. She would inspect the mess in great detail. "Mom, they have poops, too! Does it come out of their bums like ours does? Where is the hole for the wee-wee? Is it the same one as the baby guinea pig comes out of?"

Mrs. Lee was hard put to answer all of Minnie's questions, but she had sensed that they were telling her something important. Mrs. Lee would explore, listen to what Minnie already knew and figure out what her unanswered questions might be. Pets are a wonderful source of questions about sexuality, nature, and death. They are also opportunities for reinforcing care-taking skills. When Minnie picked up the guinea pig to love it, or to try it out on a slanted surface, Mrs. Lee would encourage her. Don't discourage tender or exploratory interaction (unless the animal could be injured or it could injure the child). Often, a child's hidden feelings surface during play with a pet. A child who tortures a pet is warning us about his hidden, unresolved anger. This must be attended to.

What if Minnie didn't want to take care of Agula? Her loss of enthusiasm for the daily chores is common. Children must have supervision with a pet. At this point, a parent's choices are (1) to do the caregiving herself; (2) to set up a schedule of sharing the chores—but of expecting Minnie to live up to her side of it; (3) finding Agula a new home where she can be well cared for. Haranguing the child daily is no solution and it won't work for long. What might work is a chart for the chores, supervised by the adult, coupled with praise for accomplishing the goals and a mild penance for not.

"It's your job to remember to change Agula's water after school every day. If you want me to remind you, I will. You could find a way to remind yourself, maybe by putting her cage near the front door when you leave for school." Giving a child a positive sense of responsibility should be your goal. Her actual help may be more symbolic than anything else at this age, but it's an important start. Meanwhile, parents should demonstrate by example how to be responsible for an animal's needs. A child will not learn about this responsibility if adults neglect to teach them, or if they buy pets on a whim and later have to give them away.

When Agula died, Minnie realized that she hadn't really paid attention to her animal for a long time. It made her feel guilty. When she went to Agula's cage one morning and found her stiffened beside her empty water dish with her mouth open, her eyes wide, Minnie felt as if her pet were looking at her reproachfully. Minnie knew in her heart that she'd lost interest in the animal and that she'd not played with her for a long time. She had fed and watered her a few days ago, but her mother had had to fill in. Minnie felt responsible.

Minnie was crushed. She wept. She stormed. "Why did she have to die?" "What happens when you die?" Mrs. Lee began to tell Minnie that "the angels had come and taken Agula away in her sleep." This did not have the comforting effect that Mrs. Lee had hoped for. She realized that sleep could now become a frightening time for Minnie. And why would "angels" suddenly appear on the scene to take Agula away? Mrs. Lee decided to tell the truth as she knew it.

"Agula's body just stopped working. That's what death is. Your body can't keep going." "Will I die?" "Yes, someday everyone dies, but you won't die for a long time." "When will you die? If I don't take care of you, like Agula, will you die?" "No, I won't. I can take care of myself. I intend to for as long as I can. Maybe when I'm very old, you'll take care of me. But not for a long time." Minnie started to cry. "Sometimes I wish you were dead. Could that make you die?" "No, Minnie, everyone wishes things like that once in a while about people they love. But wishing it won't make it happen. Are you worried that thoughts like that made Agula die?" "Yeah." "Well I don't think they did. Pets get old, like people, and they have to die. But we loved Agula for a long time and she had a good life with us." Minnie looked very serious, and seemed to be taking it all in. "I still wish I'd been better to her." Her mother nodded. "You feel responsible. Good for you. Agula must know that."

A Grandparent's Death

Tim's grandfather had been ill for some time. Not only was he ill but he showed it. He looked wasted; his eyes were dull, his body was weak and shrunken. Everyone catered to him. They all wanted to help him. "Can I get you a pillow, Grandpa?" "Would you like a glass of iced tea?" They showered him with attention.

Tim thought the attention was more than his grandfather really wanted. When he made pained faces after some of these offers, Tim felt it was in response to being treated as if he were a baby. He wished that everything could be the way it was before his grandfather got sick. He was sure his grandfather did, too. Tim tried to cheer his grandfather up. Whenever he tried to tell him a story, making them up from stories he remembered from his nighttime reading, his grandfather brightened up as if to thank him. But his grandfather soon faded, falling asleep and snoring with the most terrible sound. Tim had never heard such a deep-throated, rasping sound, and it frightened him. He fled and hid in his mother's lap. His mother tried to comfort him: "Grandfather is just so sick. He knows you're trying to make him feel better and he's grateful. But he just can't stay awake to listen. Tim, I am so proud of you for trying hard to help him."

Tim had many different feelings. He resented his grandfather's snoring, his weakness, his lack of fight when everyone treated him like an invalid who couldn't do anything. "Why don't you get better?" kept running through his mind. He knew he'd heard it over and over about himself.

Tim began to have nightmares again. He'd had them at four, but they'd disappeared. No one knew why they came and just as suddenly stopped. Now, Tim would wake up sobbing loudly, crying out, "No, no! Leave me alone!" His parents would come rushing in to him. They'd try to comfort him as he sobbed in their arms. He couldn't remember the bad dreams, and he didn't know why he was having them. He knew he felt helpless and weak after each one, but that wasn't anything new for Tim. At school, though, he was conscious of being more outgoing. He was more responsive to the children around him.

When Tim's grandfather died the next week, Mrs. McCormick was hit hard. She'd known it was coming, but nothing could have prepared her for how she would feel with her father gone. She and her sisters sat around, quietly remembering stories about their father. Tim didn't want to be drawn into it, for it was too painful to see his mother so devastated. He wanted to comfort her and try to smooth it over. Each of them tried to help the other. "He must be so relieved," said Tim's mother. "It was terrible being so ill and now he's free of it. I can almost imagine he's flying around, looking down on us and saying, 'Why are they sad?'"

Tim listened carefully. One day soon after, when his parents were driving him home after school, he asked, "Why did Grandpa die?" "Because he was old, his body was giving out. His heart wasn't good any longer." "What happens to dead people? Do they just fall asleep? Couldn't he wake up again?" "No, Tim, your body just stops functioning and you aren't conscious any longer. It's not the same as sleep, because you don't wake up." "What about angels? Do they come and get you?" "We don't know what happens to someone's spirit after they die. We like to make up things to comfort ourselves. We hate to give Grandpa up. We try to think that he's looking down at us and watching over us. But we are just making that up, because we don't know that that's true." "Maybe it is. I miss him already." "We all do. It helps to talk about him and to share our memories of him." "I don't think so. It just makes me miss him even more. I wish I'd helped him more when he was alive. I should have been nicer to him."

"Tim, everyone feels bad about something they haven't done for a person after he dies," said his father. "I feel just like you. I never even bought him a book to read when he was so sick. I kept meaning to, but I never did." Tim looked up at his father gratefully. He wished he'd done so much more for his grandfather.

Now one of Tim's only ways of showing how sad he was would be to help his mother. He set the table. He helped her in the kitchen. She looked at him with grateful eyes, but she started weeping all over again. That wasn't what he wanted. He wanted to comfort her and protect her from all those tears.

A six-year-old is bound to have questions—about death, about funerals, about religious and ethnic beliefs. This is a time to share beliefs, to share the grieving, to open up to a child, and to listen. The stirring up of guilt and memories of missed opportunities will all come to the surface in the next weeks. When a parent has attended to her own grieving and begins to share the child's, the time has come to listen and to be ready to answer questions, even about one's own feelings. Meanwhile, it is important for Tim to be able to see his mother's grief at the loss of her father. (What would it have meant to him had there been no grief, or none that he could witness?) It is also important for him to experience the protective feelings his grandfather's death has called up in him. Tim found it comforting to be able to express the guilty, empty feelings of not having done his part for his grandfather. When he told his father how he felt, it paved the way for his father's own guilty admission.

Parents' attempts to explain death are difficult for them, but necessary. Children cannot trust such statements as "He died in his sleep," "He flew up to heaven," or "He'll be back later." At the same time, six-year-olds cannot readily understand the irreversibility of death. None of us understands death. Everyone suffers fears and guilty feelings. Religious beliefs are one of our ways of trying to explain the unexplainable. A child needs honesty and shared feelings and the freedom to unload and share his own. Tim is fortunate to be able to learn about loss and grief from his parents. This loss has brought them all closer.

Self-esteem in First Grade

As a child becomes more independent and enters the world of first grade, self-esteem becomes at risk. Everyday brings more evaluations—by peers, by teachers, by the child himself. Marcy had to face her reading disability. Billy was confronted with Tim's superior scholastic abilities. Billy is a confident child and can make a kind of trade in self-esteem. He can turn to Tim for the help he needs in reading and writing. In return, he gives Tim a feeling of being looked up to, of being cared for; this helps Tim feel good about himself. Billy was confident enough in himself to slow down to listen and encourage Tim. He was able to sense Tim's needs and to accept Tim's help.

An important measure of a six-year-old's self-esteem is how sensitive he is toward his peers. His sensitivity helps his peers accept him and like him. If they like him, adults can be reassured that he has qualities that other children can relate to and respect. But at six there are limits to his sensitivity.

Minnie came home bursting with news for her parents. "I have a best friend. It's Marcy. She's fun and she likes me. She's great in school. She's the best drawer in the whole class. She draws beautiful pictures. She's almost as good as I am."

Even with the new room they make for others and the caring they are now capable of, six-year-olds are still "me" oriented. Many six-year-olds brag without recognizing how they sound when they do. Minnie knows that she isn't the best artist in her class, but she wants to be. She wants it so much that she pushes herself to be the best, and she almost believes that her fantasies are true. When she was three, she would have been utterly convinced. Such braggadocio is a natural responses to the big, new demands of school, but it can collide with the six-year-old's attentiveness to others.

Changes in behavior can be dramatic at this age. Often now, Minnie would sit quietly in a chair and stare at the wall. She was so quiet and unreachable. Her mother was struck by this because Minnie had never been a child who could "just sit." Mrs. Lee's own fears about Minnie's being affected by family problems were mobilized. "Does she know too much about the trouble her father and I are having? Are we affecting the children? Is Minnie depressed?" Certainly, a change in behavior associated with family problems can't be ruled out. But parents may be too quick to blame themselves when their child is hurting. Minnie might also be taxed by her efforts to make friends.

Minnie's athletic ability became her forte. She showed all the other girls how to jump rope. She delighted in showing all the other girls how to jump from side to side in one twirl. The others couldn't come close. Minnie showed off to them as long as they would watch. But after a few demonstrations, they'd turn away and ignore her. Then she'd feel deserted and vulnerable. She'd retreat to the steps and sit alone, watching as the other girls gathered in a group to giggle and to gossip. Minnie felt completely left out.

One day, Marcy noticed her sitting by herself. "Minnie, come on over." Minnie brightened. She dragged her feet, but she joined the group. As the girls accepted her, she began to show off again. But this only turned them away from her. Children are beginning to face competitive feelings at this age. All six-year-olds are aware of "who's best" and at what. Being best at something in the absence of social skills can be a liability at six. Minnie's athletic skills were threatening to the other girls. When they demonstrated their feelings by excluding her, she was driven to more showing off. Her behavior could turn into a vicious cycle.

Was Minnie trying to make up for something? All the energy she put into developing her athletic skills was at the expense of learning how to get along with other children. Arrogance covered up her awareness of the effect her showing off was having on others. Children who have been pushed to learn a skill too early are often at a loss in other domains; they pay a price, like Minnie. Minnie's parents need to help their daughter develop social skills and encourage her to divert some of her energy into making friends. But they will also need to make sure she leaves room for the drive that has led her to her physical accomplishments.

Mr. and Mrs. Lee need to establish and stick to expectations for social interactions in the family: hellos, good-byes, please and thank you, mealtime conversation, and so forth. They need to go out of their way to set up play dates for Minnie. These should offer planned activities that will appeal to both children. Initially, activities need not require a lot of direct interaction (a video or a trip to a movie, an outing for pizza or ice cream, miniature golf, the zoo). Such activities would give Minnie a chance to warm up slowly, to make the children's time together successful enough to encourage Minnie to try again. Pointing out her failures won't help, but a little feedback on how she might be perceived, how she might affect others, could. It might help to ask her how she would respond to someone who was showing off to her. Minnie might then be open to a few suggestions as to what she could do instead of showing off, what to say, or how to handle a particular situation. Some children like Minnie need help from adults in planning their social scripts.

If Minnie could have more confidence in herself, she would be more independent, less at the mercy of her peers. When she sat at home feeling miserable, her feelings of vulnerability at school ground her down, even though she would not say so. Her peers' approval was almost as important as that of her parents. Minnie needs her successful accomplishments, but she also needs to learn to handle her peers without having to impress them. "Minnie, you're looking sad. Is it so hard at school?" "Yeah, sometimes it is." "Can we talk about it? I'd like to hear." No response. "You know, I had a tough time at your age. I wasn't popular with anyone. Kids didn't really like me, and I was scared because I didn't know what to do about it." Minnie perked up a bit. "Then I made a friend. She liked me. She told me the other kids thought I was too bossy and a show-off. I didn't even know what bossy meant." "What's bossy, Mom?" "It's when you try to tell other kids what to do. When you show off, you show people you can do things better than they can." "Oh." Minnie had taken this in and was silently considering it. Mrs. Lee had tried hard to understand and to support her daughter, but she realized that she'd intruded enough. She didn't continue.

Meanwhile, Minnie deserved backup for what she could do. She helped with the chores at home. She set the table. She helped with

the dishes. She needed recognition for this, as well as encouragement for her athletics. Team playing could be even more helpful for
Minnie than it was when she was younger. She was ready now to
learn the rules and to fit in with the rest of the team. She might have
a chance not only to make a friend but to learn to hold back for the
good of the team.

Her fragility with her peers was an indication of her shaky self-
esteem—but it certainly wasn't a lost cause. Minnie had assets that
could be counted on to help her as long as she didn't give up on the
things that didn't come naturally. Like all children, she would need
skills in many areas, and it was too soon to tell where her talents
would take her.

Praising her would not be enough. She needed the approval of
her peers as well as of her family. Minnie needed a sensitive, ap-
proving teacher and the acceptance of a team. But her most important goal was to be able to approve of herself, even in moments
when no one else seemed to. No wonder it is so hard for six-year-
olds to face their weaknesses and their mistakes! If her mother

took Minnie's regression personally and blamed it on family troubles alone, she might miss opportunities to reinforce Minnie's self-esteem. Mrs. Lee was right, though, to worry that if Minnie blamed herself for her parents' arguing, she could take whatever momentary adversity comes her way as evidence of her own "badness."

In an effort to grow up and become independent, children of six are likely to try out tasks that are beyond their capacity. Marcy wanted to become a babysitter. She had played with the two- and three-year-old children next door. Their mother had complimented her. "Marcy, you're a natural. You really know what kids need. You could be a teacher or a baby doctor when you grow up."

Marcy wondered why she couldn't baby-sit for other children if she was so good with them. The children next door loved her and followed her around. Why couldn't she take them somewhere? Marcy decided to take them down the street to a pet store where they could look at the fish and the birds. As she started down the street with the toddlers, their mother came rushing out to stop her. "Marcy, where in the world are you going with the children? Don't you know any better? They could run out in the street and be killed."

What a crushing blow! Just as she'd begun to see herself as able to take care of small children, she'd failed completely. Marcy was overwhelmed. She ran home, crying loudly, "I'm no good! I want to die!" Mrs. Jackson was shaken. She gathered Marcy up, sat down in a rocking chair and rocked. Marcy's sobbing began to subside. She put her thumb in her mouth, fingering her mother's dress with the other hand. This had been her pattern of self-comfort when she was two years old. Marcy's eyes were unfocused. She was racked with dry sobs. Mrs. Jackson was frightened. She called her neighbor to learn what had happened.

"I know you meant to be helpful. It's just that taking small children off by yourself is too much for you. What if one of them tried to run away? What would you do? If you want to play with them, do it at home where their mother or I can help you if you need it. They love you and you love them. You are so good with them. But you are only six, and small kids need a grown-up to look after them." No response. But Marcy's sobs were quieter. Mrs. Jackson realized how hard the last few days had been for Marcy and how fragile she was. Her self-esteem, which had been such an asset for her, had been seriously challenged. It was time to face the blow the diagnosis of a learning problem had been.

What could be done? First of all, Mr. and Mrs. Jackson still need to face their own disappointment. Then they can pay more attention to Marcy and her fractured self-image. Simple reassurance won't help; it can even be insensitive. Acknowledgement of the feelings Marcy has about her difficulties must come first. "This is hard, isn't it, Marcy? You've never had to face anything like this." Her parents can help Marcy see that it's not the end of the world, but they first need to convince themselves of that. Marcy may be sensing their discouragement and fear for the future. She needs to feel that there are people who know how to help her with her problem, who can lead her to find her own way of learning. More cuddling, more understanding of the thumb sucking and the need to regress will also help. She needs a chance to unload her fears. Reassurance will help only after acknowledging how hard her self-image has been hit. Then she'll be ready to hear, "We can pull out of this together." She'll become convinced that she can be stronger and more secure when she's learned the coping skills she needs: "Let's go to work to find out what we need to do."

After the meltdown and the turning into herself, Mrs. Jackson could see that Marcy was beginning to bounce back. She began to stand straighter again. She had a clearer look in her eyes. She seemed to be stronger. "Mummy, can I help you with dinner tonight?" Mrs. Jackson was relieved. Only as she relaxed did she begin to recognize how tense she'd been herself. "Of course you can. What shall we cook?" "I like to have that cut-up stuff on rice." "You mean beef stroganoff?" "Yeah." "You can help me prepare the beef and vegetables. You can do it almost all by yourself, but I want to be in on it with you. Is that okay?" Mrs. Jackson's sensitivity to Marcy's desire to be on top is great. Marcy does need a boost, and Mrs. Jackson recognized the opportunity by letting her be in charge of the meal.

No matter how much support from her parents might mean, the most powerful boost to a child's self-esteem comes from within. "I can do it. I will do it," followed by "I did it. I did it myself!" Her mother's approval then becomes more meaningful than ever.

Steps into a Larger World

What a year this has been! A six-year-old is now a member of the world outside his family; he goes to a "real school" and has a "real teacher." He knows this. When his mother says eagerly, "What did you do in school today?" and the child answers, "Nothing," he really means, "Nothing I want to share, for I'm proud of being independent and having my own experiences." When a father says, "Do you have any homework?" it conjures up a picture of an older brother or an older friend who does have homework.

This new independence has also been a touchpoint for parents. They feel a loss when many of a child's most important experiences occur outside the family. A parent is likely to wonder: "Was he ready? Should I have exposed him to a world I cannot control?" These feelings are heightened by new dirty words, new behavior, new curiosity. All the intense developments are colored for parents by a feeling of losing the child they have known. "He is growing up so quickly," they will say wistfully. This powerful pull toward separation as well as the tug in the opposite direction obscure for both child and parent the fact that the ultimate developmental goal is interdependence rather than independence.

A six-year-old child will have segregated himself into a group with his own gender. He will already be learning to swagger and stride, to swear and use dirty words, to engage in gender-linked play. The strong identifications with parents from years four and five are now beginning to be played out in peer groups. Parents need to be prepared for the language, the testing out of sexual curiosity and behavior. Many children confuse and alarm their parents when they try out the other sex's customs and behavior. The child's explorations and his parents' alarm create yet another touchpoint.

The motivation to read and write dominates much of a first-grade child's time when television and media games haven't. This is a time for parents to find sensitive ways to keep the child's motivation channeled toward active learning. Television and videos are passive and can dilute this new burst of passion. Video games may be more active. Although most are narrow and repetitive, some may capture the passion. Parents find that participating in the learning efforts is thrilling—and that their participation is critical to the child, for he can then model his efforts on the excitement of the adults around him. Reading rituals that have been a part of each child's bedtime

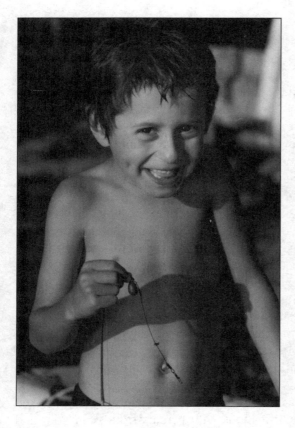

pay off for everyone now. Learning to read, however, also involves frustration. A motivated child wants to be able to read and write *now*. Parents will recognize the turmoil and regression that results as a touch-point. The frustration can be a powerful force, but it is difficult to live with.

During the first-grade year, self-esteem has been tested in every new venture. A child who believes in himself can begin to live with a learning disability or an active motor drive. Overcoming such challenges can be the beginning of a child's feeling that he can conquer his world. Learning to ride a bike, to kick a soccer goal, to woo a friend, to master a temper tantrum, to become a member of the "crowd" at school—these are all goals to be conquered *someday*. Each success makes for a surer foundation from which to face future disappointments and failures.

Learning about important relationships and about the moral codes that shape relationships has been another major quest during this year. School demands them. The urgent desire to belong with peers can be expensive for children. Parents of less adept children must suffer with them as they strive toward inclusion and acceptance by their peers. They worry whether their child's individuality and values will be lost in this fierce struggle. The turmoil in child and parent creates the regression and reorganization necessary to find ways to succeed in this new social setting.

In these years, a child might have had to learn about death—from a pet, from a beloved grandparent. By six years, a child feels passionately about such a loss. He will inevitably take it personally. "Could I have been better? Then I wouldn't have had to lose Grandpa." The themes of loss and of personal guilt must be disentangled as a six-year-old grapples with a new awareness of his own importance. Guilt and fear surface with any important separation— death, divorce, an illness, a hospitalization, even a brief separation from a traveling parent. Parents need to recognize these feelings if they are to discuss them openly with the child and help him find his own way of coping with uncertainty and sorrow. Negative passion is inevitable, and learning to live with it, and to talk together about painful feelings can be as important to a child's growth as positive passion.

Testing the limits with teasing, cheating, tattling, and stealing have all been a child's way of demonstrating his need to learn firm limits. Limits are reliable expectations. They provide a safe foundation on which children can begin to discover that they can stop themselves when they feel out of control. When a six-year-old can recognize and master his own rage, his own loss of control in a tantrum, his aggression in a battle with a peer, and his anger at a small sibling's invasion of his privacy, he is already a firmly secure child.

A six-year-old has achieved so much, and has so much yet to learn! A six-year-old's excitement and expectations about his world are unbounded.

two

FACING CHALLENGES
AS A FAMILY

ADOPTION

By the time parents finally adopt a child, they have been through a long journey of waiting, self-questioning, searching for a child, and submitting to complex adoption procedures. Many parents who adopt have had to face their inability to conceive and bear their own child. Fertility workups, repeated examinations, and tests for defects are bound to undermine any adult's self-concept. Regaining lost confidence is particularly vital for an adopting parent. When parents accept responsibility for another person's child, they are likely to question their adequacy for the task. Their zeal to provide an endangered child with a safe haven covers up insecure feelings for a while; however, the underlying questions about one's adequacy will eventually surface and will need to be resolved as the work of attachment proceeds.

A prospective parent today may need to search for a long time for a child, at home and abroad. Choices are limited. Too few agencies can be trusted. When prospective parents identify an agency they can work with, they must face a barrage of questions. Are they really able to live up to this precious responsibility? Why have they turned to adoption? Have they thoroughly explored their own chances at parenting a biological child? Many "infertile" parents adopt and later become pregnant. Even after a diagnosis of "hopeless" infertility, something about making the decision to adopt seems to free a capacity to conceive that was not identifiable during the infertility work-up. As the agency delves for reasons not to give them the child, parents question their own motives. "Why am I willing to be confronted and interrogated in this way?" Yet, as the self-questioning proceeds, parents' resolve is often strengthened. The motives become stronger. By the time they find a child, the parents-to-be are aware only of their hunger and of the long wait they have endured to satisfy it. They may not be ready for any child, but the adoption process has moved them past every parent's dream of the perfect baby; it has prepared them for the imperfections of a real one. The usual work of readying oneself that occurs during pregnancy parallels this struggle. Parents prepare themselves to fall in love with any child.

Yet, attaching oneself to an adopted child can be surprisingly complex. Although parents who have waited and searched for a child are bound to feel they are ready to give their all to her, they are surprised when they and the longed-for child can't make it with each other right away.

The younger the baby, the easier the adoption. A newborn's appearance elicits an adult's nurturing response, and the newborn's vulnerability is bound to capture hungry parents; they fall easily into a passionate bonding with a newborn. They greet every movement, every response as miraculous. Parents lucky enough to adopt a newborn know that they are in a better position to shape this baby's future as a member of the family. It is easier to develop as a parent when one starts with a newborn. But even with an older child, that potential remains.

Older infants and children will have lived in a foster or group placement before the adoption. As a child moves into the waiting family, she must make a new adjustment; even a four-month-old has adapted to the environment she has been living in. Expectancies have already developed. When the environment changes, the baby must readapt. New voices, new faces, new rhythms replace those the baby has become accustomed to. The baby will have to "grieve" over the lost environment so that she can readapt to the new. Part of the grieving will be a kind of withdrawal; the baby will become unavailable to the usual stimuli for a time. The more attractive the stimulus—a tender voice, a loving face, a nurturing cuddle—the more it will remind the baby of the previous nurturer. Even when the previous placement has been relatively empty and depriving, the baby will have adapted to that environment. New parents are likely to overwhelm the adopted baby with well-intentioned hugs and cuddles and attempts to meet her eye to eye. Parents may say, "I can't bear to put her down! Why is she turning away from me? Doesn't she like me?" The child may meet this eagerness to bond with her with hypersensitivity and averted responses. The baby's defenses are likely to be gaze aversion, arching the body, crying in protest, or sleeping a great deal.

Any parent would naturally feel rejected. The vulnerable parent who has been through so much before bringing the baby home at last is likely to feel particularly hurt. The initial period with a new adoptive child can be painful unless the parents recognize the baby's need for time to adjust. Adoptive parents must understand the baby's need for this period of withdrawal and adaptative negativism. If they don't, they are likely to take this behavior personally. Professionals can prepare parents for this period of reorganization and urge them to wait to satisfy their hunger until the child is ready. The baby's own hunger for attachment will then make the transition smoother.

The myth of a single critical period for bonding can act as extra pressure on new adoptive parents. Bonding can take place whenever the new relationship begins, but a longer process of attachment must follow. Attachment—learning about each other, each other's needs, the ways these needs are expressed, and how to respond—takes much, much longer. Learning how to be a parent to an adopted child is a challenge and an opportunity. The stresses are counterbalanced by learning about oneself and growing as a caring parent.

When does an adoptive parent begin to feel like the child's "real" parent? When does a parent become less vulnerable to such worries as, "Will she want to look up her birth parents someday—and desert me?" "Will her birth mother come and take her away from me?" "When should I tell him he's adopted—and not really mine?" "How do I tell her? Will she reject me then?" "How do I protect him from the feeling of rejection he will get when he knows his natural mother gave him up for adoption?" "How could she do it?" "What if I cause harm to her, too?"

These questions linger in the back of every adoptive parent's mind; they accompany the feeling of insecurity that adoption brings. Feelings of competition with the birth parents are bound to be there. The more an adoptive parent learns to care, the more threatening these feelings can become. An understanding of such feelings frees a parent to enjoy the process of attachment to the child. When adoptive parents move beyond the magic of falling in love and enter the working phase of staying in love, they will feel like their child's "real" parents. Adoptive parents tell me that when they've handled and survived a few crises, they are no longer vulnerable to a child's question: "Are you my real mother?" They know they are the parents their child needs.

The use of a surrogate parent can make it particularly difficult for adoptive parents to feel like a baby's "real" parents. Knowing the biological mother and making the arrangements with her forces comparisons for the adoptive mother with the mother she might have been. The anticipation of such a conflict, as well as the uncertainty about whether the "mother" will actually give up the child, or will change her mind later, makes many couples turn away from the idea of surrogacy.

When things go wrong, any new, vulnerable parent is likely to feel at fault and to look for reasons. Adoptive parents are likely to "scapegoat" the unknown—the baby's past. Parents-to-be today know so much about intrauterine conditions and their effects on the developing fetus. We know that intrauterine malnutrition can interfere with the development of the fetal brain, the thyroid, and the adrenals (organs important to activation and paying attention). The behavior of the neonate may also be affected if the pregnant mother smoked, took drugs, or drank alcohol. In former days, a parent might assign difficult behavior to "poor genes." Now, when things go wrong, a parent may also wonder whether the baby hasn't suffered a depriving pregnancy.

Fantasies about the kind of mother who would give up her baby, combined with worries about her dangerous behavior while carrying this unwanted fetus, can linger in adoptive parents' minds. As long as things go well, such worries are suppressed. But any deviance on the baby's part, any turmoil in the parent-infant relationship, can too easily lead to a label of "less-than-perfect baby," or even thoughts that this is "not *really* my baby." For example, the intractable, fussy period that occurs with most infants in the first twelve colicky weeks can lead to an unconscious reaction in new, eager, stressed parents. They think, "Uh oh—something's wrong with her. Is she damaged?" Instead of looking for the common reasons for fussiness and crying, an adoptive parent might all too easily assign a label of "damaged" to the baby.

Throughout an adoptive baby's childhood, questions about the heredity and the child's former experience will reoccur in parents' minds. Questions of their own adequacy to meet the parenting needs of their child will arise with each stress. Natural competitive feelings surface with each period of readjustment—"Would she have been better off in her natural environment? Have we failed?" Questions about adequacy arise in all parents' minds as they confront challenges with a child's adjustment. With an adoption, the tendencies toward vulnerability and a sense of personal failure are liable to be heightened.

In a cross-cultural adoption, all these issues are likely to intensify even further. As one contemplates the issues raised by an adoption of a child, the conflict about one's own identity and the identity of the "other" is raised. "How secure am I about my own cultural identity?" "What do I bring to this child that I value and want to perpetuate in her?" "What will the child bring from her culture? How much should I try to preserve the values of that culture?" "Should I become bilingual in an effort to perpetuate her language?"

A child from a distinct gene pool is likely to arrive with her own rhythms and behaviors. These will subtly or unconsciously affect her adoptive parents' reactions to her. For example, Japanese and Chinese babies observed in Asia using my Neonatal Behavioral Assessment Scale (NBAS) have demonstrated qualitatively different behavior from Caucasian babies. Their motor behavior is more fluid, slower, and smoother. Rhythms of attention and of movement are slower and lower-key. Few startles or jerky reflexes occur. Motor intensity is low compared to other groups of babies I've seen. As a result, motor behavior does not interfere with prolonged periods of attention. In this alert state, Asian babies are likely to pay attention to auditory and visual stimuli for significantly longer periods. However, the auditory and visual stimuli must be reduced in intensity and in rhythm if they are to capture the baby's attention. If the stimuli are too loud or too rapid, the baby will quickly shut them out, or will overreact by screaming loudly and inconsolably. The crying state can be impenetrable in Asian babies; crying states can be as prolonged as alert states. Asian babies can be difficult to console and may need to be fed more often and played with quietly.

On the other hand, African babies in Zambia and Kenya are excited by motoric play. Their movements are more vigorous, and appear more directed. Hand-to-mouth and self-consoling motions seem easier for African babies. They love to be played with and to be handled. In an alert state, they are more excited by visual and auditory stimuli, as well as with kinesthetic handling. As they watch and follow a face or a red ball, they become more intensely alert and throw off a startle or a jerky reflexive movement. These reflexes interrupt the period of attention. The baby then needs to be contained and quieted in order to continue to pay attention to visual and auditory cues. The intensity of interaction with sensory input from the environment, sights and sounds, may require a new parent to provide more containment, more reinforcement of self-consoling patterns such as hand-to-mouth activities.

Few new parents anticipate such differences in the thresholds that capture the adoptive child's attention, or in the rhythms and intensity necessary to maintain interaction. If the child's readjustment and period of withdrawal are prolonged after she enters her adoptive parents' home, both the child's patterns and the parent's expectations are disrupted. Adoptive parents need preparation for a cross-cultural adoption so that they can anticipate the differences in behavior as well as the first period of regression and readjustment.

In the back of any adoptive parent's mind will be the lingering question: "Will she love me or will she always wonder?" An additional worry occurs with a cross-cultural adoption: "Will she wonder, as I do, whether she'd be better off in her own culture?" The genetic dissimilarity is always a reminder. It can always resurrect the question, "Are you my 'real' mother and father?" Although research on children from adoptive situations reinforces the importance of the environment in shaping genetic endowment, each transient setback raises the question: "Am I better for her after all?" Parents need to acknowledge their vulnerability to this question. The child needs to know that her adoptive parent will always be her real parent: "I chose you. I hungered for you. I fell in love with you and I am your parent." The child needs to know that her parents are committed to her.

Some adoptions in the United States today are made by same-sex parents. Does this compound the issues their adoptive child must face? Of course. But as in all adoptions, the key is a strong, invulnerable bond the child can always count on.

Adopting an older child can be even more fraught with these issues. Separation from her old placement and the move to an adoptive home are likely to be frightening for her. The chances of the child's having endured repeated disruptive relationships in foster homes increase. She may have experienced abuse and other trauma. By the age of four or five, a child may have set up defenses—at great emotional cost—to protect herself from threatening events. These necessary defenses will have become entrenched. When the child leaves her familiar placement, her earlier learning will be questioned and shaken. The more welcoming the new adoptive home, the more of a threat she will feel if she has suffered.

Many children in orphanages develop slowly; immaturity seems to be a protective condition as well as a result of uncertain and erratic relationships. Teaching special skills is almost bound to have been neglected. Few opportunities are likely to have been presented for a child to model on and identify with reliable adults. If the child has turned to peer relationships as a way of filling the hunger for others, she has probably been let down. Peers are likely to disappear to their own adoptive homes. Adults who come and go reinforce the child's constant fear of abandonment; she dares not deepen an attachment. Attempts to assert her autonomy—a temper tantrum or holding back a bowel movement—are more likely to lead to punishment than to an understanding of her need for self-expression. Opportunities for mastery may be infrequent, and mastery leading to independence may be frightening to a child who has been abandoned. When she does make new strides, who is there to be proud of her?

All this slows a child's development. The less demanding a child is in an environment with many other children, and the more infantile and winning her superficial behavior, the more likely it is that she will be rewarded. Many children in group care learn to make shallow relationships; they dare not allow an attachment to deepen when they expect abandonment. Such children learn to withdraw into their own protective states. Their eyes dull down, their faces flatten. They are pale, their extremities become flaccid, their bodies limp. Children who have been in a hospital for a long time demonstrate the same states of waiting, of distancing, of not daring to care. Often they show either hypo- or hyper-sensitivity to auditory, visual, and tactile bids from an adult. Meanwhile, a child may not have learned the necessary steps toward impulse control. She may replace or follow withdrawal with a flaming loss of control that reminds an observer of the turmoil characteristic of a two-year-old rather than the child's actual age.

Distractibility and difficulty in relating to objects, to reading, or to learning may also be a part of this. Whereas a child in a family learns to read subtle signals, minor displays of affection, a child in an orphanage or in foster placement may not have such opportunities. A child who must protect herself by indiscriminately shutting out a threatening environment can't help but miss out on opportunities to learn.

Another "defense" may be one of hungry appeals for attention. A child I saw in an orphanage in Korea ran from one adult to another, hugging each one's legs. If you looked down to touch him or speak to him, his body would stiffen, and he'd be off to another adult. Lack of response seemed safer than a response that carried the danger of a relationship and disappointment.

Adopting an older child therefore calls for parents with considerable understanding and patience. Adoptive parents must watch the child and carefully pace their approaches to intimacy. When the child does dare to interact, she is likely either to be "too good" (with fear underneath) or use provocative behavior to test the solidity of her new relationship. If she steals or lies, can she trust you not to abandon her? If not, she's in a position she's been in before. She is prepared for being ignored or even for being rejected. If the parents are ready for these periods of testing, the child can gradually dare to trust. Each touchpoint with its regression, disorganization, and reorganization becomes an opportunity for confirming the reliability of the new relationship.

Older children who were adopted earlier experience the same kinds of conflicts when they reach a period of provocative testing. A new challenge or touchpoint in development can also upset the stability they have already achieved. An adoptive parent may not be prepared for the old feelings of vulnerability that the child's behavior revives. "Why does she need to test me? She knows I love her. Is she as disturbed as this because of earlier experiences—and I haven't recognized it before?" The child may be frightened by her own regression. When the turmoil has subsided, the parent and the child have an opportunity to reconfirm the strength of their lives together and the relationship between them. "You were awful when you had to try me out. But we made it, didn't we?"

The entry into childcare, to kindergarten, even to first grade, are typical times of vulnerability, intensified in the context of adoption.

"How will she do on her own? Have I done enough for her? Will her old experiences of abandonment surface when I must leave her? Will they like her at school—and realize how far she has come? She is such a wonderful little girl!" At the same time, parents may feel disappointed that their child may appear to need them less than before.

Behavior that is common from three to six—lying, stealing, cheating, biting, hitting—is likely to raise the deeper question of, "Is this genetic? Is she regressing to behavior that she may have inherited—or learned in her earlier placement?" Seeing this behavior as part of normal development becomes even more critical in an adoption.

With children who have experienced repeated loss, self-soothing techniques (such as thumb sucking) or turning to an adult for comfort under stress are good signs. They are evidence of resources the child can use as the parent-child relationship becomes more secure. This behavior might disturb an adoptive parent who was trying to teach the child independence. Regression can be even more disturbing to adoptive parents. If they can see it as a touchpoint, with reorganization followed by steps toward self-esteem and inner security, they can feel reassured and certain that they are indeed the "real" parents of their child.

Recommendations for adoptive parents:

1. Expect an initial period of adjustment in which the child must give up attachment to the old environment. A period of mourning and vulnerability is likely in the child's behavior. Do not take it personally.
2. Expect a feeling of vulnerability and loss in yourself as a parent when the child must become independent. This will recur with each crisis and each spurt in development (touchpoint). Be ready to examine these together with the child.
3. Share periods of readjustment with the child. Learning to cope with stress together can be a powerful force for strengthening your attachment. "When you are difficult and I get angry, it must frighten you. It does me."
4. View each readjustment as an opportunity for reaffirming: "Even though I get angry and must stop you, it doesn't mean that I don't love you. Nothing could change that."

5. Expect separations to be difficult. An adopted child will worry: "If I lost one set of parents, will these ones leave me too?"

6. Expect a lot of self-questioning: "Have we made a mistake? Are we good enough for her? Do I really understand her? Is this what it's supposed to feel like?"

7. Expect many questions, increasing over time: "Are you my 'real' parents?" "Absolutely. And we'll always be there for you. You are ours and we are yours."

8. Differences in expectations will be difficult. All parents, whether biological or adoptive, must recognize that their child will not be the person they'd planned for her to be. How much harder to accept, how much more anxiety provoking is this recognition when the biological family's past is a frightening mystery? A parent may overreact to rebellious behavior; reaching out to the child then becomes even more critical. "Sometimes I get angry and it frightens me. But you know what? After it's over, I realize I love you even more."

9. Be prepared for teasing to be difficult to face, not just for the child, but for parents, too. "They tease me because I look different from you. They know I'm adopted. What does that mean?" If parents and child are from different racial backgrounds, this will be a source of teasing. If parents are of the same sex in our homophobic culture, that will become a source of teasing. To help the child through it, face your own feelings first. Be ready to stand up for her in a way that won't embarrass your child, but will support her. When she comes home and reports such a teasing, be ready to back her up. The first step is to let the child know you feel for her: "It does hurt." The next step is to help the child protect herself. Team up with her: "Save up your hurt for home. Don't let them see how hurt you are; that will only make them feel they really can get to you. You don't have to let them. You don't have to believe the things they are saying about you. You can believe in yourself." As a parent, you can understand the teasing, but to expect a child to understand is too much. "They want to understand the things that we talk about all the time—what it feels like to be adopted, am I your real parent, what it is like to be from another culture. Children who tease you just want to know more about you."

10. Recognize that the child is likely to want to know about her birth mother. If she wants to anticipate meeting her, be sure to agree. "When you are older and we can both go together, we shall. I'd like you to know her. She gave me such a wonderful child—you!"

Expect a five- or six-year-old to test and question the solidity of your ties together. Be prepared for this again in adolescence.

ASTHMA

Asthma is becoming one of the most prevalent disorders among pre-school children; its many causes include increasingly polluted air, dust mites and uncontrollable dust, and the recirculated air in our houses. Children are paying a price. In the first volume of *Touchpoints*, I outlined a preventive model aimed at addressing the warning symptoms of allergic responses early. Such warnings as mild eczema, persistent skin rashes, bad breath, prolonged upper-respiratory-tract illness, and wheezing or shortness of breath with each upper respiratory bout should be heeded before the child and parent face an acute asthmatic attack.

In addition to dust and mites, polluted air, pollen, feather pillows, hair mattresses, and stuffed animals, aerosols can also trigger allergies. These can all act synergistically to set off an episode of asthma. Other irritants such as a cat, a food allergy (e.g., eggs, shellfish), or even severe stress can also bring on an asthma attack. If parents can eliminate as many of these factors as possible, the child may be able to avoid an acute attack. When one occurs, parents say, "But he's around them all the time without asthma; why now?" The cumulative effect may have tipped the scale. Skin tests for allergens are only partly revealing because they often identify only the major allergens; the minor ones may not show up as positive. Yet, in my experience, many children may nonetheless be affected by them. Mild allergens can be eliminated preventively. You can control asthma. Don't let it control you.

Time is on the child's side; the longer he can go without a severe respiratory episode, the more difficult it is to set one off. In families with histories of allergies, eliminating household triggers can save difficulty in advance. Another vulnerable group is premature infants who have suffered respiratory distress syndrome or who were born with immature lungs. They tend to have wheezing that is not all allergenic. Allergies can become an added insult to these children's lungs. However, maturation will help—but often not until the child is five or six years old.

An asthma attack is as frightening to the child as it is to parents. Not being able to breathe easily is terrifying. Even breathing through blocked nasal passages without asthma is exhausting. If you watch a child who must drag breath through his mouth, you see a frowning, worried child. He may not be febrile or sick enough to demand medical attention, but he surely deserves understanding and nurturing. Indeed, chronically congested breathing passages may already be suggesting an allergic mechanism—a precursor to asthma.

When a child's lungs tighten up and he begins to wheeze, he can quickly become desperate. Anxiety increases the wheezing dramatically. I have watched terrified asthmatic children who must be placed in an oxygen tent. The frantic child searches for relief. When his mother gets into the tent with him to croon and hold him, the frequency of his respirations can be cut in half. Anxiety and fear play a major role in the vicious cycle of asthma and breathing difficulty.

Parents' anxiety increases as the child worsens. Their anxiety adds to the child's, and he feels that no one knows what to do to help him. When he must go to the hospital to be taken care of by well-meaning but business-like adults, his terror is confirmed. He doesn't know these people; they don't know him. The shots and blood-letting are painful, and he may misunderstand them as evidence that nobody really cares about him. Worst of all, to him it may seem that the adults don't know what to do to help. At such a time, the delay before a medication brings relief becomes interminable. Sending a child to the hospital for treatment is a major step and should be avoided as long as is safely possible.

If possible, parents of an allergic child should arrange a reliable communication procedure with their medical provider in case of an acute episode. Such an arrangement should certainly be in place as soon as possible after the first acute attack. A person on whom the child can rely for his own fears and whom he perceives as reassuring to his parents is an important anchor to alleviate the psychological aspect of this disease. A provider who can "be there" for the parents and child can stop the spiral of anxiety and wheezing. We have effective medications now to alleviate and even prevent recurrences, but they don't address the effects of terror and vulnerability. Indeed, they may even add to the agitation a child feels at such a time.

Goals in asthma prevention:

- In an acute crisis survival is the first goal, above all else. But afterwards, it can become an opportunity for learning for the future.
- Parents need to deal with their own vulnerability so that they can plan for the future, and take steps to prevent the next attack. Planning ahead will do a lot toward calming the child's anxiety.
- The next goal is for parents and child to enter into a relationship with a doctor or nurse practitioner who is willing to assume responsibility at all times. This provider's reassuring role will help allay parents' worries; they now know they have someone reliable to turn to for help in managing the disease. The child is comforted, too: "They do know what to do to help me."
- Parent and child develop confidence in their capacity to manage the illness with the help of their doctor or nurse practitioner, and with each success in overcoming an attack before it becomes serious.

When a child starts to wheeze, or when he is in an acute episode, I recommend that he be given the medication to administer to himself, under his parent's supervision, of course. An hour later, assess his hoped-for improvement. Call it to his attention. "Remember the medicine you took all by yourself? That's made you better. We do know what to do—you and I!" The relief on the child's face indicates his awareness of his own mastery. A parent's teamwork with the child becomes an added source of strength to them both.

Whenever I had to administer medication for an asthma attack, I would ask the child either to stay in my office or to call me an hour later. Not the parent, but the child. When he called, I'd ask, "Are you better? Do you know why?" If he foundered, I'd remind him of the medication. "See, we do know what to do—you and I—and your parents." Next time, I'd ask the parents to have their child call me as soon as he started wheezing. Then, an hour later, the second phone call. Four- and five-year-olds would begin to feel in control of their disease. Even a severe episode would be accompanied by the assurance that "we know what to do." This seemed to cut down on emergency-room visits; but even when the emergency room couldn't be avoided, we would talk over the child's fears afterwards and relive them together to emphasize the importance of "knowing what to do."

Support groups for children with chronic asthma can be amazingly helpful. Children share their experiences and learn to cope with their natural and inevitable anxiety. Other children in the same situation can help your child face this disease.

For parents, an important job is the cleanup of the child's environment. Find another good home for a beloved cat, run the vacuum cleaner once a week, and cover the blown-air outlets with six layers of cheesecloth to filter dust and mites in winter; these are some of the preventative steps a parent can take. A supportive group of families can help each other face these elaborate tasks.

Asthma *can* be prevented. Allergens in the home environment *can* be removed. Our society could choose to reduce air pollution if the cost were seen as justified by the price children with asthma pay. Handling the inevitable psychological stress this illness causes is also a major factor in alleviating asthma, as important as identifying the acute allergens, cleaning the air, or prescribing the most effective medications.

ATTENTION DEFICIT HYPERACTIVITY DISORDER (ADHD)

When a child is in constant motion, cannot settle down to pay more than fleeting attention to any task, when he seems restless, fidgety, or too easily distracted by the least disturbance, he should be evaluated for attention deficit hyperactivity disorder (ADHD). A telltale sign—especially if the condition has persisted unrecognized and untreated—is that the child no longer feels accepted, either by peers, at school, or often even at home. Overdiagnosis, however, is a major problem with attention deficit hyperactivity disorder. Many children go through periods of overactivity; anxious children are likely to be hyperactive and to have short attention spans. Sometimes, children who have become anxious after being traumatized are misdiagnosed with the disorder.

About 5 percent of children may suffer from attention disorders and hyperactivity. Boys are affected four times as often as girls. Attention problems are the major symptom. Sometimes, the trouble seems to be that the child just can't pay attention long enough to accomplish tasks that he could otherwise reasonably be expected to accomplish. But for other children, the problem lies in the quality of their attention and their control over it. They may not be able to mobilize and sustain their attention, or, to do so, they may need to focus so intently on a task that that they can't take in anything else at the same time. This is why the ability to focus on a television show or a video game does not, on its own, rule this disorder in or out. Some children with ADHD may rivet themselves to a video game because it elicits the kind of "overfocus" they need if they are going to be able to pay attention at all. But this overfocusing does not allow the child to take in other information at the same time; for example, the voice of a parent telling him that it is time to stop.

Hyperactivity may be a response to an easily overloaded, hypersensitive nervous system. Activity becomes a way to discharge the tension of such a nervous system. Many of these children are hypersensitive to auditory, visual, and even tactile stimuli. Such hypersensitivity not only interferes with a child's ability to pay attention and concentrate on a task for any length of time, it is likely to lead to poor impulse control. When these children are overloaded by stimuli they can't screen out, they fall apart all too easily. It is understandable that such children would have greater difficulty handling frustration because they are using so much of their energy to manage their environment.

For the same reasons, children with ADHD also have trouble with change, with transitions. Once they've succeeded—with great effort—in managing the sensory input of one situation, they're not likely to feel ready to move on to a brand new one. Their rhythms of sleep and waking are easily disrupted, with resulting sleep problems, feeding problems, and discipline problems. These children are not intentionally provocative; their ability to concentrate on any task, or to prolong sleep or attentional cycles, is easily interfered with at an organic, brain level. Because they appear to "behave badly," they are often punished frequently; and, in turn, they quickly develop a poor self-image. They learn to expect to fail, to get into trouble. Because their nervous systems easily become overloaded in noisy or busy places, they often seem intent on misbehaving as soon as they enter a crowded or noisy room. They may appear to give up on the effort to control themselves and behave heedlessly and chaotically.

I have used a simple screening test in my office that identifies a certain number of these children. A child who is hypersensitive and has poor control over his sensory input can't shut out a stimulus that is repeated several times, even when that stimulus clearly offers him no new, useful information, and instead disrupts more important tasks. If I clap my hands (when he's not paying attention), any small child jumps and reacts the first two or three times. But a child with a normal nervous system quickly habituates himself to (or shuts out) the disturbing sounds. By the third or fourth clap, he no longer pays attention. A child with the hypersensitivity often seen with ADHD (although each can also occur separately) *must* respond each time. He may try to divert his attention to another task, but he will continue to react with a startle and/or an accelerated heart rate. His eyes may be glued to his new task, but he will blink each time I clap. Finally, a small child (from three to six) with ADHD will become over stimulated and resort to activity so that he can better handle the buildup of distress caused in his vulnerable nervous system. A normal child will have long since used his ability to filter out unimportant messages. Learning how to handle the impulsivity caused by over-stimulation can be a long-term project (see Chapter 4), but it is crucial for future learning. The child can and should understand that this is an achievable goal; otherwise, he can become hopeless and depressed.

Because children with ADHD often act before they think, they have trouble with waiting their turn, compromising, negotiating, and solving problems. This makes it difficult for them to get along with other children. The hyperactive child's impulsive behavior isolates him from other children, who are desperately trying to control their own impulsive behavior. Other children can't and don't want to identify with these children's disturbing behavior, nor do they want to be reminded of it.

It is important for parents and teachers to realize that the affected child's behavior results from his biological endowment: he is not "doing it on purpose." Hyperactivity is not his fault, even if the child must live with the consequences of his acts, intentional or not. In some cases, children profit from medication—for example, Ritalin, and sometimes others. Too many medicated children, however, do not receive the other forms of help they need if they are to become aware of their difficulties and learn to compensate for them. Some children with ADHD have "soft" neurological signs, which may show up only when the child is under stress. These signs can include clumsiness, inability to distinguish right from left, difficulty in standing on one foot, the spread or mirroring of movement (when the fingers on one hand are rapidly tapped on the thumb, the other hand mimics this). Neurological and cognitive tests, with attention to the hypersensitivity of the nervous system, help pinpoint the specific difficulties the child is having (a learning disability may also be present) and clarify the areas to be targeted for intervention. In a one-to-one situation, the child can often maintain the attention needed to succeed; but if he is tested in a noisy, active room, his test scores are likely to be lower than his potential. His inability to shut out external interference again becomes a diagnostic symptom.

Behavior modification administered by an understanding therapist can be of real help, especially if he or she can enlist the child's desire to overcome his poor controls. Parents need the help of such a therapist, too. When chemical treatment such as Ritalin is advised, let the child understand its purpose and recognize its effect on his symptoms. A child's awareness of the positive effects of medication can give him hope that he is now able to master for himself his poor impulse control and his feelings of being overloaded. But he will not feel that way if the medicine is given all the credit for the improvement. A four-year-old can learn to notice over-stimulation when he feels it coming on, turn to a sympathetic adult for help, reorganize, and go on with his learning. This is a major achievement and one that deserves high praise from the adults around him. Often adaptations in the classroom are needed as well, especially to cut down on extraneous distractions and to honor the child's need for physical activity. A special learning environment, even in an ordinary school classroom, tailored to children with ADHD, can be a major therapeutic intervention.

Many two-, three-, and four-year-olds who do not have ADHD are still working on controlling motor activity, impulses, and the capacity to focus on and screen out repetitive and unnecessary outside distractions. Therefore, diagnosis is not easy and must be done by an experienced professional. Children who go undiagnosed, or are diagnosed later (even by eight or nine years old), become discouraged and hopeless. They miss out on friendships and successes in school and on developing skills that give them the feeling that they are "good at something." Others may perceive them as troublemakers or just plain "bad." They will come to see themselves that way, too. Without motivation or hope, they find their symptoms even harder to handle. Their self-esteem plummets, and depression is too often the result. Early diagnosis (in kindergarten, or first grade), followed by a supportive and sensitive learning environment, can save the child's self-image and his hope for a successful future. (See also "Resources.")

BIRTH ORDER

How early do children in the same family begin to show distinct differences in personality? New parents are always surprised to realize what an individual their baby is. Two children in the same family demonstrate differences from the first few months. Which is at work—nature (inborn, inherited differences) or nurture (the effects of the environment)? In all likelihood, the differences are caused by a mixture of these and neither can be separated from the other.

In pregnancy, parents-to-be prepare themselves for the kind of baby they think they might have. The baby's intrauterine behavior excites conjectures. Both parents are ready to associate past experiences with the kind of baby they get. When she appears as a newborn, everyone associates memories from the past to her appearance. "She has her grandmother's eyes! She has Uncle Jim's hair! She looks right through you, like Aunt Lucy!" Parents use these expectations elicited by her appearance, along with the baby's behavior and temperament, to try to understand her, and to differentiate her.

Even in infancy, parents begin to label a child and identify expected behavioral responses. It has amazed me that a small infant can be identified as "so different" from his older sibling; indeed, every behavioral pattern is soon labeled for its difference by eager parents. "She is so easy. She just eats and sleeps. She never cries." The temperaments of two children in the same family become identified by their differences rather than their similarities. "Her older sister was never like this. She always resisted my holding her." Parents are often delighted by the differences, although this is less often the case when a "difficult" baby follows an "easy" one: "Our firstborn didn't prepare us for this!" Expectations about when and how a child negotiates a touchpoint may be difficult to adjust when a first and second child are so different.

Frank Sulloway, of the Massachusetts Institute of Technology, collected differences in sets of siblings in a large sample of normal, healthy children. Although birth order patterns may be less clear-cut than once thought, he did find that in almost every family he studied, siblings in the same family seemed to seek different roles. If the first child was feisty and active, the second was significantly more likely to be quiet and sensitive. He quantified them on several parameters: extrovert/introvert, agreeable/antagonistic, conscientiousness/carelessness, eagerness for and openness to new experiences versus lack of interest in new experiences. Two siblings were likely to polarize according to these qualities. For instance, the more forceful the behavior of the firstborn, the more likely was the second to be quiet and watchful.

In addition to this polarization effect, there were consistent differences between firstborns and later-borns. Firstborns, according to Sulloway, were likely to be more conforming and traditional, to identify with their parents' power and authority to defend their privileged position. In most cases, firstborns were tough-minded and determined, driven toward success. They were likely to be responsible, achievement-oriented, and organized; they were also more likely to be anxious and fearful than their younger siblings.

Later-borns were more likely to question parental authority, which may appear to them to serve their elder siblings' interests more than their own. More likely to challenge the status quo and its entrenched assumptions, younger siblings, Sulloway says, tend towards rebelliousness. They may also be more easygoing, cooperative, and popular because they have had to use conciliatory strategies to find their own place in the family in the face of their elders' tendencies to dominate. Later-borns' behavior seemed the opposite of that of their older siblings. Boys were more likely than girls to fit into these strong constellations.

These findings raise the question of the effects of labeling: to what extent do preconceived notions about birth order lead firstborn and later-born children to conform to such stereotypes? Sulloway's study may not provide an answer. The differences he detected, however, did seem to serve a purpose in nuclear families. Niches and labels served to reduce competition for the family resources of emotional support and interaction. Parents could be somewhat freer to react passionately to each of two very different children than if they were reacting to children with similar temperaments. Each child competes differently. One can dominate the other and roles are separate and predictable. Appeasement and rebellion are apportioned separately in the two children.

This extensive study serves to normalize the forces that exist in most families. Rather than feeling guilty and trying to change their parental reactions, perhaps parents can feel that these differences in their reactions to children in the family serve a purpose. Although parents are likely to feel that they "should" feel the same or, at least, equal about each child, that turns out to be impossible. Because of past experiences and past family relationships, a parent is bound to react to each child with a different set of emotions. Strong feelings are liable to be honest ones. All children need their parents to be desperately in love with them. Passionate love is likely to be a mixture of positive and negatives. No child is spared the negative reactions to his or her rebellious behavior. If parents avoid labeling a child's personality as "better" or "worse" and can accept the inevitable differences in their feelings for each child, no child need feel she is "second-rate."

Today, approximately 60 percent of children from three to six are cared for by working parents. It is therefore important that we as a nation provide high-quality childcare for all our children. At present, according to studies released by the University of Colorado and the Families and Work Institute, 80 percent of childcare is not of high quality. Parents are thus faced with deep concerns about their child's well-being, in addition to the pain of daily separation. A feeling of helplessness can all too easily lead to detachment, with parents giving up hope for their child's future. Parents and child all suffer.

The first requirement for a childcare center must be that care providers consider themselves parents' allies: They must recognize that parents need support and enough direct involvement in the center to know that it can be trusted. But there are several potential obstacles to parent–care provider collaboration. First of all, our society—including many childcare providers—still holds a certain bias against working parents. Yet childcare by people other than parents is not usually a matter of choice.

Another potential obstacle is "gatekeeping." Care providers and parents are likely to be in competition (often unconscious) for the same child. How many parents, already guilty and worried, struggle to subdue their child's temper tantrum at pick-up time, only to hear the childcare provider remark: "He never behaves like that with me"? Competition needs to be recognized and discussed openly.

Caregivers who are aware of a parent's feelings can be more supportive: "You know, when he gives you such a hard time at the end of the day, he's really saying how much he's missed you, and how hard he's had to work to get along without you all day long." When a caregiver can view a predictable regression as a touchpoint revealing the cost to the child of becoming more independent, the parents will feel that they and their child are valued and understood. For example, with a child who bites, a childcare provider can either reject the child and blame the parents or try to understand this behavior with the parents: "Everyone gets so upset when a child bites. But that only reinforces it. I think he's working hard at controlling his impulses and learning other ways of handling his feelings. We can't let him bite, but we certainly won't make him feel worse about it than he does already." Teamwork between parent and caregiver enhances the child's future. Preschool and kindergarten teachers who care about parents, and who include them as often as possible in thinking together about the child, find parents can be allies, not competitors.

Parents inevitably ask whether it is harmful to leave their child in substitute care. This must be answered case by case, for many interacting variables must be accounted for in assessing the effect of professional care on small children's future. Such variables include:

- The quality of the care, including staff pay and turnover.
- The group size: smaller overall numbers of children are better, even when compared to larger groups with high adult-to-child ratios.
- The ratio of children to caregivers; an optimum at each age as follows:

Birth–12 months	1 adult for 3 children
Toddlers (12–24 months)	1 adult for 3 to 4 children
Two-year-olds (24–36 months)	1 adult for 4-5 children
Three-year-olds	1 adult for 7 children
Four-year-olds	1 adult for 8 children
Five-year-olds	1 adult for 8 children
Six-year-olds	1 adult for 10 children

- Caregiver training and attitudes toward small children.
- The parents' feelings about their work.
- Parents' ability to cushion the separation and to make up for it when they and the child are together.
- The amount of time in daycare (in the years before kindergarten, half-time seems preferable to full-time).
- The timing, and adjustment the child must make.
- The temperament of the child and the "fit" between the child and the caregiver
- Physical layout: 35 square feet of indoor play space and 75 square feet of usable outside play space per child (as recommended by the National Association for the Education of Young Children)

All these variables affect the child's adjustment. I would add to these the grief of parents, who must leave their child, and whether they handle this by becoming detached or by increasing the closeness and interaction during the time they have together with the child.

A recent multi-site (fifteen sites) study (by the National Institute of Child Health and Development Early Child Care Research Network) of preschool childcare did not find a deficit in cognitive learning in children who were in childcare compared to those cared for by their own parents at home. This study was remarkable in that the researchers accounted for the quality of care, as well as the variables at home—maternal full-time versus part-time employment, maternal job satisfaction, temperament of the child, and the quality of life at home. When all these variables were accounted for, no differences were found. We *can* make childcare work. But we have not yet done so: most of our childcare does not meet the needs of babies and small children. Parents need to search for and insist upon childcare and preschools that foster their child's development. Emotional development is most important at this age. A cognitive curriculum that overpowers or presses small children to learn may ignore their more important emotional and social development. This is the biggest risk parents face today when choosing childcare.

The French researcher Hubert Montagner demonstrated that a high-quality, nurturing childcare environment fostered significant peer interactions as early as seven months; these became even more significant as the child grew older. I urge parents to look for examples of meaningful behavior between peers in searching for an appropriate center for their child. Ross Park and Alice Honig found that children who had spent their childhoods in childcare centers were no less able to perform either cognitively or emotionally at school age, but they were likely to demonstrate more "aggressive" behavior than were children who had stayed at home as infants and toddlers. This indicates the importance of enough caregivers, as just mentioned, so that they can give each child individual attention at critical times during the day.

Most locations offer a choice—center-based childcare and individual home care. In individual home care, usually a mother or grandmother cares for several children to supplement her income. Center-based care is the care we usually label "daycare." In both types of care, the ratio of adult to children must not exceed the number cited above. Beyond the adult-to-child ratio, the quality and dedication of the caregiver may be the most important factor. Next would be the dependability of the care as it supports the jobs of the parents. What happens when the child is recovering from an at-home illness but may still not be ready to join other children? What happens when the caregiver is ill and must be replaced?

Amy Laura Dombro and Patty Bryan suggest the following fact-finding questions for parents to ask:

- Are credentials, training, experience, and license up-to-date?
- Safety precautions: Does caregiver smoke?
  Observations of the caregiver:
- Is she[1] respectful of the child—or intrusive?
- Does she listen to the child and match his rhythms?
- Does she talk *with* or *at* the child?
- Does she enjoy children?
- What does she like best and least about children my child's age?
- Does she show a knowledge of developmental steps and the individual differences of the children?
- Can she step back and let the child learn by himself?
- Always watch the caregiver with your child to assess her reactions. Does she show warmth toward your child and respond to him the way you might wish?
  Observations of the environment:
- Is it homey?
- Are there bright colors and interesting toys?
- Is there room to run and climb as well as places to look at books?
- Are hooks, sinks, and toilets at a child's level?
- Is there a sense of organization, and of caring about each child?
- Health and safety—do caregivers wash their hands?

Choosing childcare is a difficult decision, and parents should make the decision with the child's individual reactions in mind. Each child accepts and adjusts differently. Visit the center or home for a day and watch for the following:

---

[1]We use "she" here because currently most childcare workers are female.

1. Evidence of individualized care. Watch to see whether the caregiver looks your child in the eye and responds in an imitative way.
2. What teachers say to a child: "I'm going to help you." "I'm going to give you a lap."
3. Established, predictable routines—a minimum of time unused or wasted in aimless activity. Routines are reassuring to children.
4. Safety and cleanliness policies re: sick children, hand washing between food preparation and after using the bathroom, changing diapers.
5. Circle time to build community and communication of ideas.
6. Coaching for positive interaction with peers—the importance of peer relationships may be the single most important thing that a child can learn from childcare.
7. The caregiver's ability to build a relationship with each child and her understanding of the child's development; reasonable expectations—does the or caregiver adjust to each child's temperament?
8. The caregiver's ability to balance discipline with encouragement.

Finally, try to ascertain the staff attitude towards parents. Do the caregivers take time to share a child's small triumphs or disappointments with parents? Do they listen to the parents' observations? Do parents and caregivers seem to be working together?

CHORES AND ALLOWANCES

Opportunities to include children as participants in parents' busy lives begin at age three. When parents return from work, everyone can sit together to compare notes on the day: "How was your day?" "Guess what happened?" When everyone is close again, parents can then face their own chores—the kitchen, the bathroom, cleaning up, setting the table. Now is the time to invite children to help; they will feel even more part of the family. Helping out is an important way for young children to feel valued.

If children find reasons to worm their way out of chores, parents can make this into a learning experience: "I'm too tired to pick up my toys." "Well, if I pick them up, they'll go in the closet where you can't play with them." "I'll pick them up. But will you help me?" Teaching responsibility is a long-term job. It can be taught in actions as much as in words if it is approached every day. From three to six is the time to introduce these opportunities for cooperation.

A child can start receiving an allowance at five. An allowance can serve as a reinforcement and a reason for the child to take a bigger role—helping with the dishes, taking out the trash. But using an allowance as a bribe won't work for long because it misses the point. Wanting to be part of an involved, hard-working family, caring for others, and feeling valued for caring are much more important goals. Allowances may send the wrong message about chores and helping each other out in a family: "I only have to help out if you pay me." But if an allowance is not seen as payment for services, it can be a useful way to help children learn how to handle money and appreciate its value.

When a child is four or five years old, parents might start regular family meetings. I recommend them once a week. Everyone sits down together. Make a list together of some of the things that need to be done around the house: feed the pets, set the table, water the garden. Everyone has a choice. Assign one or two chores to each member of the family. Each child may need an adult to be a moral support and helper in carrying out her chores; let the child decide who that will be. Together, adult and child can accomplish these tasks. Mark them up on a big chart. Decide in the meeting what the rewards are (and what the discipline might be if chores are left undone). This planning can be seen as a family's cooperative effort. In my experience, even children of four are proud to participate in the family's chores.

COMPUTERS

Computers have changed our world. Already by ages four to six, children are becoming competent in using them. My six-year-old grandson showed me how to read and print my e-mail. Scornfully, he announced, "Bapa, you're the dumbest man in the whole world." Clearly, computers offer a child the chance to master important skills.

Computer play and learning captivate most children. They are wooed by exciting colors, squirming shapes, catchy music, and surprising sound effects. But computers also offer children a special chance to act and see the immediate effects of their actions; to make choices; to make mistakes and try again; to pursue one idea or interest and then come back and try another; and, most of all, to receive positive reinforcement for their efforts. Increasingly, software allows even very young children to compose "e-mails" with pictures and symbols of their choice. The Internet allows older children to communicate with friends and relatives and to gather seemingly enormous amounts information.

More computer games are aimed at boys than at girls; as a result, fewer girls than boys begin to develop computer proficiency at an early age. Some social forecasters worry that when today's girls become young women, they will be disadvantaged in the cybernetic marketplace of the future. Once they are able to read and write, however, many girls do demonstrate an interest in computer technology—especially the social aspects, including e-mail exchanges and visiting chat rooms with friends.

For children with attentional difficulties or unique learning styles, computers (sometimes with specially adapted hardware devices and software programs) can offer a chance to discover their own potential to learn. Seeing the excitement and sense of competence of a disabled child who has learned more readily from computers than from teachers has made me aware of the forgiving nature of a machine-driven expectation. A child can quietly assemble his thoughts and responses in front of a computer at his own speed; he doesn't have to worry about a teacher's reactions.

Computer adaptations to help children with physical disabilities are impressive. A disabled child with only his fingers to generate responses can establish his thoughts, his wishes, and his competence with a computer. Children who cannot speak clearly—or at all—can show the world who they are through a computer keyboard; and children who cannot use their hands can use voice-activated software. When both fingers and speech are compromised, special pointers can be used. Opportunities for success and self-expression for such children can lift their spirits, renew their motivation, and, sometimes, even rekindle their will to live. A computer can say, "You just did it. Aren't you great!" All children need this kind of reward for demanding achievements, but particularly a disabled child who has had to work harder for success.

The potential of the computer to enhance children's learning is still far from being fully understood. Nor do we know yet what long-term effects early exposure to computers will have on physical health, and emotional, social, and intellectual development. Some of the more immediate costs to the child, though, are already evident. Some of the advantages, the privacy of this pathway for learning, and its absorbing, demanding, and immediately reinforcing activities, are also the source of some of the risks:

1. Attention that demands physiological and motor passivity.
2. The seduction of the computer as a babysitter when busy parents wish they had more time to be involved.
3. Isolation from the rest of the world.
4. Self-absorption, and the lack of rewards shared with others.
5. Interference with learning to communicate face-to-face and to understand peer relations. Time away from peers is replaced by dreaming and fantasy in a virtual world.

6. Distraction from or even loss of involvement with other activities important to well-being, health, and development. Social and physical activities may be missed out on, or avoided if these are challenging to a particular child.
7. Overeating (as with watching television), if food is permitted at the keyboard.
8. Poor posture, eyestrain, strain on hands, arms, neck, and back—all these are risks of prolonged repeated use; they are aggravated if seating and positioning of equipment are not ergonomically appropriate.
9. Possible health hazards of electromagnetic radiation from television and computer monitors (these remain unconfirmed and controversial).
10. Immediate rewards: The computer's capacity to gratify a child unfailingly can be a drawback as much as a boon. Children also need a chance to be frustrated and to tolerate frustration, to delay gratification, and to find satisfaction within themselves for their efforts.

These risks demand that a parent participate and assume control over the uses and misuses of this ever-evolving and consuming new technology.

Many parents are eager to have their young children develop computer skills in the hope of preparing them for a future that may not leave room for individuals without them. Yet, many of the skills (comparing, categorizing, decoding, discriminating, planning, hand-eye coordination, memorization, and others) that children using computers will need are readily absorbed through other activities: building blocks, drawing and painting, reading, sports, even fantasy play. Young children who show more interest in these and other activities deserve encouragement. They will have time later to become computer literate, and they are bound to bring what they have learned in their play to this task. Some parents yearn for educational software to help their children learn academic skills early, hoping they'll be ready for the competitive world parents fear they must face. Although well meant, all this pressure is bound to tip the balance towards too much time with the computer—already a powerfully captivating toy. Attention to children's nonverbal behavior will reveal the cost and the benefits of computerized media learning. A wise parent will measure these against the intellectual benefits at these ages.

Parents also need to be familiar with the content of software and Internet sites a child is using. They will want to shield their children from violent computer games. These are unlikely to help children work out angry feelings, nor do they serve any other constructive purpose. Violent images have been shown to induce aggressive behavior in young children, and although some children may be able to manage this sort of over-stimulation, others may become overwhelmed and preoccupied. Some are so frightened that they try to compensate by imagining themselves capable of violent acts. Other computer games, though nonviolent, offer limited new experiences while having an addictive quality. A child who loses interest in other activities and who always wants to play the same computer game may not demand much attention, but he surely needs it.

The Internet must be seen as uncharted territory in which—without software blocking devices—a child of almost any age can readily navigate his way to explicit sexual and violent material. When children are old enough to read and write, direct communication with unknown adults in chat rooms is another risk. With the opportunities of computer learning come new burdens and responsibilities for today's already besieged parents.

But there are straightforward ways to manage these new challenges. I recommend that extra-curricular computer time be limited to one hour a day on weekdays and not more than two hours a day on weekends. Ideally, a parent should participate for half that time; and, at a minimum, a parent should view all games and sites before giving a child permission to use them. I would advise parents to put the computer and the television in a high-traffic room—the den or living room (not the kitchen, a place that should be saved for family time together)—that everyone in the family uses. The struggles over whose turn it is are well worth having; they are part of learning to become part of a family. The television or computer should not be located in the child's room—no child this age can benefit from such extensive access! (The Academy of Pediatrics has made the same recommendation.)

Whether we like it or not, computers are likely to play an increasing role in our lives. We will soon take them for granted, if we don't already, like cars and televisions. As with these other technological advances, computers can be used for both bad and good purposes. We can choose to let them run our lives, or we can insist that they serve our needs and those of our children. Computers have enormous potential for learning and communication, but they are also competitors for our children's hearts and minds. As parents (and grandparents), we must be aware of their power.

Here are a few suggestions on how to prepare your child to use the Internet safely, some of which are adapted from *Safety Net,* by Zachary Britton (see "Bibliography"). To these, we would add the recommendation that a child never go online without parental supervision unless effective software blocks are in place to limit a child's access to developmentally appropriate sites selected by parents.

Steps:

1. Choose an Internet service provider that offers special controls for parents to block access to inappropriate Web pages, chat rooms, newsgroups, and so forth.

2. Find and install software programs that block access to objectionable sites and prevent children from disclosing personal information on the Internet.

3. Make clear to the child that it is dangerous to give out personal information, agree to meet in person, or send personal photographs to anyone they "meet" online; or to respond to messages containing offensive or threatening language. Also forbid the child to surf to a Web site requiring payment without your permission.

4. Talk to other parents about Internet safety concerns, software guidelines, and blocks. Find out whether your child's online computer use will be monitored when he is a guest in their homes.

5. If your child receives threats or pornography via e-mail or Internet messages, save the message and contact both the sender's Internet service provider and your local law enforcement agency.

6. Your child's behavior while he is at his computer will tell you a lot. If he appears unusually excited, nervous, or secretive as you walk in while he is online, you may want to talk over his recent virtual journeys with him, check your computer's record of recently visited sites, or plan to be present whenever he is permitted to log on.

DIFFERENCES

How early can parents start to prepare a child for the job of accepting differences? Fortunately, children answer this question for us: When they become aware of their own bodies, they begin to ask about differences in others.

Awareness of differences starts early. During infancy, babies become aware of repeated patterns of caretaking from those around them. As early as six to eight weeks, they begin to detect reliable differences between mothers' and fathers' interactive behaviors; their own responses with each parent begin to differ by that time. By twelve weeks, if the parent changes or violates an expected pattern, they react with surprise and try to reconstitute it with the parent. At each subsequent stage of development—at five months with peek-a-boo, at eight months with awareness of strangers and their heightened wariness of them, at twelve months with hide-and-seek behavior as they learn to cling and to walk away—they are learning to balance their needs for constancy in their environment with their attempts to deal with the unexpected, with differences.

Four- and five-year-olds become more aware of differences between themselves and others. If you ask two four-year-olds, "Who is the strongest?" both will flex their muscles and show them off. Following this display, however, they will each feel the other's muscle to see which one is stronger. When a four-year-old meets another child for the first time, she looks the child over carefully. Then, she may feel her own hair and face to be sure of her own as-

sets. As the two play together and become more familiar, they express curiosity: "Why is your hair yellow?" "Can I touch it?" "Why is your skin dark?" "Did you paint it?" These questions and comments are typical of four-year-olds who are learning about each other—and learning about differences.

All this peaks in the fifth year (it will peak again in early adolescence) as they become more aware of themselves and their effect on others. This new cognitive step leads them to an increasing concern with differences. "Why am I different? Is it okay to be different? Will I be loved if I am different?" Once this awareness sets in, a child needs to know that her differences are accepted if she is to feel safe and important. These questions underlie the new curiosity of four- and five-year-olds. New uncertainty about being worthy of acceptance accompanies an awareness of differences. Showing off demands for parents' attention when a child must compete with the telephone or a new visitor, may all increase at this time.

Awareness of differences leads to attaching values to various characteristics. In the fifth year, children compare and compete openly because they want so much to be like those they admire. This is an age of "falling in love" with one parent or the other to be like him or her. This is an age when a teacher becomes a critical attachment figure. Brothers and sisters are admired from afar or as close up as the child dares. Mimicking and modeling on siblings' behavior is to be expected. Friends and friendships become more selective as a child recognizes and can express the individuality of the friend: "She's so funny. Her face wrinkles up when she laughs." "He's faster than me. But I can still beat him up." Teasing about differences is not only inevitable, it is a way that four- and five-year-olds can try out observations and learn how other people react to differences. At the same time, they are learning how to accept their own differences. As they compare, some differences may be hard to face. Sometimes, teasing is an attempt to push away differences that a child finds disconcerting, that call up uncertainties about herself. While children at this stage tease, they are also vulnerable.

Parents must be prepared for the teasing and ready to accept and support the child. Parents of children with ethnic differences, especially, need to have worked out their own issues so they can see them from the child's side; the prejudices parents have endured during their own childhoods can add to the pain of seeing their own child hurt. As James Comer and Alvin Poussaint say in their excellent book, *Raising Black Children,* every signal in our mainstream United States culture seems to say that being white and middle class is best. Children who are poor, or of African, Asian, Hispanic, or other backgrounds must face prejudice in their neighborhoods, in school, on television. Many books and films carry a bias that being white is better. Even in the same family, children with different skin tones may sense that lighter skin color is more valued than darker. Minority parents feel that they must protect a child from implied racism in teachers, teaching materials, and on the playground. All caring parents fervently wants that "best" for their children. Yet racial self-doubt can add to a child's confusion about differences at this age.

Although we have begun to make advances toward racial acceptance, we still need to face our underlying prejudices more openly with each other and with ourselves. In this way only can we set a new pattern for our children.

Parents must first face the issues they bring from past experiences. If they don't, they will be overwhelmed the first time a child comes home in tears. Anger or despair will frighten a child, although that is bound to be any parent's reaction. Parents' vulnerability will only add to hers and make the slurs or teasing more memorable and believable. Parents would do well first to acknowledge the hurt and then to show examples of strength: "It really hurts, doesn't it? I can remember how much it hurt me at your age. I came home in tears. My mom said, 'Don't show them how it hurts. Save it for home. Try to stand proud and let them see that you feel good about yourself.' That's the strongest way to be. Remember how straight and tall your grandma was? I always think it's from all the teasing she took when she was little. She just stood up to them."

What does one say when a child says, "When they tease me, I want to be white [or tall, or blonde or rich]"? Comer and Poussaint say that this is a time to stop and listen. Let your child share her own ideas with you: "Tell me why you'd like so much to change yourself?" It may be that she has a friend with these characteristics with whom she's close. She may have been bullied, but maybe not; she may just be testing you for your reactions. She may make statements that will lead you to her ideas of vulnerability. These may be different from yours. Parents are likely to be driven by their own need to protect the child. Indeed, watching for her own ways of dealing with the issues she must face, and reinforcing them, could be more effective. There may be an inevitable tension between a child's (a new generation's) need to find her own way and parents' wishes to protect their child from the prejudice generations before her have faced. Parents of children from ethnic minorities in this country have a double job; they must try to raise children who are free of prejudice as they face prejudice around them every day.

Not all minority parents want their children to face the treatment that minorities are exposed to—present or past—without anger and resistance. Some Jewish parents may feel, for example, that their children should know about their history of persecution; many African Americans believe that their children should know about and share their feelings of anger toward slavery; some Japanese Americans may tell their children about the internment of their elders during World War II, while American Indians pass on the story of their ancestors' genocide. Parents like these feel that missing an opportunity to teach children about their heritage would be smoothing it over, that part of their children's identity is wrapped in their historic struggles. Many parents who do not want to perpetuate hatred by burdening their children with these old scars believe, nonetheless, that remembering history is necessary if we are to overcome it and not repeat its mistakes.

Each family must work out its own approach to these matters, and both parents should agree in advance so that they can present a united approach. My concern (as a white, middle-class pediatrician) is in moving beyond the anger and separatism that exists. These cannot be good for small children, or our future, although I surely do understand their sources, which cannot be forgotten.

I would rather see all parents search to bring out the particular strength and cultural values of their own heritage. In the attempt to melt everyone into the same mold, our society may unconsciously be asking cultures other than mainstream ones to give up their unique heritage without providing anything that could replace them. As a nation, we need to respect differences in ethnic traditions, and support parents in handing them on to their children. We need to value these traditions as strengths for children and for our society. We have a lot of work to do. Our small children will do better than we have done if we can give them the strong self-images they need to work on adult mistakes!

Ways to help children accept and value differences:

- Do not make derogatory statements about other ethnic or socioeconomic groups.
- Value friends from a range of ethnic, cultural, and social groups.
- Introduce dolls, stories, and toys reflecting a variety of nationalities, cultures, and races.
- Don't force your opinions, however worthy.
- Don't overprotect children, but face feelings openly.
- Set a model of tolerance and respect within the family.
- Model a realistic, positive sense of self.
- Try to avoid overreactions to teasing while expressing appropriate disapproval of such behavior.
- Learn about and cherish your own family, culture, history, and values. Share them with your children, and teach them to be proud of the differences that make them special.

Self-acceptance is a first step towards tolerance of differences in others.

DISABILITIES: CHILDREN'S QUESTIONS AND REACTIONS

A disabled person can be frightening to a child. Such vulnerability to differences in others represents a need to reassure himself that he's intact, that it can't happen to him. "If he can be disabled or different, will I be, too? Am I already?" His awareness of ways in which he does not measure up to bigger or older children makes him feel inadequate at times anyway. At four and five, when recognition of differences is at a peak, he recognizes and magnifies any disability.

"She's in a wheelchair. She can't walk or run. I don't like her." Fascination accompanies a child's awareness of differences. Teasing about them is a way children try to understand more about disabilities and to differentiate themselves, to distance themselves. This kind of teasing surfaces at a time when four-year-olds are becoming aware of their effect on others. To test these effects, they may be mean to others when they themselves are vulnerable.

The chance to teach children how to become sensitive and helpful to people who are frail or disabled is one that parents of four-year-olds will want to think about. A child's first experience in facing a disability may be with a grandparent. Children can begin to understand the disabilities and changes that come because of age in a close and loving context. Fears of being disabled themselves or of losing someone are bound to come up. All the questions—"Why is she so wrinkled? Why does he have to use a cane? Will they die soon? Where will she go when she dies?"—need to be answered honestly. But the child must be protected from feeling responsible for the infirmity or loss, and from feeling he must make reparations that are not his burden to bear.

In school, we see an increasing effort to include disabled children in regular classes. They are entitled to appropriate academic and social opportunities, just like any other child. The goal is for the disabled child to learn coping skills from other children and for both to make important relationships in a regular classroom. Problems can easily arise. Disabled children may need extra attention from the teacher. Unless the teacher and the class can share their feelings openly from time to time, resentments can smolder. Open discussions of the kind of disability and how it affects the disabled child's functioning will surely help. Then, most important, is allowing children to discuss their feelings; eventually, they may be helped to recognize what a disabled child gives back to the classroom. Children without disabilities have much to learn from those who do, and will be more open to such learning in these early years if they are first helped to face their fears.

Can children be protected from the competition for resources? Do the siblings of disabled children need to be protected? When I studied children in Cambridge, Massachusetts, who were disappearing into the drug culture in the early 1970s, I could not predict which ones would, in adolescence, disappear from their families. They were not the first or last children born into a family; they were not rejected or abused children; they were not less loved than others in the family. There seemed to be no variables that made predictions possible. But I found that I could predict which children were *not* going to disappear. These were children who were not vulnerable to peer pressure. Sometimes they were athletes or musicians, or they had some burning interest of their own. Or they were in families who together had faced family stress, such as a disabled sibling. The children in these families had learned to cope with a serious situation and were stronger for it. I learned that protecting a child from stress may not be in a child's best interest. Participating in the care of a disabled child is among the important learning experiences. In a classroom, nurturing a disabled child could be a learning experience for all the children. They could learn from the disabled child's strength, bravery, and resourceful adaptations.

Recently I visited a very sophisticated center for the disabled to talk to the children who were being treated there. The center had all the assets of computer-assisted techniques for learning and for assisting movement in the children's impaired bodies. In addition, the center had adopted the marvelous new techniques in physiotherapy. Instead of using "passive" techniques, therapists now induce motivation in the patient to want to perform the necessary movements himself. This new approach has protected the self-esteem of incapacitated children. The active participation of the child motivates him to unlock his potential, and when he succeeds, he feels an enormous sense of achievement. His self-image is strengthened and fed each time. Improvement of motor function—however limited—is empowered by the child's inner sense of "I can do it myself." The children in such a center are quite different today from the more passive, depressed children we used to see in such institutions.

As I sat down to talk to a group of four teenagers in wheelchairs, one young man spoke up. I'd noticed he was almost incapacitated from the neck down by the spasticity of his limbs caused by cerebral palsy. His difficulties, however, didn't include his sensitivity or his thinking. "Dr. Brazelton, how do I help people accept my disability?" I was stunned by such a question. "How do you know they can't accept it?" "Oh, I can tell when I first meet someone." "How?" "By their eyes. They either cloud over or they turn away, as if they were shielding their faces. Their whole body pulls away from me. Their voices sound as if they were talking to a child. They treat me as if I was mentally retarded. I can tell right away. If I knew how to help them, maybe they'd be better at talking to me. Otherwise, they give up and walk away. They act as if I embarrassed them."

What a set of sensitive observations he had to make every time he met someone! I said, "My God, you not only have to deal with your own disability, but you have to be prepared for others' inability to accept it. What a double job you have! I'm so impressed with what you've learned about observing other people. How perceptive you've had to become!" With that exchange as a starter, each of the four young men was eager to share his experiences with facing the unspoken and often unconscious prejudice of people around them.

These boys taught me an invaluable lesson. Anyone with a disability must learn to face his own difference, but then he has to deal with the reactions of others. Mainstreaming can be a positive learning experience for all children, but it requires that the adults help the other children handle their fears and their vulnerability. The children can then profit by learning to accept their disabled peers, by feeling useful to them. Disabled children, in turn, can feel useful to their nondisabled peers. Indeed, children without disabilities learn from the unique strengths disabled children have had to develop.

DIVORCE

By the time a couple has come to a divorce, they will have been through tension and angry confrontations; even a three-year-old will be aware of the impending separation. She feels a need to try to keep her parents together, but when it doesn't work, she feels a sense of responsibility. "Wasn't I good enough? Was it me they fought over? If I'd been good, would they still be leaving me?" As we have seen in Part I, from at least this age and upwards, and for emotional and cognitive reasons, children always assume responsibility for major events in the family. This feeling of responsibility is too heavy a burden. A child is likely to try too hard to be "good," or she may well become rebellious and provocative—as if to prove to herself that she is really "that bad." She isn't likely to dare to keep asking the questions that underlie her behavior: "Why?" or "Is it really my fault?" Parents must constantly reiterate their own responsibility—without requiring that the child understand or offer absolution. "Mummy and Daddy just couldn't love each other. But we both love you."

When the divorce is final and parents begin to recover, they are bound to regret the tension the child has witnessed. They are bound to regret the withdrawal from the child that they could not avoid while preoccupied with anger or grief. Parents often expect or need too much from a child during this period. Is it too late to repair the trauma? Perhaps the most difficult and powerful way to help is for each parent to foster the child's relationship with the other parent.

Divorce is responsible for most single-parent families, and the non-resident parent is often available, or could be. For the child, this availability is positive and tantalizing. "Doesn't he want to come live with me?" At four and five it is especially important that each parent respect the child's need for the other. The nonresident parent must:

1. Plan carefully and never promise a visit unless it can be carried out.
2. Show up on time.
3. Talk about how you've missed the child, but be careful not to blame this on the other parent.
4. Be at the child's disposal while you are with her.
5. Leave her with a memento of you—a videotape or a special toy as a reminder. Gifts should not be lavish or too abundant, though, and must not compete with the other parent's relationship with the child. She needs you to stand up for her other parent, despite the divorce. Affection won at the other parent's expense does not serve the child.

Children wonder: "Will Daddy ever return?" "Does he care about me?" "Was I bad and that's why Daddy left me?" "Will Mummy leave me, too?" Fear of desertion and the feeling of being responsible are bound to be underlying a child's behavior. During this period, the fear and guilt may lead her either to be "too" good or to test the resident parent.

A five-year-old whom I know confronted her recently divorced mother: "I want to live with my daddy. You are always mean, and he's not." The mother reacted out of her vulnerability. "Well, just go to him, then." That night, the child had nightmares. For the next few days, the mother noticed that her daughter was more clingy than usual. The nightmares and clinging continued until the mother sat down with the child to share her unstated fears. "You are bound to want to run away when I'm angry. But I won't let you go, and I won't leave you, even if you are mad at me. I love you. So does your daddy." A child in a one-parent family is bound to fear any loss. A child this age needs to test and to try out independence, but doesn't dare to turn on the single parent. She needs to identify with others around her and occasionally turn away from the resident parent. But she won't dare to if she thinks that a parent might desert her. The resident parent needs to reassure her that—even with all the testing in the world—she will never be deserted.

When parents divorce, the following recommendations will help protect the children:

1. Stay in as positive a relationship as possible with the other parent, or at least agree to put your anger aside when discussing the children. Agree to put their needs first, and commit to working towards consensus whenever the children are concerned.
2. Never use the child as a football between you.
3. Arrange reliable and regular visiting from the absent parent— talk about it in between.
4. Arrange phone calls and videos from the absent parent.
5. For the resident parent, arrange as much available support— extended family, reliable and regular friends—as possible.
6. Be available to talk to the child about losses and about her hunger for others.
7. Maintain the usual rules and routines. Discipline matters now even more. Divorced parents must make a concerted effort to agree on these, or at least to accept and support the other's approach when that parent is caring for the child. Be prepared for fears of loss or separation. Be prepared for behavior that stems from and increases a child's sense of guilt at having caused the divorce and loss of the other parent.
8. Face the child's difficulties in changing households. For any child this is tough. For a child with social, learning, or attentional difficulties, it is even more difficult. In some cases, I have recommended that one permanent household be established for the children and that parents switch residences; when parents consider why they can't accept this for themselves, they begin to see the challenges for their children more clearly.

Guidelines for custody arrangements are laid out in the book I wrote with Dr. Stanley Greenspan, *The Irreducible Needs of Children*. In certain situations, the risks of harm to the children in a divorce are increased. These include:

1. Parents whose persistent hostility leads them to use the child to get at each other.
2. Children with developmental or medical problems who need two parents to handle the demands.
3. Children from homes troubled before the divorce by alcohol, drugs, violence, or overwhelming hostility.
4. "No one at home" families—divorces between parents who are not available to the child anyway.

In such situations, counseling is called for. Parents should seek referrals to mental health professionals and family service agencies, as well as turn to family members who could offer support. Although the goal for divorced parents is to put aside their hostility and make decisions together in the child's best interest, it is sometimes unattainable. Then, a court-appointed guardian *ad litem* may be needed to ensure that a child's needs are understood and respected despite ongoing parental conflict.

FAMILIES OF ALL KINDS

Stepparents

Adjusting to a family that has been through divorce and the loss of one of the parents is never easy. A child yearns to replace the lost parent, yet stepparents need to realize that they can never replace the lost parent—nor is that their role. Stepparents need to understand that their role is different. The security they bring—the reassurance that they can love this child and won't leave him——becomes an important boost to the child's future self-image.

A stepparent reassures a child by loving him and his parent openly and confidently. By forming a triangle, they bring back the security lost in a single-parent family. Consistent discipline, feelings safely expressed, reassurance against loss, someone to relieve the child of the burden of nurturing his own parent—all these can be gradually offered in a newly constituted family.

A child can be expected to test the limits of the new relationship. "Will he [she] like me if I'm bad?" is a constant and recurrent theme. Regressions become opportunities for the new parent. When a child goes into a meltdown you can expect to hear the hurt and angry feelings turned against the most recent addition to the household: "You're not my *real* Daddy! My mommy makes decisions for me, not you!" Then the stepparent can say, "That's right. But sometimes I need to help your mommy and to be there for you. You and I both know you've gone too far."

When children from two families are brought together, any upset is magnified. A stepparent may feel protective. "You always take *your* children's side. They are so sassy and difficult. I don't want mine to start behaving like that." Children from two families will have unresolved concerns; they will *all* need to test the strengths of the new arrangement. When the children don't live together, the resident children will need to demonstrate their control and their territoriality. The visiting children will be bound to show off, to put on superior airs, to test the old and the new parent for security and discipline. The danger is to let this natural competition lead to destructive scapegoating, or the rejection of one or the other families. Blended families need each other. They will never be as close as siblings because they aren't siblings; but they can form new and different relationships. The children's ability to get along with each other will depend on where they are in their adjustment to their parents' divorce. They may be conflicted, but it will help if the new marriages are solid. If each parent backs up the other at a time of conflict, the children will eventually model on the solidarity, even if at first they test it and try to undermine it.

Will a stepparent ever feel equally about his own child and a stepchild? No, not likely. And the question will come up. The truth is that parents always feel differently, even about two of their own. Children will recognize this: "You like her better than me." If they can see it as a difference (I'm Danny's dad, just as Mommy is your mother") and not a rejection, they can face it.

Living "in step" as Lofas and Sova put it in their book *Stepparenting* (see Bibliography) is not easy, but it can be rewarding. For a child to feel secure in two families, parents must move past their own anger and support each other. Getting to know and to depend on the stepfamily is an essential process for a child who has lived through divorce. The inevitable stresses can serve as opportunities to learn more about each other, and to share each other's pain and joy.

At critical times, the step relationship will be questioned; birthdays, holidays, graduations, and disciplinary crises are among these times. "When is my *real* father coming?" "My *real* mom would let me do that." In confronting a stepparent, a child may feel guilty for turning back to a biological parent; this seems to be a recurring attempt to reconstitute the loss. There may also be a recurrent feeling that a child's "badness" was the cause of a divorce. Children need repeated reassurance that it was the parents who did not get along, and that each parent will always be a "real parent" and present in the child's life. A stepparent can reassure the child by emphasizing that he is not a replacement, that he is there because he loves the child's mother (or she is there because she loves the child's father) and is a new and loving figure who is there to stay. But the child is not likely to take these reassurances seriously if they are offered only when a parent is feeling guilty rather than at the times a child needs them most. A parent needs to listen carefully during those moments when the child brings up his misconceptions, and to help the child understand what he is feeling when his behavior seems driven by emotions he can't otherwise express.

Single Parents

At ages three to six, a child's identification with one parent is intense. Yet, half of all children spend a significant amount of time in a single-parent family; this means that only a single role model is in residence. How can a child in a single-parent family work out an identity? At the ages of four and five, when a child is searching for identities with both sexes, it is important to understand that a child in a single family will be "hungry": "Why don't I have two parents like everyone else? Will my daddy come back if I'm good? If Daddy left me, Mommy could, too."

Any male who visits the son of a single mother will feel the boy's hunger. The cloying, hungry behavior a child with only one resident parent is likely to demonstrate at this age toward any susceptible adult of the right gender is an example of an attempt to fill the need for identification. Such behavior will naturally make the residing parent feel guilty and even angry. Understanding why the child feels this way may help. Addressing it with him gives him the chance to face it more openly. Children work hard to fill up the real need for more than one relationship; the remarkable aspect of this is the child's energy and ingenuity in filling such a gap. Given a stable home situation with only one parent, the child will capture bits and pieces of others around the family to serve this purpose. Given the opportunity, a child will optimize his own chances of making up for the loss and absence of a parent.

Often a parent is faced with a look or statement from the child: "What's wrong with you that you can't get me a daddy (or a mommy)?" This is certain to exacerbate the single parent's sense of failure, so it hurts. It may even drive the parent to accept a substitute who isn't at all appropriate. Be sure about your own motives, for the child's neediness can push you to act inappropriately.

Lucky is the single parent who can provide a role model from the other sex; it certainly is a reason for parents to remain close to their own parents and brothers and sisters or cousins. A single parent who has extended family members available should certainly involve them. Not only can the child portion out his attachments but he can "turn from one to another," testing rejection and devotion. He can dare to identify with a stable and loving relative.

An unrelated friend cannot be as reliable. The danger of making a close relationship only to have it dashed again is always present. Finding a temporary "significant other" to fill the gap brings the obvious problem of losing that figure. A new loss touches too close to the earlier one. Some parents choose a relationship in which they do not involve the children, at least not until the relationship develops a long-term commitment. Such a situation has its costs, but also certain benefits.

A single parent may also decide to be celibate to avoid this kind of trauma. Single parents may lead a lonely life in which their children become their significant associates. With this closeness, though, the child can be burdened. He may sense a need to fill more gaps in a parent's life than a child can. A tendency for a lonely single parent may be to unwittingly press the oldest child into becoming a substitute parent; indeed, even the fear of doing this may make it a self-fulfilling prophecy. Yet valuing the child's childishness is easier said than done.

Single parents always feel alone. They have to face each crisis and deal with it alone. They have no one to talk to at the end of a busy day—no one to ask "How was your day?" As a result, their raw emotions are hard to hide from children who are more vigilant than ever. A parent is likely to feel guilty. "I didn't mean to be so hard on her. But I just didn't have anyone else on whom to take out my feelings. I can't hold them in all the time, even though I try to."

But a child whose family structure has changed feels alone, too. A child who fears losing the resident parent—after the loss of the other parent, —is bound to cling. "Don't leave me. Come upstairs with me. I can't go to bed alone. It's too scary." All this clinging reaches out to the parent's loneliness; it becomes very difficult to respect the child's need for independence, and difficult not to hover.

Yet there is never any reliable or spontaneous independence for the parent. Even going to the grocery store or trying to talk on the telephone may make the child irritable and competitive. No venture alone can be anticipated without planning, without providing a substitute.

A single parent must be both mother and father at every turn, disciplinarian as well as loving comforter. Discipline is easier to impose when it is shared. Yet discipline for children in a single-parent family may be even more necessary and comforting. They will need to test the limits frequently to be sure that the single parent is not too fragile, not too preoccupied to respond, to find out how "bad" they really are. Shared discipline, although a challenge to agree on and impose, can be more consistent and unassailable. Loving may also be less complicated when sharing can dilute its intensity.

Touchpoints and the regressions that accompany them are bound to heighten the vulnerability that accompanies this lonely job. The more responsible and caring the parent feels, the more likely it is that a sense of helpless failure will accompany every regression.

Children of teenage single parents have these same needs. If the young parent is accepted back into her family, and if family members are willing to support her and her offspring in a protective, loving envelope, the child will get a good start. He will seek his identity with his grandparents as well as with his mother. If the teenage parent is rejected by her own parents (and the father of her child), the future of her child may be seriously at risk. She and her baby need nurturing if they are to start a family of their own.

Parents with Disabilities

How does a disabled parent help a child learn to live with the parent's own disability? Parents who must care for small children while facing their own disabilities have a strenuous adjustment to make. Their first task is to handle their own feelings about loss and impairment. No matter how well they've adjusted to their disabilities beforehand, the demands of children at these ages can mobilize a disabled parent's feelings of inadequacy, a magnification of those felt by all parents of small children. "How can I nurture a child if I am disabled? Might I have to leave too much to her?" The fear of demonstrating one's sadness and worries in front of the child recurs at times of stress. Denial and other defenses that are necessary must be valued as ways of managing one's own fears. When a parent can share feelings of frustration, of anger at being held down or disabled, the child may feel he can share his feelings without adding another burden. This is often therapeutic for the child as he tries to understand a parent's disability and to take a protective, nurturing role toward the parent.

I remember a young patient whose parents were both blind; at only two years old, this child was already capable of leading her blind father on the sidewalk. When they approached the street and the curb, to my amazement, the two-year-old tugged at her father's sleeve. Her father stopped, reached out with his cane to feel the gutter, patted his toddler on the head, and said, "Thank you." They both stepped into the street as the walking light came on. Both father and daughter held up a hand to warn the motorists. I was touched by this precocious ability to fill a necessary role; it made me realize how much this toddler had already learned about responsibility for others. How prepared she was for future stresses! Did it cost her a great deal? Perhaps. But it was a necessary adjustment from which no one could possibly have protected her. Learned responsibility for others far outweighed the cost. This toddler is now grown and in charge of an early intervention center for special needs children. She is a sensitive, fulfilled adult.

Children of disabled parents will be curious about the disability and attempt to understand it. They need regular opportunities to unload their concerns:

1. Identifying with the parent. I remember a child whose mother was in a wheelchair was interested in its mechanisms. She demanded to be allowed to ride in it, to learn about its workings, to master it as a way of confronting her mother's lack of mobility. She could take care of her mother later on. This learning had been critical to her.
2. "Did I bring this on my parent? If I'd been better, would it never have happened?" Taking responsibility for any stress is part of a child's attempt to understand and join the parent in the work of facing the disability.

3. A child will attempt to understand the disability and the feelings that he senses it engenders in his parent. Such a discussion can bring intimacy and sharing. But don't tell the child what to think. Let him ask you what he needs to know. His questions and his understanding of your situation may be different from yours and may surprise you.

4. "My classmates tease me about my mommy who can't walk. They say you're lazy and just don't want to. They even said you're crippled because you did something bad when you were little." These attempts at understanding deserve honest answers. They demand that a parent first face her own feelings—"Why me?"—so that she can hear her child's plea for understanding. The child is trying to face his own responsibility in handling your disability.

5. Imagined distortions of the disability are always out of proportion to reality. Also, whether a child has reason to or not, he will worry, "Will this happen to me?" or, "Is Mommy's problem going to get worse?" Although many details are beyond the comprehension of children this age, discussing his main concerns openly and realistically is healthy. Your willingness to share your adjustment, and even to be able to be dependent, is a gift to your child.

6. If a child makes demands that are beyond you, see his "selfishness" as a sign of health, and of what he feels able to expect from you. I have often been surprised by how unrealistic a child's expectations of a disabled parent can be; he seems completely unaware of whatever limitations there are. He isn't, but his demands show he's learned to use denial to protect himself and his need to idealize you. It may not be until he is an adult that he can realistically understand the limitations imposed by your disability in a consistent way.

Older Parents

Are special feelings and reactions associated with being an "older parent"? Probably. I remember when our last child, born eight years after the last of our other three, was old enough to realize that I was twenty years older than his friends' parents. He asked, "Dad, will you last me out?" My reply was, "I expect to. You've made me young." Having a baby as an older parent is a miracle. It is an opportunity to recapture a younger time—to be a parent after one feels that time has taken that away. It heightens both the excitement and the vulnerability. "Will I be too tired? Will I be flexible enough? Can I keep up with his peers' parents?"

With these questions come practical questions. "Can I give up my job, or at least compromise it enough to parent him as I wish? I've worked so hard and sacrificed so much to get where I am. I feel torn." These feelings are heightened when this is the first child, when special efforts were required to have this child, and when this one is expected to be the last.

Next, parents face the danger to the fetus of being nurtured in an older parent's womb. It is well-known that the incidence of Down syndrome is significantly increased for older mothers. What about other genetic disorders? It is thought to be critical that older pregnant women be tested for genetic defects in the fetus—unless they plan to keep the baby no matter what the risk. (Even then, preparation can be useful for parents, and for the new baby, who may require intervention at birth or before.) Genetic testing, amniocentesis, and ultrasound explorations stir up anxiety in a pregnant woman. "Will my baby be okay?" becomes a constant refrain in all mothers-to-be. An older mother today knows too much not to be worried even more because of her age. "Will my age harm my baby?" is added to the universal concern of "Can I nurture her?"

If parents have waited to have the baby, or if they have not been able to conceive, their vulnerability increases. In-vitro fertilization or implants of fertilized ova intensify the importance of this baby. The birth can take on an almost miraculous meaning, and the baby can become godlike in significance. The danger is that the infant (and later, the child) may be treated as if he were vulnerable, in need of excessive protection. Parents who have waited or have striven against odds are almost bound to treat the child as if he were *too* precious. Too precious to be exposed to the normal stresses of growing up. Too precious to dare to take chances. Too precious to be disciplined. Too precious to be frustrated about each step in development. The danger of not leaving the child to master the stress and frustration of achieving each step by himself is that he will inevitably feel that he can't, that he isn't adequate to master his own steps in development. Discipline and learning how to achieve his own limits are critical to every child. An older, vulnerable parent must guard against the overprotection that can undermine self-esteem in their child. It's not easy.

At the same time, older parents bring enormous assets to parenting. They have often mastered the stress of their own lives and bring an inner security. They often have achieved a sense of assurance about themselves. Although these assets may not be reflected in their parenting, the child will recognize them. Older parents' poise and self-assurance will provide a firm base for their child. If parents come to parenting late, they are almost bound to be "ready to parent."

A danger that older parents need to guard against is that of being too much of a perfectionist. High expectations of oneself, and unconsciously high expectations of the child, are likely to magnify the sense of failure and disorganization of each normal touchpoint. An older parent is likely to want to be a "perfect" parent and to raise a "perfect" child. Perfection in each case is a fantasy. When anything goes wrong, older parents need to pull back and examine the pressure on themselves, and on their child. A child who presses himself to please a perfectionist parent is bound to be under unnecessary inner pressure. Let up on the child and on yourself. Let mistakes happen. You and he will learn from each other's mistakes.

The saddest thing about older parenting may be the parents' feeling of being alone. Too often, grandparents are not around or are too elderly to participate in raising the child. Too often, the parents' siblings have finished with parenting their preschool children and have little patience for new stresses. Too often, your child's friends seem to have younger, more energetic, resilient parents. Look for a support group or another set of "older parents" to lock on to. You can share the wonder, the excitement of each new step—and the fatigue when the healthy disorganization of a touchpoint in development occurs. Above all, have fun! A sense of humor is a great gift to a child, and a sense of humor only gets better with age.

Same-Sex Parents

A significant number of children are growing up with same-sex parents. What does this mean to a four-year-old whose job it is to search for diverse attributes and to identify with two persons? All the research to date of families with two parents of the same gender shows that their children can and do turn from one parent to the other; in doing so, the child finds the differences he needs. He identifies with one, then the other, as we have described in heterosexual families. The same playing off of parents occur, the same fears, dreams, and even nightmares. At times, each parent is seen as bad, as a monster. Bad dreams help to justify the temporary alienation from each parent and to diminish the temporary loss of that parent. A child's play during the day will reflect the cost of such "rejection."

A four-year-old may turn on one of her gay or lesbian parents, just as she would on a heterosexual parent. She might act as if that parent were not there. This can go on for some time and become a painful issue for everyone in the family. Same-sex parents, like all parents, look for reasons. "Have I been too hard on her? Is this because she knows she's adopted?" Every feeling of guilt is dredged up in an attempt to explain the child's behavior. The rejected parent will assume that it is his or her fault. Of course, it isn't, and an overreaction won't help. Anxiety about the effects on a child of the parents' sexual orientation make them vulnerable. A child at these ages is almost bound to hit upon any vulnerability that parents may be prey to while the child searches for an identity of his own and plays one parent against another. This rejection is normal and inevitable. It is critical that parents recognize the reasons behind their child's behavior. The vulnerability of parents whose situation differs in any way from a norm they themselves idealize can make this difficult.

Research on same-sex parents has shown that a child can grow up well in these families. If he is lucky enough to have two adults who love him, a child's needs for affection and understanding are likely to be met. These studies show no evidence that a child's sexual identification will be influenced one way or another in the absence of exposure to parents of both genders. Parents in a same-sex union need not feel vulnerable or guilty when a child shows his craving for the nonresident gender.

As with heterosexual couples, the importance of stable roles within the family cannot be overstated. It is important for parents to be consistent in their behavior toward the child. Of course, this is not always possible for any two parents. Parents in enduring unions can rely on their child's own ability to sort out and identify with the parental behaviors he needs. Research is reassuring in regard to that question. Despite the research, though, many remain concerned about the effects of same-sex parents on children's development. Ironically, this lack of acceptance may be one of the main problems the children of same-sex parents face as they grow up.

FOOD AND FOOD PROBLEMS

Meals should be valued as opportunities for sharing each other's ideas and company. Too often, however, they can be hectic, or missed altogether. Family mealtimes are even more important as opportunities for togetherness in the stressed lives of single parents and dual-career families. Routines such as breakfast and dinner with conversation that shares experiences can compensate for a great deal of separation. Busy working families need to do all they can to maintain shared mealtimes as a way of strengthening stretched ties. I recommend that working parents aim, at the very least, for shared breakfasts:

- Set the alarm half an hour earlier.
- Lay out clothes the night before for the preschool child so arguments the next morning will be minimal.
- Because low blood sugar (hypoglycemia) in the morning leads to crankiness, why not put a glass of juice by the child's bed for her to drink before she gets up and starts moving? She'll be readier for breakfast if her blood sugar is adequate.
- Encourage conversation that makes room for each family member. Meals are a social event, a time for communication. Breakfast is a chance to look forward to the day together and prepare for separations as a family.

- Keep breakfast offerings to a minimum. Use routines such as, "We always have cereal. You can have this one or that one." "Here's your toast and milk." Extensive choices are sure to lead to struggles.

Whether a child eats or not may not be worth a struggle; you can always send her to school with the toast, fruit, or dry cereal in a bag, and a drink. Let the less involved school teacher handle the child's negativism. Most learning occurs in the morning. Although some sugar, as in juice, will help a child who is hypoglycemic, a child's ability to stay attentive is best served by a balance of proteins, complex carbohydrates, and small amounts of fat, rather than by foods coated in pure sugar.

To structure mealtimes so they aren't too full of conflict for parents and child, here are a few suggestions:

- No feeding between meals. If the child wants a snack, it should be as regular and predictable as meals are.
- No eating in front of the television or computers.
- Limit eating to the kitchen (this will cut down on time spent cleaning, too) except for special occasions.
- Let the answering machine get phone messages during meals; these are times for the family to be together without interruption.
- Let the child help with planning the meal (although she may still need to rebel).
- Each child is given a smaller amount of each item than she may want; she can always ask for a second helping.
- At three, allow a child to eat with her fingers or a spoon, but be realistic about manners; she'll model herself on your expectations later.
- If a child has strong feelings about a few items, these can be eliminated, but make no substitutions, because they open the door to struggles.
- Whether the child is eating or not does not need to be discussed.
- No punitive approaches! "Of course you're still hungry. You didn't eat your beans." She'll figure out that connection without you.

- At the end of a leisurely meal, all food is cleared away. No bargains.
- Dessert is the conclusion of a satisfying meal, not a reward for "eating what Mommy wants us to eat."

Mealtime is an opportunity for children to experience their own autonomy while being together as a family. Meals need to be fun, not a struggle. Too many choices lead to conflict. A child can eat what the family eats, or not eat at all. Food can all too easily become a destructive struggle that becomes rewarding in itself; food then comes second. Food can be used as barter for affection: "Eat that just for me"; as coercion: "If you don't eat that, you won't get any dessert"; as a reward: "If you clean your plate for Mommy, you can have an M&M." Bartering clouds the point of meals. Food and the atmosphere around it are intimately tied together. Parents can provide the food, but they can't force a child to eat it. If a child is to value food and to look forward to it, it must be associated with her own motivation, appetite, and pleasure. Valuing her ability to make her own decisions about what she will eat or not is the surest way out of the struggle. All too often, parents struggle over refusals over which they have no control. Parents don't need to jump to make substitutions. Sticking to a few limited choices, combined with the choice not to eat what is offered, say to the child that "eating is important, but we aren't going to struggle over it." Starting with less than what she may want reduces pressure.

Feeding is one of the first activities to express both a parent's caring and a child's need for autonomy; feelings, then, are likely to be intense, and struggles difficult to avoid. Both parent and child are too invested. A caring parent must feel a responsibility to keep the child well-fed and to provide a "balanced diet." The child struggles between dependence (being fed) and independence (feeding oneself). Although the role of food in this struggle should have long since been put to rest, the tension between dependence and independence will be a recurring theme during a child's development. In the midst of a touchpoint and a regression, for example, a preschool child can rediscover the potential for stirring up an exciting confrontation by refusing food. Even though she may have a good appetite most of the time, even one instance of refusal can create powerful reactions in parents, who then risk reinforcing this behavior unwittingly.

A four- or five-year-old may use binges, pickiness, or refusals of food to establish independence or as a chance to play out her conflict about independence. Altered eating can become a message, a chance to become the center of attention, or to divert family attention from more stressful events or interactions. In addition, if given the opportunity, a child will be likely to try "junk" food as a way of imitating her peers. The influence of television and the media add pressure to "try things out." Once introduced, junk food can become another source of struggle. But children at this age can't be expected to resist the seductive flavorings of unhealthy junk foods. Dramatic prohibition of junk foods (and the television commercials that push them) may make them even more intriguing. Rigidity is bound to backfire. Without any fanfare, however, parents can keep junk food out of the house. Every now and then, a matter-of-fact bite is fine, but not on special occasions, and not as rewards. Simple information about what a body needs to grow and be strong can't hurt, either. Filling children's plates from the first with satisfying alternatives to junk food (and their time with activities more rewarding than television) is likely to be most effective.

At four and five, when children are beginning to imitate parental behavior, imitating table manners and trying out grown-up foods comes naturally. If parents have not set up mealtimes as a struggle, a four- to six-year-old begins to fall into family patterns. It seems incredible when a five-year-old says, "Pass the butter, please" or, "Thank you for the milk." And it's even more unbelievable when a five-year-old asks for "more string beans, please." But it can happen.

Food refusal in an otherwise healthy child that persists over several months may mean that it is time to seek help. (Complete shutdown, or food refusal combined with evidence of illness, of course, require more immediate attention.) If the child is not gaining weight (or is losing weight) and is not advancing on the weight curve her pediatrician tracks, it is time to seek outside advice. Your doctor can advise you about whether and where to find appropriate help from a child psychiatrist or psychologist. Because many illnesses affect appetite, the doctor will first want to rule out a medical problem. If there is no medical illness, a therapist can evaluate the child and help both of you with your side of feeding issues. Don't despair and don't wait too long.

GRANDPARENTS

In a generation looking for values to instill in their children, parents would do well to turn to the cultural, ethnic, and religious values of their parents. Grandparents can reach back further with rituals, traditions, and stories from their own pasts. They should take every opportunity to share memories with their grandchildren. Children will pick out the values from these stories.

In our frantic, often chaotic lives, tradition and rituals are too often lost, but grandparents can create occasions to maintain these. A meal every Sunday. A vacation together. A weekly visit. A phone call to absent family. A videotape or an e-mail sent regularly to grandchildren. A letter containing a special story about the past can become a cherished memento—and an important tie between generations.

My grandparents shaped my view of the past and of the future. My grandmother encouraged me to take care of all my little cousins as a babysitter. She would say, "Berry is so good with babies!" That statement gave me the encouragement I needed to find my way to my present career. When grandparents and grandchildren dream together and make up stories, the dreams and stories can become windows into the future. A child can dream with his grandparents without the pressure of parents' wishes.

The involvement of grandparents is needed more than ever today. Many parents have lost touch with the instinctive child-rearing traditions of the past and are confronted with a dizzying array of choices for raising their children. They are besieged with information and advice from many conflicting sources—print, television, the Internet. They know a great deal about child development, and even about parent development, but often find it difficult to make choices from all these sources. When I am criticized for being yet another source of advice, I can honestly say, "Parents were always surrounded with multiple sources of advice—aunts, uncles, teachers, ministers. They had to make their own choices then, and they do now." But with all these choices and pressures, the support of one's own parents, or the reference points of one's own upbringing, may supply a missing, clarifying perspective. Parents need the support—whether the advice is accepted or not—from their own caring parents.

Single parents especially need to be near their own parents for their children's sake. A young parent can be comforted by her own parent's advice, can be grateful for the well-meant support. But she also needs to digest it and then turn away from the parts that are not useful as parenting brings her to a new level of independence from, and interdependence with, her own parents.

This takes time and understanding on both sides. "It's so hard for me to call my mom when I've got problems. Sooner or later, she'll say, 'You deserve that kid. You were just like her yourself.' That's the last thing I need to hear." Why is the young mother so wary of her own mother's advice? In meetings with pregnant couples, one or the other parent-to-be will uncover a common conflict: "I don't want to be a parent like *my* parents." And yet, both parents know that their own experience in being parented is bound to dominate their decision making. The desire to be "different" and "free of grandparent prejudices" is universal. But it doesn't have to interfere with the potential support from grandparents, or in efforts parents make to find their own way. A discussion with their parents may alleviate their confusion. After all, even if parents decide *never* to take their parents' advice, half the potential courses of action are eliminated, and parents can relish their turn to make their own mistakes.

The truth is that we are all dominated, often unconsciously, by "ghosts from our own nurseries." When we are under stress, these experiences surface and influence our behavior. They may not be active under usual circumstances, but with the stress a touchpoint can bring, parents' anxious indecision is likely to be guided by experiences from their own past. Whether a parent conforms or rebels, the effects of the past generation are present. When a child resists repeatedly, it is time for parents to pull back and reconsider their position. Most likely, a parent is overreacting because of something echoing from his or her own past. By looking at their reactions more carefully, parents can recognize the power of the past in their interactions with their own child.

Every baby pushes parents toward a new relationship with their own childhoods and with their own parents. No longer are they dependent or rebellious adolescents. They have no choice but to be in charge. It is exciting for grandparents to watch their children grow up before their eyes as they assume the roles of parenting their own children.

At the same time, it is difficult for grandparents to refrain from giving advice. Every well-meant criticism can be perceived as a barb that can undermine as well as support. A "new" grandparent needs to learn how to wait before offering advice. You catch more flies with honey. Any unsolicited suggestion can be perceived as a criticism. Being a grandparent can be like walking on a tightrope.

Grandparents *can* be of inestimable value if they can remain nonjudgmental both about their children as parents and their grandchildren's behavior. Courtesy, manners, and generosity can be modeled rather than lectured about. The unconditional affection and caring of a grandparent is a great boost to self-esteem. A grandparent's best role is to encourage and support a child.

Having grandchildren is like dessert. The burdens of discipline and full-time responsibility do not dominate the relationship. Being able to give encouragement and admiration unreservedly builds a very special bond between a grandparent and grandchild. A relationship with grandchildren can be pure pleasure. I recommend to other grandparents that we get on with grandparenting without trying to be the parent as well.

It is difficult not to overpower your children and grandchildren. I learned very early that when I entered my children's houses I needed to suppress my eagerness. Wait until they come to you. If I charged up, looked my grandson in the face, and hugged him in greeting, he would disappear for the rest of my visit. But if I waited, pulled back, looked just past him until he made the first bid, he was less overwhelmed. After a short wait, he'd push on my leg to say, "Hi, Bapa." Then, and only then, was he ready for my eager hug. In

that visit, I'd shown him a respect for his sensitivity, for his readiness to take me in. It wasn't easy, but we've developed a more relaxed relationship, and it deepens with each visit.

Grandparents have told us that the following are the most help in strengthening a relationship with grandchildren:

1. Regular family celebrations.
2. Making grandchildren feel special.
3. Telling family stories.
4. Supporting your children as parents.
5. A special regular date with each grandchild.
6. Having fun together.

7. A videotape of grandparents reading to their grandchild.
8. Sending postcards to grandchildren.

The "new" generation of grandparents, who are still actively working themselves, find it harder to be a major backup to their children and children-in-law. When both parents are also working, everyone wishes that grandparents could fill this gap. But it is not possible when grandparents are working or are infirm.

Some grandparents are thrust into having to parent their grandchildren. Teenage pregnancies, divorces that lead young mothers back to work, and illnesses such as AIDS or drug abuse lead to such situations. Awareness is increasing of the need for support systems (and instructional material about child development) for grandparents who are primary caregivers of their grandchildren. This group of grandparents are indeed "heroes." In the research examining development of children of unwed teenage mothers, the most important positive factor is whether the grandmother accepts and continues to nurture her daughter and her baby.

Elderly grandparents can feel the cloud of illness and death hovering; it is present in the awareness of all three generations. However, shared experiences and passions make a base for accepting losses later on.

Grandparents, and great-grandparents in fortunate families, serve a major purpose and should be a part of their grandchildren's lives. The opportunity for children to love and respect the elderly is an important one. They will understand that disabilities and changes because of age are part of life. Fears of being disabled themselves or of losing family members are bound to come up. All the questions need to be answered honestly. Many fears and fantasies are aroused in a small child by illness and loss. Listen to what a child is worried about, and answer as honestly, and simply, as you can. "Grandpa's body got worn out and couldn't do much any more. We shall miss all the good times with him, won't we?" Also, grandparents themselves can explain in simple terms to children their own outlook on life and death.

HABITS

Many preschool children go through a period of various self-comforting habits such as hair-pulling, rocking, or biting their nails and the skin around them. As if they were exploring the behavior that bothers parents, they seem to run the gamut of habits. Habit patterns have deep roots. My first child sucked her middle two fingers as a newborn to comfort herself—an unusual pattern—and I found myself taking them out of her mouth. My wife said, "You'd never recommend trying to stop this to your patients. Why do you try to interfere with her sucking?" I couldn't answer her. A week later, my mother came up from Texas to see her new grandchild. "Isn't that amazing? She sucks the same two fingers you used to suck! In those days, finger sucking was considered a bad habit. We tried to stop you, but we never could. You were determined." I realized then why I'd tried so hard to stop my daughter. Attention to a habit pattern is more likely to set it as a problem than to eradicate it. Thumb bandages, terrible-tasting ointments, or other ingenious measures have the opposite effect from that intended.

An older child can be helped to see that she resorts to self-comforting habits when she's stressed and needs to calm down. These are signs of tension. Parents can evaluate the pressures on a child who is resorting often to such habits. The pressure isn't always from the outside. An over-charged, hard-driving child may need such a habit pattern to help her manage her temperamental intensity.

One child, on being reprimanded for her nail-biting, pleaded, "Mummy, can you take my head off? My mouth just bites my fingers. I don't like it and I don't know what to do." This shows the depth of feeling in a child who is trying to control such a symptom. Do we want to add our own pressure to it? Why not say, "Most people bite their nails. Sooner or later you will stop. In the meanwhile, worrying about it won't help. I've made you feel guilty about it, and I'm sorry." Better to reassure her that the habit is likely to go away. This is more likely to happen if everyone (including the child) can ignore it.

The various habits common at these ages—thumb sucking, pulling out hair, nail-biting, stuttering, and the many others that parents encounter—can show a common pattern. The following guidelines may be helpful:

1. Many three- and four-year-old children run the gamut of habits. They last only a few weeks or months. Many of these habits may be imitative of a parent, a sibling, or a peer.

2. Habits may serve a self-calming purpose at a peak of frustration or excitement. A child turns to this behavior as she might have to her thumb earlier. A special doll or other treasured object to hold and touch might help to redirect the child's need for self-comfort.

3. When a parent sets up a prohibition, this surrounds a habit with heightened interest or excitement and tends to reinforce it. Either the added attention or the use of it as a kind of rebellion makes it satisfying. All this is unconscious on the part of the child. In this way, what might have been transient behavior becomes more fixed—a habit.

4. Much less commonly, more unusual kinds of involuntary behavior (for example, repetitive hand washing or staring spells, among others) may seem to take on a life of their own and seriously interfere with a child's daily life. If they have a more bizarre quality, are more repetitive or disruptive throughout the range of a child's activities, they require professional attention. A mental health professional is needed to determine whether these are habits or something more serious (such as obsessive compulsive disorder, Tourette's syndrome, or certain seizure disorders) for which treatment is needed. Your pediatrician can refer you to a pediatric neurologist or child psychiatrist.

Criticizing the child for a habit makes her feel inadequate, unable to "break" the habit. For these reasons, a parent would be best advised to ignore the behavior from the first. Because all parents are loaded with their own past experiences, this is not easy. Nail-biting was a habit to be "broken" for the last generation. A parent today who was broken of this habit during his own childhood will find it extra hard to "ignore" such behavior today.

HOME SCHOOLING

Home schooling is rapidly becoming more widespread. Advocated by the educator John Holt in the aftermath of the school reform movement of the 1960s, which he felt had not accomplished its mission, it has grown significantly in recent years. Home school advocates emphasize the need to integrate living and learning and also the importance of gearing education to the pace and learning pattern of each child. Over 700,000 children are estimated to be home-schooled today. State regulations differ, but most states require that parents submit a planned curriculum. Home-schooled children often participate in sports and other school programs or take courses at local schools and colleges. Local home-schooling groups are the best source of information. The organization Holt Associates, founded by John Holt, is a good information source (see "Resources"). Various publishers offer packaged curricula as well as test preparation booklets for examinations such as the SAT.

Home schooling creates a demanding role for parents, but many have done so successfully and many home-schooled children are now in college and hold challenging jobs. Because it takes strong-minded parents to rebel against an institution as powerful as the school system, their children may reflect the independent, enterprising environments in which they have been raised.

Children who have been labeled in their school settings (learning-disabled, shy, sissy, bully), and who are being undermined by these labels, might well profit from learning at home with support-

ive parents. Children who indeed do have unique learning styles or particularly difficult-to-manage temperaments may also benefit, especially when schools are unable to adjust to their needs. In localities not endowed with adequate schools, home schooling can offer an alternative. Nonetheless, our public schools should be held to their mission of providing adequate education for all children, including those who have been negatively labeled, whose learning styles or temperaments present special challenges, and others with special needs.

Among the caveats to consider, two are of particular concern:

1. *Autonomy*. Because the parent is the teacher year after year, the temptation to hover and to encase the child in a protective cocoon is all too easy. Children need the opportunity to learn how to adjust to different adults—even demanding ones. They also need to learn how to handle stressful and demanding environments other than home.

2. *Socialization*. Home schooling potentially endangers the opportunities for children to adjust to and learn from their peers. Peer relationships are critical for small children. Not only must they learn about handling other children and adjusting to them but they need the learning about themselves that comes with these relationships.

These two needs, for *autonomy* and *socialization,* should be uppermost in the minds of parents deciding whether to engage in home schooling. Community-based after-school groups for children to experience athletics and social encounters are commonplace nowadays and can be of great benefit for children whose parents have chosen home schooling. Covering a set academic curriculum is only one of the responsibilities of a home teacher. Learning how to foster independence and provide a variety of social experiences is equally important.

Although home schooling may serve as an alternative for some children, or a supplement to inadequate educational resources, I find it frightening to think of the consequences of giving up on public education altogether. Education is a social endeavor; it prepares children to play a productive role in their society. As their children begin school, parents face a touchpoint in which they must reconcile the instinct to protect their child's interests above all others with the understanding that the child will have to balance his or her interests with those of others. If home schooling became the predominant educational experience, when would children begin to learn how to submit their individual needs or their family's needs to the common good? Public schools must be supported to adapt to the individual learning styles and temperaments of children if they are to continue to be entrusted with this crucial socializing role.

HONESTY

A parent of a three-year-old who had just hit her one-year-old sister said to her daughter, "Did you hit the baby?" "Yes I did, Mommy." "Why did you do that? Don't you know it hurt her?" "I just wanted to." The mother was stunned by her daughter's naïve honesty. Should she discipline her and then set the stage for lying in the future? Or should she let the child find her own remorse? This is the setting in which future morality is shaped, although it is not to come, even in its most basic form, for another year or so.

Learning to be honest is a long-term process, and it is just beginning at this age. The child has lessons to learn as she struggles with wishful thinking and the desire to change the world to be the way she would like it to be. Imagination and fantasy are important at three and four—even at five—for enlarging a child's world. As she tries to bring about her dreams she uses make-believe, even lying and stealing if she must. How does a child learn that lying and stealing are not acceptable? What will motivate her to comply? She will learn most from modeling on her parents' morals and from their values, and her reward will be their approval and the thrill of being just like them. Meanwhile, parents feel great pressure to help their children take these important steps.

Lawrence Kohlberg has outlined the stages of moral development in children:

1. Avoiding punishment: "I won't lie or steal because I might get into trouble"; or, "My parents tell me I can't tell a lie, and they'll be angry if I do."
2. Doing right for self-serving reasons: "You scratch my back and I'll scratch yours."
3. Pleasing others and fitting in: "I didn't mean to do it" means a child knows what she should have done.
4. Doing one's duty: "Rules are rules. Everyone has to follow them."
5. Reaching consensus: "We can agree on rules that serve us all, and we can stick to them."
6. Acting on principles to satisfy one's own conscience.

Don't expect children ages three to six to be motivated to be honest for reasons other than avoiding punishment, self-serving purposes, and a desire to please and fit in. Unfortunately, even some adults never make it all the way to being honest for its own sake and the sake of their consciences.

Diana Baumrind, a researcher on families and social contexts, categorized three parenting styles—authoritarian, authoritative, and permissive. An authoritarian parent controls children's behavior and coerces them into compliance with the earliest stage of moral development; but the outcome of such parental pressure might be a child who is secretive and dishonest, or who is constantly fearful of the consequences of her dishonesty. Too tight a rein can make a child depend on outer controls instead of building inner ones. The balance would be lost between a child's need for fantasy and make-believe, on the one hand, and the need to control her urge to lie and to steal, on the other. A child might be paralyzed in Kohlberg's first stage if she does not have a chance to feel motives other than fear of punishment.

An authoritative parent understands the motivations for a child to learn each stage, as well as the costs. Such a parent helps a child balance her need for make-believe with the value of fitting her behavior into the real world. "When you tell me one thing, and I know it's not true, I can't believe what you say anymore. We need to be able to believe each other. When you tell me that your friend wrecked my computer, I know you feel so badly that you wish it hadn't been you. But I want to trust you and I want you to learn how to use the computer. I need to know that I can depend on you."

A permissive parent is likely to leave the child looking for her own boundaries. "When will the ax fall? When can I get away with dishonesty? What if I feel too badly about it?" An inconsistent, erratic parent leaves the child afloat, without any dependable expectations for honesty. Dishonesty can become a way of life, accompanied by the constant fear of consequences, or worse, a lack of awareness of consequences. Either way, a child does not feel worthy of respect.

Both the child and the parent know what to expect. "When you can be brave enough to tell me the truth, I'll know I can believe what you say again." The child will first try to protect herself; she fears the consequences of "losing" her parent because of her behavior, and of giving up her make-believe world. A parent needs to be aware of the cost to the child of giving up these dreams, and the feeling of being able to change her world. Saying "I'm so disappointed in you" can be devastating to a child. It can take away the hope of doing better next time. But a parent who says, "I love you, but I don't like to hear you lie," is still facing the child with the responsibility for having lied while implying that the child can do better.

Listening to the child's reasons is important: "I want to know why you told me that." "I was afraid." "Afraid of what?" "Afraid you'd be mad." "I am mad. But we both can stand that. Why did you do it?" "I wanted to learn how to work the computer like Daddy does." "But you aren't Daddy, and it's very hard to learn. He will teach you, but you will have to learn it with him. He'll help you. I know you feel badly now, so apologize to him. He may get mad at first, but then he'll understand how much you wanted to learn about it."

Listening to the child gives her respect and support. Understanding her reasons does not take away the responsibility she must feel for her act and for her dishonesty. Instead, you have given her hope for learning in the future how to handle a difficult situation without lying.

White lies are in a gray zone, often used by adults to save the feelings of others. They are bound to be confusing to a child and need to be explained.

Tattling can become a problem in the fifth and sixth years. A child is now able to understand when the other child has told a lie. If she tells, she is likely to please the adult, but she is betraying her sibling or friend. It is a dilemma for both the child and the adult. How should a parent respond? "I am proud of you for knowing it's not right for him to tell a lie like that, but I am worried that you had to hurt him in order to tell me. Could you have asked him to tell me himself?" In this way, you have recognized her dilemma at recognizing the lie and of ignoring it versus hurting the other child. No one likes a tattletale. She should be aware of that, and of the importance of relationships with her peers. Such dilemmas are often even more complex than this, and offer early opportunities for moral learning. Children may need their parents' guidance for this. When a child's safety is involved, or if the "tattling" is a cry for help, a parent must listen and respond accordingly.

HUMOR

It is so wonderful to hear a child laugh. A small child's reaction to an event with laughter and humor makes the world around him laugh. Humor and laughter point to a child who is balanced and whose "states" are under control. Even in infancy, humor brings about a shift from an intensely involved state to a more relaxed one. A stressed child is not likely to laugh. A tired child cannot laugh.

What's So Funny?

For a young child, as with us all, humor may take the form of the unexpected. When a parent plays peek-a-boo with a one-year-old child, the violation of the expected rhythms that have been set up leads the child to giggle. Tickling, which is also more amusing when an initial pattern is suddenly disrupted, can produce a relief from tension and a change in state.

An older child recognizes the context and the expectancy associated with an event. When a parent introduces something out of context or a change in the expected, the child smiles, recognizing the violation. "That's not how you're supposed to do it!" he will say with delight; or, "I know it doesn't fit here." Humor depends on a cognitive capacity to compare and store memories and develop a general sense of what usually happens. Then the child must be able to compare the immediate situation to his understanding of what usually happens, to sort through similarities and identify differences. For a child, the fun of nonsense is the satisfaction he feels in knowing that he can tell the difference between what makes sense and what doesn't.

The Uses of Humor

Humor can be used to make an intolerable condition tolerable. "You are teasing me. I can take it. I can laugh." A child's laughter softens his teaser, who is then bound to be on his side. At three, a child can already use humor to defuse a parent's anger with something the child knows he shouldn't have done. He demonstrates that he can anticipate and change his parent's response. Silliness or teasing can turn an angry reaction into a tolerant one when the child shows that he recognizes his error and protects himself from the consequences.

Older children, too, will use humor to disarm their parents, and they can be expected to laugh or become giddy when they know they have misbehaved. An adult's reaction might be "When you are silly, I know that what you did wasn't right. I can laugh with you, but I still can't let you get away with it. You and I know it was wrong, don't we?"

Silliness and giddiness are also ways of dealing with tension in the child's environment. A four- or five-year-old draws everyone into his giddy play. He can enlist every child around him to participate in silly behavior. Adults tire of it quickly. Watch a child who enters a scene giddily. He will be observing the adults, expecting that they won't join in. The adults react with stern reproaches. The child then knows that safe limits will apply to his giddy behavior; he knows the adults will stop his buildup.

Humor and laughter are common forms of communication among siblings and peers at these ages. In their fantasy play, they use humor to try out and understand the limits of an imaginary situation and to distinguish it from expectable reality. Children use hu-

mor to test the limits of what is real, and to test it safely. "Wouldn't it be funny if I jumped off this table and tried to fly? I'd just plop down and fall on my bum."

Why do children laugh when someone is hurt? Laughter can be seen as a way of handling the anxiety that another child's injury sets up: "Will he be okay? What if that happened to me? Maybe it will." Early recognition of differences in appearance among children (based on race, gender, or disability) can also make children worry that something might alter their own bodies. Laughter disperses the understandable anxiety a child is bound to feel about his own fragility, or at least reduces it to a tolerable level. Laughter is not necessarily a mark of insensitivity. Although a child may not be able to admit it, these seemingly cruel reactions are more likely a sign of feeling vulnerable.

At five and six, as children give up their fantasies of being invincible and are forced, by their new cognitive accomplishments, to face how small and relatively defenseless they really are, the laughter can stem from fright. Adding to this are fears arising from the guilt that children of this age experience in response to their aggressive feelings: "Something bad could happen to me for being so mad at Mommy." A parent who understands this can respond to displays of inappropriate laughter with reassurance: "It is scary to see someone hurt. But laughing won't help her. We can help her get fixed and then we'll all feel better."

Parents can use humor, just as young children do, to defuse a tense situation. When a small child has pushed parents over the edge, humor can be a safe (but not always readily available) way for them to regain their ground. Irritated parents who can use humor to manage their own reactions, taking a fresh perspective on behavior that still must be faced, are modeling effective ways of handling feelings for their child. A parent who can help an angry child see the humor in her position without making her feel ridiculed is showing her an effective way of calming down. When parent and child can laugh together, they can become close again.

Humor serves many purposes for children of these ages, and for their parents, too. When a child can laugh at himself, he is demonstrating that he has a strong self-image. Other children like him. Adults feel reassured and responsive toward him. Humor can be one of the surest ways of gathering everyone's support.

ILLNESS AND HOSPITALIZATION

A child's illness is a time for family solidarity. Working parents must struggle for time off to be with the sick child. The development of separate sick-child rooms in childcare and preschool centers is a step towards shortening the duration of the child's need to be at home while not exposing other children. But the truth is that these centers create increased opportunities for cross-infections between ill and vulnerable children. An even more important concern is that a recovering child needs the psychological nurturing of home and parents. I will never forget the warm mustard plasters on my chest and the sweet, cool liquids that came with every chest cold—and my mother's caring presence! A parent's care during a child's illness is a testament to the importance of the parent-child relationship that no child ever forgets. Unfortunately, this care can be undermined by the pressures of work. We need more support from employers, and the implementation of legislation to free parents (including fathers, because mothers still bear the brunt of this responsibility) for these times with their small children. Parents need to make every effort not to miss this chance to be at home with their child!

Visits to the doctor or hospital are potentially frightening for any child. My book *Going to the Doctor* was inspired by a four-year-old boy's request that I "write a book for children." "Write about why I go to the doctor, and what you're looking for. Are you just looking for my badness?" This gave me a new insight into the reluctance children display about going to the doctor. They express fears of needles and of being undressed (probably derived from our warnings to them). More subtle and more important may be the fear that we will find their "badness." Children from three- to six-years-old are very concerned with their own responsibility for anything that goes wrong; they correlate it with their new awareness of their effect on the world around them. When a child catches a cold, any parent is bound to say, "I told you to wear your sweater yesterday!" The child also picks up on the added stress her illness imposes on parents, which makes her even more likely to feel that becoming sick is her own fault. To allay these fears, a parent might try this: "Everyone gets colds, and we do know how to make you feel better. Would you like to play cards or read a book with me?"

Hospitalizations can present a major challenge for the child and her family. They are frightening. They involve separation and painful procedures. In the hospital, the child feels helpless and senses the helplessness of her parents. "No one knows what to do for me" was the cry of my twelve-year-old daughter when she needed to be hospitalized and examined. I recommend that parents use the advance preparation now offered by most hospitals; then they can join the child in facing the experiences by explaining in simple, matter-of-fact but honest terms what lies ahead.

On a pediatric surgical service a study was done of thirty cardiac surgical patients. When parents had prepared the children, they recovered significantly more quickly. Such preparation included reading a book together about hospitalization and surgery, bringing the child in ahead to see the surgical floor and to climb in and out of an oxygen tent, to enter the treatment room, to meet the nurses, and to meet another child who had been through the same procedures and was recovering. With this preparation, even the incidence of deaths and complications after surgery were reduced significantly. The parents' presence at the time of pre-medication, before entering the operating room, and during the days of recovery were also critical to the child's optimal recovery.

Children of these ages need to cry, to moan and groan, and to regress in behavior after such an insult as hospitalization. Parents should prepare for these regressions and share them with the child. "No wonder you are wetting your pants. Anyone who has been through the frightening time you have would be likely to wet afterward." This explanation is reassuring to the child, who feels guilty about the whole experience.

After the child comes home, plan opportunities for her to play out her feelings. Fantasy play and drawing about the experience are two wonderful ways to let the child express herself about the trauma and the fears it has created. In addition to accompanying the child through the experience, playing it out afterwards is therapeutic and speeds the child's recovery. Parents often feel guilty about not being able to protect a child from the trauma of hospitalization and surgery. Their preoccupation with their own grief, or their own denial, may prevent them from facing their responsibility in preparing the child. Don't let this happen!

When the hospitalization is unplanned and is the result of an emergency admission, preparations become even more important, even though they must be briefer. Be as honest as you can about the pain and separations that are necessary, and why the child must enter the hospital. Be there when you can for all transitions. If the hospital is so antiquated that it doesn't encourage parents to be present, change hospitals if you can, or use support from other parents and from professionals from more enlightened institutions to insist that you stay with your child. If you must argue to stay with your child, be prepared for an intense reaction, as professionals are as susceptible to gatekeeping (when adults compete with each other to care for a child) as anyone else. We know that complications and poor outcomes are significantly more likely when parents cannot be present to cushion an anxious, sick child. Be there as much as you can. Encourage the child to share her fears and her feelings. Share them with her afterwards. Each illness and each hospitalization can be an opportunity—however unfortunate and unwanted—for learning how to handle stress together as a family.

Chronic illness can be debilitating both physically and psychologically. In a severely ill child's development, touchpoints may be delayed, altered, or missed. An illness with unpredictable exacerbations or an uncertain but deteriorating course leaves everyone anxious about how and whether the child can grow cognitively and emotionally. The worries about the effects of illness on a child's development can intensify the pressures, the parents' hovering, and the child's regression.

A child who is chronically ill is understandably susceptible to depression, especially with a flare up of her symptoms, with a turn for the worse, when she seems to be losing ground, or when she reaches a touchpoint her illness won't let her master. She may feel like a failure. She can easily lose the hope of being able to conquer her world. Depression can reinforce her illness and may even reduce her capacity to fight for recovery. Even if a child escapes this, some aspects of her development are likely to regress at such a time.

This is no time to push a child socially or cognitively. Follow her lead. If she wants to become a baby, treat her like one. Even use baby talk and cuddling. Don't push her to eat or to conform to previous expectations. Her dependency at such a time is necessary and healthy. Although your child's renewed dependency may worry you, your struggle against it will only reinforce it. (There will be time for her to catch up later. If there isn't, you will feel grateful that you put aside the struggles to be close.) Look, instead, for opportunities to give the child a feeling of mastery. Toys that allow her to succeed, artistic creations, or computer-assisted techniques for encouraging communication are all useful in restoring a child's feeling of being independent and able to leave her mark on her world.

A child's chronic illness can also foster depression and grief in the parents. When this happens, many chronically ill children work hard at being "good patients," even when that means keeping their suffering to themselves and feeling more alone. I would encourage you to find support groups or outside resources to help you with your own feelings so you can face those of your child. Parents who can support each other through the stress and regression of a child's chronic illness will reinforce their family's resilience and strengthen the bonds of caring and affection that hold them together—even though the grief over an incurably ill child never entirely ceases.

LOSS AND GRIEF

We all wish we could protect children from losses, but we can't. Many kinds of losses are likely to occur in childhood. The death of a pet may be the first. A child will wonder, "Why? Where has she gone? Why did she leave me? Is it my fault? Can we get another one soon?" A friend moving away—and not being able to see him again, is another. An impaired sibling who demands parental attention, and for whom everyone must grieve, marks a child—for better, and for worse—indelibly. Each of these losses demands that the child face unfamiliar emotions in himself. There will be uncertainty and questions.

Adults go through predictable stages of shock, denial, anger, depression, bargaining, and learning to cope at a different level; these are eventually followed by acceptance. A child's ability to cope with painful feelings is more limited. Parents can anticipate a time of regression leading to recurrence of earlier behavior as the child attempts to grieve.

A grandparent's death affects every family member. Parents' grief draws them inward and away from their children at such times. A parent's tears are an unavoidable shock to a child. A parent without an answer, a parent unable to make everything all better is an unfamiliar parent. The usual comforting support is no longer reliable. A loss such as this disrupts the routine and structure on which a child depends. These events cannot be controlled and the child's feeling of security is threatened.

In the earliest years, a child struggles to understand that some things don't change about himself and others, and that important people come back when they go away. Now all of a sudden a parent says, "We lost grandfather" or "Grandma is gone." "Where? Why?" Where does a lost grandparent go? If he's gone, what happens to his body? Grandfather seemed as reliable a presence as any other adult. "If he can get lost, who is next? Will I also lose my parents?" If one parent has been unavailable or not present—as in divorce or even as in hard-working families—the child may worry anew about being abandoned. One loss brings up his fears about losing other important people and revives any previous loss for the child. It also creates an awareness of the child's own vulnerability: "Can it happen to me?" All of these frightening questions and uncertainties make a child hungry for explanations: "Is it my fault? Whose fault is it?"

Magical thinking is a way of trying to explain the incomprehensible. A child can think only of his own impact—real or imagined—on the world. "I shouldn't have told that lie. I shouldn't have stayed home that day. I shouldn't have wished I didn't have to go to see him. If I'd been good, would it have happened?" When parents are distressed and distant, a child must suppress these questions, these fears. When his parents become available again, the child will once more be able to face his fears.

A child's distress might show as a change in behavior—either too good or too bad. Negative or provocative behavior is often triggered by something unrelated to the loss. A child who is fearful due to a loss may react to any stress or frustration as he did when he was much younger. Bedwetting recurs. A parent can expect clinging behavior, tantrums, and fragility. Testing limits with behavior that has already been conquered can recur months later. A parent may have to work hard to understand what this regression is saying. Newly achieved skills are most likely to be beyond the child's grasp during this period.

If grieving parents are to help, they must first face their own grief. Rituals such as curing ceremonies in some Native American cultures or sitting shivah in the Jewish religion are ways people have found to confront grief. Such ceremonies demand that adults openly face their grieving. Adults can be more available to the rest of the family after they have openly faced guilty, fearful, or angry feelings. Adults use three expectable coping behaviors to face a loss; these make the intolerable tolerable, but at a cost. *Denial—*

avoiding and distorting reality, not hearing anything related to the loss. *Avoidance*—changing the focus to other, safer areas. *Detachment*—consciously or unconsciously distancing oneself from important relationships. This last defense is the most frightening to the child.

As long as a parent denies the loss or is immobilized or detached, children will flounder on their own. Although they long to feel protected, they may react by trying to take care of the parent. Rather than lose a grieving mother, five- or six-year-olds will try to take over her duties. They may even pat their mother or put an arm around her at vulnerable times. One loss paves the way to worries about another and more frightening loss. "If grandpa can die, can mommy die, too? She misses him so much. She can't even hear me sometimes."

When a parent is ready to deal with the child's grief, these suggestions may help: Listen—let the child unload his questions. "Where has Grandpa gone?" "He died." "What is dying?" "Your body just stops working." "You mean you can't walk?" "Or breathe, or talk." "Oh. Will I die?" "Someday, but not soon." "Will you die?"—the real question in his mind. "Not soon. I want to take care of you until you grow up." "Oh." (In this way, you've shared the child's concerns. You've answered honestly and directly, not leading him into areas that you can't confirm. And you've dealt with his real question, "Will you leave me?").

The questions may be unanswerable, but sharing them is critical. Help the child with his own loss of control. "Don't worry so much. I am upset, too. Sometimes when I think about Grandpa, I cry, too." Let a child talk about the person who has died. You can reminisce about "the old days." Commemorating someone helps to keep that person's memory alive, but it also gives both of you a chance to deal more openly with the loss. It becomes a shared and therefore more tolerable event. "Even though we won't get Aunt Lucy back, we can remember her. She wanted you to have her photo album. Last time you were over there, you looked at it. She was glad you liked it."

MANNERS

With a child's increased awareness of how her behavior affects others, a new opportunity arises. When she says, "Thank you" or "Please," she receives a reward from those around her. Adults react with admiration. Parents have probably worked hard to set up these patterns. I call them "learn to please Grandma" patterns. In the second, and certainly by the third, year, a parent will automatically look the child in the face and say appealingly, "Now, say 'thank you.'" Or, if she is optimistic, she may say, "Hold out your hand to Mrs. Strauss and say, 'How do you do?' Remember how we practiced this?" The three- or four-year-old's eyes may cloud over. Her arms will drop to her sides. She may look or she may run away. If she's an especially docile child, she may put out her hand. But she will do it with the kind of passivity that overlies negativism. A child's hands can feel like dead fish at this age; they reflect the lack of enthusiasm for parental instructions in situations like this. You can expect negativism, but don't give up. I still believe in introducing manners at this age.

Watch your four-year-old when someone special arrives. Without instruction, she may even put out her hand to the new person. The person may say, "Aren't you a big girl? You know how to say, 'How do you do?!'" Your instrumental teaching has finally paid off. You have introduced behavior that she appeared to resist, but she has taken it in and has even absorbed its purpose. She is now even able to anticipate that this behavior will bring a reward. As long as the manners are yours—responding, for example, to "Say 'please' to Grandma,"—and not hers, they are only remotely effective. But they are still worth teaching. Sooner or later she will "slip up" and use one of the greetings on her own. When she does, the reward becomes her own. She has found a way of mastering this world of manners—a big step at this age. You may wish she went further on her own, but not yet. She's bound to fail as often as she succeeds. You may feel it's your failure when she does.

The risk in this kind of teaching is obvious: if a child is only compliant and only mimics your instructions, she will not have experienced the behavior as rewarding. Parents can balance the instructions with opportunities for independence. If she has a favorite uncle, don't practice a greeting ahead of time. Instead, see whether she tries out these wiles on her own. You may want to prepare the uncle in advance. Urge him to be ready to stick out his own hand and to reward the child for any reciprocal behavior that it may induce.

A parent can prepare a child for an opportunity like this: "Today we are going to lunch at grandma's. There will be people there who haven't met you yet. Even grandma doesn't know how big you've gotten. She will be so surprised to see you put out your hand and say, 'Hi, I'm glad to see you!' Some of her friends really want to meet you. She has talked so much about you." Make it sound like fun. Then let the child handle it. You've planted the seed. If she can live up to it, it will be a real achievement; if not, you may have to wait for the next occasion.

If it does work, don't overwhelm her with praise. When you do, you are taking away her own role in the achievement. Let her experience the reward herself. At most, you might ask, "Did you see how impressed Grandma was?" Your goal is to give her opportunities to affect the world around her, to realize that what she does affects others. She is intellectually and developmentally ready to reap the reward of her own actions and realize that these matter to others around her. She is beginning to develop a public conscience.

What about mealtimes and family gatherings? In the chaos that comes with shared excitement, children can create a nightmare. The response can be either punitive—"You can settle down or go to the other room to finish"—or focused on a positive outcome. "Let's play a game. You start a story, only one sentence, then everyone takes a turn. Each person, one idea. Let's see where the story goes. No inter-rupting. If you want to be ready for your turn, you have to listen." Manners need to serve a family's time together, not overwhelm it.

Manners matter in friendships, too. Children these ages are strug-gling with sharing and taking turns with their peers. A child who is left alone because she fails to share or won't take turns may need help making the connection between her behavior and the other child's response. A child who struggles to master her urge to hoard her toy to herself, or to take all the turns, takes pride in her own gen-erosity when she wins out against these urges and shares. Would the lesson have been the same if a parent had enforced the sharing? A parent might model it, suggest it, help a child care about the other child's feelings and imagine what they might be. But a parent can't show generosity in the child's place; any attempt to do so is likely to make the child feel more stingy, not glad to give. Parents may want their children to be further along than they are—but skipping steps doesn't work.

When does a parent start teaching manners? The first year. Every time a diaper is changed on a squirmy baby with any success and cooperation, a parent can say, "Thank you." Every time parents of-fer a cookie, they prompt a "please." When an elderly adult is al-lowed to enter a door first, say, "Grandma deserves to go first." Children today may be cheated of the opportunities to think gener-ously about others. We are all in a hurry, and most families are stressed. Manners may be left out or forgotten.

Demonstrations of respect for others need to be modeled from early childhood. They matter. They are an important part of the cul-tural values that parents pass on to their children. "Children can play Ping-Pong when the grown-ups are through." Our own children now must pass on family rules like this for their own fives and sixes. I have found that grandchildren value their "own time" even more when they have had to wait and honor a rule like this, especially if holding back required some effort. Manners carry an important message.

Manners today may matter more than ever. In our frantic lives, barging ahead and road rage all too frequently displace courtesy. In Texas, there are signs on the road: DRIVE FRIENDLY. These signs mean pull over when someone wants to pass. Our children were awed by this behavior: "Dad, you let him pass! You'd never do that in Boston!"

Children learn manners from adults around them. "Please" and "Thank you" can be expected by four and five if they have been a longstanding expectation in the family. These are words that acknowledge the efforts of the person being spoken to. They may not always be remembered, but often, they can be seen in action. A parent's patience and repetition will still be needed, and are more effective than nagging. Each time these important words are received with appreciation, they are more likely to become second nature. Manners matter in your child's future.

MOVING

When a parent says, "We're moving," what does this mean to a pre-school child? At first, it may be an exciting idea. "We'll all go in the car together. You can take your best toys. We'll stop at special places along the way, and you can have a hamburger or a hot dog." But as the time approaches, the reality of leaving everything the child is used to—the house, his room, his neighborhood, his friends, his teacher at school—begins to sink in. "When will I ever see my friends again?" If he is old enough (four or five) to be aware of the losses this move will entail, it will challenge his newly conquered understanding that people don't stop existing when they are not visible. He must struggle to believe that his friends and his teacher will still be there, maybe even waiting and missing him, even though he can't see them or talk to them. Moving also brings up more frightening prospects: "If I can lose my old house and friends, maybe I can lose you." A parent needs to remember this. Every loss challenges and reminds a child of his most feared loss—you.

A child may cling more. Every time his parents are out of sight, a child who has just moved may cry seemingly for no reason. A child who is about to move may be overwhelmed by his parents' busy preoccupations, and his own anticipation and fear of the unknown. He may feel frightened, and frighten his parents because he seems changed. The change may be his new sensitivity to noisy streets or to the grocery store. Nightmares may occur more frequently. Bed-wetting may recur and diapers may need to be used temporarily. It may be hard for parents to understand why a previously imperturbable four-year-old might suddenly become so dependent. He may recently have become independent enough to go to his friend's house next door or to leave his preschool room by himself to go down the hall to the bathroom. These steps are sources of pride for a child this age; they are built on familiarity, routine, and the security of ongoing relationships. It can be hard for parents to face their child's loss and their own sense of responsibility.

A move is an adult decision and parents may have underestimated the cost to the child. But in any event, the move could not be avoided. When parents recognize their own feelings of guilt and sadness, they can begin to understand the child's feelings of vulnerability. At four and five, the losses may be harder to define, but by six the loss of a newly won peer group is a distinct disappointment. The more a child can put this into words and grieve ahead of time, the easier it may be in the long run.

Parents can help a child with a move in the following ways:

1. Prepare—the longer ahead, the better. This way a big change becomes expectable, a plan rather than a crisis. Talk about it with the child: "We'll go out there and meet some new friends for you. We already know of a family with children your age in the new neighborhood. We'll ask them over. I'll take you out to meet your new teacher and see your new school." Fill in the unknown with as many details, as much information as you can. If possible, visit the new house and the new school ahead of time. Find a schoolmate or neighboring child before you go, if possible. Talk about where her bed will go, where you'll eat morning and evening. Let her meet her new teacher in advance. All the mundane, everyday routines will become even more important. Talk about them in advance. Explain your plans as soon as you know them.

2. Share your feelings, and model your ways of handling them. "I hate to leave my friends. I feel a sinking feeling every time I think about it. I know how sad you are to be leaving yours. Do they know how much you will miss them?" Have a good-bye party. Don't be afraid to cry. Let the child see that you are all facing the losses together—but also that you are anticipating the new home together. "Well eat supper together on the porch."

3. Let the child unload his feelings when he can; create special occasions alone when he can do this. Show your child that you can stand to hear how unhappy or scared he is, that these feelings are legitimate and acceptable to you. The change will be frightening enough; the feelings don't have to be.

4. Expect a regression. Help the child understand it. "Of course you're upset. So am I." Different children handle such a loss in different ways. Respect these. Help the five-year-old see that his fragility at school, his return to babyish habits—even bed-wetting—are understandable.

5. Expect a child to be angry and testing. "If we move, I'll kill you, Mommy."

6. Keep some familiar and important things with you. Don't wait for the moving van to bring a favorite toy, book, or beloved stuffed animal.

7. Once you're there, locate the important areas for routines, for play, and for meeting new friends immediately. "Here's your room. This one is Mommy and Daddy's. This is the closet for your things. We can put your pictures on the walls, and the same blanket on your bed. Here's where we'll eat breakfast and supper together." Fixing up the child's room, locating his toothbrush, sitting down for supper together make this new place feel like home. This is no longer just a strange new geographical location, it's a new home and a revival of the familiar and shared routines. Rituals are even more important— read the old favorites such as *Good Night Moon* over and over and over. Say good night to everything in the house. Hug and rock a lot.

8. As soon as possible, locate a new friend for your child. Identify children at school, at church, in the playground. Look for their parents and make an effort to meet them. "I'm new here. My son would love to make some friends here and I was hoping I could invite your little boy over to play with mine." Take the friend on a little outing with you.

9. Get to know other parents at school drop-off and pickup times. Look for shared activities with them—coaching, parent meetings at school, church meetings. It takes time and effort to become part of a community. Share an evening with your child's teacher. Ask him over for dinner. Model new relation-

ships for your child. He needs to learn from you how to make new relationships, how to start anew.

10. Call the old friends frequently. Tears and whining after a call may seem meant to punish you. But the importance of your child's friendships need to be honored. Look for opportunities to stay connected, and give them up only gradually, if you must. Write cards and letters.

This is a time of mourning losses and of regression, but also of discovery and adventure. These can all be shared. Make it fun when you can, but don't minimize your child's feelings of loss, or your own. Moving is a time for a family to draw close, to discover new places and make new friends, to share feelings, and to learn how to cope with stresses—*together*.

SADNESS AND DEPRESSION

Sadness is inevitable and necessary. It goes with many important events in our lives, and is another way for us to know how important someone or something we've lost has been to us. Every touchpoint in growing up brings the likelihood of sadness—both to parent and child; it is part of the cycle of giving up old ways and of being ready for the next step in independence. Often a parent's sadness is caused by the loss of a child's innocence or the impossibility of protecting a child from a less-than-perfect world.

All children experience sadness. At such a time, the body shuts down; other demands and emotions are either shut out or assigned secondary importance to give the child a chance to slow down, to withdraw and reorganize. The guilt and self-absorption that often accompany sadness need to be sorted through and put aside. During periods of sadness, children are learning to cope with disappointments or grief, and are mustering defenses and techniques for handling vulnerability in the future.

Sadness follows losses, criticisms, and perceived inadequacies. A broken toy leads to tears and the inescapable thought: "I did it! Why am I so dumb? Let me hide it quickly or Mommy will see and make me feel even dumber." The loss of a special blanket, stuffed animal, or pacifier is like losing a part of one's self. "What else will I lose?"

The loss of an important person is, too, and may also come with self-reproach and guilt: "What did I do wrong?" Sadness in parents can feel like a loss, too. A parent's depression will not go unnoticed by young children. They are likely to feel that a parent has "gone away" and feel responsible; this can be frightening if it is not openly acknowledged. Criticisms and slights or teasing can be devastating for young children who already feel smaller and less competent than the adults who care for them. Their self-esteem is less firmly established and more vulnerable to everyday events.

Children of different temperaments are likely to show their sadness in different ways. The commonest expressions are irritability, tantrums, angry outbursts, and aggressive behavior. These are aimed at the outer world. Children also turn their sadness inward—they may not eat, their sleeping and other normal behavior may be disrupted. They may seem pale, despondent—"not the same child." Parents' frustration and overprotection often prolongs the period of sadness, and changes it from a self-contained feeling into misbehavior to test these altered parental responses.

Parents naturally want to protect their children from sadness, but they cannot. It is painful to see a child sad. Although childhood is supposed to be fun, joyous, rewarding, every child can tell you this is not always the case. Adults remember the sad moments of their own childhood at least as readily as the happy occasions.

Here are some ways a parent can help a sad child:

1. Examine your own natural tendency as a parent to suffer when your child is in pain. Do you see her pain as your own failure? Do you feel that you must protect her from these feelings? Had you hoped you could protect her from the sadness you remember from your own childhood? Try to understand your reactions to her sadness; she needs to know that you can stand to hear how badly she's been feeling. Your desire to protect her from her sadness can prevent this.
2. Don't rush in and overpower your child. Leave her time and space to try to handle her sadness on her own. If you rush in, you may not allow time for her to feel that she is being heard and accepted. She needs time for herself. She is learning to cope. She will have to deal with disappointment and sadness eventually, and it is not too soon to begin.

3. Help the child say what she's feeling out loud: "Sometimes it helps to tell someone how you are feeling." The relief she will feel will reinforce future communication.
4. Listen. Don't try to read her mind. You may want her to know that you know just how she feels. But no one ever really can. Listening and wanting to understand are enough.
5. Share and verbalize a child's sadness without "trying to fix it." You rarely can, and you risk giving her the feeling that you can't face her hopelessness. Things don't have to stay hopeless, but a child may not begin to revive until she knows you really see just how serious her feelings are.
6. The extremes either of hovering over the child or of making light of her sadness are both likely to devalue her feelings and her efforts to handle them.
7. Share your own sadness and let her know you can still handle it. Adversity can be an opportunity to model ways of coping for your child.

Sadness is an emotion; it is not the same as depression, which is an illness. Although feelings of sadness come and go like passing clouds, depression settles in like thick fog. Depression makes it hard to see what is really going on. Everything seems joyless and without purpose. The child sees herself as "no good," grown-ups as "no help," and the world as "no fun" and gloomy. This distortion of a child's perceptions may interfere with concentration, friendships, frustration toleration, even eating and sleeping. More persistent and pervasive than sadness, depression may seem like a change in a child's personality. It may also seem more like anger than sadness. More commonly than in adults, depression in a child may give her the appearance of being angry all the time.

The following are a few ways to tell depression from sadness. If you have any doubt, mental health professionals should be called in early to evaluate the child.

- Long duration versus passing, short-lived.
- All-pervasive versus context-specific.
- Invading many areas of the child's life at once, interfering with sleep, peer relationships, and school adjustment, versus resulting from an identifiable cause.

- Peers' hostility or avoidance can signal depression in the avoided child. Often other children are the best guide; they do not like a child who calls up their own struggles and who cannot handle them.

A child who is depressed deserves prompt evaluation and treatment by a child psychiatrist or psychologist. Children have so much important growing and learning to do that they cannot afford to be drained and derailed by this readily treatable condition.

SAFETY

Children's safety is always uppermost in parents' minds. We obsess about it. We wake up at night with a lurch: "Has anything happened?" As our children face a more and more complex society, our fears increase. If we are afraid, so are our children. How can a parent alert a child to dangers that can be avoided without frightening him unnecessarily? The reality that we are all vulnerable is hard to face, so we balance it with the thought that accidents happen only to others. But no one is exempt.

The good news is that the unintentional injury-related death rate among children ages fourteen and under declined 33 percent during the 1990s.[1] However, unintentional injury remains the leading cause of death among children ages fourteen and under in the United States. These injuries are caused primarily by motor vehicle accidents, pedestrian and bicycle accidents, drowning, fires and burns, suffocation, choking, accidental firearm injuries, falls, and poisonings. In addition, each year nearly 120,000 children become permanently disabled.

Among children ages fourteen and under, it is estimated that 40 percent of deaths and 50 percent of nonfatal unintentional injuries occur in and around the home.

---

[1]Much of the information in this section has been adapted from material issued by the National Safe Kids Campaign (see "Resources").

Unintentional injury-related death rates vary with a child's age, gender, race, and socioeconomic status. Children living in rural areas, males, younger children, minorities, and poor children suffer disproportionately. Poverty is the primary predictor of injury. Racial differences in unintentional-injury rates have much to do with impoverished environments. Reducing economic barriers to safety devices and improving the safety of the environment can lower death and injury rates for children at highest risk.

The major causes of accidental deaths vary throughout childhood with changes in a child's developmental abilities and exposure to potential hazards. Parents' perceptions of the child's abilities and injury risk are also factors. Injuries are likely when the demands of a task exceed the child's ability to complete it safely. Infants have higher rates of unintentional injury-related death and are more likely to die or to sustain nonfatal injuries—especially from suffocation and car accidents—than older children. Preschoolers' new motor skills can leave them at the mercy of their still-limited impulse control and judgment. Children of this age are more likely to die from drowning, fire and burn injury, motor vehicle occupant injury, pedestrian injury, choking, and poisoning. Car accidents are the leading cause of unintentional injury-related death among children ages five to fourteen, followed by pedestrian injury and drowning, with bicycle accidents and burns also major causes of death.

As if this weren't enough, parents also worry about abductions and molestation.

When I was ten years old, a car pulled up beside me as I was walking to school one day. "Wanna ride, kid?" I'd been carefully schooled not to accept rides. As the man in the car became more insistent, I sensed danger and broke into a run. I ran across the open field and up onto the porch of the nearest house. Fortunately, the woman who lived in the house was at home, and her front door was open. I rushed in and asked to telephone my mother. She came to get me, but no one *ever* said a word about the episode. When I tried to talk about it, I was pooh-poohed. I was never allowed to walk to school again, but no one in my family shared my fright with me. My experience was treated as if it I had imagined it. I felt deserted and angry, as if no one believed and respected me. Leaving a child alone with fears like these is not the answer. We need to be able to talk to our children about possible dangers if they are to learn to protect themselves.

My first suggestion is that you share your efforts to protect your children openly with them, and to listen attentively to their fears. Although we can't protect them completely, we can help them learn to protect themselves and to put their anxiety, and ours, into perspective. By the age of three and four, we can talk to them about some ways they can help protect themselves:

- Hold my hand when we cross the street.
- Don't leave my side in crowds.
- Never get into a car with anyone you don't know.
- Learn to call our phone number and 911.
- Learn our address.
- Call out to the nearest adult if someone touches you in a way you don't like.

The protection of young children, though, is ultimately up to parents. Encouraging children to become aware of dangers and to learn how to protect themselves is nurturing and a sign of respect. But they must not be made to feel responsible for self-protection beyond their capabilities. Children who can't say they are afraid or can't ask for help are children in danger.

We can also prevent some accidents by understanding how a child sees the world. When our expectations for a child's capability to protect himself match his level of development, we can supply the protection he needs from us.

Before a child begins to crawl, we check his immediate surroundings for potential dangers—proper temperature, adequate ventilation, secure positioning to avoid unexpected rollovers and falls, and a safe distance from plastic bags or sheets that can cause suffocation. At this age, a child uses his mouth to explore his world; small objects and toxic substances, including lead paint chips and dust, must be kept out of reach. When a child first becomes mobile, get down on your hands and knees and take a look at the potential dangers from your child's perspective. You'll want to repeat this every few months for the next few years.

A newly mobile child is at greatest risk because mobility precedes judgment; he has not yet developed coordination and protective reflexes, nor has he learned about the potential dangers of his physical environment. When crawling begins, heights and drops are most dangerous because a child has no fear of them. The risks don't stop after the first month, though. A child this age still explores with his mouth, but he has greater access to toxic materials, including lead paint chips, and small objects that may cause choking. He uses his recently acquired pointing and grasping skills to pick up sharp objects and to stick his fingers in electrical sockets.

Under one year of age, a child doesn't understand basic cause and effect principles of the physical world that adults and even older children take for granted. A child who has just learned to climb up the bookshelves in the living room does not yet know that his weight can topple them on top of him.

From about nine months on, a child learns about the dangers of his world by watching his parents' faces as they react to his explorations. If his parents' reactions are not clear, or are intriguingly excited, he is likely to test the danger again. The surest way to push a child to repeat his socket poking is to overreact. Don't expect a child under two to respond to verbal warnings alone. He is likely to "do it again" to see what you really meant. At this age, a child often needs to be physically removed from the danger (safety plugs are indispensable) and to be told "no" firmly, yet without the excitement that is likely to make him try it again.

During the first years that a child walks, he will be working on motor planning, or thinking in advance about the sequence of actions he must take to get where he wants to go. Until he has mastered this planning, he is likely to stumble, trip, bump into furniture and doors, and knock things down.

Later, when a child's coordination, reflexes, motor planning, and understanding of basic physical principles (like gravity) and cause and effect have developed enough that he is able to anticipate some physical dangers on his own, a parent will still have other reasons to expect him to need help. A child's new abilities may not be available to him if his attention is already consumed by what he is doing. A distracted child may be less able to use his new skills and understanding to protect himself from predictable dangers. Impulse control and attention to more than one thing at a time are some of the skills that come later.

Although the dangers for children in our world and the ways to protect against them are too numerous to address here exhaustively, here are a few suggestions for protection (for more, see the National Safe Kids Campaign Web site and other sites listed in the "Resources" section).

- *Safety manuals.* Available from the National Safe Kids Campaign or your local children's hospital.
- *Safety checklists.* These are available for every stage of your child's development and can be obtained at your pediatrician's office.
- *First-aid kits.* See the National Safe Kids Campaign Web site for recommended contents.
- *Cribs.* Place infants on their backs on a firm, flat crib mattress in a crib that meets national safety standards; look for a Juvenile Products Manufacturers Association certification label. Remove pillows, comforters, toys, and other soft products from the crib. A safe crib will be certified to meet national safety standards and will have no more than 2 3/8 inches of space between slats or spindles; it will have a mattress that fits snugly. The drop-side latches must work properly and be safe from unintentional release or release by a baby inside the crib. Crib corner post extensions or protrusions should not ex-

ceed 1/16 inch, including decorative knobs. Always keep the side rail locked in its up position when the baby is in the crib. Never use a pillow in the crib and remove all crib toys when your child is asleep. Do not place cribs near radiators, heating vents, windows, venetian blind strings, drapery cords, or other hanging strings.

- *Car seats.* Start your baby off in a car seat (rear- facing until one year old and at least twenty pounds) on the way home from the maternity ward. Car seats are safest in the backseat, preferably in the center of the back seat if there is a middle seat belt. Children over one year and between twenty and forty pounds should be in forward-facing child safety seats. In addition, children ages four to eight (about forty to eighty pounds) should be in a car booster seat and restrained with lap/shoulder belt every time they ride. Follow instructions from car *and* car seat manufacturers. (See "Resources" for Web sites dealing with car safety.)

- *Seat belts:* Must be used to secure car seats tightly; seat belts must be worn at all times by children old enough to be out of car seats.

- *Air bags.* Air bags are dangerous for young children; they are not safe for children twelve and under, who must be properly restrained in the backseat. Never put a rear-facing infant seat in the front passenger seat of a vehicle with an active passenger-side air bag. Follow instructions from your car's manufacturer.

- *Street crossing and pedestrian safety.* Adult supervision is needed until a child is at least ten years old. Always model and teach proper pedestrian behavior. Cross streets at a corner and use traffic signals and crosswalks whenever possible. Make eye contact with drivers before crossing in front of them. Don't assume that because you can see the driver, the driver has seen you. Instruct children to look left-right-left again when crossing a street and to continue looking as they cross. Children should never run into the street. Require children to wear retro-reflective materials and carry a flashlight at dawn and dusk. Teach children to walk facing traffic, as far to the left as possible, when there are no sidewalks. Prohibit play in driveways, in adjacent, unfenced yards, and in streets or parking lots. Teach children to cross the street at least ten feet in front of a school bus and to wait for adults on the same side of the street as the school bus loading/unloading zone. Teach children not to play in or around cars. To protect children from becoming trapped in car trunks, always lock car doors and trunks and keep the keys out of children's sight and reach. Supervise young children closely when they are around cars. Be especially careful when loading or unloading the trunk. Keep rear fold-down seats closed to help prevent kids from climbing into the trunk from inside the car.

- *Bike helmets. Must* be properly fitted, positioned, and snugly fastened. Make sure the bike helmet meets safety standards. Look for an ASTM, Snell, or ANSI sticker or the new federal standard certification sticker inside the helmet and on the box. The bike helmet should sit squarely on your child's head, cover his forehead, and not rock from side to side or forward to back. Children are more likely to wear bike helmets when their parents wear them.

- *Bicycling safety.* Children must learn the rules of the road and obey all traffic laws. All bicyclists should ride on the right side of the road, with the traffic, not against it; use appropriate hand signals; respect traffic signals; stop at all stop signs and stop lights; and stop and look left, right and left again before entering a street. Expect children to model parents' example. Cycling should be restricted to sidewalks and paths until a child is ten years old and able to show how well he rides and observes the basic rules of the road.

- *Small objects.* Pennies, marbles, staples, tacks, paper clips and balloons are among the hazards to look out for. Toys with small parts, especially those intended for older children, are also a risk. A small-parts tester, or "choke tube," costs a dollar or two in hardware stores. Do not allow children under six to eat small or round or hard foods such as peanuts, grapes, and hard candy.

- *Lead.* Test children for lead exposure, and test homes built before 1978 for lead-based paint. Cover lead paint with a sealant or hire a professional abatement company to remove the paint. Wash children's hands and faces often, as well as toys and pacifiers to reduce your child's risk of ingesting lead-contaminated dust. Soil around old houses is often contaminated with lead paint.

- *Poisoning prevention.* Cleaning fluids and other chemicals should be stored in cabinets with childproof safety latches, or high above a child's reach. Post the Poison Control 24-hour information phone number by your kitchen phone. Check for poisoning prevention at grandparents' homes.
- *Medicine bottles.* Make sure these are childproof and stored out of children's reach. Check for these at grandparents' homes.
- *Cabinet safety latches.*
- *Window guards.*
- *Stair guards.* Should be installed at both the top and bottom of stairs. Don't use baby walkers with wheels.
- *Pool fences.* Install on all four sides. Pool covers do not protect children from drowning. Fencing should have self-closing and self-latching gates.
- *Water safety.* Never leave a child unsupervised in or around water. Empty all containers immediately after use and store out of reach. *Never* leave a child unsupervised in or around a swimming pool or spa, even for a moment. Never rely on a PFD (personal flotation device) or swimming lessons to protect a child. Learn CPR and keep rescue equipment, a telephone, and emergency numbers poolside. Always wear a U.S. Coast Guard-approved PFD when on a boat or near open bodies of water or when participating in water sports. Air-filled swimming aids, such as "water wings," are not considered safety devices and are not substitutes for PFDs. Never dive into water less than nine feet deep.
- *Fire safety.* —Keep matches, gasoline, lighters and all other flammable materials locked away and out of children's reach.

Install smoke alarms in your home on every level and in every sleeping area. Central locations such as the living room, the top of the stairwell, and outside bedroom doors are good places. Test them once a month, replace the batteries at least once a year (unless the batteries are designed for longer life), and replace the alarms every ten years. For the best protection against different types of fires, consider installing both ionization alarms (better at sensing flaming fires) and photoelectric alarms (better at sensing slow, smoky fires).

Plan and practice several fire escape routes from each room of the home and identify an outside meeting place. Practicing an escape plan may help children who become frightened and confused in a fire escape to safety.

- *Hot-water heaters.* Set at 120 degrees Fahrenheit or below in order to avoid scald burns to children.
- *Guns.* Be sure to equip guns with safety locks. Keep guns unloaded in locked cabinets well out of children's reach—separately from ammunition. Talk to your children about the dangers of guns. Check with adults in houses your children may visit.
- *Carbon monoxide (CO) detectors.* You can't hear, see, taste, or smell carbon monoxide. Place CO detectors outside sleeping areas and at least fifteen feet away from fuel-burning appliances such as furnaces, wood stoves, and fuel-burning kitchen stoves. Ensure that space heaters, furnaces, fireplaces, and wood-burning stoves are vented properly and inspected annually. If your CO detector goes off, ventilate the home immediately by opening windows and outside doors. If anyone starts to experience flulike symptoms, evacuate the house and call the fire department. After ventilating the home, you should turn off all fuel-burning appliances and call a qualified technician to inspect for sources of CO.
- *New surroundings.* Every time you take your child to a new setting, you'll have to start childproofing all over again. Grandparents' homes, garages, and medicine cabinets are especially important to childproof.
- *New stages.* As your child grows, the kinds of dangers he is exposed to will change. Your house will need to be rechecked for dangers every few months as your child's range of action increases. When your child is old enough to be trusted out of your sight, a new world of dangers faces him.

Much more information is available on how to protect your children from danger than we can possibly include in this chapter. For more information, see "Resources." See also in the "Bibliography" *Children's Hospital Guide to Your Child's Health and Development,* by Children's Hospital, Boston.

SENSORY INTEGRATION DYSFUNCTION

The concept of sensory integration dysfunction (SID) can be a helpful one to some parents who find their children's behavior not only difficult, but mysterious and hard to comprehend. The condition can occur along with ADHD and other disorders, but may be present separately. SID is the inability to process information received through the senses: ineffective neurological processing. The child may have difficulty in receiving (often due to hypersensitivity in one or more sensory modalities—touch, hearing, vision), analyzing, organizing, or integrating sensory messages. These difficulties may be reflected in their effects on motor activity. The result is costly to the child, interfering with his ability to plan, organize, and respond in a meaningful way. Clumsy, disorganized behavior creates a sense of failure that only adds to his distress.

A child can rarely describe his sensory experiences to others, for he has no internal baseline with which to compare them. Overwhelmingly loud sounds or prickly, tingly skin sensations may be all he knows. His reactions to these often don't help his parents understand what is going on. The child may refuse to eat certain foods, or to wear certain clothes; he may panic and throw tantrums—without ever being able to say why. He may appear shy and isolated as he attempts to protect himself from sounds (of peers shouting, of traffic, even of the quiet hum of a refrigerator) over which he has no control. Bodily contacts may feel painful and frightening, which may lead him to avoid the gross motor activities needed to develop his body and to learn to use it. Even cuddling can be more uncomfortable than pleasurable. Parents may feel useless, even pushed away, even though their child desperately needs them.

Unexpected or sudden transitions that demand changes in sensory input become painful; such a child will dread them and try to avoid them at all costs. A hypersensitive child may hide from the world as if it were a scary and dangerous place. Friendships and the self-confidence that comes from taking risks and mastering them may suffer. He and his parents will see only his failure *unless* they can understand the underlying problem that his behavior represents. Compounding the problem is parents' difficulty in describing to their health care providers and school authorities the various ways SID manifests itself. This can make it hard to find the specific help they and the child may need.

Dr. Larry Silver of Georgetown University Medical School has seen many of these children, who are often referred to him to "change their behavior." "We need to understand their behavior and what it suggests as the underlying reason," says Dr. Silver. The troublesome behavior is a set of symptoms, not a diagnosis. These symptoms may point, though, to the underlying sensory processes that go astray, and the resulting experience the child has of his world. Parents need help understanding these and identifying the specific situations that stress the child. The child, too, needs explicit information about the way his senses let in sounds and sights and other sensations so that he can began to work on protecting himself from what must feel like a barrage of over-stimulation. Many of these children are bright and have excellent potential if they can be helped to compensate for their sensory dysfunction. (Some may learn to turn their hypersensitivity into a strength—some gifted musicians have had to learn to cope with their auditory hypersensitivity.)

Carol Kantrowitz, a teacher who has worked for twenty years in the field of sensory integration dysfunction, has described SID's various symptoms and developed a program for early identification of SID by screening for the various symptoms. Her observations are adapted in the following list:

- Poor adaptive behavior, the inability to respond to new circumstances, especially when expectations are high and/or new people are involved.

- Impaired motor learning, such as clumsiness and difficulty with complex movements (e.g., learning to use a pencil) or with complex sequencing of movements (e.g., getting around a chair to reach an object on a table without bumping into something along the way).
- Problems with academic learning. The child's compensatory efforts to screen out overwhelming external stimulation may lead her to screen out needed information as well. Additionally, the energy such efforts require may take away from the ability to mobilize and sustain attention and focus on academic tasks.
- Touch avoidance—hypersensitivity to a tactile stimulus.
- Visual hypersensitivity—avoiding eye contact or bright light. A child can become hypervigilant as a result.
- Auditory hypersensitivity, e.g., to vacuum cleaners, blenders, etc. The child ignores voices when loud noises are present.
- Avoidance of odors and tastes that appear normal to others.
- Giving up easily because of frustration.
- Self-regulation problems—unable to rev up or calm down.

Other problems resulting from these difficulties include social problems (difficulty making friends and holding on to them); eating problems (not chewing or swallowing properly); and sleep problems (poor regulation of going to sleep and then awakening). Allergic reactions are also common, as is low self-esteem.

Far too many children with this (and other) disorders are diagnosed as having ADHD and are treated with drugs such as Ritalin. An evaluation by a skilled professional is necessary to differentiate between these disorders, which may coexist. Therapy in the case of SID is best directed at the processing abilities that have gone awry. Occupational therapists often know a great deal about helping such a child learn integration techniques. Most important is to seek techniques that are fun for the child, that he will be motivated to learn, and that he can eventually use for himself. Learning how not to overload or meltdown is one of the most important steps. A therapist is more likely to find and identify a technique for impulse control than is an already besieged parent. The goal is for the child to understand his sensitivities and how to protect himself from overstimulation, how to soothe himself when his senses have been overwhelmed.

SEXUALITY

Awareness of Gender Differences

Boys and girls are aware of their differences by four years. At age three, they began sorting out the differences between their genitals and anuses. Now, they recognize that boys and girls are made differently: "How do you know it's a boy?" "By his hair and his clothes." "Any other way?" With embarrassment: "You can tell by the noodle." A four-year-old is already perceptive and self-conscious.

When children discover their own genitalia, they ask questions about "the other kind." Parents should be prepared for the predictable questions: "Why are we different?" "What's that sticking out of him?" "Where has *her* hot-dog gone?" "What's the difference?"

When a little boy asks, "What happened to her pee-pee?" a parent might answer, "Little girls have vaginas, not penises. Yours is an outside kind, hers is an inside kind. Your penis will always be there and her vagina will always be there. Later, her babies will come out of there." Or, as Fred Rogers explains (on his show *Mr. Rogers' Neighborhood*), "Girls are fancy on the inside, boys are fancy on the outside." Parents can tell by these questions that children's urge to explore themselves and each other is right around the corner.

425

Masturbation

In toddlers, masturbation is a common result of exploration. The genitals are a highly sensitive part of the body and, having been covered by diapers, they have become heightened as a focus for exploration. Girls may insert objects into their vaginas to "find out how deep it is." Both sexes find that self-stimulation is exciting. What should a parent say? Very little. If children believe that these are their own private discoveries, they are more likely to feel that they have completed their explorations. However, children who seem absorbed in masturbation for prolonged periods may have a special need for self-soothing and can be helped to learn other ways to calm themselves; or they may be letting their parents know that they have been sexually overstimulated—or even traumatized.

Children need to learn that this self-stimulation is best done in private; parents can teach this without conveying a sense of disapproval. If children are exposing themselves, it's time for parents to share the difference between private and public exploration. They can set limits on where masturbation is done rather than on the act itself. "People do that because it feels nice. But it's a private thing to do, so wait until you are in your room."

Gender-Specific Play

By the time a child is four, play is likely to be gender-specific; she shuns the other sex and focuses on her own gender. Five- and six-year-old girls are likely to say that boys are loud and babyish. Boys this age are liable to brag: "We never play with girls. They're silly." Parents wonder where children learned such things. Girls and boys are less likely to associate with each other now, unless they are playing games such as "girls are poison/boys are poison." Their curiosity about each other, though, persists.

Mutual Exploration

"Playing doctor," as we saw in Part I, is an exciting way to investigate differences. Every four-year-old remembers being examined by the doctor. Many four-year-olds act this out with a friend of the same age: "Lie down and I'll test you!" After a few harmless explorations of each other, they are usually satisfied. When they examine each others' bodies, children are able to see and find out about differences. They may play doctor with other children of the same or of the opposite sex. Playing doctor tells parents that the child is ready for an explanation about gender differences. However, a parent needs to listen and respond only as far as the child wants to go; there will be plenty of time for more discussion. The goal is to set up precedents for open communication.

A child does not think about her body, or about being naked with another child, in the same way that an adult does. This may seem obvious, but it is hard to remember when children are caught playing doctor. It is important not to frighten or shame the child. Playing doctor is normal, healthy behavior. The more attention that it generates from parents, the more heightened it may become; indeed, parents' horrified responses may be counterproductive. Exploratory games are more likely to be self-limited when they receive scant attention from parents. If a parent becomes so upset that she frightens the child, she immediately sets the experience up as more intriguing. The child will feel guilty, but she will search more surreptitiously for opportunities to test the reasons for the overreaction.

When "playing doctor" occurs, parents may find it helpful to talk the matter over with the parents of the other child and agree together on an approach. Then each parent can talk it over with her own child as calmly and matter-of-factly as possible. Parents can also prevent such games from becoming a main focus by arranging activities that don't lend themselves to such play; for example, trips to the park or playing ball in the yard. Games in which a parent participates can replace some of the time children spend in bedrooms or otherwise out of sight of parents. Parents will also want to watch for behavior that goes beyond mutual exploration between peers; for example, playing doctor with an older child may be exploitative.

Parents who punish "playing doctor" are likely to shove these questions and feelings underground. An open discussion takes the exciting guilt out of the experience and satisfies curiosity. The kind of mutual exploration of each other's bodies that children of this age normally engage in does not damage later developmental adjustments. Children will not keep it up as long as adults do not overreact. Parents can have calm, open discussions of what is okay. When the child makes it clear that she is curious, she may have set it up for her parents to find out. The parents' task is to let children know they can tell and ask whatever they need to; at the same time, parents should not say so much that they close their children off.

When you discuss where the limits are in your family, you are giving the child a chance to identify with you and your values. A child can also learn to value and to take personal responsibility for her own body as a goal of these discussions. No one discussion will do it.

Any parent will have concerns about this kind of sex play in a small child. "Will she go too far? Will she repeat it over and over?" When exploration becomes repetitive and preoccupying, and when exploratory behavior takes on a more overtly sexual nature—especially any kind of penetration or oral-genital contact—it is time to worry about exposure to over-stimulating and sexually explicit materials, or even about molestation by an adult or an older child, or a child who has herself been molested. Children who have been molested or are being molested may be more likely to show signs other than telling an adult: these include resistance to or fear of getting undressed, bathing, going to the toilet, changing clothes, and going to bed—along with abrupt changes in behavior. Ask your pediatrician for help: referral to a specialist, if needed, should not be delayed

Gender Roles and Identification

Gender awareness leads a child to study each parent intently and to try on their distinctly male and female behavior. The urge to identify provides children with gestures, feelings, defenses, and self-images that help them sort out their own sexuality. Girls and boys imitate both male and female behavior. Both will want to wear daddy's hat or mother's high-heeled shoes and try on her lipstick. Halloween parties and other dress-up times are opportunities to identify. It is easier to accept such imitation when you understand what is behind it.

During this time, children discover the differences in their feelings for each parent, and these shift over time. They find that they feel especially drawn to or excited by one parent. At the same time, they fear the resentment of the parent they want to leave out, or they suffer guilty feelings about that parent. As we saw in Part I, turning to one parent and away from the other is the way children balance their feelings for each parent. Their sense of closeness to the temporarily favored parent can be uncomfortable for parents. The intense longing the child expresses stirs up a confusion of feelings they may need to untangle.

Parental Nudity

Four-year-olds become more conscious of their parents' bodies. Nudity and bathroom behavior become of great interest. This is a time to pull back a bit. Children learn important attitudes toward nudity and sexuality from their parents. Attitudes are personal or cultural, and they vary considerably in a multicultural society such as ours. A child's cues should guide parents in determining whether their nudity is overwhelming for their child, or is overwhelming at a particular point in their child's development. Parents can also learn to recognize when the absence of information about sexuality, or a furtive, uncomfortable attitude on the part of adults about nudity, is overstimulating a child's curiosity. This will differ as the child grows—at three, a child may be mildly curious about the anatomical differences spotted during occasional glimpses of her naked parents. But at four and five, children may make comparisons with their own bodies and find them frightening or disheartening.

Gender Identity in Single-Parent Families

In single-parent families, the child's need to sort out gender identity is similar to that in other families, although it is sometimes heightened. A boy may still say, "Mummy, I want to marry you. Couldn't we go off together?" This seems to be such a deep-seated need that it makes me wonder what a five-year-old's notion of having Mummy to himself (or Daddy to herself) really is. I certainly can't believe that it is about sexual feelings in the way that adults think about them. For the child, other aspects of the wished-for relationship are more important: having a parent all of one's own, being dominant enough to control him or her, being rid of outsiders such as siblings, grandparents, and people on the phone.

All children want to own their parents, but verbalizing this is difficult. At four and five, a child wants to be "like" each parent. At other times, the child needs to explore what it would be like to have the parent of the other sex all to herself. As the force to separate and become independent of these two important caregivers increases, children turn to other models—siblings, older playmates, teachers, sitters. They imitate the model, absorb his or her characteristics, and play at becoming that admired person. Children in single-parent families work especially hard to find and take in adults beyond the immediate family, and may allot them a larger place to make a balance. Adults exploit this need in a child or shy away from it, or they can follow a child's lead.

Children's Questions About Sex and Reproduction

Children from three to six ask questions in the language available to them: "Why doesn't Daddy have breasts?" "What is my belly button for?" "What's this bag under my penis?" "Why is my penis covered with skin? Neil's isn't." "Will I hurt if I stick my finger in my vagina?" "Can I stand and pee like boys?" "Girls don't look the same. Did theirs fall off?"

Parents need not get into complicated answers. By watching a child's eyes and face, you can tell when you have gone too far. The child's own questions might surprise you. You will keep the lines of communication open if you listen and give simple replies.

The more honest a child feels you are in answering her questions, the more satisfying your conversation will be for her. Each of us, however, has personal and cultural values that determine the way these sensitive issues are handled.

Each question is an opportunity for sharing information at a very intimate level. Each question is a window into what is going on in the child's mind, and a chance for her to become confident that she can trust the future. Dismissing the questions or allowing her to sense your disapproval will heighten the questions she has and close off communication.

Children let parents know when they have more information than they need by looking away or glazing over. A parent can tell when the question has, for the time being, been answered to the child's satisfaction. Your openness and honest replies are likely to be reassuring—unlike television and gossip among peers.

When should children be given a full description of intercourse? As soon as a child asks about how babies are made, her parents can give a simple and honest explanation. A child will ask elsewhere if she feels she can't find out from a parent. Discovering the truth from giggly peers after listening for years to parents' stork stories is bound to upset a child far more than simple, straightforward answers from parents right from the first. If parents can establish honest communication about sexuality now, the child is more likely to rely on them for more critical information about sexuality in later years.

SLEEP

Sleep issues are one of the biggest problems today for young children and their families. More parents than ever are having trouble turning the task of learning to get to sleep over to the child. Since sleep is a separation issue for parents and an autonomy issue for the child, it is important to try to distinguish between the two.

In infancy, the child learns to cycle regularly from deep sleep up to light sleep, and then finds an independent and comfortable way to return to deep sleep; this is not easy and must be a learned process. We all sleep in three to four-hour cycles. Every three to four hours, a child moves from deep sleep into an agitated light sleep. Most children cry out and scrabble around in bed to find a way of comforting themselves before they can get back to sleep. Over the first few months of life, a baby learns how to help herself manage these cycles. By four months, if she has learned this, she is likely to be able to sleep eight hours, coming up to light sleep twice. By six to eight months, if she can sleep ten to twelve hours, she manages these agitated periods three times. This is a big job, and requires learning to become independent at night. Many children rely on a thumb or a blanket or toy—as a "lovey"—when they rouse.

A child learning to sleep alone also depends upon her parents' ability to separate from her at night. If a parent cannot support the child in learning how to get back to sleep on her own, if she either feeds or rocks or cuddles her at each light sleep episode, she becomes part of her child's sleep pattern. Reliance on the parent's intervention is likely to become part of the baby's sleep pattern for the future.

The most common reason for sleep problems today is that parents who are too stressed or who are away all day feel cut off from the child. They feel so separated during the day that they instinctively want to make up for it at night. When the child rouses at three- to four-hour intervals, they often go to the child, pick her up to love and comfort her, and nestle her until she falls back asleep.

Experts on sleep issues feel that early patterns of learning to sleep lead to reliable sleep habits later on. Children of three to five sleep from eleven to fourteen hours a night (and from ten to thirteen hours by six years). If daytime naps are continued at three and four years, the child actually sleeps even longer and more deeply at night. There is some evidence that the more deeply a child sleeps at night, the more available is her attention for learning in the daytime.

Sleep patterns are likely to be tied to a child's temperament. A driven, active child is much more likely to have sleep difficulties than a child who is more easy-going. Naps in the afternoon (which should end before three o'clock) can enhance a child's ability to settle down and to manage state control (level of alertness) over the afternoon and evening.

Going to bed alone is a problem in the three-to-five age group. Bedtime is an opportunity for a child to test parents' intentions—and it will continue into six if parents are ambivalent. After being away all day, parents feel committed to time with their child in the evening—and so they should, because the child needs this closeness. If possible, ask childcare workers and kindergarten teachers to arrange the afternoon rest period to accommodate the evening schedule. A child who can rest in the period from one to three o'-clock will be ready to join parents for supper and then enjoy a period of closeness from seven to eight o'clock. This can be a quiet time of reading together, a song and/or a prayer. After that, parents must stick to a predetermined number (one to two) of glasses of water and returns to the potty. A firm end to these returns is necessary. No mercy thereafter, unless an emergency arises—an illness or a bad day. Be ready to help the child in distress, but see it as an exception. A firm, nonambivalent approach helps the child with her own limits, and discourages her from making demands for the parents' attention at night. No child can stop teasing for "one more time" if parents are still ambivalent.

When a child rouses during the night, should you go to her? Of course. No child deserves to be deserted. No parent can tolerate such a drastic measure. I have never felt that "crying it out" helped a child learn to get to sleep or a parent to learn to separate. But a definite separation becomes necessary at these ages. Both parents need to be firmly committed to a time of separating. The following list outlines the necessary steps:

1. Parents need to agree with each other that separation at night is critical.
2. Parents need to agree with each other that their child can learn how to go to sleep. Offer her necessary supports (a teddy, a blanket, her thumb, quiet lullabies).
3. Decide upon a limited number of times to go to her after you've read to her, cuddled her, and put her to bed.
4. Stick to them, reminding her, "You can manage now."
5. When she rouses during the night, go to her, comfort her, but do not take her out of bed.

6. Don't react or interact unless the action is soothing. A verbal battle does not soothe. Be quietly firm, but determined.
7. If she climbs out of bed, allow her to sleep on a mattress on the floor. But the door of her room is the limit.
8. No wandering around the house—it's not safe.
9. As an extraordinary measure, and only if it's necessary, let the child understand that you may have to equip her door with a chain so that she can call out but not come out.
10. Often, the "other" parent can settle it more easily at these awakenings. Take turns going to the child. It symbolizes your joint resolution to be separate.
11. Set up her room so you can sit by her bed without interacting.
12. Continue to croon quietly: "You can do it! You can do it!"
13. Turn your chair away so that you can't interact with her.
14. Gradually move your chair farther away, to the doorway, and then out of her room.
15. Encourage a "lovey" or "soother" such as a doll, stuffed animal, or special blanket during the day; give it to her at night for rousing and sleeping.
16. Eliminating naps eventually becomes necessary—but they should always be avoided after three in the afternoon.
17. If you waken a child as you go to bed, before she wakes you, you break into her regular cycle; she may learn to sleep through more easily after such an awakening, but you may have to comfort her back down.

Co-sleeping

Many parents today (from 30 to 40 percent in this country, according to some surveys) sleep with their children in a family bed. When a small baby awakens every three to four hours, it is then easier to respond to her and to feed her. It may be less difficult emotionally to have her nearby than to separate from her. Certain SIDS (sudden infant death syndrome) researchers claim that SIDS is less likely with co-sleeping. Our culture is one of the few that doesn't sanction co-sleeping. In Asia and Africa, and in many cultures worldwide, co-sleeping is accepted. But the eventual separation is never made easily. Many cultures terminate co-sleeping abruptly. The child mourns and is often depressed for a period until she learns to sleep alone.

In our culture, most babies and children are expected to sleep alone and in their own bedrooms. The taboo in this country against co-sleeping arose from our emphasis on the child's independence. Some believe that a child who co-sleeps will have more difficulty learning to become independent in the daytime. In addition, some people believe that "a child who sleeps between parents interferes with their marriage" and that "sexual abuse is more likely if the child is co-sleeping."

Parents who feel the child needs them at her predictable periods of rousing because they are torn away in the daytime find it hard to "push the baby away" to learn independent sleeping patterns. When parents contemplate or conceive a second child, they often begin to rethink co-sleeping with their first. However, if they are undertaken shortly before or after a second birth, changes in sleeping arrangements, from crib or parental bed to "big-girl" bed, are bound to fail, or to leave a child feeling even more left out.

By three or four, co-sleeping often becomes a burden. Parents want to be together without the child. They often become aware that the child has maintained immature waking patterns every three to four hours and they are all subject to interrupted sleep. Parents are tired. They may begin to feel that a child who is ready for kindergarten should be ready to conform to the sleep patterns of the culture. But now it will be harder for the child to learn to sleep on her own, for she has been allowed to depend upon her parents at night.

Before they attempt to separate from the child at night, parents must be ready to deal with their own issues. Then, after discussing it with the child, set up a cot next to the family bed. Encourage the child to use the cot for napping. Encourage her to use her lovey. First, she can learn to sleep alone next to the parents; then, a room and "big" bed of her own becomes the next step. When she calls, be ready to go and comfort her. Pointing out times during the day when she demonstrates her independence can help her work toward independent sleeping. She will be even more proud and relieved than you.

Naps

Naps provide a wonderful break for a parent. An active child can certainly use a break, but parents may need it even more. Naps should be planned from one to three in the afternoon. Most children do not need to sleep at nap time after the age of three or four, but a time to read or to get away from peer stimulation can be therapeutic. Introduce a quiet time for shared reading and cuddling. Then allow the child to settle on her own, but encourage a non-exciting activity—not television or media games because they do not provide a physiological break. Soft music, reading a book, playing with dolls, or quiet games may all help a child to settle down and refuel. Naps won't usually last after the age of four, but the routine of having a quiet time in the afternoon may be a helpful one to keep.

Nighttime Fears

As we suggested in Part I, fears and nightmares are common in four-, five-, and six-year-old. Boys worry about "bad guys," lions, tigers, and monsters. Girls worry about witches and bad people. These night problems occur at the same time as a fear of dogs, loud noises, sirens, ambulances. These herald the child's more openly aggressive feelings, which she sees—in exaggerated form—beyond herself. After they have dealt with fears of separation in the third year, children want to test their own limits more openly. They want to act out aggressive and rebellious play. Such feelings are important to a child's personality and sense of security. They need to know they can feel angry and not lose control. Firm discipline and consistent limits are reassuring to a child at this time: "You may not wander around the house at night. I may well have to fix your door. I can come to you, but you cannot come out alone."

What helps a child learn to cope with fears and nightmares?

1. Comfort the child and take the fears seriously, but don't add your own anxiety to hers.
2. Look under the bed, in the closet. Let her understand that this is for her comfort, not because you recognize danger.

3. Firm limits on bedtime are reassuring.

4. Once again, a comforting lovey helps.

5. Help a child learn ways of comforting herself when she wakes in fear. She can learn to "talk herself down" by repeating to herself all the ways she knows that her fear is unjustified; or, she can distract herself by singing songs, remembering songs, making up stories, or thinking pleasant thoughts. In modified form, adapted to other situations, she will use these skills for the rest of her life.

6. Help the child learn "safe" aggression during the day. Modeling your own ways of handling your aggression becomes even more important. Talk about them with the child when they occur.

7. Read fairy tales together; these encourage young children to face their own fears and angry feelings. Also read such books as *There's a Monster in My Closet* (Mercer Mayer), *Where the Wild Things Are* (Maurice Sendak), and *Much Bigger Than Martin* (Steven Kellogg), among many others. Books allow a child to face and eventually master these feelings—she can turn the pages at her own pace, study a picture as long as she likes, go backwards, or close the book tight. Television and movies have a pace of their own—they present scary situations too vividly and fail to respect the child's need to control how quickly and how much she is able to confront.

Among the possible causes for sleep disturbances or overwhelming fears that your child's pediatrician may need to help you sort through are the following:

1. "Night terrors" need to be ruled out. These occur in deep sleep, when a child suddenly sits bolt upright and shrieks in terror. Characteristically, because she still is asleep, the child is unreachable for several minutes as a parent attempts to soothe her (see *Touchpoints*).

2. If a child seems too overwhelmed by her fears, be sure she hasn't been traumatized or molested. If fears abruptly seem to take on a life of their own, dominating her life and interfering with a broad range of usual activities, a mental health professional's help will be needed to interpret these worrisome behavioral changes. Of particular concern is a child who sud-

denly becomes fearful about undressing to change clothes, for bath time, for using the toilet, and for bedtime.

3. Repeated sleepwalking, which is rare, can be disruptive. Confinement to a safe sleeping environment by fixing the child's door with a chain may be necessary if she is a wanderer or a sleepwalker. Sleepwalking is worth reporting to your pediatrician, who will refer you to a sleep specialist if necessary.

SPECIAL NEEDS

For parents of children with special needs, specified times for each developmental step are daunting. The timing and outcome of some developmental steps may be affected by the disability. Any "developmental calendar" can make it harder for parents to encourage a disabled child to take the steps he is able to take on his own time, and to help him discover the strengths within himself that he needs.

Understanding the cost of a touchpoint (regression and disorganization) to a child can be especially important to parents of a child with special needs. Such an understanding may be important to the child, too. Most four-year-olds know some of the steps a child of their age is expected to make. A child's disability may interfere with his development, but not necessarily with his awareness of an eagerly anticipated or "unattained" touchpoint. He may try to fight harder, and he may regress further.

When parents must give up their dream of the "perfect child," they are bound to grieve. "Why us? Why did it happen? What did we do? Will we ever be able to nurture this child as he deserves? Am I really sure I want to?" As they grieve, adults need to muster defenses. In the hospital, the three defenses that we see after the birth of a child with a problem are:

1. Denial—denying that it has happened, denying that it matters.
   The necessity of such a defense to handle grief makes it critical

that caregivers understand and accept the parents' reaction of denial. Because it can seriously interfere with parents' ability to meet the child's needs, denial must be worked through so that this will not happen. Parents cannot do this by "confronting" the denial; they can face denied reality only when they can tolerate the intolerable feelings that go with it. Rallying support from family and friends and teaming up with trusted healthcare professionals can help. Sometimes denial takes the form of a search from doctor to doctor for a tolerable diagnosis. Occasionally, a second opinion is needed.

2. Projection—projecting onto others the responsibility for the child's condition and inability to "catch up." The guilt that parents experience can be intolerable. Blaming others and/or taking all the blame for the problem are two ends of the same spectrum.

3. Detachment—detaching from the child and the implications of his condition, not because the parent doesn't care but because it hurts so much to care so passionately. Parents who abuse or neglect their special needs children may be driven by this misdirected passion.

These defenses are necessary. Unless they interfere with the child's progress and recovery, they are healthy. Respecting them and bringing them to conscious sharing may be the best role of a provider. I have found that a parent in denial is constantly asking, "When will he catch up? Where should he be in his development?" The energy spent in comparing the child to a "normal" child could be used so much more productively in understanding and valuing the child for where he is. A caregiver or medical provider can model such an approach.

Parents of a child with a disability are likely to wait for the next shoe to drop. The parent who is preparing for more bad news may want to consider the possibility that an impairment in one area may drain the child's energy from others as he adapts, or when greater demands are made on the area of impairment. Intact abilities (e.g., motor, cognitive, emotional) can be valued as resources for the child's overall development even though they may be less available when the child tries to meet a developmental challenge intensified by the disability. Increasing the child's awareness of his own effort to push himself along boosts his self-esteem.

We have learned so much about children with special needs and their ability to recover in certain areas when they participate in early-intervention programs. Most programs are aimed at infancy because this is when redundant pathways in the brain have a chance to take over for those that have been damaged. Early intervention alerts parents to techniques that further the child's development. Awareness of the immature nervous system's plasticity, as well as of the importance of respecting the child's hypersensitivity to certain kinds of stimulation, makes the work of therapists and parents much more effective. Sensory integration techniques help a child gradually learn to master incoming stimuli that might otherwise overwhelm him. These techniques have enlarged our capacity to help a child's adaptation.

Most early-intervention centers are funded to work with and follow the progress of children only up to three; after that, children are—more often now than ever—being mainstreamed. When a child must be transferred to a new center, he can feel deserted. Because Head Start or school programs may not offer the intense support that had been available earlier, parents need to become their own experts and advocates. But it can be overwhelming to take this task on alone; instead, seek out the most supportive person in the new school setting and assess that person's advice and advocacy.

Nowadays, with managed care and the pressure on physicians and nurses in HMOs, it is increasingly difficult for parents to find a professional who will advocate for the complex care and follow-up that most special needs children require. I urge parents to ask around in the community, in the parents' groups, and in early-intervention settings, for an advocate who can help sort out options for treatment and school programs.

All parents wonder, "Why? Is it my fault?" So do grandparents; indeed, they feel that the difficulties are theirs as well. Their inability to protect and help the grandchild and their own child can make them want to intervene. Including them in the diagnosis and therapy can offer them a realistic way of being of value.

Healthy Siblings

Siblings of special needs children deserve our attention because they are bound to be caught between positive and negative feelings. A sibling may feel proud of helping out and will enjoy the praise that goes with it. But he is also likely to resent the extra efforts he has to make as well as all the attention the special needs sibling receives. "Why is he so different? Why does he have to embarrass me in front of my friends? I don't want to bring anyone home to see how gross he is." Such reactions generate guilt. If he is allowed to express negative feelings, a sibling may become more nurturing and supportive. Many become protective and nurturing, especially when parents share their understanding of the child's special needs. An impaired child learns so much from a sibling. An older sibling can model systems of behavior; a younger sibling of an autistic or disorganized, delayed child often becomes a model, too.

As in so many other stressful situations, a young sibling is likely to think, "Did my bad thoughts do it to him? I didn't want a brother like him." Discussion with parents to open up these questions can be priceless. Parents worry about the price a sibling must pay for all the attention the disabled child needs. They fear that the siblings will have to face society's hidden prejudices. It may be true. But children whose families face such an issue together are often stronger for it.

I urge parents to give siblings as much information as they can handle for their ages. Let the children join in caregiving and therapeutic maneuvers with the special needs child. Point out early how dependent the special child is on learning from his sibling. But most important of all, listen. Let the sibling share his feelings—both positive and negative. Don't be afraid to hear about the ambivalence and the searching; answer the questions the sibling is trying to understand. Also, allow the sibling his own independent life. A sibling can be a caregiver when he shows he wants to help, but he shouldn't be pressured into it. Expect feelings of guilt, and be wary of pat or premature reassurance. The sibling of a disabled child may feel that he needs to take care of you; he may also be afraid of making his own needs known for fear of over-burdening you. To be ready to attend to siblings' needs, parents have to face their own grief and feelings so that they can be ready to listen. By the time he is three or four, a child needs his parent to attend to the reactions and needs the disabled sibling arouses in him.

We have found that peer groups for siblings can be a valuable support. Try to locate one by asking at the early-intervention center or the nearest pediatric center. In groups, peers can share their questions, their feelings, and their ambivalence with each other. They can find friends who are going through the same turmoil. It helps them all when they can work it out with each other.

Inclusion

In recent years, we have expanded the range of children who can be included in "regular" classrooms and benefit from the opportunities for learning these afford; however, parents should consider the pros and cons of mainstreaming for a special needs child. Whether to seek it for your child depends on many variables, including

1. the condition of the child and his responsiveness to social and intellectual stimulation;
2. the temperament and threshold for stimulation and over-stimulation (too much stimulation can drive a hypersensitive child into himself—although this can be a problem in any setting);
3. the availability of the teacher to absorb a special child into the class while attending to the other students' needs;
4. class size; and
5. interference with more directed intervention for the child.

These considerations may balance out differently for the same child over time.

Parents' decisions will also be influenced by the support their school system provides for mainstreaming. Special equipment and accommodations may be necessary. Teachers' aides can be added to the mainstream classroom to assist the special needs child as well as the other students. Consultation with healthcare professionals can help teaching staff understand the child's needs and effective therapeutic strategies. Specialists such as speech pathologists or occupational therapists can provide targeted help for the special needs child in the "regular" classroom or during "pull-out" hours.

Inclusion presents the opportunity for a child to model on and learn from other children. In particular, he may learn how to handle himself in a group and how to socialize with a variety of peers. He may learn how to handle his disability and even become motivated to overcome it.

But he may also be overwhelmed. An inevitable risk in a class of children the same age is that he may be labeled "special" or "slow," although such labeling can't be always be avoided in a separate special class, either. Will it affect his self-esteem? Will the contrast make it more difficult for his grieving parents? Will it interfere with ongoing therapy? As with any touchpoint in development, he is likely to regress when he enters a new school program. He will need time to adjust and to profit from the experience.

Nondisabled children in the mainstreaming class can profit enormously—if their teachers are not overburdened. Classmates can learn how to nurture the special needs child; they can learn from the differences in his development. His determination, courage, and capacity to adapt can serve as a positive model. Classmates can learn to participate in a few carefully selected therapeutic maneuvers. I have seen examples of altruism in such a class—and the way that experiences with special needs children can be a rare opportunity for other children.

Estate Planning

Every parent of a special needs child wonders, "Will he survive me? If he does, who will take care of him?" Parents should plan for this in advance. The type of planning depends on the child's disabilities and a family's means. Financial and practical planning for placement can put parents' minds at ease. Professional advice about a disabled child's eligibility for social security income may also be needed. Such matters are difficult for parents to face during their special needs child's preschool years, but the day will come when they will be glad they did. (See also "Resources.")

SPEECH DELAYS

The connection between speech and behavior begins to consolidate in the third year. Watch a child use her body to express an idea—or a question: "Why? Why?" Her words and her explorations show that she is entering a new phase of wondering and wanting to understand—even things beyond her comprehension.

By age three, a child who can't use speech is already at a disadvantage. Roberta Golinkoff, a linguist at the University of Delaware, points out that language development occurs during a critical period; a child who can't use speech to communicate by the time she is three years old is losing potential richness in linguistic self-expression and is missing important opportunities to socialize, to reach out for and receive all sorts of responses from peers and the adults around them. Children between two and four not only learn to talk but also learn the ability to communicate ideas and feelings. Recognizing a child's inability to speak before the age of three can be critical to her future social development. At this age, a child who can't speak is also missing out on language as a way to make her needs known, and to discover that she can have an effect on the world around her.

The first step a parent might take to determine whether professional assessment should be sought is to determine whether a child is receptive to language. Give her three directions: "Go into the bedroom. Find my slippers and bring them to me." If she can understand and carry out these directions and others like them, her receptive language is intact. If she must watch your face to understand you, she may have a hearing deficit for which she is compensating by lip-reading. Some children may have intact hearing and receptive language, but suffer impaired auditory memory; if this is the case, they may not remember the information even when they have understood it. (Other children, even without speech, language, or hearing impairments, may have trouble focusing, staying on task, avoiding distractions, or planning a sequence of actions, all of which can also interfere with following through on a short list of instructions.)

Children who come from bilingual homes may be delayed in their expressive speech because they have to learn how to sort out the differing phonemes from each language; putting them together and assigning them to each person appropriately may delay speech until the third year. When a child does speak two languages, however, it's worth the wait; indeed, a child who learns two languages between three and seven is likely to be better equipped for future language learning. Not only will she speak both languages but she will assign the appropriate language to the appropriate person or situation. A major feat!

Dr. Golinkoff suggests another way to evaluate a child's language: "Does my child tell coherent narratives? Can she make up a story?" Many children enjoy practicing stories and conversations at bedtime, a relaxed time. After reading to her, ask her to respond with her own story. Another useful question is: "Does my child know how to use social speech?" Some children may speak fluently and understand language that refers to material things, but have trouble understanding or using language that serves a social purpose, language used in making friends, in understanding the world of feelings. Children with limitations in these areas need an evaluation by a speech and language pathologist.

A three-year-old should be talking in short sentences; if she is not, she should be evaluated. Seek an evaluation with a speech therapist who understands small children. A hearing test would be the first step. Even a minimal hearing loss, which can result from repeated ear infections, can delay and confuse a child who is trying to learn to talk. The incidence of earaches and chronic ear infections has risen. Children in early daycare contribute to a pool of infections to which each baby must become immune; most babies in infant day care, or toddlers in childcare, must have approximately four bouts of ear infection before immunity is established. With the fluid that collects in the inner ears, there can be mild or major interruptions of hearing. A toddler who is learning speech by imitation may easily hear the sound "ood" instead of "good." Or "ood-eye" instead of "good-bye." A complete hearing test is needed to rule out such an interference in a three-year-old delayed speaker.

In addition, other signs demand professional attention when there are delays:

- Gaze aversion after a question, as if the child is trying to hide her inability to respond; she won't enter into reciprocal exchanges. She may be hypersensitive to auditory signals and easily overwhelmed, or she may be unable to handle a complex situation.
- Children who are in constant motion and on the move, unable to calm down long enough to communicate. A short attention span interferes with the child's ability to receive language from her environment.
- Blank, inattentive eyes and self-focused, repetitive behavior that increases in response to a bid for communication from an adult.
- No signs of gestural speech. When a child leads you to where she wants to go, or points to something that interests her, she probably understands but can't find the appropriate language. A speech therapist who understands small children can sort out the reason for delay.
- Loss of previously acquired language skills.
- Frustration with her inability to speak, and aggressive behavior as an outlet and alternative form of communication.

SWEARING AND DIRTY WORDS

Children first hear "dirty words" at three and four; their understanding of language at these ages is sophisticated enough for them take note of the special intonations and contexts associated with such words. But if they are to understand what is different about dirty words, they need to experiment, to try them out. No one takes them too seriously: "Mommy, you're a poo-poo face." "Daddy is a fat bum-bum." At most, each parent reacts with a cringe, then a laugh. "Where did you hear that?" "From you." Parents are usually not satisfied with that, even when it's true. "Whom did he play with yesterday? Did he learn it from him, or did he hear it on that television show?"

Parents do need to be concerned because they must teach their children about language, its uses, and its power. Their job is to model behavior and create an environment in which children can learn how their words and actions affect others. Parents' work is harder than ever as offensive sexual talk (not all talk about sex need be) becomes ubiquitous on television, radio, and the Internet. But overreactions just make the swearing and dirty words more intriguing to children and give them a power they will want to try out.

Why do parents overreact? A child who swears challenges a parent's desire for him to fit in and please others. Dirty words may seem like another sign of growing up and that parents are losing their control; they may appear to signify loss of innocence—so hard for parents to face. Already parents have fears about how a child will fare in a dangerous world. It may frighten them to see their child so vulnerable to imitating peers. Everyone in the family knows it will get worse. Kids from down the street will become models, and a young child is bound to imitate their dirty words and bring them home to try out on parents (see the end of Chapter 4). Sexual curiosity and four-letter words are right around the corner. A child's way to discover the limits of a taboo is by testing his parents over and over after an initial overreaction. Innocence has now turned into outright provocative behavior. A parent worries, "Will he use it in public? What does it mean? Could he have been molested?" All these fears may run through parents' minds as they respond: "We don't say words like that! We don't swear in this family!" But often it's not that simple. Parents who sometimes say swearwords themselves may now wish they hadn't. How confusing for a child to understand that what comes out of his mouth is treated differently!

Instead of being offended when a child's swears, a parent might try to discover the reason for it. When you can damp down your response, the offensive words will begin to lose their interest and you will hear them less often. If your child uses them too freely in public, use such an incident as a teaching opportunity: "When you say these words, people are upset. Those are words we don't say unless we want to bother other people. Is that what you mean to do—or does it just slip out?" In saying this, you are attempting to place your negative view of swearing and dirty words in context—that of sensitivity to other's feelings.

In the relative hierarchy of offensive behavior, swearing is more innocuous than most, especially if ignored, and thereby eventually extinguished. Children aren't likely to become chronically foul-mouthed in an environment that doesn't value swearing and dirty words.

TELEVISION

We are all frightened by the aggression and violence we live with today—and so are small children. How are they affected by the violence they can see on television many times each day? Even without violence, television is a compelling and demanding medium, prominent in many homes and daily lives. When I watch my grandchildren in front of the television, they are literally entranced: their color drains, their hearts race, their breathing becomes deep and regular, but not in response to anything in the room. If you speak or call out to a child in this state, she doesn't answer. She is "hooked": the television is more powerful than you are. When the show is over, she demonstrates the physical cost to her with jumpy and irritable behavior, and perhaps she even cries. A parent finds it difficult to reach her through directions or by cuddling her. The child has to shut out the overstimulating messages, but at what cost? The cost will vary with the child's temperament. With exuberant play, an active child may be able to discharge the overwhelming feelings induced by a violent television show. A quiet child may not appear overstimulated; inside, though, such a child may be upset, her stomach churning at the sights she has seen. This child may grow quieter and more withdrawn. Her feelings may have no outlet. The cost to her of violent television may be harder to see.

Television is a major competitor for our children's hearts and minds. At this age, a child may confuse aggression on the screen with what it might do to her. A three-year-old has not developed defenses or controls for the fears induced in her by images that come not from her world, but from an adult's imagination. Parents need to limit a child's television watching, need to monitor what she is watching, and need to know what is likely to happen on that show. They should be with the child as much as possible when she watches television. A parent who does watch with her child will quickly overcome the feeling that she might be "depriving" the child by limiting television. If a child feels overwhelmed, listening to her fears and her reactions can help her deal with the raw feelings that are stirred up—even at three. Being out of control is always scary.

No matter how resistant to guns and aggressive behavior parents may be, guns and aggression are a main preoccupation of children around the age of five. Television and computer games reinforce this aggression, and their vivid sounds and images leave no room for the imagination of children's fantasy play. Children today who watch television see so many shootings and murders that they are likely to think of these as normal adult behavior. Study after study has shown that aggression and warlike behavior in young children is significantly more likely after a television show that portrays aggression or warfare. Limiting television is therefore important, although it will not stop aggressive behavior. At this age, playing with guns is not about preparation for future warfare; it is about learning to deal with feelings. The job for parents today is to teach children how to be aggressive safely and when to stop the behavior. Most television shows do not contain such messages. Watching television together can create opportunities to discuss aggressive feelings.

Television, or an Internet version of it, is here to stay. It is unrealistic to think that a child can be raised without any exposure to it whatsoever, but parents can certainly keep it to a minimum. Besides, some television programming (although not enough) can open new worlds for children. (Unfortunately, commercials on any show can be counterproductive to a child's needs.) When they are a little older, children can learn more actively by making their own videos; such a creative activity will help them see through television's powerful technical illusions and give them a better grasp of how these can affect anyone's thoughts and feelings.

Parents must foster media literacy from the very beginning. Help your child develop a critical attitude towards what she watches on television. Even a very young child can be encouraged to wonder if what she is seeing is "real," to wonder what happens to all the people who are getting hurt, and so on. Your child needs you to help her dismantle commercials from the very first: "How do you know that that cereal is really better than all the others? Why do you think the people who made up that commercial might want you to think that?"

Parents need to be aware of the risks of letting their children watch television excessively. Among the recommendations from the Academy of Pediatrics are the following guidelines:

- Children under two should not watch television.
- Television should be limited to no more then one hour on weekdays, two on weekends. (A parent need not allow a child to watch even this much, and certainly the choice of programs during this time is critical.)
- Children should never have television sets in their bedrooms.
- Parents should realize that children who spend a lot of time in front of the television or media games tend to gain weight; obesity in childhood is a major health issue. (Lack of physical activity associated with television and repetitive movements required by computer games are likely to cause other health problems as well.)

Watching television with your children gives you a chance to share their experience and listen to their questions and concerns. Some parents are resistant to such advice. They may have relied on television as a babysitter from early on, and now may feel that they have no right to take it away. In a busy household, they may not have the energy to hold firm and insist on determining the quality and quantity of television consumption. They may even feel that it is hopeless to try to buck this national addiction. They may worry that their child will feel out of place and be ostracized if she doesn't share this common culture. This does not have to be the case. A child who models herself on parents with interests and skills other than television and who has had the time available to become passionate about other activities because she has not lost her afternoons and evenings to television and video games will certainly be an exciting and competent playmate for her peers.

Recognize your child's need for routines, structure, and activities. Fill a drawer with special activities for your child—they needn't be expensive, but keep each one a surprise until needed. Keep a list of everything else your child can do—alone, with a friend, or with you: indoors, outdoors, season by season. Look the list over with your child. Your enthusiasm about other activities will be contagious. Help her plan her day before boredom sets in and the television appears to be the only solution. Spontaneity, of course, can be even better; but here, too, television and video games get in the way. Children are resourceful, though, and may not need all this help if you can keep the television and video games out of their reach.

The right kind of television and media can be positive in shaping a child's behavior. Four- to six-year-olds are ready and eager to identify with adults. We can surely influence their choices of additional role models if we help them become selective about the television shows or videos they watch.

TOILET LEARNING PROBLEMS REVISITED

Toilet problems are on the rise. More child abuse occurs from toilet failures than from any other area of development. Approaches to toilet training have changed over the years. After a child-oriented approach to training was introduced in the 1960s, problems such as constipation, smearing feces, daytime wetting, and even nocturnal enuresis (nighttime wetting) diminished. Over the past thirty-five years, we have been able to give children control of their own toilet training. In a study I conducted of a child-oriented approach, even bed-wetting was reduced from 8 percent to 1 percent of six-year-olds. Other problems were also significantly affected. Many children were not ready to comply until the third or fourth year, but they did well when allowed to be "late bloomers."

Since the early 1990s, we have seen a gradual but definite increase in late bloomers and in the problems associated with toilet training. Increasing tension in the environments around these children and a hurried approach to toilet training seem to be the culprits. Nursery schools or childcare centers that demand three-year-olds be trained before accepting them have added to the pressure. Working parents who need child care are anxious to train a toddler. This leads to resistance and problems are likely to result. If the nursery school you apply to demands a trained three-year-old, find one that doesn't. However, parents who find schools willing to take

455

children in diapers usually share training efforts with the school's caregivers—and so another dimension of challenge is added to the busy parent's burden.

Many children have not completely mastered this big task by three. Conforming to the demands of society is a daunting but necessary process for a toddler; it demands a great deal of compliance and voluntary imitation of people around him. Potty learning should be built upon communication between parents and child. Each step that parents introduce as they show the child what society expects should be left to the child. The steps are easy and the child will decide when he is ready.

The steps of a child-oriented approach to toilet training are outlined in the first volume of *Touchpoints;* they are set up to capture the child's interest and abilities. As he accomplishes each step, parents can commend him and respect what he has contributed to his toilet training. If they push him or take his own contribution away from him, they have missed an opportunity for encouraging his sense of mastery. His success will be its own reward. Rewards from parents interfere with the child's appreciation of his accomplishment for its own sake.

An infant starts out being "covered up" in the diaper. He has to be freed from the diaper to become aware of his urine and bowel movements. In the second year, he becomes aware of sphincter sensations. As he begins to control them, he can even begin to think about them. After the introduction of toilet-training techniques, a two- or three-year-old ties his heightened feelings about sphincter control to the events associated with urination and defecation. A child associates his productions with his own and everyone else's interest. When he gains control over his productions, a toddler feels pride and senses mastery. Such awareness becomes connected with his increasing interest in his body and what he can do with it. A world of mastery opens up for him when he is allowed to feel that he has achieved these steps for himself. A three-year-old may be highly sensitive to interference or comment from his parents. They should be quietly observant. If they are not, the child will experience their comments as interference in what is still a fragile mastery. Parents need to pull back and to recognize the enormous will it has taken for the child to gain this control. He needs to be encouraged to value his own achievement because his self-esteem is at stake.

Feeding and toilet learning are two areas that rely on the child's motivation. Until he is ready to assume the responsibility for each step, it is not "his." The child can comply in an effort to please everyone around him, but that is not the goal. Each step must be his own and he must be able to feel proud of it. A parent needs to share each step with him, but not with pressure—spoken or unspoken. When parents feel pressure, either as a result of their own past experi-

ences or from the outside (nursery school requirements, for example), they are almost bound to pressure the child to perform.

Constipation and Soiling

Withholding bowel movements can be a result of too much pressure; chronic constipation will result. Passing a hard bowel movement can cause a painful crack in the anal sphincter. The child begins to fear passing stools because each stool causes pain. The sphincter reacts to hold back the bowel movement. Out of the fear of pain, the child voluntarily holds back; he may retain stools for a week, or sometimes even longer. Liquid stool leaking around the retained hard one causes soiling. To counteract this vicious cycle, a parent must be sure that the bowel movement is softened with a bowel softener designed for children. (The child's pediatrician should be consulted at this point to rule out other causes of constipation.) Reassure the child about pain, and allow him to wear diapers or pull-ups. Meanwhile, the child must know that this is his decision. No mention or attention to it is possible without adding pressure. Parents must withdraw, leaving decisions to the child.

Bed-wetting

Enuresis, or bed-wetting, is another likely result of pressure on a child to perform, although it may have other causes that require a pediatrician's attention. Bed-wetting can last until the teens, whether it is due to pressure, to so-called familial enuresis, or a combination of the two. Bed-wetting should not be treated as a problem until the child is six or seven—unless the child has been dry at night for a prolonged period but suddenly begins repeated bed-wetting all over again. A sudden recurrence may be associated with a touchpoint, but it can also be a sign of infection, undiagnosed illness, or even sexual abuse; in such cases, other symptoms often accompany the bed-wetting.

Young children's sleep is deep and immature. Their bladders are immature and, so far, they've had little practice at controlling their urinary flow in the daytime. At three, nightmares and nighttime fears occur frequently. I would never recommend putting pressure on a child to remain alert, to wake up, or to get up and go to urinate in another room. If he is ready and eager to accomplish this step, then help him. The parent can reassure him: "It will happen when you are ready." The drive to imitate adults and older children is powerful enough at this age. Don't add more pressure.

The child's own readiness is worth waiting for. If not already motivated, he will be when he cannot spend an overnight in a friend's house, or when other children find out and begin to tease him. His self-image is at stake.

With the child's permission, the following steps may help:

1. Ask him to hold onto urine for a slightly longer time in the daytime.
2. Offer to awaken him before you go to bed. Let him go to the pot and perform on his own. Taking him is not the same, and it does not encourage self-motivation in the child.
3. An alarm clock can be used to awaken him when he needs it to remind him.
4. A special potty, painted with luminous paint, can be placed next to his bed. The child can be awakened and asked to use it; he will find it easier to get to when he is half asleep than to the toilet down the hall. Call it his "night pot."

By six or seven years, bed-wetting inevitably becomes a problem for the child. A parent will need to help, not punish. By this time, the child needs a pediatric and perhaps a psychological evaluation. Such evaluations must respect the child's self-image, for protection of the child's feelings about himself will be a major goal of any treatment.

TOYS

In our culture, toys play a major part in many children's lives. In the first few months, a child is given a "lovey" to hold on to and to use for major transitions such as going to sleep, or when she's hurt or lonely. The lovey—often a blanket, a piece of soft material or a beloved teddy bear—becomes an extension of herself and her caregiver. With it, she feels secure and ready to face her world of transitions. Without it, she must rely on adults who can't always be there, no matter how reliable they are.

From the time a child looks at or reaches for objects, some parents equip the crib with the latest toys for infants. "Learning" toys soon supplement cuddly ones. Musical, speaking, and reading toys become representative of parents' concern to provide their toddlers with enough "brain stimulation" to excel in our competitive preschools and schools. In this way, even toys can cause pressure rather than stimulate exploration and play. Media toys—such as video and computer games—are becoming part of many three- and four-year-old's life. Parents who are away all day or are leading stressful lives may feel that they need to satisfy the demands of a preschooler with constructive and educational replacements of themselves. Toys can become surrogates by filling the isolation in which many of us live. Toys don't have to be used in this way.

Toys are a child's world. They extend a child's dreams. A parent can attend seriously to a child's choice of toys, and observe closely how she plays with them. If a parent can help choose a toy as a way

to learn about the child and who she is becoming, the process can become a communication. (Toy stores, too stimulating for most children of this age, are rarely set up to encourage such communication.) For a toddler, pots and pans give her an opportunity to mimic her mother's kitchen chores. At three, four, and five, simple dolls and toy soldiers help children live out fantasies. The distorted anatomies of Barbies and pumped-up action figures are intriguing to some children, as is the mysterious adult sexuality they evoke. But toys like these impose adult preoccupations on child's play and do not encourage a child's self-discovery and self-expression. Many children turn to safer toys, such as toy animals and puppets when they play out the aggressive feelings that they need to test. Simpler toys leave room for a child to try out her own dreams and wishes, her own aggressive or sexual fantasies. Toys offer the child a link for play with a peer as well as an opportunity to learn about others. The child can trade them and collect them; toys even provide the child a chance to show her skills to her friends.

In choosing toys, a parent must consider whether they allow the child to interact with them or with a friend or sibling. Does the toy elicit her own fantasies and imagination and allow her to spin them into dreams that sustain the play? Does it challenge her, while leading her to find her own solutions? How much room does the toy leave for her—or does it take over and make her give in to it?

Other considerations include:

Safety. Inspect toys for parts that are small enough to be inhaled or swallowed. A toy should not be breakable or easily taken apart. Some of the plastics with which toys are made contain potentially toxic materials; remember that all children mouth and suck on a favorite toy. Toys' safety is regulated, but not always enforced, so parents still need to be careful.

Durability. Will the toys last the experimentation, the torturing that is a necessary part of their future?

Noise. Can you as a parent stand the repetitious music or crooning speech that accompanies some toys?

Interest. Can the toy hold the child's long-term interest, or will it soon be forgotten?

Age appropriateness. Many toys are labeled with the different uses of the toy at successive ages. If these labels described the cognitive and emotional capacities elicited by the toys, parents could be sure to enjoy and participate in the child's growing involvement with them.

Temperamental appropriateness. One child may need a quiet, solitary toy that challenges her intellectually; another might prefer an activity-based toy.

If toys were geared toward the optimal development of the child, their characteristics might be:

Rewarding, after a moderately frustrating beginning, demanding the child's intellectual investment.

Individuated, so each child feels rewarded for her special contribution.

Memorable from past or for future experiences associated with family or special events, perhaps even transmitted over the generations.

Interactive, requiring two participants and challenging them to pay attention to each other's contribution. Also toys could appeal to important adults as well as to the child.

WORKING AND CARING

In most families, both parents are in the workforce; 63 percent of mothers (of children under eighteen) work outside the home. This isn't likely to change, and we need to find ways to adjust that will consider children's best interests first. Today, we are asking both parents to split themselves in two—for the workplace and for nurturing at home. We are asking children to adjust to the split and to participate in our efforts to "make it" in a working family.

Another revolution in the workplace that will alter once again the relationships of parents to each other and to their children is also underway. The promise of new technologies to bring more leisure time to families has been overshadowed by their capacity to bring the workplace into the home. Beepers, cellular phones, fax machines, e-mail, and the Internet have made it possible for more and more Americans to work at home, and for many others to bring a part of their work with them into times and places meant for family to be together.

For some parents, technological changes in the way we work have meant increased flexibility, winning back time once lost on commuting, and more availability to the family, even if there isn't really more time. For others, though, these changes have brought a new intrusion of work into the home, and further demands of work have eroded family time.

Fax machines and e-mail create new expectations for rapid turn-around, pushing the pace of work to new and frenetic heights. Children feel the stress their parents are under. Some turn away, as if to prevent themselves from causing their parents further stress. They seem to have given up on moments when they might have their parents to themselves. Others lobby hard to keep their parents tuned in to them, even if it means behavior that wrecks the little time they have together.

Beepers and cell phones mean unpredictable interruptions at all times and further infringement on family time; routines—so critical to young children—are thrown off course. More subtle, but more disruptive, is the way these devices keep parents emotionally "on call" to their work, requiring them to divide their attention between their careers and their children even when they're home. Children can tell when we're only partially tuned in to them.

Although the time working fathers spend with their children has increased, so far no accounting has been made for the intrusion of beepers, phone calls, e-mail, and so on. What child doesn't feel a sense of rejection and loss when his father turns away from a game in which they are both involved to answer his cellular phone? There may be no other way to protect parent-child interactions than to declare specific hours every day when parental attention is entirely available: Beepers are turned off, answering machines are left to field phone calls, and computers are left alone.

On the whole, American parents must work many hours more in a week to come close to maintaining the standard of living they had a few decades ago. Parents in increasing numbers are working two full-time jobs and can't possibly have the time and energy they would like to devote to their children. This is a time when parents need to sit down together to evaluate their priorities and their options. They should ask themselves whether their children's early years are a time for such frenetic activity.

Work has not only invaded the home but also stepped past the nine-to-five boundaries into evenings, nights, and weekends. Children have had to adjust to their parents' absence after school, at suppertimes, at bedtimes, and now, sadly, even through the night. In many two-parents families, each parent works a different shift so that both can be available to their children—but the children never see their parents together. This can create strain on the marital relationship, and a lost opportunity for children to model their behavior after their parents' interactions with each other.

Worst of all, perhaps, is that it has become a mark of success in our society to be busy—the more frantic, the more over-extended we are, the better. Have we become so dependent on being busy that we can no longer afford the time to stop and consider what has become of our priorities? If we insist on strong priorities, children and families could benefit from the changes in our communications and computer know-how instead of being at their mercy. The new technologies are redefining the ways we use time and space; they also have the potential to alter the way we communicate with each other, to change the nature of our relationships. We must decide whether these technologies are to be used to strengthen family structures or to wear them down.

In planning solutions for families in which both parents must work, each parent needs to share in these decisions. If their children are old enough, they may be included in the decision-making. Then, when the questions arise, "Did you see Joey's flashy new car? Are we ever going to get rid of our old junk heap?" or "She gets an allowance to buy her own toys. Why can't I have one? You don't ever buy me anything," the parent can point to the family's decisions, trade-offs, and the values behind them. These decisions can be a mainstay for parents determined to hold out for family time as they face workplace pressures and financial burdens. Part-time jobs are worth considering, so that one parent can be at home when the children return from childcare or school. Sharing child-care with each other also benefits the child.

The "take your child to work" campaign symbolizes the value of letting your children understand the meaning of work to you and to the family. When I moved my pediatric office into my home, I did so with serious misgivings. I thought my children would resent my giving shots to their friends, and examining them in our house. Instead, they came down to visit with their friends, to see how they felt after I'd examined them. They delighted in sharing my job with me. Parents who allow the child to experience their passion for their work are already preparing the child for his future.

For both parents who must work outside the home, the following suggestions may help:

- Openly discuss the need to work and the necessary adjustments to the two jobs—at home and in the workplace.
- Share the work at home. Children can help as they grow up.
- Be aware of feelings of grief over being away.
- Learn to compartmentalize office worries and home concerns. Leave work at the job, non-critical home problems at home.
- Stay in contact regularly with each child and his caregiver.
- Prepare each child for separation in the morning and yourself for reunion at night.
- Learn to "cheat" on the workplace. Save up energy during the day for close family times at the end of the day.
- Recognize that all children will be tired and disintegrating when you return. They'll save up their protests for you. Be prepared and save energy for them.
- Tend to children and their needs *first*.
- When you arrive home, gather everyone up in a big rocking chair to rock and catch up together. "How was your day?" "I missed you so."
- As soon as you are close again, *then*, and only then, attend to household chores.

- Invite children into the kitchen with you to help. Even though their helping may take more time, it is important to let them participate. Commend them for helping.
- Plan weekly family meetings to go over the positives and the negatives of the week.
- Lay out the family chores to be done. Allow children some choice, and share these around the family. List the rewards and the penalties for each chore well done or not done.
- Plan regular celebrations for the family that works together!
- Remember that your children are learning how to manage the two jobs for their own future.

More time is the universal need of working parents. "I never can get anywhere on time; when I do get there, my mind hasn't caught up with me. I am always two steps behind. When I walk into my workplace, my mind is on the sobbing child I left with his sitter. When I arrive home at night, I find it so difficult to change rhythms. I can't put the unfinished tasks or the work hanging over me out of my mind. Changing diapers or sitting down to rock isn't hard, but I'm not really home yet—I'm still at work and my child knows it. I'm not entirely with him. I'm still wound up."

Parents who are away aren't just missing the time with their children; they worry about missing each step in the child's development. "How did he learn it? Without me! I'm missing his childhood." There simply is not enough time for the family to be together. No time for just dreaming and thinking. No time for oneself. No time for one's spouse. No time for the children. "No time" is a universal cry of distress. We are raising our children in an atmosphere of pressure.

Children benefit when parents attempt to strike a reasonable balance. Ellen Galinsky, director of Work Family Directions in New York, asked children what they thought about their mothers' working outside the home. Most quickly stood up for their mothers: "Even if she hates her job, we need the money and she knows it." Clearly, these children felt that their mothers were "the most important person for me. She's always there when I'm sick or I need her." Their mothers' working or not was not their issue. They wanted "focus time" with their mothers, time in which they were uppermost in her thoughts. The most satisfied children valued the "hanging out" time they had with their mothers. Rather than so-called quality time spent on planned excursions or planned togetherness, all these children preferred just hanging out with their parents. It became apparent from Galinsky's study that these children wanted to be a part of the family's effort; they wanted to understand their parents' jobs, to be included in the family's efforts to "make it." If the family is working together, children do not feel shortchanged. "School is kids' workplace. My mom and dad have theirs. But we have each other to help us."

Parents Who Travel

More and more parents are now required to travel regularly as part of their jobs. Parents who have had to combine parenthood with life as a road warrior probably already know that, no matter what they say, spouses and children hate it when they're away. When a parent returns home from a business trip, she expects a warm welcome. She may get one. But after dramatic hugs and inquiries about gifts, the family may barely acknowledge the returning parent—as if to show that they can get along without her. The icier the indifference, the more she's been missed. If she respects her family's need to hold her at bay, the distance won't last long. She would do well to put off the mail and phone messages, to make herself available for the moment when they are ready for her. She should follow the children's lead as they gradually warm up. She's the one who went away. Now they need to take control of the pace in coming together again.

Children from three to six may worry, cling, and become apprehensive of subsequent separations, even brief ones. Such behaviors show how deeply involved with parents these children are, and they are healthy signs. Children of this age do need clear explanations as to where a parent is going, for how long, and especially why a parent must go away. "Where" can be located on a map, or illustrated with pictures or photographs; in this way, it becomes less unknown and less frightening. "How long" can be shown on a calendar, on a clock, or by counting nights and days, bedtimes and breakfasts. Minimizing the trip may make a parent feel better in the short run, but will only make it harder for a child to trust the parent in the long run. "Why" a parent must go away is crucial—a clear, simple explanation about work helps a child know that it is not because he has been "bad." Although a parent can state that she would prefer not to travel and would rather stay with her children, there is no need to be negative about work. Children need to identify with parents who take pleasure and pride in what they do.

Parents need as much help as children do to stay "connected" when away and to "connect" again once back home. The following tips are adapted from James Levine's book *Working Fathers* (clearly, working mothers who travel need help, too):

- Prepare yourself and your spouse first. Be sure you both feel the trip is necessary. Acknowledge the other's feelings and prepare for a reunion afterwards.
- Explain the trip in terms children can understand. A three-year-old may think that you're never coming back. A five-year-old may even have your car crashing in his fantasy. Listen to their concerns.
- Prepare a project that you will finish together when you return. Explain your timetable in their terms. Perhaps leave a calendar with stars to paste on each day you're away.
- Use leave-taking rituals and always say good-bye—accompanying the parent to the airport can be an expedition to wish Daddy or Mommy a good trip.
- Share a ritual phone call each day you're away. Find out what the child has been doing and ask him about it.
- Make a VHS video or a cassette tape of you reading good-night stories that can be played each day.
- Mail postcards.

Avoid traveling at symbolically important times—birthdays, religious holidays, school performances. These are powerful opportunities to say—with your availability—that your child, your family matters. A child knows that these are special times, and he will respond to the priorities you set, especially when you have to fight for them.

Make the most of the time you do have together. For example, when you are with your child, let him know this is "his" time. No beepers, no cellular phones, no fax machines. Look for innovative ways to let him know you are "his." Follow his suggestions. Use age-appropriate toys and games. Dr. Stanley Greenspan's concept of "Floor time" is useful here. When you get on the floor with a child, that child knows you are "his." Then, follow his lead, play his games, not yours. You may just want to watch at first so that you can match his rhythms, and enter the play at his level. It is difficult not to lead, or to teach, rather than to follow. But remember that the play is his and the message you want to convey is, "I'm yours."

resources

This is a selective list of national organizations that can advise you:

American Academy of Child
   and Adolescent Psychiatry
3615 Wisconsin Ave NW
Washington DC 20016
(202) 966–7300
www.aacap.org

American Academy of Pediatrics
P.O. Box 927
Elk Grove Village IL 60009
(847) 434–4000
www.aap.org

American Association on
    Mental Retardation (AAMR)
444 N. Capitol St. NW, Suite 846
Washington, DC 20001-1512
www.aamr.org
email: aamr@access.digex.net

American Council of the Blind
1155 15th St. NW, Suite 720
Washington, DC 20005
800-424-8666 (toll free)
202-467-5081 (voice)
202-467-5058 (fax)
http://acb.org

American Foundation for
   the Blind (AFB)
11 Penn Plaza, Suite 300
New York, NY 10001
800-AFB-LINE (232-5463)
   (toll free)
http://afb.org
email: afbinfo@afb.org

American Speech-Language-
Hearing Association (ASHA)
10801 Rockville Pike
Rockville, MD 20852
800-498-2071 (toll free; voice)
301-897-5700 (TT)
301-571-0457 (Fax)
http://www.asha.org

Autism Society of America
7910 Woodmont Avenue, Suite 650
Bethesda, MD 20814-3015
800-AUTISM (toll free; voice)
301-657-0869 (Fax)
http://www.autism-society.org

Center for School Mental Health
Assistance (CSMHA)
680 W. Lexington St.
Baltimore, MD 21201-1570
888-706-0980 (toll free; voice)
410-706-0984 (Fax)
http://csmha.ab.umd.edu/index.html

Children & Adults with Attention
Deficit Disorders (Ch.A.D.D.)
499 NW 70th Avenue
Plantation, FL 33317
800-233-4050 (toll free; voice)
954-587-4599 (Fax)
http://www.chadd.org

Children's Defense Fund
25 E Street NW
Washington, DC 20001
202–628–8787
www.childrensdefense.org

Council for Exceptional Children
(CEC)
1920 Association Drive
Reston, VA 20191-1589
703-264-9446 (Voice)
703-264-9494 (Fax)
http://www.cec.sped.org
email: cec@cec.sped.org

Council for Learning Disabilities
PO Box 40303
Overland Park, KS 66204
913-492-8755 (Voice)
913-492-2546 (Fax)
(202) 638–2952
http://coe.winthrop.edu/CLD

ERIC Clearinghouse on Disabilities
and Gifted Education
The Council for Exceptional
Children (CEC)
1920 Association Drive
Reston, VA 20101-1589
800-328-0272
703-620-3660 (TTY)
http://www.cec.sped.org/ericec.htm

Families and Work Institute
330 Seventh Ave.
New York, NY 10001
(212) 465–2044
www.familiesandwork.org

Federation for Children with
Special Needs
95 Berkeley Street, Suite 104
Boston, MA 02116
617-482-2915
www.fesn.org

Growing Without Schooling
2380 Massachusetts Avenue
Suite 104
Cambridge, MA 02140
(617) 864-3100
www.holtgws.org

Joseph P. Kennedy Foundation
(for mental retardation)
1325 G Street, NW, Suite 500
Washington, DC 20005-4709
202-393-1250 (Voice)
202-824-0351 (Fax)
www.familyvillage.wisc.edu/jpkf/

Kids First!
The Coalition for Quality
   Children's Media (CQCM)
112 W. San Francisco St., Suite
   305A
Santa Fe, NM 87501
505-989-8076 (Voice)
505-986-8477 (Fax)
email: kidsfirst@cqcm.org
www.cqcm.org

Learning Disabilities Association
   (LDA)
4156 Library Road
Pittsburgh, PA 15234-1349
412-341-1515 (Voice)
412-344—224 (Fax)
email: ldanatl@usaor.net
www.ldanatl.org

National Adoption Information
   Clearinghouse
330 C St., SW
Washington, DC 20447
888-251-0075 or 703-352-3488
   (Voice)
703-385-3206 (Fax)
email: naic@calib.com
www.calib.com/naic

National Alliance for the Mentally Ill
200 N. Glebe Road, Suite 1015
Arlington, VA 22203-3754
800-950-6264 (Toll free; helpline)
703-516-7991 (TT)
703-524-9094 (Fax)
email: namiofc@aol.com
www.nami.org

National Association for
   Developmental Disabilities
   Council (NADDC)
1234 Massachusetts Avenue NW,
   Suite 103
Washington, DC 20005
202-347-1234 (Voice)
202-347-4023 (Fax)
www.igc.apc.org/NADDC/

National Association for the Deaf
814 Thayer Avenue
Silver Spring, MD 20910-4500
301-587-1788 (Voice)
301-587-1789 (TT)
301-587-1791 (Fax)
email: NADHQ@juno.com
http://www.nad.com

National Association for the
   Education of Young Children
1509 16th St. NW
Washington DC 20036
800-424-2460 or 202-232–8777
202-328-1846 (Fax)
email: naeyc@naeyc.org
www.naeyc.org

National Association of State
   Directors of Special Education
   (NASDSE)
703-519-3808 (Voice)

National Attention Deficit Disorder
   Association
9930 Johnnycake Ridge Road,
Suite 3E
Mentor, OH 44060
216-350-9595 (Voice)
216-350-0223 (Fax)
email: natladd@aol.com
http://www.add.org
National Child Abuse Hotline
800-422-4453

National Easter Seal Society
230 W. Monroe St., Suite 1800
Chicago, IL 60606
800-221-6827 (Toll free; Vioce)
312-726-6200 (Voice)
312-726-4258 (TT)
http://seals.com

National Safe Kids Campaign
1301 Pennsylvania Ave., NW;
  Suite 1000
Washington, DC 20004-1707
800-441-1888 or 202-662-0600
  (Voice)
202-393-2072 (Fax)
email: info@safekids.org
www.safekids.org

National Tourette Syndrome
  Association
42-40 Bell Boulevard
Bayside, NY 11361-2820
718-224-2999 (Voice)
718-279-9596 (Fax)
http://tsa.mgh.harvard.edu

SafetyBeltSafeUSA
www.carseat.org

Sibling Information Network
c/o A.J. Pappanikou Center
249 Glenbrook Road
U-64, Storrs. CT 06269-2064
860-486-4985 (Voice)
860-486-5087 (Fax)

Sibling Support Project
http://www.seatttlechildrens.org/
  sibsupp

Spinal Bifida Association of
  America
4590 MacArthur Boulevard NW,
  Suite 250
Washington, DC 20007-4226
800-621-31 1 (Toll free; Voice)
202-944-328 (Voice)
202-944-3295 (Fax)
email: ir@sbaa.org
http://www.sbaa.org

Stepfamily Association of America
650 J St., Suite 205
Lincoln, NE 68508
800-735-0329 (Toll free, Voice)
402-477-8317 (Fax)
email: stepfamFS@aol.com
http://www.stepfam.org

Touchpoints Project
Children's Hospital—Boston
1295 Boylston St. Suite 320
Boston MA 02215
617-355-6947
www.touchpoints.org

UNICEF
UNICEF House
3 United Nations Plaza
New York NY 10017
www.unicef.org

United Cerebral Palsy Association
1660 L Street NW
Washington DC 20036-5602
800-USA-5UCP (Toll free; Voice)
202-776-0406 (Voice)
202-776-0414 (Fax)

bibliography

Ames, Louise B., and F. L. Ilg. *Your Three Year Old.* New York: Gesell Institute, Delacorte Press, 1976.

_____. *Your Four Year Old.* New York: Gesell Institute, Delacorte Press, 1976.

Barnet, Ann B., and R. J. Barnet. *The Youngest Mind*s. New York: Simon & Schuster, 1998.

Baumrind, Diana. *Child Maltreatment and Optimal Caregiving in Social Contexts.* New York: Garland, 1995.

Benkov, Laura. *Reinventing the Family: The Emerging Story of Gay and Lesbian Families.* New York: Random House, 1997.

Bennett, Steve. *The Plugged-In Parent: What You Should Know About Kids and Computers.* New York: Times Books, 1998.

Bentz, Detective Rick, and C. Allen. *Start Smart for Kids.* New York: Ballantine, 1999.

Bernstein, Amy. *Flight of the Stork: What Children Think (and When) About Sex and Family Building.* Indianapolis, Ind.: Perspectives Press, 1994.

Beckart, T. S., D. T. Dodge, and J. R. Jablon. *What Every Parent Needs to Know About First, Second, and Third Grades.* Naperville, Ill.: Sourcebooks, 1997.

Bergson, Henri. *Le Rire: Essai sur la signification du comique.* Paris: Presses Universitaires de France, 1946.

Bettelheim, Bruno. *The Uses of Enchantment: The Meaning and Importance of Fairy Tales.* New York: Vintage, 1989.

Bodnar, Janet. *Money-Smart Kids.* Washington, D.C.: Kiplinger, 1993.

Bok, Sissela. *Mayhem: Violence as Public Entertainment.* Cambridge, Mass.: Perseus Publishing/Merloyd Lawrence, 1998.

Brazelton, T. Berry. *Going to the Doctor.* Cambridge, Mass.: Perseus Publishing/Merloyd Lawrence, 1999.

Brazelton, T. Berry. *Touchpoints: Your Child's Emotional and Behavioral Development.* Cambridge, Mass.: Perseus Publishing/Merloyd Lawrence, 1992.

Brazelton, T. Berry, and S. Greenspan. *The Irreducible Needs of Children.* Cambridge, Mass.: Perseus Publishing/Merloyd Lawrence, 2000.

Britton, Zachary. Safety Net: Guiding and Guarding Your Children on the Internet. Eugene, Ore.: Harvest House, 1998.

Calderone, M. S., and J. S. Ramsey. *Talking with Your Child About Sex.* New York: Random House, 1982.

Chess, Stella, and A. Thomas. *Know Your Child: An Authoritative Guide for Today's Parents.* New York: Basic Books, 1987.

Cantor, Joanne. *Mommy, I'm Scared: How T.V. and Movies Frighten Children and What We Can Do.* San Diego: Harcourt Brace, 1998.

Children's Hospital, Boston. *Children's Hospital Guide to Your Child's Health and Development.* Cambridge, Mass.: Perseus Publishing/Merloyd Lawrence, 2001.

Coll, Cynthia Garcia, J. L. Surrey, and K. Weingarten. *Mothering Against the Odds: Diverse Voices of Contemporary Mothers.* New York: Guilford, 1998.

Comer, James P., and A. Poussaint. *Raising Black Children: Two Leading Psychiatrists Confront the Educational, Social and Emotional Problems Facing Black Children.* New York: Penguin, 1992.

Cooney, Barbara. *Miss Rumphius.* New York: Puffin Books, 1982

DeGangi, Georgia. *Pediatric Disorders of Regulation in Affect and Behavior: A Therapist's Guide.* New York: Academic Press, 2000.

Deutsch, F. M. *Halving It All: How Equally Shared Parenting Works.* Cambridge, Mass.: Harvard University Press, 1999.

Diamond, M., and J. Hopson. *Magic Trees of the Mind: How to Nurture Your Child's Intelligence, Creativity, and Healthy Emotions.* New York: Penguin, 1988.

Dixon, Suzanne, and M. Stein. *Encounters with Children.* St. Louis: Mosby, 1999.

Doka, Ken. *Living with Life-Threatening Illness: A Guide for Patients, Their Families, and Caregivers.* San Francisco: Jossey-Bass, 1993.

————. *Living with Grief When Illness Is Prolonged.* Philadelphia: Taylor & Francis, 1997.

Dombro, Amy L., and P. Bryan. *Sharing and Caring: Childcare and Making It Work.* New York: Simon & Schuster, 1991.

Elkind, David. *The Hurried Child: Growing Up Too Fast Too Soon.* Reading, Mass.: Addison-Wesley, 1981.

———. *A Sympathetic Understanding of the Child: Birth to Sixteen.* Needham Heights, Mass.: Paramount Publications, 1994.

Erikson, Erik H. *Childhood and Society.* New York: Norton, 1963.

Fawcett, Parry. *The Parents' Guide to Protecting Children in Cyberspace.* New York: McGraw-Hill, 2000.

Fraiberg, Selma. *The Magic Years.* New York: Scribner, 1959.

Galinsky, Ellen. *The Six Stages of Parenthood.* Cambridge, Mass.: Perseus Publishing/Merloyd Lawrence, 1987.

Galinsky, Ellen, and J. Davis. *The Preschool Years.* New York: Times Books, 1988.

Galinsky, Ellen, C. Howes, S. Kontos, and M. Shinn. *The Study of Children in Family Child Care and Relative Care: Highlights of Findings.* Boston: Families and Work Institute, 1994.

Gallin, Pamela. *The Savvy Mom's Guide to Medical Care.* New York: Golden Books/Babies' and Children's Hospital of New York, 1999.

Gardner, Howard. *Frames of Mind: The Theory of Multiple Intelligences.* New York: Basic Books, 1983.

Gesell, Arnold. *The First Five Years of Life: The Preschool Years.* New York: Harper Brothers, 1940.

Gilligan, Carol. *In a Different Voice: Psychological Theory and Women's Development.* Cambridge, Mass.: Harvard University Press, 1982.

Golinkoff, Roberta. M., and K. Hersch-Pasck. *How Babies Talk: The Magic and Mystery of Language in the First Three Years.* New York: Dutton, 1999.

Goleman, Daniel. *Emotional Intelligence.* New York: Bantam, 1997.

Gopnik, A., A. N. Meltzoff, and P. K. Kuhl. *The Scientist in the Crib: Minds, Brains, and How Children Learn.* New York: Morrow, 1994.

Gottlieb, Susan. *Keys to Parenting Your Three Year Old.* Hauppaug, N.Y.: Barron's Educational Services, 1995.

Greene, Ross W. *The Explosive Child: A New Approach for Understanding and Parenting Easily Frustrated, "Chronically Inflexible" Children.* New York: HarperCollins, 1998.

Greenspan, Stanley. *Floortime: Tuning in to Each Child.* New York: Scholastics, 1997.

Greenspan, Stanley I., with B. L. Benderly. *The Growth of the Mind.* Cambridge, Mass.: Perseus Publishing/Merloyd Lawrence, 1997.

Greenspan, Stanley, and S. Wieder, with R. Simons. *The Child with Special Needs: Encouraging Intellectual and Emotional Growth.* New York: Perseus Publishing/Merloyd Lawrence, 1998.

Haffner, D. W. *From Diapers to Dating: A Parents' Guide to Raising Sexually Healthy Children.* New York: Newmarket Press, 1998.

Hallowell, Edward M., and J. J. Ratey. *Driven to Distraction: Recognizing and Coping with Attention Deficit Disorder from Childhood Through Adulthood.* New York: Pantheon, 1994.

Harris, Robie H. *It's So Amazing!: A Book About Eggs, Sperm, Birth, Babies, and Families.* Illustrated by Michael Emberley. Cambridge, Mass.: Candlewick Press, 1999.

Helburn, S. W., et al. *Cost, Quality, and Child Outcomes in Child Care Centers.* Public Report. Denver. Department of Economics, Center for Research in Economic and Social Policy. Denver, Colo.: University of Colorado, 1995.

Hobbs, N., and J. Perrin, eds. *Issues in the Care of Children with Chronic Illness.* San Francisco: Jossey-Bass, 1985.

Howes, Carolyn. "Continuity of Care." *Zero to Three* 18 (June 1998).

Joslin, Karen R. *Positive Parenting from A to Z.* New York: Fawcett Books, 1994.

Kagan, Jerome. *Three Seductive Ideas.* Cambridge, Mass.: Harvard University Press, 2000.

Kantrowitz, Carol. *The Out of Sync Child.* New York: Skylight Press, 1998.

Kellogg, Steven. *Much Bigger Than Martin.* New York: Dial Books, 1978.

Kessler, Daniel, and P. Dawson. *Failure to Thrive and Pediatric Undernutrition.* Baltimore: Brookes, 1999.

Kindlon, Dan, and M. Thompson. *Raising Cain: Protecting the Emotional Life of Boys.* New York: Ballantine, 1999.

Kohlberg, Lawrence. "The Child as Moral Philosopher." In *Vice and Virtue in Everyday Life.* Chicago: University of Chicago Press, 1971.

Lebato, D. *Brothers, Sisters, and Special Needs.* Baltimore: Brookes, 1990

Lesser, Gerald S. *Children and Television: Lessons from Sesame Street.* New York: Vintage, 1974.

Levine, James, and T. Pittinsky. *Working Fathers—Balancing Work and Family.* Cambridge, Mass.: Perseus Publishing, 1997.

Levine, R. A., S. Levine, S. Dixon, A. Richman, P. H. Liederman, C. H. Keefer, and T. B. Brazelton. *Child Care and Culture.* Cambridge, England: Cambridge University Press, 1996.

Lofas, Jeanette. *Helping Stepfamilies and Single Parents Build Happy Homes.* New York: Kensington Books, 1998.

Lofas, Jeanette, and D. B. Sova. *Stepparenting.* New York: Kensington Books, 1985.

Ludtke, Melissa. *On Our Own: Unmarried Motherhood in America.* New York: Random House, 1997.

Lynch, E. W., and M. J. Hanson. *Developing Cross-cultural Competence.* Baltimore: Brookes, 1992.

Masters, Kim J. *The Angry Child: Sleeping Giant or Paper Tiger.* Santa Monica, Calif.: National Medical Enterprises, 1992.

Mayer, Mercer. *There's a Monster in My Closet.* New York: Penguin Books, 1976.

Maynard, R. A. *Kids Having Kids: A Robin Hood Foundation Special.* New York: Robin Hood Foundation, 1996.

Mclanahan, S., and G. Sandefur. *Growing Up with a Single Parent: What Hurts, What Helps.* Cambridge, Mass.: Harvard University Press, 1994.

Meltz, Barbara. *Put Yourself in Their Shoes.* New York: Dell, 1999.

Miranker, Cathy, and A. Elliott. *The Computer Museum Guide to the Best Software for Kids.* New York: HarperCollins, 1995.

Montagner, Hubert. *L'Attachement: Les Débuts de la tendresse.* Paris: Odile Jacob, 1988.

National Institute of Child Health Development Early Child Care Research Network. "Effects of Infant Care on Infant Mother Security." *Child Development* 68, no. 5 (October 1977).

Osofsky, Joy. *Children in a Violent Society.* New York: Guilford Press, 1997.

Papert, Seymour. *The Children's Machine: Rethinking School in the Age of the Computer.* New York: Basic Books, 1993.

Piaget, Jean. *The Origins of Intelligence in Children.* New York: International Universities Press, 1952.

Plaut, Thomas F. *Children with Asthma: A Manual for Parents.* Amherst, Mass.: Pedi Press, 1983.

Prend, Ashley. *Transcending Loss: Understanding the Lifelong Impact of Grief and How to Make It Meaningful.* New York: Berkley, 1997.

Prothrow-Stith, Deborah, and M. Weissman. *Deadly Consequences.* New York: HarperCollins, 1993.

Pruett, Kyle. *Me, Myself, and I: How Children Build Their Sense of Self.* New York: Goddard Press, 1999.

_____. *Father Need: Why Father Care Is As Essential as Mother Care for the Young Child* New York: Free Press, 2000.

Rodriguez, Gloria G. *Raising Nuestros Niños: Bringing Up Latino Children in a Bicultural World.* New York: Fireside, 1999.

Samalin, N. *Loving Each One Best: A Caring and Practical Approach to Raising Siblings.* New York: Bantam Books, 1997.

Schor, Juliet. *The Overworked American: The Unexpected Decline of Leisure.* New York: Basic Books, 1993.

Schore, Allan. *Affect Regulation and the Origin of the Self: The Neurobiology of Emotional Development.* Hillsdale, N.J.: L. Erlbaum Associates, 1994.

Segal, M. *Your Child at Play: 3–5 Years.* New York: Newmarket Press, 1998.

Sendak, Maurice. *Where the Wild Things Are.* New York: HarperCollins, 1984.

Simons, R. *After the Tears: Parents Talk About Raising a Child with a Disability.* New York: Harcourt Brace, 1987.

Sluckin, Andy. *Growing Up in the Playground: The Social Development of Children.* London: Routledge & Kegan Paul, 1981.

Smith, B., J. L. Surrey, and M. Watkins. " 'Real' Mothers." in Cynthia Coll et al., eds.,. *Mothering Against the Odds: Diverse Voices of Contemporary Mothers.* New York: Guilford, 1998.

Sourkes, Barbara. *Armfuls of Time: The Psychological Experience of the Child with a Life-Threatening Illness.* Pittsburgh: University of Pittsburgh Press, 1982.

Steiner, Hans, ed. *Treating Preschool Children.* San Francisco: Jossey-Bass, 1997.

Stern, Daniel, and N. Bruschweiler-Stern. *The Birth of a Mother.* New York: Basic Books, 1999.

Sulloway, Frank. *Born to Rebel: Birth Order, Family Dynamics, and Creative Lives.* New York: Random House, 1996.

Trozzi, Maria. *Talking with Children About Loss.* New York: Perigee, 1999.

Turecki, Stanley, and L. Tonner. *The Difficult Child.* New York: Bantam Books, 2000.

Unell, Barbara, and J. Wyckoff. *The Eight Seasons of Parenthood.* New York: Times Books, 2000.

Wallace, M. *Keys to Parenting Your Four-Year-Old.* Hauppauge, N.Y.: Barron's Educational Services, 1997.

_____. *Birth Order Blues: How Parents Can Help Their Children Meet the Challenges of Birth Order.* New York: Henry Holt, 1999.

Wallerstein, Judith, and S. Blakeslee. *Second Chances: Men, Women, and Children a Decade After Divorce.* New York: Ticknor & Fields, 1989.

Wallerstein, Judith, J. Lewis, and M. S. Blakeslee. *The Unexpected Legacy of Divorce: A 25-Year Landmark Study.* New York: Hyperion, 1999.

Weissbluth, M. *Healthy Sleep Habits, Happy Child.* New York: Fawcett Books, 1987, 1999.

White, E. B. *Charlotte's Web.* New York: HarperCollins, 1974.

Winnicott, D. W. *Babies and Their Mothers.* Cambridge, Mass.: Perseus Publishing/Merloyd Lawrence, 1988.

_____. *The Child, the Family, and the Outside World.* Cambridge, Mass.: Perseus Publishing/Merloyd Lawrence, 1987.

_____. *Talking to Parents.* Cambridge, Mass.: Perseus Publishing/Merloyd Lawrence, 1993.

Wood, Chip. *Yardsticks: Children in the Classroom, Ages 4–12.* Greenfield, Mass.: Northeast Foundation for Children, 1995.

Zeitlin, Shirley, and G. Williamson. *Coping in Young Children: Early Intervention Practices to Enhance Adaptive Behavior and Resilience.* Baltimore: Brookes, 1994.

Ziegler, Robert. *Homemade Books to Help Kids Cope.* New York: Magination Press, 1992.

Zigler, Edward, and M. Lang. *Child Care Choices.* New York: Free Press, 1991.

Zill, Nicholas, and C. W. Nord. *Running in Place: How American Families Are Faring in a Changing Economy and an Individualistic Society.* Washington, D.C.: Child Trends, Inc., 1994.

index

For age-specific references see Babies, Three-year-olds, Four-year-olds; Five-year-olds, Six-year-olds. For temperament-specific references see Temperaments.

photo credits

Photos by

Dorothy Littell Greco (pages 1, 7, 45, 90, 94, 98, 99, 100, 103, 106, 118, 121, 125, 127, 131, 133, 136, 157, 163, 165, 196, 220, 221, 238, 246, 247, 252, 274, 275, 294, 302, 306, 309, 331, 383, 391, 414, 434, 461, 465)
Marilyn Nolt (pages 2, 12, 15, 17, 29, 70, 79, 179, 183, 185, 193, 205, 213, 244, 257, 271, 334, 347, 457)
Sam Ogden (pages 26, 41, 57, 377)
Janice Fullman (pages 22, 172, 231, 289, 399)

about the authors

T. Berry Brazelton, M.D., founder of the Child Development Unit at Children's Hospital, Boston, is Clinical Professor of Pediatrics Emeritus at Harvard Medical School. Currently Professor of Pediatrics and Human Development at Brown University, he is also past president of the Society for Research in Child Development and Zero to Three: The National Center for Infants, Toddlers, and Families. A practicing pediatrician for over forty-five years, he introduced the concept of "anticipatory guidance" for parents into pediatric training. The author of over 200 scholarly papers, Dr. Brazelton has written thirty books for both a professional and a lay audience, including *Touchpoints* (translated into eighteen languages), *To Listen to a Child,* and the now-classic trilogy *Infants and Mothers, Toddlers and Parents,* and *On Becoming a Family.* His television show, "What Every Baby Knows" has run for fourteen years and won an Emmy and three Ace Awards.

To continue his important research and implement its findings, Dr. Brazelton founded, and co-directs two programs at Children's Hospital: the Brazelton Institute (furthering work with the NBAS) and the Brazelton Touchpoints Center (training health and child care professionals across the country in the Touchpoints preventive outreach approach).

Dr. Brazelton, who has served on the National Commission for Children appointed by the U.S. Congress, is the recipient, among his very numerous awards, of the C. Anderson Aldrich Award for Distinguished Contributions to the Field of Child Development, given by the American Academy of Pediatrics, and the Woodrow Wilson Award for Outstanding Public Service from Princeton University.

Joshua D. Sparrow, M.D., Instructor in Psychiatry, Harvard Medical School, is Supervisor, Inpatient Psychiatry, Children's Hospital, Boston and Associate Director for Training, Brazelton Touchpoints Center at Children's Hospital. He has held appointments in psychiatry at the School of Medicine, University of Marseilles, France.
Dr. Sparrow also has co-authored articles with Dr. Brazelton for the New York Times Syndicate, and lectures on child development nationally and internationally.

The Brazelton Foundation supports and expands the training programs begun by Dr Brazelton. These programs train healthcare and childcare professionals in a new model of preventive healthcare and positive relationships between the provider, the child, the family and community.

Website: www.brazelton.org

Email: brazfound@aol.com